Developments in Sociology

edited by

Robert G. Burgess
and Anne Murcott

Prentice
Hall

An imprint of **Pearson Education**

Harlow, England · London · New York · Reading, Massachusetts · San Francisco · Toronto · Don Mills, Ontario · Sydney
Tokyo · Singapore · Hong Kong · Seoul · Taipei · Cape Town · Madrid · Mexico City · Amsterdam · Munich · Paris · Milan

Pearson Education Limited
Edinburgh Gate
Harlow
Essex CM20 2JE

and Associated Companies throughout the world.

Visit us on the World Wide Web at:
www.pearsoneduc.com

First published 2001

© Pearson Education Limited 2001

ISBN 0582 41855 0

British Library Cataloguing-in-Publication Data
A catalogue record for this book is available from the British Library

Library of Congress Cataloging-in-Publication Data
Burgess, Robert G.
    Developments in sociology / Robert G. Burgess and Anne Murcott.
      p.   cm. — (Longman sociology series)
    Includes bibliographical references and index.
    ISBN 0-582-41855-0
     1. Sociology. I. Murcott, Anne. II. Title. III. Series.

  HM585 .B87 2001
  301—dc21   00–045641

10 9 8 7 6 5 4 3 2 1
05 04 03 02 01

Typeset in Stone Serif 9/13.5 pt by 35
Produced by Pearson Education Malaysia Sdn Bhd
Printed in Malaysia

contents

Tables   vii
Notes on contributors   viii
Series preface   xiii
Preface   xv

Introduction   *1*
Robert G. Burgess and Anne Murcott

Part One: Theory, methodology and methods   *9*

Chapter 1

Sociologists and the survey: potential and pitfalls   *11*
Sara Arber

Chapter 2

Never mind the quality . . . ? Developments in ethnographic and
qualitative research   *35*
Robert G. Burgess

Chapter 3

Theory, meta-theory and discourse: reflections on post-empiricism   *51*
Christopher G.A. Bryant

Chapter 4

On the cusp of the cultural   *79*
John Eldridge

Chapter 5

Feminism and postmodernism in social theory   *99*
Mary Maynard

Chapter 6

Developments in the sociology of gender and women's studies   *121*
Sylvia Walby

Part Two: Substantive areas *141*

Chapter 7

Developments in the sociology of religion *143*
James A. Beckford

Chapter 8

Developments in the sociology of education since 1950:
from structural functionalism to 'policy sociology' *165*
Kevin J. Brehony

Chapter 9

The sociology of work and employment: new perspectives on
new issues *185*
Richard K. Brown

Chapter 10

Science and technology studies – the environmentally
friendly cottage industry *207*
Peter Glasner

Chapter 11

Family sociology in from the fringe: the three 'economies'
of family life *227*
David H.J. Morgan

Chapter 12

Sociology and health: creating the agenda *249*
Anne Murcott

Part Three: Policy and problems *273*

Chapter 13

Poverty and the welfare state at century's end:
paradoxes and prospects *275*
Mick Carpenter

Chapter 14

Rediscovering the underclass *301*
Robert Moore

Index 327

tables

Table 12.1 Institutional affiliation of those who submitted a return for inclusion in the BSA Medical Sociology Group Register of Research and Teaching, first, fourth, sixth and eighth editions *264*

Table 13.1 Comparison of causes of poverty, 1899 and 1987 *283*

Acknowledgements

We are grateful to the following for permission to reproduce copyright material:

Table 13.1 from Lewis, J. and Piachaud, D. (1992) 'Women and poverty in the twentieth century', in C. Glendinning and J. Millar (eds) *Women and Poverty in Britain: The 1990s*, Harvester Wheatsheaf, Pearson Education.

Whilst every effort has been made to trace the owners of copyright material, in a few cases this has proved impossible and we take this opportunity to offer our apologies to any copyright holders whose rights we may have unwittingly infringed.

Sara Arber is Professor of Sociology and Head of Department at the University of Surrey. She is President of the British Sociological Association (1999–2001) and was previously Honorary Treasurer of the BSA (1988–90). She has written on survey methodology, and is co-author of *Doing Secondary Analysis* (Allen and Unwin 1988). Her research focuses mainly on gender and ageing, and inequalities in women's health. Publications include *Gender and Later Life* (Sage 1991 with Jay Ginn), *Ageing, Independence and the Life Course* (Jessica Kingsley 1993 with Maria Evandrou), *Connecting Gender and Ageing* (Open University Press 1995 with Jay Ginn), and *The Myth of Generational Conflict* (Routledge 2000 with Claudine Attias-Donfut).

James A. Beckford is Professor of Sociology at the University of Warwick. He was President of the Association for the Sociology of Religion in 1988–9, a Vice-President of the International Sociological Association from 1994 to 1998, and is currently President of the International Society for the Sociology of Religion. His main publications include *Religious Organization* (Mouton 1973), *The Trumpet of Prophecy. A Sociological Analysis of Jehovah's Witnesses* (Blackwell 1975), *Cult Controversies. The Societal Response to New Religious Movements* (Tavistock 1985), *Religion and Advanced Industrial Society* (Unwin-Hyman 1989) and (with Sophie Gilliat) *Religion in Prison. Equal Rites in a Multi-Faith Society?* (Cambridge 1998). He is the editor of *New Religious Movements and Rapid Social Change* (Sage 1986), and co-editor of *The Changing Face of Religion* (Sage 1989) and *Secularization, Rationalism and Sectarianism* (Oxford 1993). His next book will be on religion and social theory.

Kevin J. Brehony is Senior Lecturer in Education at the University of Reading where he teaches, among others, an MA course on the sociology of education. He is a former Honorary Treasurer, Executive Committee member and Education Study Group Convenor of the British Sociological Association. He has published numerous articles in the fields of sociologically informed histories of child-centred education and education policy. With Rosemary Deem and Sue Heath he is the author of *Active Citizenship and the Governing of Schools* (Buckingham, Open University Press 1995) and editor, with Naz Rassool, of *Nationalisms Old and New* (Houndmills, Macmillan Press 1999). With Rosemary Deem he is currently writing a book for Macmillan entitled *Rethinking Sociologies of Education* and he is researching the introduction of performance-related pay for teachers.

Richard K. Brown studied history at the University of Cambridge and personnel management at the LSE. After nearly eight years working as research officer and then Lecturer in Sociology in the University of Leicester he was appointed Lecturer in Sociology in the University of Durham in 1966, became Professor of Sociology in 1982, and retired in 1993. His research has focused on the sociology of work and employment, including studies of women hosiery workers, the shipbuilding industry, and local labour markets. He is the author of *Understanding Industrial Organisations* (Routledge 1992) and editor of *The Changing Shape of Work* (Macmillan 1997), and he was the founding editor of *Work, Employment and Society*. Recent research and publications have included studies of the work of sign language interpreters, notably Mary Brennan and Richard Brown, *Equality before the Law. Deaf People's Access to Justice* (DSRU, Durham 1997).

Christopher G.A. Bryant, a graduate of Leicester and Southampton Universities, has been Professor of Sociology at Salford University since 1982 and is now Dean of the Faculty of Arts, Media and Social Sciences. He has held visiting appointments in Germany, America, the Netherlands and Poland and is a member of the Advisory Board of the Central European University in Warsaw. He researches in social theory and political sociology and is currently writing a book on nations and national identities in Britain. His publications include *Sociology in Action* (Allen and Unwin 1976), *Positivism in Social Theory and Research* (Macmillan 1985), *What Has Sociology Achieved?* (co-edited Henk Becker, Macmillan 1990), *Giddens' Theory of Structuration* (co-editor David Jary, Routledge 1991), *The New Great Transformation? Change and Continuity in East-Central Europe* (co-editor Edmund Mokrzycki, Routledge 1994), *Practical Sociology: Postempiricism and the Reconstruction of Theory and Application*, Polity 1995), *Civil Society, Pluralism and Democracy* (co-editor Edmund Mokrzycki, IfiS 1995), *Anthony Giddens: Critical Assessments* (co-editor David Jary, 4 vols., Routledge 1997) and *The Contemporary Giddens* (co-editor David Jary, Macmillan 2001).

Robert G. Burgess is Vice-Chancellor of the University of Leicester. He was Senior Pro-Vice-Chancellor, Director of CEDAR (Centre for

Educational Development, Appraisal and Research) and Professor of Sociology at the University of Warwick until August 1999. His main teaching and research interests are in social research methodology (particularly qualitative methods) and the sociology of education (especially the study of schools, classrooms and curricula). He has conducted ethnographic studies of secondary schools and universities. His main publications include: *Experiencing Comprehensive Education* (Methuen 1983), *In the Field: An Introduction to Field Research* (Allen and Unwin 1984), *Education, Schools and Schooling* (Macmillan 1985), *Sociology, Education and Schools* (Batsford 1986), *Schools at Work* (Open University Press 1988 with Rosemary Deem), *Implementing In-Service Education and Training* (Falmer Press 1993 with John Connor, Sheila Galloway, Marlene Morrison and Malcolm Newton), and *Research Methods* (Nelson 1993), together with over twenty edited volumes on qualitative methods and education. He was President of the British Sociological Association, President of the Association for the Teaching of the Social Sciences, Founding Chair of the UK Council for Graduate Education and has been a member of the Council and Chair of the Postgraduate Training Board of the Economic and Social Research Council, UK.

Mick Carpenter is Reader in the Department of Social Policy and Social Work, and co-Director of the Centre for Research in Health, Medicine and Society, both at the University of Warwick. He trained as a general nurse before entering higher education to study for a sociology degree. His doctoral research focused on the history of nursing trade unionism in Britain, and he has since researched and published widely in the field of public service industrial relations, and health and social policy. Recently published work has focused on the role of public service trade unions in community care and social policy (for example, *Normality is Hard Work: Trade Unions and the Politics of Community Care*, 1994 Lawrence and Wishart), gender inequalities of health, and the comparative sociology of mental health policy. He has acted as a policy advisor to the public services union, UNISON.

John Eldridge is Professor of Sociology at the University of Glasgow. He is a founder member of the Glasgow Media Group. His research work has been in the areas of industrial sociology and the sociology of the mass media. He has also written monographs on Wright Mills and (with L. Eldridge) on Raymond Williams. He is a former President of the BSA and served as the first chairperson for the Association of Learned Societies in the Social Sciences.

Peter Glasner is Research Professor in Sociology, and a Director of the Science and Technology Policy Unit, at the University of the West of England, Bristol, where he was previously Executive Dean of the Faculty of Economics and Social Science. He has been an Honorary General Secretary of the BSA, a vice-president of the Sociology Section of the British Association for the Advancement of Science, and President of the Association of Learned Societies in the Social Sciences. He has also held a Morris Ginsberg Fellowship at the London School of Economics. His publications include six books and over sixty articles and reports on the sociology of religion, the sociology of science, and science policy, and his current interests are in the management of the new genetic technologies, and in public participation in techno-scientific decision-making. He is a founding editor of the international journal *New Genetics and Society* published by Carfax/Taylor and Francis.

Mary Maynard is a Professor in the Department of Social Policy and Social Work at the University of York, UK, where she is also Head of the Social Policy Section. She previously lectured in the Department of Sociology at York and was Director of the Centre for Women's Studies there from 1984 to 1996. Her major research interests are in social and feminist theories, research methodologies, gender and women's studies, ethnicities, ageing and later life and she has published in all of these areas. She is currently working on an ESRC-funded project focusing on successful ageing, which draws on the comparative experiences of Afro-Caribbean, Asian and white British women.

Robert Moore has been Eleanor Rathbone Professor in Liverpool University since 1989; previously he was Professor of Sociology in the University of Aberdeen. He taught at Durham University from 1965 to 1969, having graduated from Hull University in 1964. Prior to 1961 he was an officer in the Royal Navy. His publications include: *Race, Community and Conflict* (with John Rex, OUP 1967); *Pitmen, Preachers and Politics* (CUP 1974); *Slamming the Door: the Administration of Immigration Control* (with Tina Wallace, Martin Robertson 1975); *Racism and Black Resistance in Britain* (Pluto Press 1975); *The Social Impact of Oil: the Case of Peterhead* (Routledge 1983); *Women in the North Sea Oil Industry* (with Peter Wybrow, EOC 1984); *The Black Population of Inner Liverpool in the 1991 Census* (Runnymede Trust 1995); *Positive Action in Action: Equal Opportunities and Declining Opportunities on Merseyside* (Ashgate, Danish Centre for Migration and Ethnic Studies 1997).

David H.J. Morgan recently retired from Manchester University after teaching and researching there for over thirty years. He is currently

Emeritus Professor in Sociology at Manchester and also has a part-time, 'Professor 2', appointment at Norges teknisk-naturvitenskapelige universitet (NTNU), Trondheim. In addition to family sociology, his main academic interests include the study of men and masculinities and the uses of auto/biography in sociological enquiry. His most recent book is *Family Connections* (Polity 1996). He has been an active member of the British Sociological Association and was President of that body from 1997 to 1999.

Anne Murcott, a graduate of the Universities of Edinburgh and Wales, began developing sociological work on food and eating in the late 1970s. She has published extensively in the area, including *The Sociology of Food: Eating, Diet and Culture* (with Stephen Mennell and Anneke van Otterloo, Sage 1992) is a past co-executive editor of *Appetite* and is an editorial board member of the newly founded *Gastronomica*. She was Director of the Economic and Social Research Council (UK) Research Programme ' "The Nation's Diet": the social science of food choice' (1992–8) and edited an associated volume under the same title, published in 1998 by Longman. She sustains her broader interest in the sociology of health professions, and served as editor of *Sociology of Health and Illness* from 1982 to 1987. Having taught sociology in both the social science and medical faculties in the University of Wales (Cardiff) for more than twenty years, she moved briefly to London University (the London School of Hygiene and Tropical Medicine) and now holds a research post as Professor of the Sociology of Health at South Bank University, London.

Sylvia Walby is Professor of Sociology at the University of Leeds. She has previously been Professor of Sociology at the University of Bristol, founding Director of the Gender Institute and Reader in Sociology at the London School of Economics, and founding Director of the Women's Studies Research Centre at Lancaster University. She has been the Chair of the Women's Studies Network (UK) and was the founding President of the European Sociological Association. Her books include: *Gender Transformations* (Routledge 1997), *Theorising Patriarchy* (Blackwell 1990), *Patriarchy at Work* (Polity 1986); co-authorship of *Localities Class and Gender* (Pion 1985), *Restructuring: Place Class and Gender* (Sage 1990), *Contemporary British Society* (Polity 2000), *Sex Crime in the News* (Routledge 1991) and *Medicine and Nursing: Professions in a Changing Health Service* (Sage 1994); editorship of *Gender Segregation at Work* (Open University 1988) and *New Agendas for Women* (Macmillan 1999); and co-editorship of *Out of the Margins: Women's Studies in the Nineties* (Falmer 1991), and *European Societies: Fusion or Fission* (Routledge 1999).

series preface

The New Sociologies Series provides an alternative to the standard texts available. It also provides an insight into the range of contributions that sociologists can make to our understanding of contemporary issues. The Series is, therefore, forward looking and builds upon discussions and debates that open up 'new' fields of social enquiry. Each volume contributes to debates in the discipline and raises issues of relevance to contemporary policy and practice in the twenty-first century.

A hallmark of the Series is the development of theoretically informed empirical work which will be of interest to undergraduate and graduate students of sociology, researchers, scholars and teachers. All together the volumes in the Series will include authored books as well as edited collections that assess and contribute to the development of the discipline.

This volume brings together specially-commissioned chapters from major British sociologists. Each chapter provides an assessment of the scale and scope of a field of study and outlines ways in which researchers have explored their subject and developed the discipline. All the chapters in this volume provide an account of major trends in British sociology, which will be of interest to students, researchers and teachers.

Robert G. Burgess
University of Leicester

Series Editor

preface

This volume has long ago outstripped its origins. It began in a symposium that Robert Burgess organized when he was President of the British Sociological Association. He invited a number of friends and colleagues to participate in a series of linked seminars that would briefly outline key developments in a particular field of study in sociology, and highlight areas of future development. Subsequently, this idea found sufficient general favour that in time it not only grew larger but developed into something much more substantial, entailing the commissioning of a number of additional contributions to make for a broader coverage of sociology.

The purpose of this collection of newly commissioned papers is to provide an illustration of the way in which major developments have occurred within sociology. Even though the scope of the volume was widened, it has still not been possible to include every area of study – attempting comprehensive coverage is not feasible in a volume of this kind. Rather we aim to give a taste of some of the key issues and debates in sociology, and of the light they can shed on the nature of contemporary society. So we hope the volume will not simply provide an introduction to some less familiar areas for specialists as well as for newcomers, but even serve as a small landmark that will provide grist to the mill of future sociologists examining how the discipline developed.

Some of the participants in the original seminars agreed to develop their contributions, including Cathie Marsh, whose all too early death deprived sociology of further distinguished contributions from her for the development of the discipline. The field of study she covered at the seminar was on survey research and has been generously taken on by Sara Arber who dedicates her chapter to the memory of Cathie Marsh.

The work began when Robert Burgess was at the University of Warwick and has been completed following his move to the University of Leicester. The task of editing the papers has been greatly assisted by Anne Murcott, who was one of the contributors to the original symposium, and who has collaborated with him in the later stages of this volume's editing.

Finally, it remains for us both to thank all the authors for producing a set of essays which we hope will contribute to advancing our understanding of the ways in which sociology can provide important insights on contemporary society.

Robert Burgess
University of Leicester

Anne Murcott
South Bank University, London

June 2000

introduction

Robert G. Burgess and Anne Murcott

British sociology is predominantly a post-Second World War development, and now spans several decades of research. The problem for teachers and students of sociology today is how to come to terms with the subject matter. This is neatly summed up in a book on British society by Obelkevich and Catterall, when they state:

> British society is a complicated affair, full of loose ends and bits that don't fit. This may be a good thing for the people who live in it, but it is a source of frustration for those who study it and try to understand it. Every attempt to sum it up in a simple formula – as a 'class society' or what-ever – has proved to have so many exceptions and qualifications that it was more trouble than it was worth. The first thing to understand about British society is that there are no shortcuts, no master keys.
>
> (Obelkevich and Catterall 1994: 1)

This problem is central for sociologists studying their own society, but is multiplied when attempting to engage in comparative work (Burgess 1994) – a direction in which sociologists are increasingly likely to move in future. Given these difficulties, we might ask how sociologists have coped over the last four decades. In what ways have theories and methods been developed? How has the shape of sub-fields been defined and redefined? What 'new' perspectives have been used to study 'old' problems? What 'old' perspectives persist to tackle 'new' problems? What future possibilities exist for sociologists to develop the research agenda within their subject?

To address such questions, some sociologists have produced neatly packaged accounts which attempt to cover the total stock of sociological knowledge under the title 'Sociology'. While such an approach may appear helpful to the beginning student, it also has the potential to mislead, as all loose ends are tied together, rough edges are smoothed, and unresolved problems are omitted. As Horowitz has commented: 'One is often tempted to assume that the rationality of the final sociological product is a consequence of the rationality of the method for realizing that product' (Horowitz 1969: 9). Instead, he suggests it is important to avoid the perpetuation of such myths and in so doing to point up the fragility of theories and methods that are used in an attempt to grapple with the complexity of the social world. Sociology is an intricate set of styles and approaches that attempt to deal with a set of complex phenomena by embarking on critical activities, challenging assumptions, raising doubts, teasing out the policy relevance of an issue and its consequences. For sociology is a discipline marked by discussion and debate. The subject is not static; the shape and substance of the discipline change over time as disputes arise and dialogue occurs over what should be included or excluded from the field of study or what might constitute a new disciplinary area in its own right. In such circumstances, sociologists raise new questions, devise new methods and adopt new theoretical frameworks. And so we might ask a further question: how has this applied to British sociology in the last forty years?

There are now several assessments of the work of British sociology (e.g. Eldridge 1980) and British empirical studies over the last forty years (e.g. Marshall 1990) but, as both these particular authors are quick to point out, the volume of research is now so great that it is impossible to provide a complete coverage of British sociological work.

Accordingly, the present volume, like those that have gone before, only includes a selection of some of the main developments and key debates within various sub-fields of the discipline. Correspondingly, the identification of topics, developments or debates themselves is perennially provisional. Some of these appear in this volume represented as whole chapters. Others, however, run across chapters; an example is race and ethnicity which is at issue in several, including the final chapter on the underclass. In any case, sociology and sociologists are no strangers to controversy, so the authors who were invited to contribute the chapters were asked to:

(a) provide an outline of key developments within their subject field;
(b) provide an assessment of the main issues and debates;
(c) identify the key changes that have occurred;
(d) point towards future developments and difficulties that researchers need to confront.

Each author was invited to focus on the achievements of the discipline; however, the time period in which this occurs is arbitrary as far as their subject is concerned. Accordingly, each writer has been permitted to interpret the issues in whatever way was considered most appropriate for the topic under consideration. The picture that emerges is not a neat sequence of clearly demarcated sub-fields, but a ragged set of developments where theories, methods and substantive topics combine and recombine. In short, the essays demonstrate the richness of the sociological enterprise which has contributed to the development of other disciplines and other fields, especially cultural studies and women's studies. This volume of essays therefore covers a vast terrain: theory, meta-theory and discourse, postmodernism, and feminism, as well as methods involving cross-sectional surveys, panels, longitudinal studies, ethnographies and qualitative approaches. A range of questions is raised such as: Has religion continued to decline? Is there evidence that the underclass creates a culture of dependency that is transmitted across generations? How has the study of violence in the domestic context developed? What are the implications for social relations of the declining proportion of 'permanent' jobs and the corresponding increase in jobs which are non-regular? How do members of the public react to efforts to engage them in thinking about up-to-the-minute advances in science and technology? Many of the essays demonstrate the links that exist between their area of study and other branches of the subject.

The vastness of the terrain and the unavoidable selectivity in the group of contributions are not neatly reconcilable. In order to provide the roughest of guides to the former, the essays are grouped into three sections, under simple enough headings: theory, methodology and methods; substantive areas; policy and problems. In order simultaneously to acknowledge the spread of the coverage as well as the contrast between each, and thus avoid imposing an arbitrary thematic scheme, the essays appear within each group in alphabetical order of the authors' surnames.

Rather than provide a detailed review of all the essays in this volume, we can pick out some of the questions and topics they address. In the opening chapter, Sara Arber traces some of the main concerns of sociologists engaged in surveys. The potential value of surveys conducted by governments and other organizations points to future opportunities for the development of secondary data analysis. Meanwhile, as Robert G. Burgess illustrates in the next chapter, qualitative strategies based on observation and interview have the potential to be used in a range of research and evaluation projects that are concerned with the policy process, as well as with 'basic' research questions that are fundamental to the discipline.

Although these approaches are dealt with in separate chapters, it is often the case that they need to be used together to advance our understanding of the social world – and it is still too often the case that they are presented as if mutually exclusive or methodologically antagonistic.

Some of the complex theoretical issues that run through different methodological approaches are reflected in the concerns examined by Christopher Bryant. This is an extremely broad terrain in which some of the theoretical developments that have been at the cutting edge of social theory are those surrounding postmodernism and feminism. Yet among some sociologists there are fears that theory proper has yielded to meta-theory, which may be superseded by reference to discourse. What has been given prominence in recent work, however, is diversity, especially in relation to ethnicity. Among the current preoccupations of some sociologists is whether postmodernist approaches to theorizing can deal with questions of power and complexity.

The next three contributions – which between them may well have no ready or clear counterpart in any overview of sociology of only a couple of decades ago – all treat some of the themes whose relevance is established in Bryant's discussion. Indeed, some fields, such as cultural studies and women's studies, have helped to reshape sociology and the debates within the discipline. John Eldridge addresses the former by providing a tour of the way theorizing culture is taking new guises. A key illustration of the impact of a sub-field of the discipline on sociological analysis is provided both by Mary Maynard, who examines intricacies in social theory of postmodernism and feminism, and Sylvia Walby, who provides an overview of the current variety of work still developing in women's studies and the sociology of gender. The variety covered in Walby's chapter illustrates how women's studies and the sociology of gender have focused on diversity and difference among women, as well as on equity, segregation and inequality in employment, male violence, science, reproductive technologies, sexuality and health and the restructuring of the family and household. In this respect, a 'new' field of study has resulted in fruitful developments through a reconceptualization within sociology alongside the development of cross-disciplinary and inter-disciplinary activities.

Walby's chapter thus treats several key substantive topics and conveniently provides a bridge between the book's first section and those which follow. At the same time, many of the themes from studies of theory and method also arise in the context of a number of the sub-fields discussed in the rest of this volume. Several of the sub-fields of sociology (for example, the family or education, health or religion) have had a marginal existence on the fringes of the discipline, but recent trends and possible future developments may well bring these areas more into the mainstream. For example, David Morgan demonstrates how the family and family issues may have increased in significance in other areas of the subject – such as work, gender and stratification – with potential for further developments through the sociology of the body and the study of the home.

In the sociology of education, Kevin Brehony traces major changes and developments since the mid-1950s. He highlights the relationship between this sub-field and sociology in general. Finally, he turns to the area of 'policy sociology' in education that some would argue is a recent development. However, as several writers have shown, policy concerns have always been a significant aspect of the discipline from its early days of development at the London School of Economics (Halsey 1985). Brehony's contribution paves the way, however, for seeing different, possibly novel versions of the manner in which the relation between the two is playing out at the end of the twentieth century.

The troubled and troublesome relation between sociology on the one hand and the sociology of education on the other is similar to that between sociology and health. The particulars of the politics may differ, as does the terminology which has arisen to deal with it, but Anne Murcott's outline of developments associated with, among other things, changes of name – from medical sociology to the sociology of health and illness – tracks something of a parallel trajectory.

Within the sociology of religion, James Beckford indicates how the subject has been dominated by issues that were on the margins of mainstream sociology. However, he concludes that two recent developments in the sociology of religion build useful bridges to theoretical debates in other fields of sociology. The first is the application of rational choice theory to religious phenomena in the USA, while the second has occurred among French sociologists who argue that modernization creates its own religious opportunities with attention being devoted to emotional styles of religiosity and to subjective identity and religious traditions. In this context, links are made not only between a sub-field and other areas of sociology, but also to developments in the USA and Europe that have had an impact upon British work and to which British sociologists actively contribute. Along the way, Beckford points out that the now prominent notion of globalization has its origins in thinking on the status of religion in modern society.

Science and technology studies represent a significant field, one that is not simply burgeoning, but whose substantive focus is set to become a central and extensive social, political and economic concern. Here, as Peter

Glasner demonstrates, 'new' and 'old' perspectives rub shoulders in devising approaches which need to encompass rapid and far-reaching developments. All the same, in some other areas of sociology, there is evidence of 'new' approaches being taken to examine 'old' problems. The problem of poverty may be only too longstanding, but as Mick Carpenter's chapter suggests, it is made the more serious by its persistence in the midst of mounting prosperity. Together with Robert Moore's discussion of the underclass, the final two chapters in the volume demonstrate the continued relevance of sociological thinking in sharp examinations of old and new terminologies for poverty, and in subjecting old explanations to sustained critical analysis.

These illustrations taken from the contributions highlight some of the themes that are common to many of the chapters in this volume, and which exemplify the continuing diversity and vigour of British contributions that allow Britain to take a notable place in international developments in the discipline (cf. Mohan and Wilke 1994). They include:

(a) the influence of theorizing, conceptualization and reconceptualization in the development of sociology;
(b) the impact of a range of methodologies upon substantive development;
(c) the links between fields of study;
(d) the reconceptualization of the discipline and the extension of fields of study;
(e) the acquisition of sociological analysis and sociological insights for policy development;
(f) the potential of sociology to engage in multi-disciplinary and inter-disciplinary studies.

The list is extensive. Altogether, it points to a discipline where there is a rich and varied tradition of theoretical, methodological and substantive work that is subsequently available as a springboard into new areas. For sociology is open to numerous developments and interpretations which are reflected in the essays that follow in this volume. Indeed the time is ripe for sociologists to make a strong series of contributions to debates about contemporary societies and the policy issues they confront.

References

Burgess, R.G. (1994) 'Some issues and problems in cross-cultural case study research', paper presented to ESRC Field Research Seminar, University of Warwick, May.

Eldridge, J. (1980) *Recent British Sociology*, London: Macmillan.

Halsey, A.H. (1985) 'Provincials and professionals: the post war sociologists', in M. Bulmer (ed.) *Essays on the History of British Sociological Research*, Cambridge: Cambridge University Press.

Horowitz, I.L. (ed.) (1969) *Sociological Self Images*, Oxford: Pergamon Press.

Marshall, G. (1990) *In Praise of Sociology*, London: Unwin Hyman.

Mohan, R.P. and Wilke, A.S. (eds) (1994) *International Handbook of Contemporary Developments in Sociology*, London: Mansell.

Obelkevich, J. and Catterall, P. (eds) (1994) *Understanding British Society*, London: Routledge.

part 1

Theory, methodology and methods

chapter 1

Sociologists and the survey: potential and pitfalls

Sara Arber

This chapter is dedicated to Cathie Marsh who presented a paper on developments in quantitative methodology to the President's Symposium at the British Sociological Association annual conference in 1991. It was a great loss to British sociology that Cathie died of cancer on New Year's Day 1993.

Introduction

British sociology has never whole-heartedly embraced the survey, unlike our North American cousins. During the postwar period, the dominance of surveys in American sociology led to numerous critiques, which had a profound impact on a generation of British sociologists. Students still quote C. Wright Mills' (1959) characterization of social surveys as representing 'abstracted empiricism' which involves no sociological imagination, and Cicourel's (1964) argument that surveys impose a 'deterministic grid' on respondents which artificially generates attitudes and obscures respondents' meanings. Cathie Marsh played a key role in re-establishing the value of surveys within British sociology. Her book *The Survey Method* (1982), provided a trenchant critique of Cicourel (1964) and the 'anti-positivists', and argued convincingly that social surveys can measure respondents' meanings.

British sociologists, and particularly graduate students, are usually encouraged to collect their own data. This emphasis, together with constraints of time and money, has led to a preponderance of smaller-scale qualitative research in British sociology, as well as many poor-quality surveys. Although an increasing amount of high-quality national survey data is available, it is only analyzed by a small number of sociologists and few graduate students. Government surveys are rich sources of data for secondary analysis, since many are underanalyzed, both from a statistical and a theoretical viewpoint.

This chapter demonstrates that survey researchers require sociological imagination, that surveys have contributed much to sociological under-standing, and that the secondary analysis of large, primarily government, surveys has untapped potential as a source of sociological insights. Although such data are 'official statistics', government surveys must be distinguished from official statistics based on administrative sources, such as crime, suicide, and unemployment statistics. The problems associated with administrative statistics (Kitsuse and Cicourel 1963; Hindess 1973; Scott 1990; Levitas and Guy 1996; Dorling and Simpson 1999) are distinct from those associated with government surveys.

Developments in surveys

Surveys comprise the collection of standardized data from a sample of individuals or aggregate units, such as households or small businesses, using structured interviews or self-completion questionnaires. The defining characteristic of a survey is that questions are standardized, allowing the comparison of responses, and surveys aim to be representative of a speci-fied population, so that inferences can be made from the survey results to the wider population from which the sample was drawn.

The methodology of surveys has developed in numerous ways since the 1950s. Telephone surveys are more common and in some areas of market research have largely replaced face-to-face interviews because of the cost advantages (Lavrakas 1986; Frey 1989). Telephone surveys developed hand-in-hand with the development of computer-assisted telephone interviewing (CATI), which alters the process of coding, data entry and editing, as well as the relationship between the interviewer and respondent. The fall in the cost of laptop computers in the 1990s prompted the development of computer-assisted personal interviewing (CAPI), which is now used on nearly all government surveys and surveys conducted by large research organizations (Sainsbury *et al.* 1993; Couper *et al.* 1998). For example, the British government Labour Force Survey (LFS) uses CAPI to collect data at the first household interview, with subsequent interviews using CATI, if the respondent has a telephone and is agreeable (OPCS 1993a).

Many parts of the survey process are increasingly being controlled through computer programs, a development known as CASIC (computer-assisted survey information collection) (Couper *et al.* 1998; Westlake *et al.* 1998). This trend is transforming the survey data collection process and is likely to continue. The required substantial investment in hardware and software means that CASIC can be embraced by government and large survey organizations, but is largely outside the reach of sociologists wishing to conduct their own one-off survey.

Over recent years developments in sampling have led to modifications in sample designs to reduce sampling errors, e.g. by improving the precision of stratification factors (Bruce 1993). The representativeness of samples has been enhanced by using sampling frames with more complete coverage. For example, government surveys have changed from using the electoral register to the Postcode Address File (PAF) as a sampling frame of the population, because of its improved coverage (Butcher and Dodd 1983; Dodd 1987; Butcher 1988; Foster 1993).

Technical advances in data storage, processing and handling, together with the reduction in the cost of computing, have encouraged the growth in the number and size of surveys. In the 1960s, all computing was undertaken on mainframe computers with limited capacity to hold and analyze large datasets; overnight turnaround was the norm and statistical analysis packages, such as SPSS, were only beginning to be developed. By the early 1980s, personal computers had become more common, but at first only had two floppy disk drives and insufficient disk capacity to hold most survey datasets, let alone the statistical packages to analyze them. By the late 1990s, personal computers had sufficient disk space to run the largest statistical analysis packages and hold and analyze surveys containing upwards of 20,000 cases. In addition, statistical packages have become more user-friendly, capable of handling more complex survey data structures, and produce high-quality graphical output.

The growth of surveys has also been stimulated by social and political changes. The information needs of government and other organizations have increased alongside the speed of change in society. In the early 1990s, Conservative political ideology, encapsulated in the Citizen's Charter and the Patient's Charter (DoH 1992), emphasized that services should respond to the needs and priorities of the individual consumer. Thus, surveys were designed to identify the customer's priorities and attitudes towards the services provided. The Labour government has continued this emphasis: for example, in 1998, the Cabinet Office launched a people's panel of 5000 adults to monitor change over time in views about a wide range of public services (Page 1998; Cabinet Office 1999).

The proliferation of survey research makes it all the more important to evaluate the adequacy of survey data, and for sociologists to analyze only data which are considered to meet criteria of reliability, validity and representativeness. A further issue relates to the conceptual assumptions embedded in surveys. These are often implicit, reflecting the underlying conceptual framework of the organization or individuals conducting the research. Inevitably surveys, like sociologists, are prisoners of specific values and theoretical assumptions, which need to be subjected to critical scrutiny. Irvine *et al.* (1979) and Dorling and Simpson (1999) demonstrate that the collection of official survey statistics is not a purely technical matter, showing how conceptual assumptions influence both the production and presentation of official statistics. Only certain types of data are collected by the government. Data of interest to the sociologist may be collected in government surveys, but are presented in a way that reflects contested conceptual assumptions: for example, sexist assumptions about the identity of the head of household or that the husband's occupation is an adequate measure of the social class of married women (Oakley and Oakley 1979). However, secondary analysts may be able to apply alternative conceptual assumptions in their own analyses, for example by classifying women by their own rather than their husband's occupation or characterizing the household by the characteristics of the highest income earner rather than the head of household (Arber 1997).

The purposes of surveys

Surveys of value to sociologists are conducted for a wide variety of purposes. Bulmer (1978) provides a framework which distinguishes four types of purpose. 'Intelligence and monitoring' is an essentially descriptive enterprise, whereby the survey originator is interested in 'fact-finding', relating to the collection of demographic and socio-economic data, or information about attitudes and knowledge. Primary research undertaken by sociologists is rarely of this type, but this is the major type of survey research conducted by central government, local authorities and health authorities.

'Specific problem-orientated research' is geared towards providing solutions and recommendations to a specific problem, with the problem defined by a particular 'customer', such as a government department or health authority. Problem-orientated research may be conducted by sociologists working on government research contracts or for a specified 'paymaster'.

Bulmer characterizes 'strategic social science' as theoretical, but orientated towards providing a better understanding of a social problem, with the aim of producing policy-relevant results, referred to by the Economic and Social Research Council (ESRC) as 'applied strategic' research, whereas Bulmer's fourth type, 'basic social science', aims to advance knowledge through theory building and is not designed to have any direct practical implications, referred to by ESRC as 'basic research'. Both these types are orientated to advancing knowledge and theoretical understanding, and are the main province of the academic sociologist. The ESRC and charitable trusts are the main funders of both 'basic' and 'strategic' social science, but such funders increasingly emphasize the latter, with a concern that research addresses the needs of 'users and beneficiaries'.

Surveys conducted by sociologists

This section focuses on surveys designed by sociologists, and the next section outlines surveys conducted by government and other organizations which may be used to address sociological questions.

The restricted amount of funding available from the ESRC for surveys has been one reason why the number of major British sociological surveys barely reaches double figures. Conforming to the canons of conventional sociological enquiry, most of these surveys have explicitly aimed to test specific hypotheses. A classic is *The Affluent Worker* study in the early 1960s which tested 'the embourgeoisement thesis' among affluent male workers in Luton (Goldthorpe *et al.* 1969). Social mobility and class analysis have been repeatedly investigated by surveys. Glass (1954) examined intergenerational social mobility in the early postwar period and the Oxford Mobility Study surveyed a national sample of men in 1972 (Goldthorpe and Hope 1974; Goldthorpe 1980). Roberts *et al.* (1977) surveyed economically active men to examine class imagery. Male manual workers were interviewed to examine the degree of constraint and choice in their working lives (Blackburn and Mann 1979). The Cambridge Social Stratification Group later conducted a survey of friendship patterns among men which formed the basis of the Cambridge Social Class scale (Stewart *et al.* 1980).

The tradition of surveys on social class culminated in the Essex Social Class survey (Marshall *et al.* 1988), which formed part of a cross-national project researching class structure and class consciousness, initiated by Erik Olin Wright in the USA. For the first time, women as well as men were interviewed, but the survey questions were firmly locked in a male-stream concern with paid employment. Surveys have sometimes been used in community studies, such as the second study of Banbury, which interviewed 1500 men and women, alongside participant observation, examination of documentary sources and neighbourhood studies (Stacey *et al.* 1975).

Structural changes within the British economy, and particularly the growth of male unemployment, led to surveys to examine the social consequences of economic restructuring. For example, Harris (1987) conducted a survey among redundant South Wales steel workers funded by the ESRC. Pahl's interest in the 'informal' (or black) economy developed into the Isle of Sheppey study (Pahl 1984). He examined unpaid as well as paid work, taking the household as the unit of survey analysis, thereby examining women's as well as men's contribution to the household economy. This survey represents a milestone in its conceptualization of work, and its inclusion of young people's employment within a household context (Wallace 1987).

Sociological surveys relating to class and labour markets reached their zenith with the ambitious ESRC-funded Social Change and Economic Life Initiative (SCELI). In six local labour markets, surveys were conducted of men and women under 60, followed by a household survey which included interviews with the respondent and their partner, and a telephone survey of some 200 employers in each locality (Gallie 1988; Gallie *et al.* 1994). A great deal of attention went into the design of complex survey instruments, including the collection of full work, employment, family and migration histories. The detailed work and family histories produced data which captured the complexity of individuals' working and everyday lives, but sacrificed ease of analysis, although the development of easily used software for analyzing event history data has tended to lag behind methods to collect such data.

Surveys funded by ESRC include Finch and Mason (1993), who used the innovative approach of vignettes to assess the normative obligations of caring for older relatives according to the history of inter-family rela-tionships (Finch 1987). Some sociological surveys involve rela-tively small samples, e.g. a team at the University of Keele (Bernard *et al.* 2000) received ESRC funding to resurvey the family lives of older people in three communities previously studied over forty years earlier. This study only interviewed 200 people in each community, making it difficult to undertake more detailed statistical analysis.

It seems likely that the 'academic-survey gap' in Britain (McKennell *et al.* 1987) will remain substantial or increase, as the expertise of professional survey experts in government and large organizations becomes increasingly divorced from that of academic sociologists. The high costs of surveys and lack of technical survey infrastructure within university sociology departments means that, in future, sociologists are less likely to seek funding to conduct their own surveys. Where they do so, however, they are likely to use a survey organization to collect the survey data rather than directly conduct the survey themselves.

Surveys collected by other organizations and used by sociologists

Surveys conducted by government and other organizations are an important source of sociological data, providing a valuable resource for secondary analysis, because of the relative lack of 'tailor-made' socio-logical surveys. Central government collects a wide range of statistical data about the characteristics of the population which is of interest to soci-ologists: for example, the Labour Force Survey collects information about the social and demographic characteristics of the employed, self-employed and those seeking work (OPCS 1993a).

The descriptive data collected in government surveys, such as the General Household Survey (GHS), reflect the policy concerns of specific government departments. For example, during the late 1980s, Conservative government policy was to expand share ownership and increase the uptake of personal pensions and private medical insurance, and it was therefore no surprise that questions were asked in the GHS about these topics at this time. Childcare for working mothers became an issue in the 1990s and the 1991 GHS included a section on formal providers of care for children under 11 and the cost of childcare.

Some government surveys address specific problems: for example, the DHSS cohort study of unemployed men (Moylan 1984) examined the income replacement ratios of unemployed men, comparing their earnings in work with their income while unemployed. As well as specific problem-orientated research, government surveys may aim to illuminate a policy area of current concern to better understand a policy issue or client group and provide background information to inform possible future policy changes. Many one-off government surveys have played this role, includ-ing the Women and Employment Survey (Martin and Roberts 1984) and the OPCS (Office of Population Censuses and Surveys) Disability Surveys (Martin *et al.* 1988).

A number of government surveys have explored issues of interest to feminist sociologists, such as the Women and Employment Survey (Martin and Roberts 1984), and the section on carers in the 1985 GHS, published as the *Informal Carers Survey* (Green 1988). The Policy Studies Institute (PSI) surveys on the impact of maternity rights on women's employment following childbirth (Daniel 1980; McRae 1991) were particularly influential. Earlier criticisms that surveys are male-stream (Abbott and Wallace 1990) largely reflected the choice of topics previously studied by sociologists using surveys rather than anything inherent in the survey as not being an appropriate research method to investigate topics of concern to feminist sociologists (see Roberts 1990).

The decennial population census provides 'benchmark' data about the social characteristics of the population, the extent of geographical migration and housing conditions in local areas (OPCS 1993b). In the USA, public-use microdata samples have been available for each census since 1960 (Marsh *et al.* 1991), and have provided a major source of data for sociological research on issues such as occupational attainment and residential segregation according to ethnicity. In Britain, microdata for secondary analysis is available from the 1991 population census as Samples of Anonymized Records (SARs): a 2 per cent sample of individuals and an independent 1 per cent sample of households (Marsh 1993). There are proposals to increase the 'individual' SAR to 3 per cent for the 2001 census (Dale and Elliot 2000).

Surveys may be designed because of a perceived lack of information about an area of policy interest. The 1991 National Survey of Sexual Attitudes and Lifestyles (NATSAL) was conducted because of concerns about the spread of HIV/AIDS and the lack of knowledge about the sexual behaviour of adults. Nearly 19,000 men and women aged 16–59 were interviewed, with funding provided by the Wellcome Trust (Wadsworth *et al.* 1993). Another example is the Policy Studies Institute Fourth National Survey of Ethnic Minorities (Modood *et al.* 1997) which provided important data on the health and socio-economic characteristics of black and minority ethnic groups.

The British Social Attitudes Survey (BSAS) provides a major time series to document changes in attitudes to a wide range of issues and has been conducted annually since 1983 by Social and Community Planning Research (now the National Centre for Social Research, NCSR) (Jowell *et al.* 1998).

Studying time: panel and longitudinal studies

Time can be taken into account in cross-sectional surveys by collecting retrospective data about the respondent's work, family or migration history, and in prospective studies which collect data at a number of points in time, i.e. panel, longitudinal or cohort studies. Although life course and life history analyses have been emphasized more by qualitative than quantitative researchers, their insights are equally applicable to survey researchers. The life course approach focuses on the interlinkage between phases of the life course and the ways in which an individual's life is interwoven with the lives of others (Hareven and Adams 1982; Arber and Evandrou 1993).

Some surveys which collected retrospective event histories, such as the Women and Employment Survey (Martin and Roberts 1984) and SCELI (Gallie 1988), have developed techniques to aid the accurate recall of past events. However, retrospective data can only be accurately collected on topics which are salient to the individual (Moss and Goldstein 1979; Dex 1991). Many issues of interest to sociologists cannot be accurately asked about retrospectively, for example an individual's past attitudes, domestic division of labour prior to marriage, income in the past, and health or behaviour as a child. These issues can only be studied using a panel or longitudinal study, which obtains information about the individual's current attitudes or behaviour, and resurveys them periodically.

Cross-sectional surveys often reveal associations but cannot determine the causal ordering of variables. For example, unemployment is correlated with poor health, but the theoretical and policy implications of this association depend on the direction of causation: whether being unemployed causes poor health or poor health leads people to lose their job or not obtain a new job (Fox *et al.* 1985; Bartley 1991; Blane *et al.* 1993). The direction of causation can only be resolved with panel or longitudinal studies, which accurately measure health status at varying points in time. The three British birth cohort studies were not originally designed to clarify the direction of causation in relation to inequalities in health, but have been used extensively to address this issue (Wadsworth 1986, 1991; Power *et al.* 1991).

Longitudinal studies allow an accurate assessment of the effects of time (period), age and cohort (generation). Panel and longitudinal studies may be collected by academic social scientists, government or other organizations, and seldom fit neatly into Bulmer's (1978) four types of purposes of research. Collecting longitudinal and panel studies is very expensive, and may involve a range of funders, either funding different waves or co-funding within the same wave. The British government has played an important role in funding most British longitudinal studies, often together with the ESRC, the Medical Research Council and other funders.

Britain is fortunate to have three birth cohort studies, based on births in one week in March 1946 (National Survey of Health and

Development), in March 1958 (National Child Development Study, NCDS), and in March 1970 (the British Cohort Study (BCS), formerly Child Health and Education Study). In each case the child was followed up at intervals by collecting survey data from the mother and the child, as well as from teachers and health professionals, and subsequently data collected during adulthood. The 1946 and 1958 cohort studies have also surveyed the next generation, collecting data about the children of cohort members, and the 1991 wave of NCDS collected data from the partners of cohort members (Ferri 1993). Further surveys collecting data for the NCDS and BCS are being undertaken in 1999/2000.

The ONS (Office for National Statistics) Longitudinal Study (LS) contains data on 1 per cent of the population of England and Wales, linking census records from 1971, 1981 and 1991 for the same individuals and other members of their household, as well as data about death, births and other vital events (Dale 1993). For reasons of confidentiality LS data are not available from the Data Archive at Essex, but can only be analyzed in association with the Centre for Longitudinal Studies at the Institute of Education, London (which is part of the Joint Centre for Longitudinal Research).

The ESRC-funded British Household Panel Study (BHPS), University of Essex, began in 1991, interviewing all adults in about 5000 households annually (Buck *et al.* 1994). The aim was to produce a 'basic resource for both strategic, fundamental research in the social sciences and for policy-relevant research' (Rose *et al.* 1992: 6). It therefore does not fit solely into one of the types of purposes of primary research identified by Bulmer (1978). The Institute of Social and Economic Research (ISER) at Essex has been highly successful in promoting the use of the BHPS as a data resource, although it has hitherto been analyzed to a much greater extent by economists than sociologists. BHPS data are of high quality and are made available rapidly to users; comprehensive and user-friendly information about the BHPS is available on their exemplary website (http://www.iser.ac.uk/bhps/).

Thus, increasing amounts of longitudinal data are now available for secondary analysis, and there have been developments in statistical techniques for analyzing event history data collected as part of cross-sectional surveys and longitudinal/panel survey data (Dale and Davies 1994). The Analysis of Large and Complex Datasets (ALCD) programme, funded by ESRC, has led to major advances in statistical modelling, but this programme has been dominated by the concerns of statisticians rather than driven by the agendas of substantive social scientists.

Annual surveys contain many questions that are repeated each year or on a periodic basis. The General Household Survey (GHS) has been running since 1971 (apart from two years – 1997/98 and 1999/2000), the Family Expenditure Survey (FES) since 1957 and the British Social Attitudes Survey (BSAS) since 1983. These annual surveys allow the analysis of trends over time: for example, to monitor the impact of policy changes over the last fifteen years on poverty and attitudes towards welfare and moral issues.

Social scientists can also use repeated cross-sectional surveys as quasi- or synthetic cohorts to address some of the policy issues which require an understanding of the impact of time, cohort and age (Harding 1990; Waldfogel 1993). Pseudo-cohorts can be constructed by using successive years of cross-sectional data such as the GHS to track a particular cohort through time. Although the same individuals are not surveyed each year, individuals from the same birth cohort are. Thus the characteristics of one cohort can be compared with those of a group which represents them demographically five or ten years later. However, such an approach is limited in that it focuses on the average group characteristics or behaviour, rather than that of individuals, and fails to capture the various changes in people's circumstances over time. It may be complemented by analysis of longitudinal data such as the NCDS (Waldfogel 1993).

Secondary analysis

The government has a near monopoly over the funding of large-scale survey data, some of which are collected in-house. However, funded government research is now usually subject to competitive tendering and undertaken by survey organizations, such as the National Centre for Social Research (NCSR, formerly SCPR). There is an increasing amount of survey data available to British social scientists for secondary analysis. Secondary analysis is the re-analysis of existing microdata for the researcher's own purposes, using data available in an anonymized computer datafile (Hakim 1982; Dale et al. 1988; Procter 1993).

The UK has a national archive where datasets are deposited and distributed to the academic community: the Data Archive at the University of Essex (http://dawww.essex.ac.uk/). An outstanding success of the Data Archive has been the negotiation of rights to distribute virtually all British-government-funded surveys for secondary analysis at no cost to academics. Datasets are supplied free of charge to students and academics, except where research is externally funded from sources other than the ESRC. The only charge is for supplying the documentation about the survey, such as interview schedules and codebooks, but these are increasingly available electronically, thus eliminating this cost. The Data Archive holds overseas datasets and provides a gateway to non-UK data for UK researchers and vice versa. There is an on-line catalogue and information retrieval system, BIRON, and datasets can be ordered and despatched electronically.

The questionnaires for the main government surveys and other key surveys, such as the BHPS and BSAS, are available on-line through the ESRC-funded Question Bank (http://www.soc.surrey.ac.uk/qb1). The Question Bank is designed as a knowledge resource to increase the sharing of good practice on ways of designing questions to measure social scientific concepts, to document data collection instruments and to provide insight into underlying conceptual and design issues. The full questionnaires are on-line and can be easily downloaded for use by researchers or in teaching.

Academics face no restrictions in how they analyze most datasets supplied by the Data Archive. For government surveys, researchers must submit a short proposal outlining the research purposes for which they plan to use the data, required for information by the Data Archive and the relevant government department rather than to prevent researchers analyzing data for specific purposes. A contractual user form must also be signed. Publications are not vetted in advance, so secondary analysts' work is not controlled in any way. The only requirement is that two copies of publications must be submitted to the Data Archive after publication, one of which is forwarded to the data depositor.

The potential of secondary analysis

There are a number of advantages of secondary analysis compared with the collection of primary survey data for addressing sociological issues. These will be outlined, focusing particularly on the potential of government and other large surveys.

Cost-effectiveness

The cost to a sociologist of designing and conducting their own survey is generally prohibitive, yet government and other large surveys are available from the Data Archive at no cost. Government surveys produce high-quality data from nationally representative samples, usually with a high response rate. The annual cost of collecting GHS data is about

£2 million, so secondary analysts have a very valuable and costly dataset at their fingertips to interrogate in whatever way they wish.

Convenience

Datasets supplied by the Data Archive are usually fully labelled as SPSS files, and can be supplied electronically or on a range of media, e.g. diskette or CD-ROM. Current computing power means that all except the very largest datasets can be analyzed on a PC. Once the researcher is familiar with the dataset, analyses can be performed relatively quickly, allowing sociologists to engage in current policy debates.

Richness of data

Secondary analysis of government and other large surveys is more akin to primary analysis, because sociological issues can be addressed which were not envisaged by the survey originators. Government surveys are conducted primarily to provide policy-related descriptive information for specific government departments. Only a small proportion of these analyses are published. For example, annual reports consist largely of multi-way cross-tabulations and often a limited amount of commentary, such as the annual report of the Labour Force Survey (OPCS 1993a).

The secondary analyst of government surveys can go beyond the published government analyses in several ways. First, multivariate statistical techniques may be more appropriate than relying on multi-way cross-tabulations, for example, in analyzing the interconnnections between structural and family factors in influencing ill health (Arber 1991, 1997; Cooper *et al.* 1999). Second, government survey reports are written within the value framework of the government department and usually little attempt is made to address particular theoretical issues. The secondary analyst can use the same data to address theoretical questions which are outside the remit of the survey originators. Third, the secondary analyst need not be locked into the same conceptual assumptions as those embedded within the published survey report. For example, occupational unit groups are collected in the GHS and can be used to construct alternative social class categorizations (see Rose and O'Reilly 1997). Similarly, although the GHS annual reports analyze married women's health by their husband's social class, the secondary analyst can analyze married women's health by their own social class and compare this 'individualistic' approach with the 'conventional' approach (Arber 1989, 1990, 1997).

Source of representative samples of small sub-groups

Many issues of sociological interest relate to proportionately small sub-groups of the population. For such groups it is usually impossible to identify a complete sampling frame and thus draw a representative sample, so research is often biased in significant ways. An alternative is to use large government surveys, where necessary combining data from consecutive years to increase the sample size of the sub-group of interest. For example, sociologists may be interested in people who cohabit or the income consequences of lone fatherhood compared with lone motherhood. There are no available sampling frames for people who cohabit or on lone parents, but the GHS annually yields a representative sample of such groups. Cooper *et al.* (1998a, 1998b) combined three years of the GHS to give a sufficiently large sample to produce reliable analyses on the health of children of lone parents and the health of children from minority ethnic groups.

Even for research which does not involve small population sub-groups, it is often beneficial to combine a number of years of data. Our research on factors influencing mid-life women's labour force participation used a combined dataset from the 1988–90 GHS yielding a sample of 14,000 women aged 40–59, allowing reliable analyses by marital status and detailed age groups in the years before women's statutory retirement age (Ginn and Arber 1994).

Studying social contexts

A key concern of sociologists is to analyze social relationships and how an individual's behaviour is influenced by the behaviour of significant others, and the wider groupings of which they are a part. Multi-level analysis takes into account the impact of larger social groupings on the behaviour and attitudes of individuals.

Many government surveys collect data on all adults in the household, allowing the researcher to analyze the interrelationships between the characteristics of different household members (Dale *et al.* 1988). Exploiting the hierarchical properties of households allows researchers to rebuild connections between household members. For example, Payne (1987) used the GHS to analyze young people's unemployment and how this related to whether their fathers and/or mothers were unemployed. Since women's employment participation is influenced by their partner's employment status and level of earnings, as well as the ages and number of their children, household surveys like the GHS provide sufficient data for such analyses.

Sociologists of education have made particular advances in the study of school effects on educational attainment, after controlling for the child's characteristics and their family background. An early influential study was Rutter *et al.* (1979), and many subsequent studies have yielded important substantive and statistical advances (Aitkin and Longford 1986; Goldstein 1987; Paterson 1991; Raudenbush and Willms 1991). A key concern of the ESRC-funded ALCD programme has been to develop new techniques for multi-level modelling.

Comparative analysis

The growth of government surveys has occurred across most industrialized countries. This opens up the possibility of cross-national analysis which addresses social policy or sociological issues. For example, Finland conducts a Level of Living Survey which is very similar to the British GHS. In Finland, women's labour market participation is comparable to that of men, with nearly 90 per cent of women employed full-time during their child-bearing years; this contrasts with British women's high rate of part-time employment and lower overall employment participation rate. Arber and Lahelma (1993) compared the impact of employment participation on inequalities in women's health in these two societies.

Validity of interpretations

A number of secondary analysts are likely to use the same survey data source; therefore they are in a position to contest each other's findings and interpretations. If a researcher has mis-specified a statistical model, the same data can be reworked by another analyst who can publish their own divergent findings leading to debate on alternative procedures and theoretical interpretations. This is unlike qualitative research, where it is rare for another researcher to rework fieldnotes or interview transcripts and disagree with an author's analysis or interpretations.

Potential pitfalls of secondary analysis

Despite the considerable advantages of secondary analysis identified in the previous section, the secondary analyst needs to be wary of a number of potential pitfalls when planning their analysis.

Complexity of data structure

The potential sociological value of many government datasets relates to their large size and/or the complexity of their data structure. Since many datasets are very large, researchers need to have sufficient computer disk space to store and analyze all the data or must obtain a sub-set of the data.

Household surveys generally have a hierarchical structure in which the amount of data varies with the number of household members, and with the number of levels of hierarchy: e.g. the GHS asks for details of all doctor consultations in the last two weeks; most respondents have none but some will have six or more. The GHS can be supplied by the Data Archive as a hierarchical file in Scientific Information Retrieval (SIR) format. Secondary analysts who wish to examine the interrelationship between the characteristics of different household members will probably need to use a data management package such as SIR (Dale *et al.* 1988). The Data Archive also supplies the GHS as a rectangular SPSS file based on either individuals or households, which is easier to use, but may not contain all the linkages between household members which the analyst requires.

It goes without saying that secondary analysts need sufficient knowledge of statistics, as well as the ability to use statistical analysis programs such as SPSS. This should no longer be a constraint as analysis programs have become more user-friendly and the teaching of computing and basic statistical analysis is a requirement for ESRC-funded postgraduate students. However, there is a lack of knowledge of more advanced methods of multivariate analysis and the management of large and complex data structures (Skinner 1999).

Assessing the validity of the data

Government surveys need to be subjected to the same critical scrutiny as any other source of data, including the quality of developmental and pilot work, interviewer training and fieldwork control, the method of sample selection, sampling frame and response rate. The secondary analyst needs to obtain as much documentation as possible about the collection of the survey data and be aware of data limitations.

For many large surveys, the Data Archive organizes workshops or user group meetings and operates an electronic bulletin board. The ESRC Survey Link Scheme offers academic social scientists the opportunity to spend one or more days finding out more about a survey, attending interviewer briefings and accompanying interviewers in the field. This scheme operates with surveys such as the GHS, LFS, British Social Attitudes Survey and British Household Panel Study.

Measurement error

The conventional research paradigm inherent within survey research is one of 'theory-testing', that is the primary researcher conducts research to test theoretical hypotheses. These are operationalized into empirical hypotheses, and questions are developed to validly measure the theoretical concepts which constitute the various elements of the researcher's theory (Gilbert 2001).

However, the secondary analyst has to work with someone else's survey questions and assess whether these questions adequately measure the theoretical concepts fundamental to the theory they wish to test. Unfortunately, it may not be possible to measure key concepts because appropriate questions have not been asked in the survey or the questions may not be ideal indicators of the relevant concepts. Alternatively, appropriate questions may have been asked but the existing coding categories do not provide theoretically meaningful analytic distinctions. For example, the 1991 GHS asked about childcare for children under 11, providing distinctions between different sources of paid care. However, all forms of unpaid care were combined into a single category of 'family and friends', with childcare by partners or others living in the same household explicitly excluded. This coding meant a researcher could not assess how much childcare was provided by grandparents or other relatives while mothers were at work.

Exploratory and confirmatory research

The secondary analyst works in a much more interactive way between existing survey questions and theory than is suggested in the 'theory-testing' model. The actual process of secondary analysis is in practice a combination of exploratory data analysis and theory-testing or confirmatory analysis (Marsh 1988; Erickson and Nosanchuk 1992). Initial stages of secondary analysis are often exploratory, since the secondary analyst needs to fully understand the data by exploratory analysis, producing a range of cross-tabulations and descriptive statistics, trying out different indicators of concepts and constructing various new derived variables. This initial descriptive phase may itself produce worthwhile analyses: for example, initial exploration of the 1985 Informal Carers Survey was published as Arber and Ginn (1990).

Timeliness of data

Government surveys are usually at least two years old before they are released to the Data Archive for secondary analysis, typically after the publication of the relevant government report. Some surveys are released very quickly: e.g. the Labour Force Survey collects data on a quarterly basis which are available from the Data Archive fourteen weeks after the end of data collection.

Most sociologists use secondary analysis to address analytic questions which are not highly time-dependent, so the time lag in the release of data is not a major constraint. For example, the theoretical significance of analyses of class inequalities in health are likely to be the same irrespective of whether the data are one or four years old. More innovative research – for example, developing alternative conceptualizations of class – may be undertaken on earlier data without detracting from its significance (e.g. Rose and O'Reilly 1997).

The future

The future use of surveys by sociologists is promising in terms of the secondary analysis of the large quantities of survey data routinely collected by government and other organizations, but is less sanguine with regard to sociologists designing and collecting their own survey data. The challenge and opportunity for sociologists is to apply their theoretical knowledge and conceptual skills to use existing survey datasets creatively to address sociological questions. The rapid fall in the real costs of computing power means that the cost advantage of secondary analysis over primary data collection is increasingly great.

Although the skills base of sociologists is slowly changing, a potential problem is that many sociologists lack the statistical and data management skills to fully exploit these large and complex datasets. The challenge is to increase the current level of expertise, while ensuring that the future generation of survey analysts do not lose sight of substantive sociological and policy issues because of their fascination with new statistical techniques.

Acknowledgements

I am grateful to Robert Burgess, Angela Dale, Nigel Gilbert, Gill Jones, Denise Lievesley and Jean Martin for their very helpful comments on an earlier draft of this chapter. The errors of commission and omission remain my own.

References

Abbott, P. and Wallace, C. (1990) *An Introduction to Sociology: Feminist Perspectives*, London: Routledge.

Aitkin, M. and Longford, N.T. (1986) 'Statistical modelling issues in school effectiveness studies', *Journal of Royal Statistical Society A* 149: 1–43.

Arber, S. (1989) 'Opening the "black" box: inequalities in women's health', in P. Abbott and G. Payne (eds) *New Directions in the Sociology of Health*, Brighton: Falmer Press.

Arber, S. (1990) 'Revealing women's health: re-analysing the General Household Survey', in H. Roberts (ed.) *Women's Health Counts*, London: Routledge.

Arber, S. (1991) 'Class, paid employment and family roles: Making sense of structural disadvantage, gender and health status', *Social Science and Medicine* 32 (4): 425–36.

Arber, S. (1997) 'Comparing inequalities in women's and men's health: Britain in the 1990s', *Social Science and Medicine* 44 (6): 773–87.

Arber, S. and Evandrou, M. (eds) (1993) *Ageing, Independence and the Life Course*, London: Jessica Kingsley.

Arber, S. and Ginn, J. (1990) 'The meaning of informal care: gender and the contribution of elderly people', *Ageing and Society* 10 (4): 429–54.

Arber, S. and Lahelma, E. (1993) 'Women, paid employment and ill-health in Britain and Finland', *Acta Sociologica* 36: 121–38.

Bartley, M. (1991) 'Health and labour force participation: "stress", selection and the reproduction costs of labour power', *Journal of Social Policy* 20 (3): 327–64.

Bernard, M., Phillips, J., Phillipson, C. and Ogg, J. (2000) in S. Arber and C. Attias-Donfut (eds) *The Myth of Generational Conflict: Family and State in Ageing Societies*, London: Routledge.

Blackburn, R.M. and Mann, M. (1979) *The Working Class in the Labour Market*, London: Macmillan.

Blane, D., Smith, G.D. and Bartley, M. (1993) 'Social selection: what does it contribute to social class differences in health?', *Sociology of Health and Illness* 15 (1): 1–15.

Bruce, S. (1993) 'Selecting stratifiers for the family resources survey', *Survey Methodology Bulletin* 32: 20–5, London: OPCS.

Buck, N., Gershuny, J., Rose, D. and Scott, J. (1994) *Changing Households: The British Household Panel Survey 1990–1992*, Colchester, Essex: ESRC Research Centre on Micro-social Change.

Bulmer, M. (1978) *Social Policy Research*, London: Allen and Unwin.

Butcher, R. (1988) 'The use of the postcode address file as a sampling frame', *Statistician* 37: 15–24.

Butcher, R. and Dodd, P. (1983) 'The electoral register – two surveys', *Population Trends* 31: 15–19.

Cabinet Office (1999) *Results from the People's Panel*, issue 2, London: Cabinet Office.

Cicourel, A.V. (1964) *Method and Measurement in Sociology*, New York: Free Press.

Cooper, H., Arber, S. and Smaje, C. (1998a) 'Social class or deprivation? Structural factors and children's limiting longstanding illness in the 1990s', *Sociology of Health and Illness* 20 (3): 289–311.

Cooper, H., Smaje, C. and Arber, S. (1998b) 'Use of health services by children and young people according to ethnicity and social class: secondary analysis of as national survey', *British Medical Journal* 317: 1047–51.

Cooper, H., Arber, S., Fee, L. and Ginn, J. (1999) *The Influence of Social Capital and Social Support on Health*, London: Health Education Authority.

Couper, M.P., Baker, R.P., Bethlehem, J., Clark, C., Martin, J., Nicholls, I. and O'Reilly, J.M. (eds) (1998) *Computer Assisted Survey Information Collection*, New York: John Wiley.

Dale, A. (1993) 'The OPCS longitudinal study', in A. Dale and C. Marsh (eds) *The 1991 Census User's Guide*, London: HMSO.

Dale, A. and Davies, R. (eds) (1994) *Analyzing Social and Political Change: A Codebook of Methods*, London: Sage.

Dale, A. and Elliot, M. (2000) 'Confidentiality work to support the specification for an individual SAR from the 2001 census', *SARS Newsletter* 14: 4–9.

Dale, A, Arber, S. and Procter, M. (1988) *Doing Secondary Analysis*, London: Allen and Unwin.

Daniel, W.W. (1980) *Maternity Rights: The Experiences of Women*, PSI report no. 588, London: Policy Studies Institute.

Department of Health (DoH) (1992) *The Patients' Charter*, London: HMSO.

Dex, S. (1991) 'The reliability of recall data: A literature review', working paper no. 11, Colchester, Essex: ESRC Research Centre on Micro-social Change.

Dodd, T. (1987) 'A further investigation into the coverage of the postcode address file', *Survey Methodology Bulletin* 21, London: Office of Population, Censuses and Surveys.

Dorling, D. and Simpson, S. (eds) (1999) *Statistics in Society: The Arithmetic of Politics*, London: Arnold.

Erickson, B.H. and Nosanchuk, T.A. (1992) *Understanding Data*, second edition, Milton Keynes: Open University Press.

Ferri, E. (ed.) (1993) *Britain's 33 Year Olds*, London: National Children's Bureau and ESRC.

Finch, J. (1987) 'The vignette technique in survey research', *Sociology* 21 (1): 105–14.

Finch, J. and Mason, J. (1993) *Negotiating Family Responsibilities*, London: Routledge.

Foster, K. (1993) 'The electoral register as a sampling frame', *Survey Methodology Bulletin* 33: 1–7, London: OPCS.

Fox, A.J., Goldblatt, P.O. and Jones, D.R. (1985) 'Social class mortality differentials: artefact, selection or life circumstances', *Journal of Epidemiology and Community Health* 39: 1–8.

Frey, J.H. (1989) *Survey Research by Telephone*, second edition, New York: Sage.

Gallie, D. (1988) *The Social Change and Economic Life Initiative: An Overview*, SCELI working paper 1, Oxford: Nuffield College.

Gallie, D., Marsh, C. and Vogler, C. (eds) (1994) *The Social Consequences of Unemployment*, Oxford: Oxford University Press.

Gilbert, N. (2001) 'Research, theory and method', in N. Gilbert (ed.) *Researching Social Life*, second edition, London: Sage.

Ginn, J. and Arber, S. (1994) 'Mid-life women's employment and pension entitlements in relation to co-resident adult children', *Journal of Marriage and the Family* 56: 813–19.

Glass, D.V. (ed.) (1954) *Social Mobility in Britain*, London: Routledge and Kegan Paul.

Goldstein, H. (1987) *Multilevel Models in Educational and Social Research*, London: Griffin.

Goldthorpe, J.H. (1980) *Social Mobility and Class Structure in Modern Britain*, Oxford: Clarendon Press.

Goldthorpe, J.H. and Hope, K. (1974) *The Social Grading of Occupations: A New Approach and Scale*, Oxford: Clarendon Press.

Goldthorpe, J.H., Lockwood, D., Bechhofer, F. and Platt, J. (1969) *The Affluent Worker in the Class Structure*, Cambridge: Cambridge University Press.

Green, H. (1988) *The Informal Carers' Survey*, London: Office of Population, Censuses and Surveys.

Hakim, C. (1982) *Secondary Analysis in Social Research*, London: Allen and Unwin.

Harding, A. (1990) 'Dynamic micro-simulation models: problems and prospects', Welfare State Programme discussion paper no. 48, London: LSE.

Hareven, T.K. and Adams, K.J. (eds) (1982) *Ageing and Life Course Transitions: An Interdisciplinary Perspective*, London: Tavistock.

Harris, C.C. (1987) 'Redundancy and class analysis', in R.M. Lee (ed.) *Redundancy, Layoffs and Plant Closures*, London: Croom Helm.

Hindess, B. (1973) *The Use of Official Statistics in Sociology*, London: Macmillan.

Irvine, J., Miles, I. and Evans, J. (1979) *Demystifying Social Statistics*, London: Pluto Press.

Jowell, R., Curtice, J., Park, A. *et al.* (1992) *British Social Attitudes: The 1992 Report*, Aldershot: Gower.

Kitsuse, J.I. and Cicourel, A.V. (1963) 'A note on the use of official statistics', *Social Problems* 11: 131–9.

Lavrakas, P.J. (1986) *Telephone Survey Methods*, Applied Social Research Methods no. 7, Newbury Park CA: Sage.

Levitas, R. and Guy, W. (eds) (1996) *Interpreting Official Statistics*, London: Routledge.

Marsh, C. (1982) *The Survey Method*, London: Allen and Unwin.

Marsh, C. (1988) *Exploring Data: An Introduction to Data Analysis for Social Scientists*, Cambridge: Polity Press.

Marsh, C. (1993) 'The sample of anonymised records', in A. Dale and C. Marsh (eds) *The 1991 Census User's Guide*, London: HMSO.

Marsh, C., Skinner, C., Arber, S., Penhale, B., Openshaw, S., Hobcraft, J., Lievesley, D. and Walford, N. (1991) 'The case for a sample of anonymised records from the 1991 census', *Journal of the Royal Statistical Society A* 154 (2): 305–40.

Marshall, G., Newby, H., Rose, D. and Vogler, C. (1988) *Social Class in Modern Britain*, London: Hutchinson Education.

Martin, J. and Roberts, C. (1984) *Women and Employment: A Lifetime Perspective*, London: HMSO.

Martin, J., Meltzer, H. and Elliot, D. (1988) *The Prevalence of Disability among Adults: Report 1*, London: HMSO.

McKennell, A., Bynner, J. and Bulmer, B. (1987) 'The links between policy, survey research and academic social science', in M. Bulmer (ed.) *Social Science Research and Government: Comparative Essays in Britain and the US*, Cambridge: Cambridge University Press.

McRae, S. (1991) *Maternity Rights in Britain: The Experience of Women and Employers*, London: Policy Studies Institute.

Mills, C.W. (1959) *The Sociological Imagination*, Oxford: Oxford University Press.

Modood, T., Berthoud, R., Lakey, J. *et al.* (1997) *Ethnic Minorities in Britain: Diversity and Disadvantage*, London: Policy Studies Institute.

Moss, L. and Goldstein, H. (eds) (1979) *The Recall Method in Social Surveys*, Institute of Education, Studies in Education no. 9, London: Institute of Education.

Moylan, S. (1984) *DHSS Cohort Study of Unemployed Men*, London: HMSO.

Oakley, A. and Oakley, R. (1979) 'Sexism in official statistics', in J. Irvine, I. Miles and J. Evans (eds) *Demystifying Social Statistics*, London: Pluto Press.

OPCS (1991) *General Household Survey, 1989*, London: HMSO.

OPCS (1993a) *Labour Force Survey*, Department of Employment, London: HMSO.

OPCS (1993b) *1991 Census: Age, Sex and Marital Status, Great Britain*, London: HMSO.

Page, B. (1998) 'The people's panel', *Social Research Association News*, November: 1–4.

Pahl, R. (1984) *Divisions of Labour*, Oxford: Blackwell.

Paterson, L. (1991) 'Socio-economic status and educational attainment: a multi-dimensional and multi-level study', *Evaluation and Research in Education* 5 (3): 97–121.

Payne, J. (1987) 'Does unemployment run in families? Some findings from the General Household Survey', *Sociology* 21 (2): 199–214.

Power, C., Manor, O. and Fox, J. (1991) *Health and Class: The Early Years*, London: Chapman and Hall.

Procter, M. (1993) 'Analysing other researchers' data', in N. Gilbert (ed.) *Researching Social Life*, London: Sage.

Raudenbush, S.W. and Willms, J.D. (eds) (1991) *Schools, Classrooms, and Pupils*, New York: Academic Press.

Roberts, H. (1990) *Women's Health Counts*, London: Routledge.

Roberts, K., Cook, F.G., Clark, S.C. and Semetonoff, E. (1977) *The Fragmentary Class Structure*, London: Heinemann.

Robertson, C. (1993) 'Participation in post-compulsory education in Scotland', *Journal of the Royal Statistical Society A* 156 (3): 423–42.

Rose, D. *et al.* (1992) 'Micro-social change in Britain: current and future research using the British Household Panel Survey', *Working Papers of the ESRC Research Centre on Micro-Social Change*, paper 21, Colchester: University of Essex.

Rose, D. and O'Reilly, K. (eds) (1997) *Constructing Classes. Towards a New Social Classification for the UK,* Swindon: ESRC/Office of National Statistics.

Rutter, M., Maughan, B., Mortimer, P. and Ouston, J. (1979) *Fifteen Thousand Hours: Secondary Schools and their Effects on Children,* London: Open Books.

Sainsbury, R., Ditch, J. and Hutton, S. (1993) 'CAPI', *Social Research Update,* no. 3, Guildford: University of Surrey.

Scott, J. (1990) *A Matter of Record,* Cambridge: Polity Press.

Skinner, C. (1999) *Review of Social Statistics, Report to the ESRC and Research Resources Board,* Swindon: ESRC (mimeo).

Stacey, M., Batstone, E., Bell, C. and Murcott, A. (1975) *Power, Persistence and Change,* London: Routledge.

Stewart, A., Prandy, K. and Blackburn, R.M. (1980) *Social Stratification and Occupations,* London: Macmillan.

Wadsworth, J., Field, J., Johnson, A.M., Bradshaw, S. and Wellings, K. (1993) 'Methodology of the National Survey of Sexual Attitudes and Lifestyles', *Journal of the Royal Statistical Society A* 156 (3): 407–21.

Wadsworth, M.E.J. (1986) 'Serious illness in childhood and its association with later-life achievement', in R.G. Wilkinson (ed.) *Class and Health: Research and Longitudinal Data,* London: Tavistock.

Wadsworth, M.E.J. (1991) *The Imprint of Time: Childhood, History and Adult Life,* Oxford: Clarendon Press.

Waldfogel, J. (1993) *Women Working for Less: A Longitudinal Analysis of the Family Gap,* Welfare State Programme discussion paper no. 93, London: LSE.

Wallace, C. (1987) *For Richer, For Poorer,* London: Tavistock.

Westlake, A., Martin, J., Rigg, M. and Skinner, C. (eds) (1998) *New Methods for Survey Research: Proceedings of an International Conference,* Chesham, Bucks: Association for Survey Computing.

chapter 2

Never mind the quality . . . ? Developments in ethnographic and qualitative research

Robert G. Burgess

Introduction

A brief glance at many current empirical projects conducted by researchers and postgraduates in sociology quickly reveals that the most popular choice of methodology is what could be described as 'qualitative' or 'field research' or 'case study' or 'ethnography'; that is, research which uses a combination of methods including observation, participant observation, in-depth or unstructured interviews alongside documentary evidence (Hammersley and Atkinson 1983; Burgess 1984). Indeed, in recent years the repertoire of qualitative research has been extended to include narrative analysis auto/biography and discourse analysis among a range of approaches (for a discussion of the range see Bryman and Burgess 1999). The predominance of those methods might suggest that a qualitative rather than a quantitative approach has always been at the forefront of British sociology. However, to assess the position of qualitative and ethnographic approaches, it is essential to put these relatively recent methodological developments into context before exploring ways in which sociologists can think about doing ethnographies. In recent years, sociologists have conducted research in familiar settings within their own society and have encouraged their postgraduate students to make links between their domestic lives, their work situations and the research that they do (Harris 1988; Hughes 1988; Stowell 1988) – all topics that are appropriate for a qualitative rather than the quantitative approach that dominated much methodological work until recent years.

Yet it is essential for sociologists to remember that the use of a particular method or methodology is not based on a simple choice. Instead, the research question that is posed determines the research strategy, or more often the strategies, that are used. Accordingly, many research projects demand a mixture of quantitative and qualitative approaches, but for the purpose of this chapter I shall focus on the development of ethnographic and qualitative research.

Speaking autobiographically

To begin autobiographically, I want to place the development of ethnography as it has been taught and used within the discipline of sociology by drawing on my own experience of ethnographic work. Thirty years ago I was introduced to ethnography. Nobody called it that at the time. Nobody said 'this is ethnography'. In the late 1960s, I was a sociology undergraduate in Durham where we were required to take a course entitled 'Social Research Methods'. The course was taught by a range of staff rather than by anyone who could be described as a methodologist or a 'methods' specialist (a situation that was quite usual at the time given the size of sociology departments, and regrettably remained so in many departments for all too long to the detriment of methodological development (Peel 1968; Burgess 1979; Wakeford 1979; Bulmer and Burgess 1981)).

Within the twenty-week lecture series, Stan Cohen came to give one lecture on participant observation. Cohen had recently completed a study of 'mods' and 'rockers' that was published subsequently as *Folk Devils and Moral Panics* (Cohen 1972) and was currently doing research on long-term prisoners that was later published as *Psychological Survival* (Cohen and Taylor 1972). As a consequence, his discussion of participant observation was illustrated by an account of the way he conducted research in settings with people who could be labelled 'deviants'. The lecture was basically a review of the advantages and disadvantages of doing participant observation drawing on Cohen's own fieldwork experience by way of illustration. In this context, emphasis was placed on the research setting and research techniques rather than the social processes associated with doing research. Accordingly, participant observation was seen in the course merely as a research technique that was evaluated alongside other research techniques in order to assess its usefulness in sociological work.

The main research techniques to which participant observation was compared were those methods associated with the social survey: the questionnaire and the formal interview. These methods were seen in the late 1960s and 1970s as the predominant mode in which sociologists went about doing research and were discussed in key 'methods' texts such as

Survey Methods in Social Investigation (Moser and Kalton 1971) and *Research Methods in Social Relations* (Selltiz *et al.* 1968) that contained relatively little on ethnographic or qualitative approaches to research. Instead, these major texts contained much on surveys and brief sections on observation and participant observation but no explicit set of chapters on ethnography as a research strategy.

Now, the purpose of discussing this issue is not to tell a story against the Durham Department of Sociology by saying 'Well, there was only one lecture on participant observation in the research methods course, and then they didn't even tell us about ethnography' – perhaps it was my fault that I never read sufficiently widely to realize that participant observation was located within the ethnographic tradition. The main point of this brief account is that it provides an insight into the status of qualitative studies and ethnographic work on undergraduate sociology courses in the 1960s, as I subsequently discovered my Durham experience was reflected in 'methods' syllabuses and recommended reading available to undergraduate students elsewhere during that period (Peel 1968). As the materials collected by Peel demonstrate, it was usual to include participant observation as one of a series of 'tools' of social research, but rare to find a department teaching about case studies, key informants, note taking and diary keeping – all aspects of ethnographic work and crucial to an understanding of the conduct of qualitative research. (In Peel's survey, this approach was only available in two departments that taught degree courses in sociology and social anthropology and probably owed more to the latter rather than the former.)

Even in the 1960s, participant observation was seen as a mere technique of social investigation and was evaluated on that basis. This was problematic as there tended not to be any wide-ranging reflective discussions on the conduct of ethnographic work which was becoming more widely used in a range of sub-fields of sociology, especially through studies of rural and urban communities in Britain (Williams 1956; Stacey 1960; Little-john 1963). One major site for the development of ethnographic work of this kind was the University of Manchester, Department of Sociology and Social Anthropology, whose staff, under the direction of Max Gluckman, were conducting ethnograpic studies in a range of locations in contemporary British society (Frankenberg 1982). Essentially, the approach that had traditionally been used by social anthropologists based in Manchester to study societies other than their own was being used by Max Gluckman and his colleagues to study factories (Lupton 1954; Cunnison 1966), schools (Hargreaves 1967; Lacey 1970), and localities (Frankenberg 1957). Yet questions were raised as to whether studies based on observation and in-depth interviews could yield data that were reliable and valid and whether such an approach could constitute research. Most sociologists would not question this approach as a research activity today, although those of us engaged in the conduct of ethnographic studies would still want to question the practice of ethnographic research, not only in terms of the ways in which we collect data, but also the strategies that can be used for data analysis (Bryman and Burgess 1994). Indeed, there is now a well-established tradition of ethnographic researchers reflecting critically on their research experience (Burgess 1984, 1990, 1992). Many of the accounts of the research process focus critically on different phases of research: gaining access, data recording, data analysis and data dissemination. Many of the texts and collections of essays containing these accounts are used on 'methods' courses at undergraduate and postgraduate levels. Indeed, there are now many specialist options on qualitative methods that are located in a discussion of theoretical and methodological issues that influence the shape of sociological study. On this basis, I would suggest that ethnographic enquiry has moved over the last thirty years from being a fringe activity to becoming more central within the discipline of sociology, where teaching and research have gone beyond the consideration of research technique towards the critical evaluation of a research approach that can be used in many social settings (Hammersley 1992).

The way in which sociologists have developed a distinctive approach to ethnographic enquiry is such that it is derived partly from social anthropology and partly through studies of urban industrial society, particularly through the Chicago school in America (see Burgess 1982). But, in turn, one of the important developments that has occurred in sociology, particularly in recent years, is the idea that ethnography can be used in the study of familiar social settings. The ethnographer no longer focuses merely on the exotic and the obscure in societies other than our own, but instead contributes studies of hospital wards, factories, classrooms and a whole range of other social settings and social groups where an ethnographic and qualitative approach is appropriate to use. But we might ask: how has ethnographic research been conducted? What have we learned in the process of doing these studies?

From techniques to processes

First, we need to look at some of the characteristics associated with the conduct of ethnographic and qualitative work. Many people would argue that central to the approach of doing this work is the researcher himself or herself (Hammersley and Atkinson 1983; Burgess 1984). It is the researcher who is central to ethnographic studies when using observational techniques, conducting in-depth or unstructured interviews and utilizing documentary evidence. While these three approaches have influenced the way in which ethnographic and qualitative studies are conducted, it is important to appreciate that ethnography cannot be discussed exclusively in terms of techniques. It becomes important to contextualize the methods and techniques associated with ethnographic work within an array of social processes associated with the conduct of research. Among the areas that ethnographers discuss are the processes associated with research design, research access, sampling and selection, analytic approaches and the social, political and ethical features of social investigation that permeate the research process.

Many ethnographers and qualitative researchers take as a central characteristic the notion that at least a year's fieldwork is required, especially when conducting this work as part of doctoral studies at postgraduate level. In these terms, it would be quite usual to design an ethnographic study where it is intended that the fieldworker should spend a whole year in the field, but recent methodological developments have taken place whereby a qualitative research approach has been adopted to conduct short periods of research and evaluation (Burgess 1993a). A further characteristic of the ethnographic approach is that it often involves the study of single cases: one factory, one school, one hospital, and so on, and the comparisons that occur are internal to that particular case, but this has also been modified so that qualitatively based multi-site case studies have been conducted in several enquiries (see Burgess *et al.* 1994a; Deem and Brehony 1994). Many ethnographic studies are designed on the basis of a lone researcher working to a long timescale while focusing on one particular social setting, as Whyte did in his classic ethnographic study of street corner gangs in *Street Corner Society* (Whyte 1955), but this has also been developed whereby qualitative research has been conducted by research teams (see Burgess *et al.* 1994b; Hill *et al.* 1994; Parry *et al.* 1994) in a range of social settings.

One of the problems associated with the conduct of ethnographic work is that the focus is upon data collection. Within many of the major texts only one chapter or section is devoted to data analysis (Burgess 1982, 1984; Hammersley and Atkinson 1983). There has been a much greater concern with data acquisition, with little attention devoted to a range of topics including proposal writing, research design, data analysis, data dissemination and links between qualitative research and policy making. Furthermore, the links between different phases of the research process have not been sufficiently explored: how proposal writing is linked to data collection and how data collection links forward to data analysis and writing. Indeed, it is only in the last ten years that sociologists have explicitly turned their attention towards looking at the writing process in ethnographic work (Atkinson 1990) by asking: how do you begin to assemble an ethnographic account? How do you decide those data you choose to write about and those data that you choose to omit? In turn, sociologists have only recently been encouraged to consider the criteria that are used when reading ethnographic studies (Hammersley 1992). For example, how do you evaluate ethnographic studies? What kinds of questions do you ask about the way in which ethnographic studies are structured? What kind of writing style has been used? How are different styles used depending on the purpose of the investigation? How far does the researcher determine how the work can be produced? To what extent are data collection and data analysis linked together? This range of work provides a much more balanced view of the ethnographic approach by taking us away from the idea that research techniques are central to ethnographic enquiry and qualitative studies. Instead, it encourages us to make links between the kinds of questions that sociologists pose when going into factories, schools, hospitals and localities with the kinds of methodological approaches that are chosen. It also encourages researchers to critically scrutinize all elements of the research process and to give greater attention to the ways in which data analysis can be conducted and the ways data are used. However, there are still further gaps in our knowledge about ethnography and qualitative research. As there are no standard approaches, but an emphasis on flexibility of approach, there is much methodological research and development that needs to take place.

One of the key elements associated with the exploration of methodological approaches in sociology is that they are not standard. The texts that are used do not provide a static portrait of how research has always been conducted and how it always will be. Indeed, I would argue that thirty years ago we had a notion that techniques were important to acquire, whereas in the intervening period we have moved towards looking at the interaction of research techniques with research processes. We need to look in methodological terms, not just at the techniques, but at the influence of the researcher upon the researched and the way in which the researcher, working with particular approaches in sociology, shapes the field of study. We have become much more attuned to this approach in sociology, particularly through some of the work that has been done in the field of ethnography and qualitative research, with the result that the discipline has developed a more questioning style about sociological practice and the ways in which sociologists conduct research. Developments in ethnographic and qualitative research have had an impact upon the ways in which sociologists discuss the research process, write about the conduct of research and teach students about doing research.

Further developments

But there are many further developments that can be made. Many courses on social research methods discuss the conduct of social research as if it is nothing but a free-floating intellectual activity with no notion of how it is sponsored and financed, and the ways in which this influences how studies are designed, conducted, analyzed and reported. If we examine the books on research methods' reading lists, we find there is relatively little material that suggests research has to be sponsored and financed and how those issues are factors in the way in which the research is conducted. We need to enquire more about the role of research sponsorship in relation to sociological activity, because to do otherwise is to suggest that research is just a sterile activity that is devoid of social, political and ethical concerns and merely based upon a series of techniques (Burgess 1993a). Many of the issues associated with sponsorship in relation to ethnographic and qualitative research have focused upon policy studies in a range of fields including education (Pettigrew 1994; Burgess 1994). Here we need to explore further the influence of contractual control on methodological development and the dissemination of research findings. There is also space to explore the impact of sponsorship upon the dynamics of qualitative research. In this way, sociologists can engage in current debates within UK higher education about the extent to which sponsors determine the kind of research that gets conducted and the way in which the purposes of the research activity might be linked to the promotion of wealth creation and the quality of life (HMSO 1993).

Now as soon as a researcher takes on these objectives, it will influence the kind of research that is conducted. But how can sociologists consider the way in which a particular methodological approach interacts with the ways in which sponsors operate? Here we need to turn to a consideration of the changing role of sponsors and sponsorship and the way this can be used positively to develop the principles of ethnographic and qualitative research. The result is that we will need to move away from some of the classic models of doing ethnographic and qualitative research that are presented in methodology textbooks (but without compromising on issues of reliability and validity or on matters concerning the integrity of the researcher to the researched or the general public).

Some recent studies: examples from case study research

If I look at the kind of work that I have been doing over the past ten years, it departs quite radically from the notion of doing a classic ethnographic study involving a single researcher going to one location for a year, after having spent six months planning the study, followed by a year writing up. Timescales are reduced and are determined by sponsors rather than by me, but these can present new challenges for the researcher to engage in qualitative work that can directly contribute to policy and practice. On the basis of the funding that is available, and the timescales that are given, sociologists have to consider how to utilize the principles associated with traditional models of doing ethnographic and qualitative enquiries, whilst at the same time being able to deliver a case study or a set of case studies at the end of the period in question. Does this mean that the days of ethnography are over or at least strictly numbered in relation to the classic approach that has been used? If we look at classic ethnographic studies, it appears that if you do not have a year to do fieldwork, then it is problematic for the researcher. Or is it?

As I have argued elsewhere (Burgess 1993a, 1993b, 1994), this need not be the case. It is possible to begin to innovate around some of the classical approaches that have been used to conduct ethnographic and qualitative studies. The researcher can consider how different methodological approaches can be utilized and developed in relation to sponsorship, funding and timescales. Budgets are small, timescales are short, sponsors expect the researcher to cover more than one site, and as a result the classic ethnographic study cannot be done. Yet the principles from such studies can be developed in a multi-site approach. In a recent project, I was invited by the Sheffield Local Education Authority to look at the local management of schools (Sheffield LEA 1992). The project was allocated a budget of £25,000 (at 1990 prices) for the research to be conducted within six months which included recruiting a team, designing the project, doing the fieldwork and writing up the report. This was the task. But the local authority did not want a survey conducted because they had hired a research team from the University of Sheffield and the Open University to do this work. Instead, our team was hired to conduct a series of qualitative case studies. Now the classic literature of ethnographic enquiry would suggest that is not possible, so we need to ask: how does a research team, engaged in a qualitatively based case study, work within the constraints of the project and develop qualitative research? We found that the Sheffield LEA wanted in-depth work that focused on process rather than product. The research, therefore, needed to be very close to a classic ethnographic study, but the constraints made this problematic. So to what extent could the principles of case study or qualitative research or ethnographic enquiry be developed in that particular context?

First of all, it was essential to consider the demands made by the research location. In a city the size of Sheffield, how do you begin to do ethnographic work? Instead of operating with a lone researcher working at one site, as in classic ethnographies, a team-based, multi-site case study approach needed to be developed. However, this automatically presents a sampling problem, similar to those problems frequently encountered in survey research, as decisions had to be made about how to select research sites. In this study, a range of sites needed to be selected to examine the ways in which local financial management operated in a range of schools across the city. Accordingly, our team needed to conduct a series of case studies that reflected different kinds of schools: nursery, primary and secondary, as well as a tertiary college. We selected nine different case study sites. The principles used to select these sites included: school type, size of school, geographical position in the city, and so on. However, with nine sites to be covered in a six-month period, we still needed to consider how intensive case studies could be done by the research team. At this point, there was a need to innovate around the notion of the classic ethnographic approach. But how can researchers develop an approach derived from a single case study for use in multi-site case studies? How can a team be used to conduct qualitative case studies? As soon as we begin to ask questions like these we start to go back to some fundamental methodological principles (Burgess *et al.* 1994a).

The first major question to address is: how are units of study selected? With several researchers going into nine case study sites, the team had to be clear about the kinds of sociological questions that were to be posed. Clarity was required about the focus of the study, the issues to be considered, the questions to be asked, both in the course of observational research and when conducting interviews. There was also a need to consider who was going to be interviewed within the nine case study sites. This was essential so that when the research team reassembled, analytic comparisons could be made between the different case studies. Some consideration also had to be given to the relationship between the project budget and the number of days that could be spent in each research site (Burgess 1994). On this basis, I would argue that the conditions under which this research was conducted were as rigourous, or calls for as great a rigour, as ethnographic research that is conducted using a lone researcher at a single site over a long time period. In multi-site case studies, careful planning in relation to the purpose of the research and research design becomes essential. However, there is also a major advantage of the multi-site case study as it allows generalization across cases and overcomes some of the problems concerning generalization that have been levelled against classic single-site ethnography (Deem and Brehony 1994). On this basis, the project allowed us to begin to investigate the extent to which a qualitative case study approach can be used to generalize within sociological work.

The multi-site approach has also been used by me in an Economic and Social Research Council sponsored project when studying postgraduate students in nine universities (Burgess *et al.* 1994b). This study examined postgraduate students studying for doctoral degrees in economics, sociology and business studies in nine institutions across the UK. Again, it becomes important to make sure that sites can be compared. However, one of the problems involved in doing research of this kind is that researchers may plan very carefully as to what the units of study are going to be, but when they arrive at the institutions to be studied things change. People do not use definitions and labels for the convenience of researchers doing sociological studies. Indeed, we found that what counted as a department in one university was not the same in another. What constituted a faculty was not the same across all the research sites. Accordingly, in doing multi-site case studies, researchers have not only to pick up similarities in terms of units of study, but also to focus on difference and to tease out the complexities involved within the cases. Now in that sense, the multi-site case study, especially in familiar settings, challenges us further to think about questions of research design on the one hand and the analysis of data on the other. If we think about issues concerning research design and research focus, we begin to consider the kinds of data that it is essential to collect and that are available for analysis at the end of the project.

If we return to questions of data collection, it is essential to consider how to collect data across nine sites in six months. On both the Sheffield project and the postgraduate project, we planned the number of days being allocated to each research location for data collection, data analysis and writing. Here, the case studies were not an end in themselves, but were used to write a theme-based report that linked into policy and practice (Burgess *et al.* 1992a, 1992b). In this sense, the research team had to think about questions that could be pitched against the case study data and the ways in which these data could be utilized to develop themes from the different sites. In this respect, researchers are utilizing the approach that ethnographers have used, but departing from it in three major ways: firstly, in terms of increasing the number of cases; secondly, by utilizing a team-based approach; thirdly, by working within a restricted time frame. Classic ethnography would normally involve one researcher in a particular locale, while multi-site case study allows us to go across cases. But we can begin to push ethnographic enquiry even further by using case studies in a longitudinal sense.

Further possibilities?

Traditionally, longitudinal research design consists of a large panel of people being followed at regular intervals from birth throughout their lifetime (Douglas 1954). This is the classic longitudinal study. But how can we adapt this approach and the case study approach to look longitudinally at organizations? How far can a longitudinal study designed in this way result in a series of portraits of an organization over time? Although in sociology we like to think we are not very conventional, I think the way in which we do research is highly conventional – new approaches to familiar problems are required if we are to advance our understanding of social situations.

When we conduct ethnography or qualitative studies, we need to consider how technology can be used to develop this approach, not only through the use of computers and qualitative software programs, but other forms of technology, including cameras, movie cameras and video machines. But how can photographs be used in sociological work? How can films and videos be used? How might we begin to innovate and develop these approaches in relation to the kind of research that we want to do? Taking photographs is a form of observation, but what problems are raised by this approach? If a camera is pointed at one particular sector of a room, I am already involved in a sampling problem, but I have also fixed the situation by freezing the action. Indeed, many advocates of the use of film in anthropological study are critical of photographic studies for these reasons (Crawford and Turton 1992). They argue that the photograph fixes on a central perspective which is itself fixed, while in film making the picture moves and the movie maker is fixed. However, counter-arguments and debates have evolved in the field. For example, Pinney (1992) argues that photographs are full of meaning and can, therefore, be used in subsequent analysis.

In a recent case study concerning education reform in English and Japanese schools, I planned that three fieldworkers would conduct multi-site case studies in Japanese schools. None of the team spoke Japanese, so the research focus required careful consideration by observing the teaching of English and practical classes such as physical education. So how can we innovate and begin to do ethnographic enquiry in that context? Photography is an approach that could be used, but consideration has to be given to the number of photographs that would be required to review the situations that have been observed. The photograph, like the written record in a notebook, is central to data analysis. We know that in the course of half an hour three or four rolls of film need to be taken to illustrate the way in which a situation unfolds.

But several issues still remain to be resolved: how might photographs be used in conjunction with text? What is the relative status of visual and written text? In turn, will greater clarity be achieved through the use of film, video and video discs (Asch 1992; Macfarlane 1992)? On the basis of this limited exploration, I feel there is sufficient evidence to suggest that there are many other approaches that we can begin to explore in relation to conventional ethnographic and qualitative methods.

Conclusion

Doing research is not a static activity. It is an activity for which we have a set of methodological principles and around which we can innovate. This is one of the fascinating things about methodological issues and the development of ethnographic and qualitative approaches in sociological enquiry. Until relatively recently, ethnographic and qualitative research was, at best, marginal to British sociology in general and to research methodology in particular. The emphasis was upon quantitative methodology. The last thirty years have witnessed considerable development with many sociologists using ethnographic and qualitative methods in their projects. Indeed, in teaching and research in sociology, qualitative work has a major role. Yet it could be argued that we have gone too far in sociology, given the difficulty of finding (let alone recruiting) a British sociologist who is fully trained in quantitative as well as qualitative research methods and is able to use them in their projects. Indeed, the Economic and Social Research Council's Postgraduate Training Guidelines

(1996) has laid out requirements for all social scientists engaged in graduate work to be given methods training. In the version that is being prepared in the year 2000 there is a higher specification of the basic quantitative and qualitative research tools that any social scientist should have as part of their core training at graduate level. In this way, there is an attempt to move beyond basic methodological literacy to a situation where young scholars can use quantitative and qualitative approaches.

Yet there is still space for further development. How research can be developed and how research takes place depend on the social and political contexts in which we work. We need to explore, develop, elaborate and above all evaluate the approaches that we use in order to engage in methodological development that is appropriate for the research question posed rather than personal preference. However, methodological development is *not* separate from research, but occurs in relation to the social context within which the researcher is placed, the research problem that is to be investigated, the kind of writing that is to be done and the form in which evidence is to be presented. There are no rules for the conduct of sociological research, but there is a vast terrain that can continue to be explored as part of the research adventure.

References

Asch, T. (1992) 'The ethics of ethnographic film making', in P.I. Crawford and D. Turton (eds) *Film as Ethnography*, Manchester: Manchester University Press.

Atkinson, P. (1990) *The Ethnographic Imagination*, London: Routledge.

Bryman, A. and Burgess, R.G. (eds) (1994) *Analysing Qualitative Data*, London: Routledge.

Bryman, A. and Burgess, R.G. (eds) (1999) *Qualitative Research* (4 vols.), London: Sage.

Bulmer, M. and Burgess, R.G. (eds) (1981) 'The teaching of research methodology' (special issue), *Sociology* 15 (4).

Burgess, R.G. (ed.) (1979) *Teaching Research Methodology to Postgraduates*, Coventry: University of Warwick.

Burgess, R.G. (ed.) (1982) *Field Research: A Sourcebook and Field Manual*, London: Allen and Unwin.

Burgess, R.G. (ed.) (1984) *In the Field: An Introduction to Field Research*, London: Unwin Hyman.

Burgess, R.G. (ed.) (1990) *Reflections on Field Experience*, London: JAI Press.

Burgess, R.G. (ed.) (1992) *Learning About Fieldwork*, London: JAI Press.

Burgess, R.G. (1993a) 'Customers and contractors: a research relationship?', in R.G. Burgess (ed.) *Educational Research and Evaluation: For Policy and Practice?* Lewes: Falmer Press.

Burgess, R.G. (1993b) 'Biting the hand that feeds you?', in R.G. Burgess (ed.) *Educational Research and Evaluation: For Policy and Practice?* Lewes: Falmer Press.

Burgess, R.G. (1994) 'Scholarship and sponsored research: contradiction, continuum or complementary activity', in D. Halpin and B. Troyna (eds) *Researching Education Policy: Ethical and Methodological Issues*, Lewes: Falmer Press.

Burgess, R.G., Hockey, J., Hughes, C. *et al.* (1992a) 'Case studies: a thematic look at issues and problems in Sheffield LEA', in *Resourcing Sheffield Schools*, Sheffield: Sheffield Local Education Authority.

Burgess, R.G. *et al.* (1992b) *Resourcing Sheffield Schools, Part Two: The Case Studies*, Sheffield: Sheffield Local Education Authority.

Burgess, R.G., Pole, C.J., Evans, K. and Priestley, C. (1994a) 'Four studies from one or one study from four? Multi-site case study research', in A. Bryman and R.G. Burgess (eds) *Analysing Qualitative Data*, London: Routledge.

Burgess, R.G., Pole, C.J. and Hockey, J. (1994b) 'Strategies for managing and supervising the social science PhD', in R.G. Burgess (ed.) *Postgraduate Education and Training in the Social Sciences, Processes and Products*, London: Jessica Kingsley.

Cohen, S. (1972) *Folk Devils and Moral Panics*, London: MacGibbon and Kee.

Cohen, S. and Taylor, I. (1972) *Psychological Survival*, Harmondsworth: Penguin.

Crawford, D.J. and Turton, D. (eds) (1992) *Film as Ethnography*, Manchester: Manchester University Press.

Cunnison, S. (1996) *Wages and Work Allocation*, London: Tavistock.

Deem, R. and Brehony, K. (1994) 'Why didn't you use a survey so you could generalise your findings? Methodological issues in a multiple site case study of school governing bodies after the 1988 Education Reform Act', in D. Halpin and B. Troyna (eds) *Researching Educational Policy: Ethical and Methodological Issues*, Lewes: Falmer Press.

Douglas, J.W.B. (1954) *The Home and the School*, London: MacGibbon and Kee.

Economic and Social Research Council (1996) *Postgraduate Training Guidelines*, Swindon: Economic and Social Research Council.

Frankenberg, R. (1957) *Village on the Border*, London: Cohen and West.

Hammersley, M. (1992) *What's Wrong with Ethnography?* London: Routledge.

Hammersley, M. and Atkinson, P. (1983) *Ethnography: Principles into Practice*, London: Tavistock.

Hargreaves, D. (1967) *Social Relations in a Secondary School*, London: Routledge and Kegan Paul.

Harris, D. (1988) 'A sociological study of workers' responses to change in the organisation of the gas industry', unpublished Ph.D. thesis, University of Warwick.

Hill, T., Acker, S. and Black, E. (1994) 'Research students and their supervisors in education and psychology', in R.G. Burgess (ed.) *Postgraduate Education and Training in the Social Sciences, Processes and Products*, London: Jessica Kingsley.

HMSO (1993) *Realising Our Potential*, London: HMSO.

Hughes, C. (1988) 'An ethnographic study of the stepfamily', unpublished Ph.D. thesis, University of Warwick.

Lacey, C. (1970) *Hightown Grammar*, Manchester: Manchester University Press.

Littlejohn, J. (1963) *Westrigg: The Sociology of a Cheviot Parish*, London: Routledge and Kegan Paul.

Lupton, T. (1954) *On the Shop Floor*, Oxford: Pergamon Press.

Macfarlane, A. (1992) 'The potential of videodisc in visual anthropology: some examples', in P.I. Crawford and D. Turton (eds) *Film as Ethnography*, Manchester: Manchester University Press.

Moser, C. and Kalton, G. (1971) *Survey Methods in Social Investigation*, second edition, London: Heinemann.

Parry, O., Atkinson, P. and Delamont, S. (1994) 'Disciplinary identities and doctoral work', in R.G. Burgess (ed.) *Postgraduate Education and Training in the Social Sciences, Processes and Products*, London: Jessica Kingsley.

Peel, J. (1968) *Courses Mainly Concerned with Sociological Theory and Methods in 29 British Universities*, London: British Sociological Association.

Pettigrew, M. (1994) 'Coming to terms with research: the contract business', in D. Halpin and B. Troyna (eds) *Researching Education Policy: Ethical and Methodological Issues*, Lewes: Falmer Press.

Pinney, C. (1992) 'The lexical spaces of eye-spy', in P.I. Crawford and D. Turton (eds) *Film as Ethnography*, Manchester: Manchester University Press.

Selltiz, C., Jahoda, M., Deutsch, M. and Cook, S.W. (1968) *Research Methods in Social Relations*, New York: Tavistock.

Sheffield LEA (1992) *Resourcing Sheffield Schools*, Sheffield: Sheffield Local Education Authority.

Stacey, M. (1960) *Tradition and Change: A Study of Banbury*, Oxford: Oxford University Press.

Stowell, M. (1988) 'Becoming a teacher: an ethnographic study', unpublished Ph.D. thesis, University of Warwick.

Wakeford, J. (1979) *Research Methods Syllabuses in Sociology Departments in the UK*, Lancaster: University of Lancaster.

Whyte, W.F. (1955) *Street Corner Society*, second edition, Chicago: University of Chicago Press.

Williams, W.M. (1956) *The Sociology of an English Village: Gosforth*, London: Routledge and Kegan Paul.

chapter 3

Theory, meta-theory and discourse: reflections on post-empiricism

Christopher G.A. Bryant

Social reality is unlike any other because of its human
constitution.
(Archer 1995: 1)

Standards of evaluation may, and indeed do, shift in the
process of the development of explanations which transform
theoretical objects and relations, but scientific judgements
are 'indeterminate' only in the sense that there is no one, pre-
given best way forward, not in the sense that judgements of
superior adequacy cannot be made.   (Holmwood 1996: 110–11)

Sociology: crisis or opportunity?

Ever since Gouldner published *The Coming Crisis of Western Sociology*
in 1970, there have been those who, with greater or lesser relish, have
proclaimed sociology to be in crisis. Most such writings also recommend
their own way out of the crisis. Jonathan Turner and Stephen Turner's 1990
account of the development of sociology in America, still the society with
more academic sociologists than any other, extended the genre by concluding that sociology is condemned to remain *The Impossible Science,* for
ever betraying all those naive enough to seek from it reliable knowledge
of practical value. What gives the notion of sociology in crisis heightened
resonance at the beginning of the new millennium is its association with
postmodernity. Modernity, reason and societal self-reflection or 'reflexivity' went hand-in-hand, as do the current exhaustion of modernity, the
distrust of reason and the disillusionment with sociology for the doubters.

Fortunately there is an alternative to the frustrations of an impossible science or the indulgences of postmodern fragmentation. As early as
1983, Bernstein invited us to go *Beyond Objectivism and Relativism*. Now
we can. Thanks to profound work by many scholars on the constitution
of society and the making and accepting of both knowledge claims and
value judgements, we can discern, at least in outline, the contours and
constituents of a new practical sociology – a social science that works. As
a consequence, we now have an opportunity, perhaps for the first time,
to promote a sociology which can realistically expect to live up to its claims.
What I am offering in this essay is, therefore, not a systematic and even-
handed general overview of British contributions to social theory, but rather
the fundamentals of a particular, and no doubt contestable, argument about
the past, present and future of sociology in Britain and elsewhere which
has at its core theoretical issues.[1] It is an argument which focuses on features of sociology itself, not the world it addresses. It is true that sociology
emerged and developed in engagement with capitalism and modernity,
and that it is re-forming itself at the same time as it engages with late/post
modernity, globalization, the relations of north and south, the transformation of postcommunist societies, the future of work, gender relations, etc.
But that engagement is a topic in its own right which would require a
different essay.[2]

Theory and theory proper

Argument about theory, meta-theory and discourse in sociology lies
at the heart of the debate about the character of sociology itself and its
claim to be a social science (cf. Boudon 1980). I shall begin with reflection
on the broad range of activities which have been practised in the name
of sociological theory over the last half century by recalling Merton's conception of theory proper and the conception of science which went with
it. I shall then consider the challenge to both presented by the linguistic
turn, anti-foundationalism and post-empiricism. I believe this challenge
has largely succeeded among specialists in sociological theory, though not
necessarily sociologists generally, but I will also address the deep anxiety
of those who fear that in the process meta-theory has triumphed over
theory proper. I shall then recommend the term 'discourse' as a way to
overcome the unprofitable theory–meta-theory distinction.

Merton's view of what properly counts as sociological theory was ex-
ceedingly influential (1957a).[3] He listed six types of work which have gone
by the name of theory in sociology – methodology; general orientations

(for example, Durkheim's generic hypothesis that 'the determining cause of a social fact should be sought among the social facts preceding it' (Durkheim 1982: 110)); analysis of concepts; *post factum* interpretations (finding an interpretation to fit the facts, such as the plausible constructions placed on documents by Thomas and Znaniecki in the *The Polish Peasant in Europe and America* (1918–20)); empirical generalizations (isolated propositions summarizing observed uniformities between two or more variables such as Engel's law of consumption which states that as household income increases the proportion spent on food declines); and the formulation of scientific laws (statements of invariance derived from a theory) – and implied a seventh – the codification of scientific laws. Of these only the last two – deduction of propositions to be empirically tested (for which the formalization of Durkheim's explanation of differential suicide rates provides an example), and their codified cumulation (which Merton illustrates in his essays on continuities in the theories of social structure and anomie and of reference group behaviour) – are deemed to constitute theory proper (Durkheim 1952; Merton 1957b, 1957c).

The growth of theory proper is central to Merton's conception of sociology which Crothers has aptly characterized as 'an advancing, accumulative science generally based on a "natural science" model and sharply demarcated from "common sense" social knowledge' (Crothers 1987: 51; also see Sztompka 1986: ch. 2). This is the theory in the theory building promoted by Lazarsfeld and Rosenberg (1955) or Stinchcombe (1968) or Dubin (1969) or Blalock (1969). It is also the theory for which Wagner (1984) makes claims of growth, whose achievements Wallace (1988) celebrates in Smelser's weighty *Handbook of Sociology* (1988) and which Jonathan Turner (1989b) lauds in a volume derived from theory papers given at the 1987 meeting of the American Sociological Association. I have characterized it as 'instrumental positivism' and have declared it the prevailing tradition in American sociological theory (Bryant 1985: ch. 5).[4] Many of its protagonists prefer to speak of the 'analytical tradition' of sociology (cf. Becker 1990: ch. 2). It is not, however, the whole story – even in America.

There were, of course, differences in the programmes for sociology put forward some four decades ago by Merton, Parsons, Lazarsfeld and Stouffer (Turner and Turner 1990: ch. 3), but there was also a broad consistency in so far as they were all modelled on natural science. As a consequence they were all doomed to disappoint. A comparison between Merton and Parsons reveals why. Parsons differentiated four levels of conceptual systematization (Parsons and Shils 1951: 49–52; Mulkay 1971: ch. 3). The progressive achievement of a scientific sociology requires movement from the first to the fourth. The four are: first, *ad hoc* classifications; second, a categorial system (an interdependent system of classes and definitions); third, a theoretical system (a categorial system plus laws which specify relations between its elements); and fourth, an empirical–theoretical system (which affords predictions under real, as distinct from experimental, conditions). Parsons thought that economics and psychology were beginning to establish themselves at the third level as evidenced by the theory of marginal utility and the stimulus–response theory of learning, but that other would-be social sciences had not even got beyond level one. This, Parsons believed, he could remedy by establishing for the first time nothing less than a categorial system, not just for sociology, but for all the social sciences. His failure to do so cannot leave us unmoved in so far as routine, but systematic, comparison and cumulation of social research findings – what Kuhn (1962) later called normal science – is impossible in the absence of conceptual consistency and routine commensurability between researches. Either we must succeed where Parsons failed or we must reconsider our theoretical goals. The latter is more realistic.

It must be emphasized that Parsons' failure has to do with his conception of scientific sociology, not the scale of his theorizing. Merton may have eschewed grand theory in favour of theories of the middle range, but that theorizing is still located on the third and fourth of Parsons' levels. It presumes the establishability, if not the establishment, of a categorial system, albeit bit by bit. 'No study can become scientific . . .', we are told, 'until it provides itself with a suitable technical nomenclature, whose every term has a single definite meaning universally accepted' (Lazarsfeld and Merton 1954: 24). Unlike Parsons, Merton did not believe generation of such a nomenclature was a task for any single theorist and his or her associates. Instead it would develop from the contributions of numerous sociologists who took care, as Merton did, to consider past and present uses of a term before engaging in concept formation. In practice, however, the labours of innumerable sociologists, whether careful or careless about concept formation, have not generated the categorial system or universal nomenclature sought by those who would model sociology on natural science.

The linguistic turn and ontologies of the social

The initial challenge to social science as Merton conceived it came from proponents of the linguistic turn, and, amongst other things, it indicates why a single categorial system for all social science, or even all sociology, is bound always to elude us. The expression 'the linguistic turn' originated in Bergmann's *Logic and Reality* (1964): 'All linguistic philosophers talk about the world by means of talking about a suitable language. This is the linguistic turn, the fundamental gambit as to method, on which ordinary and ideal language philosophers . . . agree' (Bergman 1964: 177). Rorty's use of it for the title of his 1967 volume on philosophical method made it more generally known. In sociology it has prompted what has sometimes been called 'the hermeneutic turn' (cf. Phillips 1986: 2). Social scientists who make the turn acknowledge the language and understandings of the (types of) person whose action they seek to account for and about whom they seek to generalize. 'Language use', as Giddens says, 'is embedded in the concrete activities of everyday life and is in some sense partly constitutive of those activities' (Giddens 1984: xvi). That this has important consequences for the kinds of laws and generalizations which sociologists are able to formulate is generally agreed, even if not everyone would subscribe to Giddens' version of what they are.

> Generalizations tend towards two poles, with a range and variety of possible shadings between them. Some hold because actors themselves know them – in some guise – and apply them in the enactment of what they do. The social scientific observer does not in fact have to 'discover' these generalizations, although that observer may give a new discursive form to them. Other generalizations refer to circumstances, or aspects of circumstances, of which agents are ignorant and which effectively 'act' on them, independently of whatever the agents may believe they are up to . . . and each form of generalization is unstable in respect of the other. The circumstances in which generalizations about what 'happens' to agents hold are mutable in respect of what those agents can learn knowledgeably to 'make happen'.   (Giddens 1984: xix)

The two-way tie between ordinary members' and sociologists' language and knowledge (Giddens' double hermeneutic) is inimical to Merton's conception of theory proper not only because it connects what he would separate – social science and common sense – but also because it precludes cumulation of the kind he sought.

For theory proper to be possible, societies would have to be constituted differently from the way they are. How societies are constituted – the ontology of the social – has been the subject of the micro–macro and agency–structure debates, in America and Europe respectively, which have enjoyed a renewed intensity in the last twenty years. Symposia edited by Knorr-Cetina and Cicourel (1981); by Alexander *et al.* (1987); and by Sztompka (1994) explore the issues. There are also a number of writers who have reconsidered what they call the microfoundations of macro-sociology; they include Collins (1981), Hechter (1983) and Coleman (1990). Those attempting revised ontologies of the social include Gurvitch (1958), Touraine (1965, 1973), Bhaskar (1975, 1979, 1986), Giddens (1976, 1979, 1984), Habermas (1976, 1984–7), Bourdieu (1977, 1990), Elias (1978/82, 1968, 1978), Archer (1982, 1988, 1995), Sztompka (1991) and Mouzelis (1992). Elias first formulated his position long before the present period but it has only recently been taken up by others and discussed widely. Gurvitch also wrote well before the period in question; he seldom figures in the debate but he was the first to use the term 'structuration' in sociology. Touraine's 1965 book had little follow-up and has not been translated. None of these three can therefore be said to refute the claim that the *debate* about the ontology of the social is a feature of the 1970s onwards. And the debate matters. However recondite they may sometimes seem, ontologies of the social are of great practical consequence. Misconceive the constitution of society, and strategies for the application of sociology are highly likely to go wrong.

What has the great debate achieved? Let Archer provide the beginnings of an answer.

> Social reality is unlike any other because of its human constitution. It is different from natural reality whose defining feature is self-subsistence: for its existence does not depend upon us, a fact which is not compromised by our human ability to intervene in the world of nature and change it . . . The nascent 'social sciences' had to confront this entity, society, and deal conceptually with its three unique characteristics.
>
> Firstly, that it is inseparable from its human components because the very existence of society depends in some way upon our activities. Secondly, that society is characteristically transformable; it has no immutable form or even preferred state. Thirdly, however, neither are we immutable as social agents, for what we are and what we do as social beings are also affected by the society in which we live and by our very efforts to transform it.
>
> (Archer, 1995: 1)

At a minimum, what the great debate has done is make the position Archer summarizes so neatly a commonplace. There is, however, more than one theory which is consistent with it. In Britain, scientific realism and structuration theory have been the principal contenders.

Contributors to the development of realist social theory include Bhaskar (1975, 1979, 1986), Keat and Urry (1975), Pawson (1989; Pawson and Tilley 1997) and Archer (1995). Pawson's and Archer's projects are still very much in progress. All realists claim that it is realities and their generative mechanisms which underlie actualities, realities which may not be directly observable and whose existence may have to be inferred from the observable effects they generate. The status of these underlying realities has not been agreed. In particular, Bhaskar's strong thesis of the stratification of reality and of ontological depth is not shared by all realists. There is an equally basic unresolved issue in Giddens' structuration theory. This theory has at its heart the notion of the duality of structure which treats structure 'as the medium and outcome of the conduct it recursively organizes' (Giddens 1984: 374). Structure consists of 'rules and resources, recursively implicated in the reproduction of social systems' but 'exists only as memory traces, the organic basis of human knowledgeability, and as instantiated in action' (1984: 377) – or rather has only a virtual existence. But the virtual, albeit when instantiated, has effects, and, by some accounts, to have effects is to be real. The status of the virtual in Giddens is no less problematic than the status of the real in Bhaskar. Here as elsewhere in the great micro–macro and agency–structure debates, what is at stake is specification of the relations between the actual, the real, the ideal and the virtual.

The notion of social science as moral inquiry (Haan *et al.* 1983), or what Alexander refers to as 'the distinctively evaluative nature of social science' (1988: 80), follows from that of the linguistic turn. In the 1950s and 1960s sociologists sought an objectivity and value neutrality which required that social science and moral inquiry be quite separate. Once the double hermeneutic is recognized, however, this dissociation loses all plausibility. The language sociologists use in constituting their objects of inquiry can never be purged of all normative content, and what they say and write can, and often does, enter extra-sociological discourses, either directly, or as mediated by others from politicians to social workers. The rational justification of values is thus back on the social science agenda. Especially notable contributions to the debate include Hesse (1978) on theory and value in the social sciences, Wolfe (1989) on social science and moral obligation, Habermas (1993) on discourse ethics, Cain (1990), Harding (1993), Longino (1993) and other feminists on the pros and cons of standpoint theory, Bauman (1993) on postmodern ethics and Tester (1997) on moral culture.

Anti-foundationalism

Anti-foundationalism poses a further challenge to the ideas of theory proper and cumulative science. The metaphor of a sure foundation for our knowledge originates in Descartes. Strictly speaking it belongs to epistemology but, like many notions in epistemology, it also shades into ontology in so far as ideas about how we can know are connected to ideas about what there is to be known. It refers to knowledge as a mirror of nature, to knowledge as a faithful representation of how the world is. This is how Rorty characterizes it:

> we may think of both knowledge and justification as privileged relations to the objects those propositions are about . . . If we think of knowledge in [this] way we will want to get behind reasons to causes, beyond argument to compulsion from the object known, to a situation in which argument would not be just silly but impossible, for anyone gripped by the object in the required way will be unable to doubt or to see an alternative. To reach that point is to reach the foundations of knowledge.
>
> (Rorty 1980: 159)

This is, of course, precisely the version of knowledge which Rorty goes on to demolish so compellingly later in the same book.

Anti-foundationalism goes against the historical grain of sociology as well as of philosophy. The whole point of Comte's positive philosophy and sociology was to abandon the 'intellectual anarchy' which was responsible for the 'great political and moral crisis' of the time (Martineau 1853: vol. 1, 22), in favour of sure (but circumscribed) knowledge. The same can be said of Durkheim on the *sui generis* character of society and the rules of sociological method. In the 1920s and early 1930s the Vienna Circle made its own bid to end the 'anarchy of philosophical opinions' (Schlick 1959: 54) by combining logic and empiricism – and there are filiations, albeit complicated ones, from logical positivism through particular methodologies of social research to the American tradition of empirical sociology. The quest for certainty also figures in the Marxist and hermeneutic traditions. There are elements of it, for example, in the privileged status Marx gives to the mode of production and the dialectical method, and these elements feature prominently both in readings of Marx coloured by Engels' conception of science or Lenin's materialism and empirio-criticism and in derivations from Lukács's notion of the proletariat's privileged access to truth. It is also instructive that Kolakowski (1975) related his lectures on Husserl to the quest for certitude, and in recent times a number of interpretivist sociologists have made plain their foundationalism (cf. Williams 1990). Cicourel, for example, opens his *Method and Measurement in Sociology* (1964) by expressing his critical concern for the foundations of social science research. Sure foundations for knowledge were also integral to the dominant conceptions of sociology in the mid-twentieth century, those of Parsons and Merton.

Securing the foundations for social knowledge was not just a matter of intellectual interest; it was also of great practical value and political importance. Marx sought not just to interpret the world but to change it. Comte and Durkheim in their different ways each sought to move from positive philosophy to a positive polity. And Parsons and Merton in their different ways each sought to provide for usable knowledge. Anti-foundationalism thus calls into question, as Crook (1991) notes, the whole project of 'modernist radicalism'.

What marks much contemporary sociology off from both the structural–functional orthodoxy of the 1950s and the alternative paradigms in the subsequent war of the schools is widespread doubt about the availability of any such foundation. There are a number of reasons for this. They include the impossibility of sealing off sociological discourse from natural discourse and the consequent elusiveness of a universal categorial system for all sociology, the impossibility of effecting any closure on the constitution of society, the limitations of all known research methods and the contested character of objectivity.

Once foundationalism is discarded, objectivist claims become highly problematic. By 'objectivism' I mean the idea that 'there must be some permanent, ahistorical matrix or framework to which we can ultimately appeal in determining the nature of rationality, knowledge, truth, reality, goodness, or rightness' (Bernstein 1983: 8); and by realism I mean Francis Bacon's thesis that science reveals the true and hidden nature of the world.

Anti-foundationalism is more disputed than the linguistic turn and there are a number of responses to it. One is that of Bhaskar (1975, 1979), Pawson (1989), Archer (1988, 1995) and other scientific realists who have been very influential in Britain but less so elsewhere. I have argued elsewhere that the underlying realities they posit do not have the privileged ontological status they think they do. In addition their empirical confirmation presents difficulties which are no different in principle from those which accompany attempts to establish the utility of any ideal-type, logical construction or deductive system in the explanation of the actual social world or the real economy in the economist's sense of real. In short, scientific realists fall foul of Ockham's razor; they make additional ontological assumptions for no additional explanatory benefit.

Another response is that of Habermas. I contest the attempt made by Habermas (1970), who otherwise accepts much of the anti-foundationalist case, to vest the ideal-speech situation with a transcendental character which privileges it over other idealizations, such as Weberian ideal-types, by claiming that it is anticipated in all discourse. I contend that the ideal-speech situation is better regarded as a normative counterfactual (and that the undistorted communication of the ideal-speech situation need not eventuate in rational consensus).

Alexander has readily conceded Rorty's basic point that we must 'give up the utopian hope that a single ahistorical standard of truth can ever be established' (Alexander 1988: 94), but fears that in Rorty, or perhaps in Rorty's more misguided followers, this opens the way to irrationalism. This third response to anti-foundationalism is mistaken. Rorty is better understood as playing with the interminable dialectic between 'systematic' and 'edifying' philosophy, normal and abnormal discourse. Rorty's complaint about systematic philosophy concerns its historic, but false, quest for apodictic truth. The alternative he proffers is inquiry within a framework of justification, and 'conversations' between different frameworks. The rules which guide the first, and the devices which make possible the second, are reasonable, learnable, discussable, justifiable. By application, then, sociology prosecuted within a particular framework of (non-apodictic) justification, and sociology dedicated to the construction of 'conversations' between different claims to knowledge (whether social scientific or not), are both reasonable, learnable, followable, discussable, justifiable. It is only those who will not, or cannot, engage others in conversation who succumb to solipsism. Contrary to Alexander, there would thus seem no warrant for irrationalism in Rorty.

What Rorty does warrant is a pragmatic response to post-foundationalism. This fourth response does not deny the non-availability of a single meta-language or metric but refuses to draw from this the conclusion of radical incommensurability. Instead it treats comparisons between paradigms and conceptual vocabularies, cultures and epochs, as exercises in translation in which there may be some direct equivalences but there will also have to be many discursive glosses. The object of these pragmatic exercises is to construct a 'conversation' between one's own culture, age, position, etc., and some other(s). For distinguished examples of this kind of work, one can turn to Geertz (1973); for more of its rationale, one can turn to Rorty (1980, 1982) in philosophy and Bernstein (1971, 1983) in social theory. It is a pragmatic approach in that it is guided by the notion that knowledge is better regarded not as a representation of reality but rather as an engagement with it. This response to the anti-foundationalist challenge is still being worked out, but it is already possible to discern something of its sources and its uses. The former include Rickert and Weber on theoretical and practical value-relations, and Peirce and other American pragmatists. The latter include the interactive and dialogical models of applied social research which capitalize on the double hermeneutic.

Post-empiricism

The linguistic turn and anti-foundationalism have led to what Alexander calls post-positivism but what I, in deference to Hesse (1980) who did so much to formulate it, prefer to call post-empiricism (though Hesse herself also refers to post-deductivism). Put at its simplest, post-empiricist social science is social science after the linguistic turn.

Empiricism, for Hesse, is a philosophy of natural science, developed by Carnap, Hempel, Nagel, Braithwaite and Popper, which rests on the assumptions of (i) a naive realism, (ii) a universal scientific language and (iii) a correspondence theory of truth. For empiricists:

> there is an external world which can in principle be exhaustively described in scientific language. The scientist, as both observer and language-user, can capture the external facts of the world in propositions that are true if they correspond to the facts and false if they do not. Science is ideally a linguistic system in which true propositions are in one-to-one relation to the facts, including facts that are not directly observed because they involve hidden entities or properties, or past events or far distant events. These hidden events are described in theories, and theories can be inferred from observation. Man as scientist is regarded as standing apart from the world and able to experiment and theorize about it objectively and dispassionately.
>
> (Hesse 1980: vii)

By the 1970s all three basic assumptions had been undermined by (i) more historically oriented philosophers of science, such as Kuhn, Feyerabend and Toulmin, (ii) the anti-foundationalist epistemology of Quine, which was itself partly derived from that of the historian of science, Duhem, and, one might add, of Rorty, and (iii) the linguistic philosophy of Wittgenstein.

In formulating an alternative philosophy of science, Hesse turned to the very characteristics of social science which many had insisted made it different from natural science: namely, (i) the non-detachability of theory from data, (ii) the mimetic reconstructions of facts as theories, (iii) the internal relations between the investigator and the objects investigated and between the objects themselves, (iv) the equivocity of its scientific language, and (v) the constitution of facts by meanings. Versions of all of these figure in natural science too. It was, she argued, true of both natural and social science

> that data are not detachable from theory, and that their expression is per-meated by theoretical categories; that the language of theoretical science is irreducibly metaphorical and unformalizable; and that the logic of

science is circular interpretation, reinterpretation, and self-correction of data in terms of theory, theory in terms of data.   (Hesse 1980: 173)

Hesse called the successor position which emerged from the onslaught on the old orthodoxy in the philosophy of natural science 'post-empiricism' (or sometimes 'post-deductivism').

Although Hesse made use of a contrast between natural and social science in the formulation of post-empiricism, much social science in the positivist, analytical and theory-building traditions has been broadly 'empiricist', as she understands it, in orientation. Post-empiricism has thus made an impact on social science too, an impact reinforced by the 'linguistic turn' and the revival of the hermeneutic tradition. This is Giddens and J.H. Turner's (1987) version:

> the idea that there can be theory-neutral observation is repudiated, while systems of deductively-linked laws are no longer canonized as the high-est ideal of explanation. Most importantly, science is presumed to be an interpretative endeavour, such that problems of meaning, communication and translation are immediately relevant to scientific theorizing.
>
> (Giddens and Turner 1987: 2)

In its emphases on metaphor, models, imaginary constructions, and net-works of propositions, its combination of elements of both the cor-respondence and coherence theories of truth, and its refusal to dichotomize either the pre-theoretical and the theoretical, or the theoretical and the empirical, post-empiricism clearly no longer allows a stark contrast be-tween natural science and social science, let alone between the analytical and hermeneutic traditions within the social sciences.

This is not to proclaim some new version of a unified science, how-ever, for two reasons. First, the double hermeneutic applies only to social science. Second, the underdetermination of theory by data has a different import in the social sciences in so far as the values and images which inform and complement data should not be regarded as unfortunate intrusions but rather as contributants to be argued for and justified in their own right – as assets rather than liabilities. '[T]he proposal of a social theory is more like the arguing of a political case', Hesse contends, 'than like a natural science explanation' (1978: 16) – except that there are parallels in the way claims for each are constructed and accepted in Hesse's own network theory (and in Habermas and others). One way or another, then, the philo-sophical grounds for the mutual respect of adherents to the analytical and interpretivist traditions in sociology are stronger than the partisans of each have often cared to suppose.

Discourse and the new theoretical movement

I have argued that the dichotomization of theory and meta-theory is distortive. Even works sympathetic to meta-theory, such as the collection edited by Ritzer (1992a), can sometimes mislead by treating consideration of all matters other than substantive theory building within the analytical tradition as meta-theory, instead of recognizing that many of them are integral to, not separate from, modes of substantive theorizing.[5] Holmwood (1996) is right to warn that it is often impossible to decide meta-theoretical issues without reference to real problems of explanation. In short, the distinction between theory and meta-theory is as likely to obscure as to clarify. Alexander's essay on the new theoretical movement proposes a way round the troublesome distinction which, suitably modified, I wish to endorse. Like Alexander, I believe that the term 'discourse' has merit because it combines characteristics separately attributed to theory and meta-theory by the friends and foes of each.

Discourse in ordinary English refers (among other things) to conversations and exchanges about something, to continuous processes of formulation in which various parties participate. In the social sciences, 'discourse' derives its significance from the linguistic turn and provides 'a term with which to grasp the way in which language and other forms of social semiotics not merely convey social experience, but play some major part in constituting social subjects . . . their relations, and the fields in which they exist' (Purvis and Hunt 1993: 474). And, as Foucault reminded us, there are no extra-discursive phenomena; all things are constructed within discourses.[6] In addition to all of these, Alexander (1988) contrasts the qualities of sociology as discourse with those of sociology as explanation. By 'discourse', he refers to

> modes of argument that are more consistently generalized and speculative than normal scientific discussion. The latter are directed in a more disciplined manner to specific pieces of empirical evidence, to inductive and deductive logics, to explanation through covering laws, and to the methods by which these laws can be verified or falsified. Discourse, by contrast, is ratiocinative. It focuses on the process of reasoning rather than the results of immediate experience, and it becomes significant where there is no plain and evident truth. Discourse seeks persuasion through argument rather than prediction. Its persuasiveness is based on such qualities as logical coherence, expansiveness of scope, interpretive insight, value relevance, rhetorical force, beauty, and texture of argument.
>
> (Alexander 1988: 80)

Alexander's characterization of discourse needs two modifications. First, persuasive qualities, I would insist, additionally include respect for evidence

– there being no need to make the qualities of sociology as discourse and as explanation mutually exclusive – provided always that regard be given to the constitution of evidence. Second, as 'normal scientific discussion' is itself a discourse – there being in the social sciences, as Alexander himself says, not discourse but discourses – it would be better to distinguish between the post-empiricist or post-deductivist discourse of the new theoretical movement, which Alexander supports, and the deductive-nomological discourse of the theory builders, which he rejects. In other words, sociology is a set of discourses, and sociology as discourse is shorthand for a particular discourse, namely, post-empiricist discourse.

The relatively simple conception of (post-empiricist) discourse, here derived from the linguistic turn via Alexander, incorporates all the elements internal to knowledge claims made and accepted among sociologists, but does not require attachment to either the theory of communicative action of Habermas or the poststructuralism of Foucault. For Alexander this is quite deliberate: 'Between the rationalizing discourse of Habermas and the arbitrary discourse of Foucault, this is where the actual field of social science uneasily lies' (Alexander 1988: 80).

Post-empiricist knowledge cumulation and decline

Alexander and Colomy have developed what Colomy (1990) calls a 'post-positivist model of knowledge cumulation and decline' (see also Alexander 1982; Alexander and Colomy 1992). Following Alexander (1982: 40), Colomy sets out 'the continuum of social scientific thought'. At one end is the metaphysical environment of science (non-empirical), and at the other the physical environment of science (empirical). As one moves from the metaphysical to the physical pole one encounters, in order of decreasing generality and increasing specificity, presuppositions, ideological orientations, models, concepts, definitions, classifications, laws, complex and simple propositions, methodological assumptions and observational statements – ten items in all. Colomy refers to the ten items as levels and then makes three points. First, sociology 'is carried out at different levels of generality and is conducted through distinctive modes of discourse' (Colomy 1990: xix); second, 'in the history of social thought the options at each level have been limited' (1990: xix); and third, although no intrinsic relationship exists between levels, social scientists usually presume a linkage because social science practice unfolds within powerful theoretical traditions which stipulate them.

This scheme is attractive in so far as it blurs the distinction between theory proper (the real thing) and meta-theory (a seductive diversion from the real thing) by referring to social science as discourse which properly embraces the referents of both. It is unattractive in so far as it proposes a meta-theoretical structure based on unambiguous and stratified distinctions between concepts, definitions, classifications and laws – to take the middle four levels as an example. Alexander and Colomy err, however, in assuming a quasi-foundational continuum/layering of social thought instead of the shifting clustering of components of social thought, and in positing the mediation of empirical reality instead of the constitution of society and the person. They make social thought much tidier than it is or ever can be.

Colomy (1990) argues that 'Social reality . . . is mediated by the discursive commitments of traditions, and social scientific formulations are channelled within relatively standardized paradigmatic forms' (1990: xix). Traditions afford both generalized discourse and research programmes. They can often be traced to an intellectually charismatic founder. Their theoretical cores resist change, but they are otherwise subject to elaboration, proliferation and revision. Elaboration and proliferation are true to the tradition; revision acknowledges, sometimes implicitly, strains within it, and offers reformulations accordingly. Reconstruction, on the other hand, explicitly questions elements of the tradition and opens up to alternatives offered by other traditions. Alexander and Colomy's own reconstruction of Parsonian functionalism as neo-functionalism provides an example. Traditions can also be abandoned and revived. When this happens it is not so much that they have been falsified as that they have become 'delegitimized in the eyes of the scientific community' (1990: xix).

In Alexander and Colomy's model, the 'primary motor of social scientific growth is conflict and competition between traditions' (Colomy 1990: xx). Most estimates of progess can only be estimates of progress within a tradition relative to others. Disciplinary communities change theoretical positions in response to shifts in 'scientific sensibility' which pose different questions and prompt different modes of discourse. 'The deep structure of a discipline consists of the networks and literatures produced by the contact between empirical objects, ongoing traditions and new disciplinary movements' (Colomy 1990: xx).

Instead of 'deep structure', Colomy would, I think, have done better to speak of 'dynamic structure' – the combination of factors which generate stability and change. He might also have confirmed that 'empirical objects' are 'constituted empirical objects' and he ought also to have added in 'applications'. With those amendments, however, change in a discipline or specialty can be understood as the product of contacts between old and new objects of inquiry, old and new thinking, and old and new applications, and knowledge cumulation and decline can be understood in terms of the growth and loss of support for a generalized discourse and its accompanying research programmes within a scientific community. Whether change amounts to 'progress' is something which can only be justified through dialogue within a scientific community.

Sociology in America and Britain

Anyone reading the all-American contributions to Ritzer's *Frontiers of Social Theory* (1990) is likely to conclude that it is contributors to the new theoretical movement who have made all the running. Some of the contributors reflect on relations between different paradigms or modes of theorizing, and on relations between theory and American sociology in general. They largely converge on two versions of the same story: the dignified and the down-to-earth. The dignified version notes that, with or without obeisances to Rorty or Lyotard, devotees of most modes of theorizing make non-exclusive claims for their favoured discourse and welcome exchanges and convergences with others. Hence the new syntheses of Ritzer's sub-title (and the similar new synthesis to which Giddens (1987: ch. 2) refers in a lecture given in America two years before the Maryland conference). At the same time, they reject any idea of a hegemonic paradigm, grand synthesis or master narrative. American sociology has moved, it seems agreed, from functionalist orthodoxy, through the war of the schools, to a pluralism which is both principled and pragmatic. The down-to-earth version, to which Ritzer himself refers, is similar but adds that most leading theorists find their niches and do their work without regard for the large number of lumpensociologists (my term) who would have welcomed the resurgence of neo-functionalism had they noticed that the original version had fallen into disrepute, and the even larger number of lumpensociologists whose work has no connection at all to theorists' theory.[7]

Theorists' theory has been marginalized in America; *Sociological Theory*, the American Sociological Association's theory journal, was founded in 1982 to give theory the prominence it conspicuously lacked in other journals. Instead 'instrumental positivism' has enjoyed an ever increasing ascendancy in American sociology since the 1930s (Wells and Picou 1981; Bryant 1985: ch. 5). It has displayed five main characteristics: a preoccupation with the refinement of statistical techniques and research instrumentation; a nominalist or individualistic conception of society consistent with the sample survey; a view of the cumulation of knowledge as best secured by induction, verification and incrementalism; a linkage of a (false) dichotomy of facts and values with a (mis)conception of value-freedom; and a commitment to team research and the development of centres of applied social research. Anyone doubting the persistence of this tradition has only to turn to the *American Sociological Review*. There is no doubt that it has been aligned to the pursuit of 'theory proper' in so far as it has attended to theory at all. There is, then, a danger that what I have presented as post-empiricism, and what Alexander calls the new theoretical movement, has only served to detach theorists' theory more sharply than ever from the prevailing research practice in the society in which sociologists have been most numerous.

The same point can be made the other way round. The most lauded contribution to the articulation of 'theory proper' in recent years would seem to have been J.S. Coleman's massive *The Foundations of Sociology* (1990). Like Merton before him, Coleman complains that most 'social theory' is really the history of social thought, especially nineteenth-century social thought, and as such it provides a poor basis for the analysis and explanation of a world undergoing an organizational revolution. For that, a new robust theory of action is required, and, pulling together the threads of a twenty-year personal project, Coleman heroically sets out to provide it himself in both discursive and mathematical forms. In the course of nearly a thousand pages, Coleman makes innumerable shrewd points about contemporary social phenomena but his researchers' theory is impervious to the linguistic turn, the double hermeneutic and the preoccupations of post-empiricist philosophy of science. It belongs to a time warp; it avoids not only theory conceived as the history of social thought, but also connections with almost any developments in social theory and the philosophy of the social sciences in the last quarter century. The agency–structure debates might as well not have taken place. Kuhn, Hesse, Rorty – they all laboured in vain. The new theoretical movement is beyond notice. (For that matter, so are the profound misgivings about the direction American sociology has taken, voiced by the leading proponent of causal modelling, Blalock (1984).) Most tellingly of all, Coleman seemed unaware that the very notion of the foundations of social science could be controversial. Significantly, his book was respectfully reviewed in the leading American journals and ignored altogether in the British ones.

The detachment of theorists' theory from research practice seems to have done mainstream American sociology – Turner and Turner's 'impossible science' (1990) – no favours. Their thesis is that American sociology has, since the 1950s, sold itself to the foundations, to agencies of the federal and state governments, and to prospective students on a false prospectus – basically a natural-science type prospectus – on which it has all too conspicuously proved unable to deliver. They are particularly interesting on the poisoned legacy of the 1960s. They argue that sociologists enjoyed huge increases in federal funding for research and in student numbers in the 1960s and 1970s before they had resolved fundamental questions about what their discipline could and should be and do. The reorganized ASA became an umbrella organization for enormously diverse activities.

> The result was an almost complete inability to consolidate symbolic resources around either a sense of a common professional community – as the founders of American sociology tried to do – or a common corpus and storehouse of knowledge. And when the period of decline in funding, student enrollments, ASA membership, and eventually Ph.D. production began in the mid 1970s, sociology did not have the organizational resources, such as centralized administration and control, nor the symbolic resources, such as common professional identification, consensus over a knowledge base, and prestige within the academic or lay community, to cope with the decline.
>
> (Turner and Turner 1990: 139–40)

Obsession with quantitative research techniques is simply not enough to integrate the discipline.

Each of the Turners has responded differently to the continuing plight of American sociology. Jonathan is the gnostic sectarian who cannot come to terms with post-empiricism. 'The relativistic, solipsistic, particularistic, anti-positivistic, and meta-istic (to invent a word) character of theory is no longer a challenge to debate', he tells us, but rather, 'Increasingly it is something to be ignored' (Turner 1990: 389). The fifty or so true believers in 'the realization of Comte's original vision for a "social physics"' are invited to abandon the mainstream of sociological theory. (I am reminded of the old joke about the English: 'Fog in Channel: Continent cut off'.) Stephen is the sardonic *flâneur*, self-exiled in a philosophy department. Looking at American sociology, he sees too much contentment with comfortable niches, too few students, too little connection with society, and too little prospect of theoretical integration.

I believe that the majority of American sociologists, and the minority of American theorists, who still pursue an empiricist conception of sociology will find that their holy grail continues to elude them. But sociology is only an impossible science for those who subscribe to an impossible conception of science. Unfortunately, subscribers include politicians, publics and purseholders. As a consequence, Smelser expects his fellow American sociologists to go on trying to give donor agencies and government officials what they expect irrespective of whether that strategy 'is, in the end, effective or self-defeating' (Smelser 1988: 15). Even so, I think Turner and Turner underestimate the long-term persuasiveness of post-empiricism and the new theoretical movement, and the numbers who will eventually be touched by it in their research practice. I also note with interest calls for the redirection of sociology in America. I have in mind Gans' call for more 'public sociologists', by which he means not popularizers of other people's work but researchers, analysts and theorists in their own right who have the commitment and the skills to engage the interest of the educated lay public – or, as I would prefer, to initiate and sustain a dialogue with lay publics (Gans 1988). He gives Riesman as the prime example. I also think Marris (1990) is right to call upon sociologists to pay more attention to their role as story-tellers. He argues that influential research mostly tells a story with a moral. That would account for at least part of the success of works like Bellah *et al.*'s *Habits of the Heart* (1985), Wilson's *The Truly Disadvantaged* (1987) and Lipset's *American Exceptionalism* (1996), each of which addresses aspects of the moral condition of America.

In sum, American sociological theory is alive and well, but may have more impact on sociology in general outside America than within it. In the long term, American sociology generally will probably come right, but it is questionable whether in the short term it offers many positive lessons for sociological communities elsewhere.

In Britain, as in America, sociology expanded greatly in the 1960s and early 1970s without having first secured the disciplinary integration coveted by Turner and Turner. This expansion was, however, not so great as to make possible the fragmentation of sociology into countless self-sustaining specialties – the introverted nicheism which Turner and Turner so deplore in America – and seems not to have impeded concerted responses to the cutbacks of the early 1980s. There have been some separatist tendencies in the sociology of health and illness (the largest specialty in Britain) and in ethnomethodology but they have been very much the exception and not the rule. Most British sociologists are, without doubt, less accomplished in quantitative social research methods than their American counterparts but they are probably better informed, by choice and necessity, about developments in different sociological traditions – analytical, hermeneutic and historical – and different specialties. The war of the schools is now a distant, if often fond, memory.

Departments are cohesive. Student demand for sociology – long falling until the mid-1980s – grew strongly until the mid-1990s (although it is now falling again). Instead of Margaret Thatcher's hostility to sociology, we have Tony Blair's (selective) use of Tony Giddens in the formulation of a third-way politics beyond the old left and the new right (Giddens 1994, 1998; Blair, 1998; Bryant 1999). None of this is to deny, of course, that serious problems remain. In particular the chronic and wearying under-funding of higher education in Britain in general, and the location of sociology among the poorest-funded group of disciplines in particular, has, in the context of the current rapid expansion of higher education, put sociology teachers under great strain and limited time and money for research. It has also restricted provision for in-service training, the updating of equipment and much else besides. Research institutes of the size now familiar in Germany are also conspicuous by their absence (Weymann 1990). British sociology is, however, in better shape than seemed possible in the early 1980s – partly because it is not wedded to an impossible conception of science. Compared with its American counter-part, it could perhaps be best described as poor but honest.

It is notable that the circumstances of British sociology do seem to have sustained work in theory which has been copious in volume, high in quality and rich in diversity. My list of theory writers includes Barbara Adam, Martin Albrow, Margaret Archer, Michèle Barrett, Zygmunt Bauman, Ted Benton, Tom Bottomore, Percy Cohen, Ian Craib, Gerard Delanty, Norbert Elias, David Frisby, Mike Gane, Anthony Giddens, Geoffrey Hawthorne, David Held, John Holmwood, Richard Kilminster, Derek Layder, Steven Lukes, Tim May, Stephen Mennell, Nicos Mouzelis, William Outhwaite, Ray Pawson, John Rex, Paul Rock, W.G. Runciman, Andrew Sayer, Liz Stanley, Rob Stones, John Thompson, Bryan Turner and John Urry. Others with different interests (in cultural studies or ethnomethod-ology, for example) will think differently and the names will multiply – which is precisely the point. In addition to three general sociology journals which publish many theoretical articles, Britain also has two specialist theory journals – the well-established and highly acclaimed *Theory, Culture and Society* (founded in 1982 and edited ever since by Mike Featherstone) and the new *European Journal of Social Theory* (founded in 1998 and edited by Gerard Delanty). Why has sociology in Britain proved so hospitable to social theorists? One factor is surely that British sociology has from the 1960s, the decade of its academic take-off, been less the cumulative sci-ence sought by Merton and Turner in America and more a set of discourses. Open to both the empirical and statistical traditions of American sociology and the theoretical and philosophical traditions of European sociology, it has had the singular fortune to be the meeting point for the sociologies of the world.

Practical sociology: a social science that works

Two themes run through this essay. The first is that the quest for sure foundations, whether epistemological, conceptual or real – as in the pursuit of theory proper, deductive nomologicalism, definitive reconstructionism and the establishment of a categorial system, strong scientific realism, etc. – has not just failed, but failed irretrievably. The social engineering and the exclusively instrumental reason associated with some versions of the quest have also, of necessity, failed to deliver much of what was expected of them. The product of modelling social science on different conceptions of natural science, they are misconceived, whether grand in scale or ambition like Parsons, middling like Merton, or small like the theories Warshay (1975) discusses. This is, however, most definitely not to charge that legions of able and industrious men and women have laboured for decades and produced nothing of value. Quite apart from what we might treat in the long run as their necessary but instructive failures, sociologists of various positivist, empiricist and strong realist persuasions have, on the contrary, come up with a huge number of substantive theories, concepts, research methods, empirical findings, interpretations and applications which are, or have been, of great social value. It is just that there is no way of connecting them all to yield a single integrated and cumulating body of law and evidence; it is in connection with that project, and that project only, that all those sociologists have laboured in vain. In sum, what could be called the theory-building orientation in sociology has exhausted whatever potential it might once have had.

The second theme is that the linguistic and hermeneutic turns, and anti-foundational and post-empiricist philosophies of science, have supported alternative ways of doing social science which are consistent with the ontologies of the social defined within the agency–structure debate and with the double hermeneutic and the connections identified between social scientific and lay and other discourses. They also facilitate convergences between social science and moral inquiry and open up the possibility of procedures for the rational assessment of values, and they encourage cognitive and practical ambitions which are realistic. In sum, what could be called the constitution-of-society orientation in sociology has great cognitive potential and avoids giving hostages to political fortune. It affords a pragmatic sociology, one whose practitioners are alive to the conditions and the limits of what they can do and one which enhances the capacity of citizens to engage effectively with the changing social milieus in which they move. (There are affinities here with what Brown (1989) calls 'sociology for civic competence', and Giddens' endorsement of public intellectuals.) A pragmatic sociology does not promise what it cannot deliver, but it also knows the social value of what it can deliver. It succeeds by persuasion, by informing the reasoning of agents.

Given the positive and constructive character of this second orientation, is its triumph assured? In the longer term, its prospects would seem very good, as ever more sociologists can be expected to take a realistic view of what sociology is and can be. In the short term, however, it faces considerable obstacles. First, its adoption is intolerably disorienting to colleagues habituated to the first, or theory-building, orientation. Second, politicians, publics and purseholders largely expect a social *science* worthy of the name and the funding to produce knowledge as reliable and incontestable as that they attribute, however simplistically, to the natural sciences. (That post-empiricist philosophy of science has undermined empiricist natural science, too, seems as yet to have made no difference.) Hence Smelser's dilemma, mentioned above, according to which sociologists in America continue to be locked into delivering to government and other funders what some may have come to recognize is undeliverable.

For the post-empiricist reconstruction of theory and application to succeed, sociologists have got to persuade publics, politicians and purseholders that sociology is rational even as it is contestable, that there are learnable and justifiable principles and techniques which inform both different discourses and communication between them and different kinds of research design, practice and analysis. They have also to convey that sociology is necessary: that in differentiated and changing societies there are always understandings to be reached and connections to be made, and that the principles and techniques that make sociology a set of discourses, a discipline, and not an activity in which anything goes, also ensure that it has a contribution to make to the reflexivity of contemporary societies different from anything poets, prophets and pundits can offer. This re-presentation and repositioning of sociology will be difficult and protracted, but on its success the future strength of the discipline depends.

Notes

1 An earlier draft of this essay was written for an earlier version of this book and its argument was subsequently developed at book length in my *Practical Sociology: Post-Empiricism and the Reconstruction of Theory and Application* (Bryant

1995), with chapters on concept formation, the constitution of society, values in social science and models of applied social science. This version of the essay draws on the Introduction and Conclusions of the book, but also takes account of some later writings.

2 For an excellent discussion of the issues, see Delanty (1999).

3 I have used the revised and enlarged second edition of Merton's *Social Theory and Social Structure* published in 1957. There is an earlier version of the essay, 'The bearing of sociological theory on empirical research' (Merton 1957a), which lists the types of work which have gone by the name of theory, in the first edition of 1949. Engel's law of consumption is my example of an empirical generalization, not Merton's. The two 'Continuities' essays mentioned later in the paragraph appear for the first time in the second edition.

4 The term has subsequently been used, and the claim endorsed, by Jonathan Turner (1989a); also see Wacquant (1993).

5 Neither Ritzer, nor his contributors, confine themselves to his narrow definition of meta-theorizing as 'the systematic study of the underlying structure of sociological theory' (1992b: 7). Ritzer himself broadens meta-theorizing to include the debates on the paradigmatic status of sociology, the micro–macro and agency–structure linkages and the modelling of social science on natural science, and his contributors add issues as diverse as the value of classical theory, concept standardization, reflexivity and postmodernity and theory. It is questionable whether sociological theory has any single underlying structure.

6 For a discussion of five clearly distinguishable uses of the term 'discourse' in the social sciences, including Foucault's, see Cousins and Hussain (1984: ch. 4); and for a review of the similarities and dissimilarities between different conceptions of discourse and ideology, see Purvis and Hunt (1993).

7 Menzies (1982) introduced the notion of a theory gap between theoreticians' theory and researchers' theory. His distinction is between systematic theory building and the researchers' pursuit of such limited connections between phenomena as the complexity and messiness of the social world permit. In similar vein, I have noted the big gap between the theoretical concerns – conceptual, analytical, hermeneutic, critical, 'meta-theoretical', etc. – of self-styled theorists and the narrow theoretical focus of those researchers for whom theory refers only to hypotheses for test, and the labelling of connections confirmed by test, within discrete areas of inquiry – in short to (the littlest of) what Warshay (1975) calls 'little theories' (Bryant 1995: ch. 6). It would be wrong to suppose that these two types of sociology are the only ones in America, but the number of empirical researchers so characterized is very large.

References

Alexander, Jeffrey C. (1982) *Theoretical Logic in Sociology*, vol. 1: *Positivism Presuppositions and Current Controversies*, London: Routledge and Kegan Paul.

Alexander, Jeffrey C. (1988) 'The new theoretical movement', in N.J. Smelser (ed.) *Handbook of Sociology*, Beverly Hills and London: Sage, 77–101.

Alexander, Jeffrey C. and Colomy, Paul (1992) 'Traditions and competition: preface to a postpositivist approach to knowledge cumulation', in G. Ritzer (ed.) *Metatheorizing*, Newbury Park CA: Sage.

Alexander, Jeffrey C., Giesen, Bernhard, Münch, Richard and Smelser, Neil J. (1987) *The Micro–Macro Link*, Berkeley CA: University of California Press.

Archer, Margaret S. (1982) 'Morphogenesis versus structuration: on combining structure and action', *British Journal of Sociology* 33: 455–83.

Archer, Margaret S. (1988) *Culture and Agency: The Place of Culture in Social Theory*, Cambridge: Cambridge University Press.

Archer, Margaret S. (1995) *Realist Social Theory: The Morphogenetic Approach*, Cambridge: Cambridge University Press.

Bauman, Zygmunt (1993) *Postmodern Ethics*, Oxford: Blackwell.

Becker, Henk A. (1990) 'Achievement in the analytical tradition in sociology', in C.G.A. Bryant and H.A. Becker (eds) *What Has Sociology Achieved?*, London: Macmillan, ch. 2.

Bellah, Robert N., Madsen, Richard, Sullivan, William M., Swidler, Ann and Tipton, Steven M. (1985) *Habits of the Heart: Middle America Observed*, New York: Harper and Row.

Bergmann, Gustav (1964) *Logic and Reality*, Madison: University of Wisconsin Press.

Bernstein, Richard (1971) *Praxis and Action*, Philadelphia: University of Pennsylvania Press.

Bernstein, Richard (1983) *Beyond Objectivism and Relativism*, Oxford: Blackwell.

Bhaskar, Roy (1975) *A Realist Theory of Science*, second edition, Brighton: Harvester.

Bhaskar, Roy (1979) *The Possibility of Naturalism*, Brighton: Harvester.

Bhaskar, Roy (1986) *Scientific Realism and Human Emancipation*, London: Verso.

Blair, Tony (1998) 'The third way: new politics for the new century', *Fabian Pamphlets*, no. 588, London: Fabian Society.

Blalock, Hubert M. Jr (1969) *Theory Construction*, Englewood Cliffs NJ: Prentice Hall.

Blalock, Hubert M. Jr (1984) *Basic Dilemmas in the Social Sciences*, Beverly Hills CA: Sage.

Boudon, Raymond (1980) 'Theories, theory and Theory', in R. Boudon, *The Crisis in Sociology: Problems of Sociological Epistemology*, trans. H.H. Davis, London: Macmillan, ch. 7 (first published in French, 1970).

Bourdieu, Pierre (1977) *Outline of a Theory of Practice*, trans. R. Nice, Cambridge: Cambridge University Press (first published in French, 1972).

Bourdieu, Pierre (1990) *The Logic of Practice*, trans. R. Nice, Cambridge: Polity Press (first published in French, 1980).

Brown, Richard Harvey (1989) *Social Science as Civic Discourse: Essays on the Invention, Legitimation, and Uses of Social Theory*, Chicago: University of Chicago Press.

Bryant, Christopher G.A. (1985) *Positivism in Social Theory and Research*, London: Macmillan.

Bryant, Christopher G.A. (1995) *Practical Sociology: Post-Empiricism and the Reconstruction of Theory and Application*, Cambridge: Polity Press.

Bryant, Christopher G.A. (1999) 'The third way, two Tonys – and a single vision?', *ECPR News* 10 (2): 17–18.

Bryant, Christopher G.A. and Becker H.A. (eds) (1990) *What Has Sociology Achieved?*, London: Macmillan.

Cain, Maureen, (1990) 'Realist philosophy and standpoint epistemologies or feminist criminology as a successor science', in L. Gelsthorpe and A. Morris (eds) *Feminist Perspectives in Criminology*, Milton Keynes: Open University Press.

Cicourel, Alvin V. (1964) *Method and Measurement in Sociology*, New York: Free Press.

Coleman, James S. (1990) *Foundations of Social Theory*, Cambridge MA: Belknap Press.

Collins, Randall (1981) 'On the microfoundations of macrosociology', *American Sociological Review* 86: 984–1014.

Colomy, Paul (ed.) (1990) *Functionalist Sociology*, London: Edward Elgar.

Cousins, Mark and Hussain, Athar (1984) *Michel Foucault*, London: Macmillan.

Crook, Stephen (1991) *Modernist Radicalism and its Aftermath: Foundationalism and Anti-foundationalism in Radical Social Theory*, London: Routledge.

Crothers, Charles (1987) *Robert K. Merton*, Chichester: Ellis Horwood.

Delanty, Gerard (1999) *Social Theory in a Changing World: Conceptions of Modernity*, Cambridge: Polity Press.

Dubin, Robert (1969) *Theory Building: A Practical Guide to the Construction and Testing of Theoretical Models*, New York: Free Press.

Durkheim, Emile (1952) *Suicide: A Study in Suicide*, introduction by G. Simpson, trans. by J.A. Spaulding and G. Simpson, London: Routledge and Kegan Paul (first published in French, 1897).

Durkheim, Emile (1982) *The Rules of Sociological Method*, introduction by S. Lukes, trans. W.D. Halls, in *The Rules of Sociological Method: and Selected Texts on Sociology and its Method*, London: Macmillan (first published in French, 1895).

Elias, Norbert (1978/82) *The Civilizing Process*, vol. 1: *The History of Manners* and vol. 2: *State Formation and Civilization*, Oxford: Blackwell (first published in German, 1939).

Elias, Norbert (1968) 'Introduction' to the second German edition of *The Civilizing Process*, appendix to vol. 1 of translation, 221–63.

Elias, Norbert (1978) *What is Sociology?*, trans. S. Mennell and G. Morrissey, London: Hutchinson (first published in German, 1970).

Gans, Herbert J. (1988) 'Sociology in America: the discipline and the public', in H.J. Gans (ed.) *Sociology in America*, London: Sage, Appendix B.

Gans, Herbert J. (ed.) (1990) *Sociology in America*, London: Sage.

Geertz, Clifford (1973) *The Interpretation of Cultures*, New York: Basic Books.

Giddens, Anthony (1976) *New Rules of Sociological Method*, London: Hutchinson.

Giddens, Anthony (1979) *Central Problems in Social Theory: Action, Structure and Contradiction in Social Analysis*, London: Macmillan.

Giddens, Anthony (1984) *The Constitution of Society*, Cambridge: Polity Press.

Giddens, Anthony (1987) *Social Theory and Modern Sociology*, Cambridge: Polity Press.

Giddens, Anthony (1994) *Beyond Left and Right: The Future of Radical Politics*, Cambridge: Polity Press.

Giddens, Anthony (1998) *The Third Way: The Renewal of Social Democracy*, Cambridge: Polity Press.

Giddens, Anthony and Turner Jonathan H. (eds) (1987) *Social Theory Today*, Cambridge: Polity Press.

Gurvitch, Georges (1958) 'Les Structures sociales', in G. Gurvitch (ed.) *Traité de sociologie*, Paris: Presses Universitaires de France.

Haan, Norma, Bellah, Robert N., Rabinow, Paul and Sullivan, William M. (eds) (1983) *Social Science as Moral Inquiry*, New York: Columbia University Press.

Habermas, Jürgen (1970) 'Towards a theory of communicative competence', in H.P. Dreitzel (ed.) *Recent Sociology no. 2: Patterns of Communicative Behavior*, New York: Collier-Macmillan, ch. 5.

Habermas, Jürgen (1976) *Legitimation Crisis*, trans. T. McCarthy, London: Heinemann (first published in German, 1973).

Habermas, Jürgen (1984/7) *The Theory of Communicative Action*, vol. 1: *Reason and the Rationalization of Society*, London: Heinemann; vol. 2: *The Critique of Functionalist Reason*, Cambridge: Polity Press (introductions and trans. both volumes T. McCarthy; first published in German, 1981).

Habermas, Jürgen (1993) *Justification and Application: Remarks on Discourse Ethics*, introduction and trans. C. Cronin, Cambridge: Polity Press (first published in German, 1991).

Harding, Sandra (1993) 'Rethinking standpoint epistemology: What is "strong objectivity"?', in L. Alcoff and E. Potter (eds) *Feminist Epistemologies*, New York: Routledge, ch. 3.

Hechter, Michael (ed.) (1983) *The Microfoundations of Macrosociology*, Philadelphia: Temple University Press.

Hesse, Mary (1978) 'Theory and value in the social sciences', in C. Hookway and P. Pettit (eds) *Action and Interpretation: Studies in the Philosophy of the Social Sciences*, Cambridge: Cambridge University Press, ch. 1.

Hesse, Mary (1980) *Revolutions and Reconstructions in the Philosophy of Science*, Brighton: Harvester.

Holmwood, John (1996) *Founding Sociology? Talcott Parsons and the Idea of General Sociology*, London: Longman.

Keat, Russell and Urry, John (1975) *Social Theory as Science*, London: Routledge and Kegan Paul.

Knorr-Cetina, Karin D. and Cicourel, Aaron V. (eds) (1981) *Advances in Social Theory; Toward an Integration of Micro- and Macro-Sociologies*, London: Routledge and Kegan Paul.

Kolakowski, Leszek (1975) *Husserl and the Quest for Certitude*, New Haven: Yale University Press.

Kuhn, Thomas S. (1962) *The Structure of Scientific Revolutions*, published as *International Encyclopedia of Unified Science*, vol. 2, no. 2, Chicago: University of Chicago Press.

Lazarsfeld, Paul F. and Merton, Robert K. (1954) 'Friendship as social process: a substantive and methodological analysis', in M. Berger, T. Abel and C.H. Page (eds) *Freedom and Control in Modern Society*, New York: Von Nostrand, 18–66.

Lazarsfeld, Paul F. and Rosenberg, Morris (eds) (1955) *The Language of Social Research: A Reader in the Methodology of Social Research*, Glencoe IL: Free Press.

Lipset, Seymour M. (1996) *American Exceptionalism: A Double-Edged Sword*, New York: Norton.

Longino, Helen (1993) 'Subjects, power and knowledge: description and prescription in feminist philosophies of science', in L. Alcoff and E. Potter (eds) *Feminist Epistemologies*, New York: Routledge, ch. 5.

Marris, Peter (1990) 'Witnesses, engineers or storytellers? Roles of sociologists in social policy', in H.J. Gans (ed.) *Sociology in America*, London: Sage, ch. 5.

Martineau, Harriet (1853) (ed.) *The Positive Philosophy of Auguste Comte*, 2 vols., London: Chapman. 'Freely translated and condensed' by the editor from A. Comte, *Cours de philosophie positive*, 6 vols., Paris: Bachelier, 1830–42.

Menzies, Ken (1982) *Sociological Theory in Use*, London: Routledge and Kegan Paul.

Merton, Robert K. (1957a) 'The bearing of sociological theory on empirical research', in R.K. Merton, *Social Theory and Social Structure*, revised edition, Glencoe IL: Free Press, ch. 2.

Merton, Robert K. (1957b) 'Continuities in the theory of reference groups and social structure', in R.K. Merton, *Social Theory and Social Structure*, revised edition, Glencoe IL: Free Press, ch. 9.

Merton, Robert K. (1957c) 'Continuities in the theory of social structure and anomie', in R.K. Merton, *Social Theory and Social Structure*, revised edition, Glencoe IL: Free Press, ch. 5.

Mouzelis, Nicos (1992) *Back to Sociological Theory: The Construction of Social Orders*, London: Macmillan.

Mulkay, Michael (1971) *Functionalism, Exchange and Theoretical Strategy*, London: Routledge and Kegan Paul.

Parsons, Talcott and Shils, Edward A. (eds) (1951) *Towards a General Theory of Action*, Glencoe IL: Free Press.

Pawson, Ray (1989) *A Measure for Measures: A Manifesto for Empirical Sociology*, London: Routledge.

Pawson, Ray and Tilley, Nick (1997) *Realistic Evaluation*, London: Sage.

Phillips, Derek L. (1986) 'Preface' to M.L. Wardell and S.P. Turner (eds) *Sociological Theory in Transition*, Boston: Allen and Unwin.

Purvis, Trevor and Hunt, Alan (1993) 'Discourse, ideology, discourse, ideology, discourse, ideology . . .', *British Journal of Sociology* 44: 473–99.

Ritzer, George (ed.) (1990) *Frontiers of Social Theory: The New Syntheses*, New York: Columbia University Press.

Ritzer, George (ed.) (1992a) *Metatheorizing*, Newbury Park CA: Sage.

Ritzer, George (1992b) 'Metatheorizing in America: explaining the coming of age', in G. Ritzer (ed.) *Metatheorizing*, Newbury Park CA: Sage, ch. 1.

Rorty, Richard (ed.) (1967) *The Linguistic Turn: Recent Essays in Philosophical Method*, Chicago: University of Chicago Press.

Rorty, Richard (1980) *Philosophy and the Mirror of Nature*, Princeton: Princeton University Press.

Rorty, Richard (1982) *The Consequences of Pragmatism*, Minneapolis: University of Minnesota Press.

Schlick, Moritz (1959) 'The turning point in philosophy', in A.J. Ayer (ed.) *Logical Positivism*, London: Allen and Unwin, 53–9 (first published, 1930).

Smelser, Neil J. (ed.) (1988) *Handbook of Sociology*, Beverly Hills and London: Sage.

Stinchcombe, Arthur (1968) *Constructing Social Theories*, New York: Harcourt Brace Jovanovich.

Sztompka, Piotr (1986) *Robert K. Merton: An Intellectual Profile*, London: Macmillan.

Sztompka, Piotr (1991) *Society in Action: The Theory of Social Becoming*, Cambridge: Polity Press.

Sztompka, Piotr (ed.) (1994) *Agency and Structure: Reorienting Social Theory*, Yverdon, Switzerland: Gordon and Breach.

Tester, Keith (1997) *Moral Culture*, London: Sage.

Thomas, William I. and Znaniecki, Florian (1918–20) *The Polish Peasant in Europe and America*, 5 vols., Boston: Gorham Press.

Touraine, Alain (1965) *Sociologie de l'action*, Paris: Le Seuil.

Touraine, Alain (1973) *The Self-Production of Society*, trans. D. Coltman, Chicago: University of Chicago Press.

Turner, Jonathan H. (1987) 'Analytical theorizing', in A. Giddens and J.H. Turner (eds) *Social Theory Today*, Cambridge: Polity Press, 156–94.

Turner, Jonathan H. (1989a) 'Sociology in the United States', in A. Genov (ed.) *National Traditions in Sociology*, Beverly Hills and London: Sage.

Turner, Jonathan H. (ed.) (1989b) *Theory Building in Sociology: Assessing Theoretical Cumulation*, Newbury Park CA and London: Sage.

Turner, Jonathan H. (1990) 'The Past, present and future of theory in American sociology', in G. Ritzer (ed.) *Frontiers of Social Theory*, New York: Columbia University Press, ch. 14.

Turner, Jonathan and Turner Stephen (1990) *The Impossible Science: An Analysis of American Sociology*, Newbury Park CA and London: Sage.

Wacquant, Loïc J.D. (1993) 'Positivism', in T. Bottomore and W. Outhwaite (eds) *Blackwell Dictionary of Twentieth Century Thought*, Oxford: Blackwell, 495–8.

Wagner, David G. (1964) *The Growth of Sociological Theories*, Beverly Hills and London: Sage.

Wallace, William (1988) 'Towards a disciplinary matrix in sociology', in N.J. Smelser (ed.) (1988) *Handbook of Sociology*, Beverly Hills and London: Sage, 23–76.

Warshay, Leon H. (1975) *The Current State of Sociological Theory: A Critical Interpretation*, New York: McKay.

Wells, Richard H. and Picou, J. Steven (1981) *American Sociology: Theoretical and Methodological Structure*, Washington: University Press of America.

Weymann, Ansgar (1990) 'Sociology in Germany: institutional development and paradigmatic structure', in C.G.A. Bryant and H.A. Becker (eds) *What Has Sociology Achieved?*, London: Macmillan, ch. 11.

Williams, Robin (1990) 'From cognitive style to substantive content: programmatics and pragmatics in the development of sociological knowledge', in C.G.A. Bryant and H.A. Becker (eds) *What Has Sociology Achieved?*, London: Macmillan, ch. 3.

Wilson, William J. (1987) *The Truly Disadvantaged: The Inner City, the Underclass and Public Policy*, Chicago: University of Chicago Press.

Wolfe, Alan (1989) *Whose Keeper? Social Science and Moral Obligation*, Berkeley: University of California Press.

chapter 4

On the cusp of the cultural

John Eldridge

Culture is everywhere

The issues and problems that come into view in the space labelled the sociology of culture are so variegated that only the rim of them will be observed in this short paper. There are analytic and substantive debates (Alexander and Seidman 1990; Chaney 1994; During 2000; Lovell 1995). Yet debate is too tidy a word at a time when there are culture wars and rumours of culture wars (Gitlin 1995; Sokal and Bricmont 1998; Eagleton 2000; Philo and Miller 2000).

Culture is a famously complex term (Williams 1976, 1981). There are ambiguities, shifting meanings and varying purposes in its application. If we ask how culture can be classified we quickly encounter a proliferation of descriptive and analytical terms such as:

African, European, Oriental . . .
aristocratic, bourgeois, democratic . . .
wild, garden . . .
elite, mass, popular, democratic, common . . .
dominant, residual, emergent . . .
high, low . . .
rural, urban . . .
traditional, modern, postmodern . . .

As we learn to speak of sociologies rather than sociology so it is with culture, but much more so. There is, we might suppose, a culture of everything – of science, religion, work, economy, politics, law, the arts, media, sport and leisure; of blame, shame, violence, fear, dependency, enterprise, complaint and contentment; of class, status and party, gender, ethnicity and identity. With what is culture to be contrasted or what is non-culture? Is it nature? (but is there not a culture of nature?); civilization? structure? society? As far as the sociological project is concerned we encounter issues of relativism which impinge in complex ways on questions of epistemology, morals, politics and aesthetics. There are different, sometimes competing, theoretical perspectives and methodological strategies. We are invited to consider the significance of the 'cultural turn'. Here, as elsewhere in sociology, issues concerning the relations between agency and structure, micro and macro analysis, subject and object, theory and method, can be located (McGuigan 2000; Tudor 2000).

All of this is made much more multi-faceted, though no doubt more creative, by the presence of contributors from other disciplines such as social anthropology, literary theory, semiotics, cultural studies, media studies and history. The metaphor that comes to mind is not so much that of a debating chamber as that of a bazaar: many voices telling us about one world – or is it one world (Gellner 1986)? In presenting their wares, some are confident, some diffident, some optimistic, some worried and perplexed. But can we distinguish the authentic from the fakes and forgeries (Eco 1990)? Can we evaluate what is on offer?

A walk around the bazaar

Why not start with the antiques section? Max Weber is an adornment to it. He was, after all, centrally concerned with the cultural significance of different world views and the relationship of beliefs to conduct. The significance of the Protestant ethic is only the most well-known example of his comparative and historical studies of social change as Ralph Schroeder has well illustrated (Schroeder 1992). The question of relativism is never far away. In the *Methodology of the Social Sciences*, Weber writes a great deal about the cultural sciences. In the process he argues that 'concept construction depends on the setting of the problem, and the latter varies with the content of culture itself. The relationship between concept and reality in the cultural sciences involves the transitoriness of all such syntheses . . . The greatest advances in the sphere of the social sciences are substantively tied up with the shift in practical cultural problems and take the guise of a critique of concept construction' (Weber 1949: 105–6). Indeed, that is why he thinks of the cultural sciences as having the gift of eternal youth. The task, as he saw it, is not only to understand social change through the analysis of culture but to recognize that change brings new constellations of groups, interests and values, which will require new concepts, ideal-types, to explain the meaning and consequences of these transformations.

There is, therefore, no absolutist way of conceptualizing a cultural system. For precisely this reason he explicitly rejected an approach which claimed that in the cultural sciences we should strive for a system of propositions from which reality can be deduced. This, he noted, would involve constructing 'a closed system of concepts in which reality is synthesised in some sort of permanently and universally valid classification and from which it can again be deduced' (Weber 1949: 84). What he argued for was a cultural science that in its explanations was disciplined by empirical evidence, which would allow us to make claims for their validity at the level of their meaning and in terms of their causal adequacy.

Such a sociology of culture was based on the assumption that no individual science can provide us with a copy of reality. Moreover, while Weber was constantly producing typologies and classifications, rationality itself being a notorious example, he was suspicious of the concept of system. That is why his contemporary, Albert Salomon, observed: 'Every attack on Weber's lack of system . . . is meaningless, since Weber by his fundamental theory of knowledge, rejected such a desire, and he repeatedly gave utterance to this view . . . In order to undermine this absence of system, therefore, it would be necessary to attack the logical foundations of his sociology as such' (Salomon 1935: 68).

If we linger a little at the Weber stall it is to notice that as well as recognizing the importance of religion as a cultural form and its relevance for economic, military and political activity, he also gave us a monograph on the rational and social foundations of music (Weber 1958). His discussion of the emergence of the piano as a modern keyboard instrument is a good example of the ability to combine an understanding of the social and technical conditions of production with an awareness of the role of composers, musicians and the audiences for whom they wrote and played.

We are prompted by this to take a sideways look at the Frankfurt stall. After all, Adorno not only wrote extensively about music but composed it (Rose 1978; Witkin 1998). Adorno referred to the commodity character of music and the way in which this was stimulated by new modes of mechanical reproduction and the new possibilities of exchange and distribution. In writing about 'popular' music Adorno tended to conflate jazz and 'light' music and treat them as corrupt styles of traditional music, rather than note the emergence of new musical forms and possibilities. More discriminating accounts of jazz as a cultural form are to be found in Hobsbawm's *The Jazz Scene* (1989) and Dyer's lyrical *But Beautiful* (1991).

We are drawn in closer to the Frankfurt stall at the risk of getting a little depressed. The definitive essay, which tells us what is at stake for them, is *The Culture Industry: Enlightenment as Mass Deception* (Adorno and Horkheimer 1979). There they tell us: 'In the culture industry the individual is an illusion not merely because of the standardisation of the means of production. He is tolerated only so long as his complete identification with the generality is unquestioned. Pseudo individuality is rife: from the standardised jazz improvisation to the exceptional film star whose hair curls over her eye to demonstrate her originality. What is individual is no more than the generality's power to stamp the accidental detail so firmly that it is accepted as such. The defiant reserve or elegant appearance of the individual on show is mass-produced like Yale locks, whose only difference can be measured in fractions of millimetres. The peculiarity of the self is a monopoly commodity determined by society; it is falsely represented as natural' (Adorno and Horkheimer 1979: 144).

This is confident, if depressing stuff. But how do they know this? What about their own individuality? How many millimetres of difference there? We can see the affinities with another member of the Frankfurt group, Herbert Marcuse, especially in *One Dimensional Man* (1964), although soul and jazz got a better rating from him. Marcuse became something of a media celebrity himself through his writing and because of his support for the student movements (where he achieved guru status) and for civil rights protests in the USA. Ironically, he was incorporated into the culture industry he sought to critique. A transient fame, some may say, but a little longer than fifteen minutes.

As exiles from Europe, Adorno, Horkheimer and Marcuse all lived in southern California – unlikely lotus eaters. Mike Davis, in his evocative *City of Quartz* (1990) mused on their continuing spectre-like presence even if their once ironic observations have been reduced to guidepost cliches for the benefit of postmodernism's Club Med. If the Weimar exiles appeared in Los Angeles as tragedy, then today's Fifth Republic tourists come strictly as farce. What was once anguish seems to have become fun. As a local critic has observed with regard to a recent visit of the current Parisian philosopher king: 'Baudrillard seems to enjoy himself. He loves to experience the liquidation of culture, to experience the delivery from depth . . . He goes home to France and finds it a quaint nineteenth century country. He returns to Los Angeles and feels perverse exhilaration. "There is nothing to match flying over Los Angeles by night. Only Hieronymous Boch's Hell can match the inferno effect"' (Davis 1990: 54). Baudrillard:

how easily one is distracted. He it is who tells us that culture has never been anything but the collective sharing of simulacra, as opposed to the collective sharing of the real and meaning. In such ways are truth and reality reduced to a language game (Rojek and Turner 1993).

The game has been played by others before him (Gellner 1959 and 1992). Baudrillard might seem to enjoy himself, but in the end what he has to say is as deeply pessimistic as anything from the Frankfurt school. In his world of disconnected signifiers, floating images and the interplay of simulations he offers us a book 'playfully' entitled *The Gulf War Did Not Take Place* (1995). Yet it is another story of mass deception. According to him, everyone has become trained in the unconditional reception of broadcast simulacra: 'if people are vaguely aware of being caught up in this appeasement and by this disillusion of images, they swallow the deception and remain fascinated by the evidence of the montage of this war with which we are inoculated everywhere: through the eyes, the senses and in discourse' (Baudrillard 1995: 68). All this is asserted without any empirical study of media content or the reception of media messages. Just as Adorno and Horkheimer appear to inhabit a higher ground where the deception of the masses can be observed, so too does Baudrillard. As Philo and Miller point out, 'here again we see the tendency of those who have abolished reality to make clear statements about what "actually" happens' (Philo and Miller 2000).

Still, one thing Adorno and Horkheimer knew: money was for real and so was the market. This was why they wrote about the culture *industry*. But, of course, Georg Simmel, over there with Weber, knew it too when he wrote of the fragmentation of modern life and the transitoriness of all its cultural forms (Frisby 1987). In his essay *Money in Modern Culture*, Simmel comments on the intertwining of the division of labour and the money system. It is the money economy that makes possible a means of communication and connection which is generally effective every-where, as well as the autonomy of the individual, through the process of individualization (Simmel 1991). While he argued that we cannot have fixed truths to explain modern societies that are characterized by flux and instability, there are sociological tasks that can be undertaken. As Frisby points out, Simmel reveals the illusory aesthetic of circulation and exchange in the everyday world of capitalism and, moreover, raises the possibility of excavating the 'culture of things': 'If Simmel shows that the study of everyday modern life is a difficult task, then it is not an impossible one' (Frisby 1991: 90). This need not lead, and did not lead Simmel, to a state of cultural pessimism. This differentiates him from the mass society theorists and certainly from Baudrillard.

Back to the bazaar. Apart from the Frankfurt group there is another rather noisy Marxist stall, who seem to be falling out with one another as much as with anyone else. Here is E.P. Thompson in the thick of it. The sparks of controversy fly when he is around. Evidently in the Romantic tradition – his first major work was on William Morris and his last on William Blake (Thompson 1955, 1993) – at times he appears to take on all-comers, Marxists and non-Marxists alike.

From the outset of his most famous study, *The Making of the English Working Class* (1963), Thompson makes clear his view that class is as much a cultural as an economic formation. Indeed, for him the social and the cultural do not simply follow the economic, they are immersed in the same nexus of relationship. This, of course, leads him to reject forthrightly base-superstructure models: culture is not just to be seen in the superstructure. Further, in his stress on agency, he seeks to do justice to the insight that people do make their own history but not in circumstances of their own choosing. Whether they do so wisely or successfully is another matter. This is what shapes his closely textured account of the experience of the English working class in the late eighteenth and early nineteenth centuries. It is not about the Scottish or Welsh working class for, as he pointed out, their experiences and popular culture were different. We may note in passing that when David Cannadine wrote *Class in Britain* (2000) covering a longer historical period, he argued from the premise that 'class is best understood as being what culture does to inequality and social structure: investing the many anonymous individuals with shape and significance, by moulding our perceptions of the unequal social world we live in' (Cannadine 2000: 188).

Thompson emphasizes the category of experience but when he tells us that the working class made itself as much as it was made he is drawing attention to the interaction between structure and agency in a way which exemplifies Cannadine's contention. The changing structures of work and productive relations, which the industrial revolution brought into being, were real and constraining. But they impinged not upon ciphers or puppets but upon people. They were surrounded by specific influences and traditions – Tom Paine, John Bunyan, village rights and craft traditions, the politics of Jacobinism, for example. Culture, on this reading, may be a way of life, but it has to be understood crucially as a way of struggle and resistance against tremendous pressures from more powerfully placed groups. We need look no further than this to understand the motivation that energized Thompson's extraordinary polemic against Althusser in *The Poverty of Theory* (1978). Althusser had to be confronted since, for Thompson, the very practice of historical materialism was at stake and in its place an ahistorical theoreticism was asserted, which, on inspection, turns out to be a form of idealism.

Thompson offers us one way of relating the study of culture to the problem of power. We can pause to recall that within the orbit of historical scholarship there are many fine examples of the analysis of cultural formations that are seen and interpreted in the context of power relations. We can instance the influential work of the French historian, Le Roy Ladurie: the account of the medieval community, whose heretical tradition and cultural practices brought it into direct conflict with the Church and the Inquisition; the carnival at Romans, where mocking the powerful on permitted occasions was a means of control, with, however, the potential for getting out of hand; or the beliefs about witches and witchcraft in the seventeenth century (Le Roy Ladurie 1980, 1981, 1990). Staying with France, there is Robert Danton's notable work on cultural history (Danton 1984). Why did the print workers at Rue St Severein, Paris, in the late 1730s find the massacre of the cats, which they undertook, so funny when most of us today (though presumably not badger baiters and organizers of illegal dog fights and cock fights) would be reporting it to the RSPCA? Or, on a different scale, there is Simon Schama's chronicle of the French revolution with its emphasis on agency, rather than the inexorable forces of social change and its interest in the cultural construction of citizenship (Schama 1989).

In England the historical work of Christopher Hill is justly celebrated. Here, by way of example, I will simply refer to his work on John Bunyan (Hill 1989), not least for its discussion of popular culture. To explain the changes that were taking place at the level of popular culture in sixteenth- and seventeenth-century Europe, Hill insists that, while phrases like 'the rise of individualism' or of 'capitalism' grope towards the answer, economic definitions alone are too narrow. The account is different in different countries. For England it had to do with 'an explanation of the decline of magic, of hell, of Calvinism as a dominant intellectual system, of millenarianism as a fighting revolutionary creed' (Hill 1989: 348). This does not lead Hill to romanticize popular culture or to suggest that because it emanates from the lower orders it is somehow above reproach because it is always a culture of resistance. What he has to say about this touches on questions of relativism, about which more anon:

> Puritans were censorious of some aspects of popular culture, for non-economic reasons. Philip Stubbes and Perkins disapproved of bull and bear-baiting, both because they disliked cruelty and because of the pleasure which such activities gave to spectators. Despite Macaulay, the latter

seems to me no worse a motive than dislike of cruelty. Violence was endemic in the society. The Dutch were shocked by English merchants' habit of beating their wives. Rough music and witch-rabbling were means of social control, of maintaining accepted norms: the victims might be wives who refused to accept their inferior status, or unhappy old women whom the community resented having to support. Despite social mobility, it was an intensely local society, hostile to strangers, especially those likely to become a burden on the rates . . . and there were other considerations. Before 1640, cock-fighting and bear-baiting took place in several Bedfordshire parish churches. There might be religious as well as killjoy reasons for objecting to this, or to a Bedfordshire rector acting as a Christmas Lord of Misrule.

(Hill 1989: 350–1)

One can see a good deal of affinity here between Hill and Thompson and perhaps especially in the latter's collection of essays *Customs in Common* (Thompson 1991). There Thompson argues that we can read a good deal of English history as a succession of confrontations between an innovative market economy and the customary moral economy of the plebs, which he labels 'plebian culture'. Yet, he writes, 'culture is a clumpish term, which by gathering up so many activities and attributes into one common bundle may actually confuse or disguise discriminations that should be made between them. We need to take this bundle apart, and examine the components with more care: rites, symbolic modes, and cultural attributes of hegemony, the inter-generational transmission of custom and custom's evolution within historically specific forms of working and social relations' (Thompson 1991: 13). This is certainly not an atheoretical matter and Thompson is more than ready to use Gramsci's insights into the ambivalent nature of popular culture (Gramsci 1985). The same reality may yield two different kinds of theoretical consciousness. One recognizes the need to survive in a world where the rules of the game are rigged in favour of the powerful; the other is grounded in the shared experience with fellow workers and neighbours of exploitation, hardship and repression.

It is that word again – experience. But we must mark the fact that Thompson was not one who treated the concept of experience as unproblematical. Moreover, he explicitly rejected the label of culturalism that was pinned on him: he did not like the idea of becoming paradigm fodder, as implied in Stuart Hall's well-known paper (Hall 1986) and more polemically expressed by Richard Johnson's essay (Johnson 1981). His treatment of the relation between theory and method always gave space to the concept of structure, distinguishing what he regarded as valid conceptual and heuristic organizations from structuralism. This also was one reason why he insisted that we must recognize the distinction between culture and non-culture, difficult though it might be in practice. There was, as he saw it, the raw material of life experience at one pole and 'all the infinitely complex human disciplines and systems, articulate and inarticulate, formalised in institutions or dispersed in the least formal ways, which "handle", transmit or distort this raw material . . . at the other' (Thompson 1981: 398).

The quarrel between Thompson and some fellow Marxists found its sharpest expression in *People's History and Socialist Theory* (Samuel 1981) with a discussion (too mild a word) about the adequacy of *The Poverty of Theory* (Thompson 1978). The main protagonists against Thompson were Hall and Johnson, both of whom were strongly linked with the Birmingham Centre for Contemporary Cultural Studies, although Hall had by then moved on to the Open University. As we have noted, Thompson's attack on Althusser had been forthright and comprehensive. For Thompson, Althusser had generated a Marxist theology rather than a critical approach to historical materialism and had evicted human agency from history. There is more, much more, that could be said. It suffices for present purposes to recall that the Birmingham group under Hall had paid a great deal of sympathetic attention to Althusser and to Gramsci and this was an important part of the context in which the confrontation took place.

Accounts of the work of the Birmingham group are to be found in various places and most of them are broadly sympathetic to its accomplishments (e.g. Bratlinger 1990; Turner 1990; McGuigan 1992). A number of areas in British society were opened up for scrutiny including crime, race and ethnicity, education, gender, youth and the media. But in addition to the critique of Althusser already noted, the treatment of hegemony via Gramsci has also been questioned. They are not unrelated. Harris, for example, argued that the Birmingham version of Gramsci showed itself 'far too ready to close off its investigations of social reality, to make its concepts prematurely identical with aspects of that reality in various ways . . . Sociology and other bourgeois disciplines could claim to have maintained a more open relationship to empirical evidence, in other words to have allowed for "surprise", or for historical evidence which did not fit neatly with the theory of the stages of crisis in British society' (Harris 1992: 195). A significant intervention in this debate came from Stanley Cohen in the revised edition of his seminal study *Folk Devils and Modern Panics* (1987). The treatment of moral panics was taken up by the Birmingham group, notably in *Policing the Crisis* (Hall *et al*. 1978).

In his essay, 'Symbols of trouble', which prefaced the revised edition and merits close reading, Cohen argues in similar vein to Harris that the determination to find an ideological closure led the group to a premature theoretical closure: 'The actual material selected as proof of a slide into the crisis (newspaper editorials, statements by MPs and police chiefs) does not always add up to something of monumental proportions. The diffuse normative concern about delinquency is, I think, more diffuse and less political than is suggested. And the assumption of a monolithic drift to repression gives little room for understanding why some objects are repressed more severely than others' (Cohen 1987: xxiv–xxv). And Martin Barker, again in a way which parallels the discussion of Althusser, is similarly critical when he argues that what is left out of the treatment of moral panic by the Birmingham group is a concept of agency (Barker 1992).

The social anthropologists are tugging at our sleeve. There is, after all, a lineage of writing on culture from Durkheim, Mauss, Lévy-Strauss and Bourdieu in France; Malinowski, Evans-Pritchard, Turner, Douglas and Worsley in Britain; Linton, Mead, Benedict and Geertz in the USA. It is scarcely surprising that they should want to draw attention to their presence at the bazaar – some of them even call themselves cultural anthropologists. Ruth Benedict was one such. *Patterns of Culture* (1961) was first published in 1935. She used the image of a great arc of possible interests and activities which human beings may pursue in their material environment. Out of this enormous range only some things can be selected, since that is the prerequisite for intelligibility. It is selectivity that makes for order and patterns, as in the case of language itself, and for differences between cultures. She linked the empirical truth of cultural diversity with the advocacy of tolerance between cultures, based on respect for difference.

As with other anthropologists, before and since, Benedict conveyed a sense of cultures as wholes. The people who lived in and through these cultures participated in a form of life. This was typically theorized at that time in structural functionalist terms. The interrelationships between the different parts of society were delineated; the meanings of the activities which flow from this, the beliefs, signs, symbols and rituals which accompany them and the very language which conceptualizes these meanings, constitute culture as a way of life.

But so much of human history is the story of contact between one way of life and another. Even the anthropologist who might wish to argue that a remote culture should be left untouched to preserve its distinctive way of life (as ecologists urge the preservation of bio-diversity) has to reckon with the fact that once s/he has interacted with that way of life it can never be quite the same again. Anthropologists have never been unencumbered visitors. They come with their own education, language, interests and values. The cultures from which they come have had their traders, soldiers, missionaries, colonial administrators, with whom in various combinations they have often had to relate. Such relationships could vary from mutual support to open hostility.

While anthropologists like Benedict wanted to encourage the study of lived cultures as integrated wholes, the reality, as she well knew, was one of contact between cultures of unequal physical and technological power. Part of her strategy, indeed, was to challenge the ethnocentricism which infused and sometimes motivated such contact. The 'white man's burden', after all, it was commonly supposed, was to bring western civilization and values to 'lesser breeds without the law'. Of course, to critique this western orientation in a way which has affinities with Edward Said's later influential discussion of orientalism (Said 1978) was by implication to say that to understand all was not to forgive all. In this respect there is an underlying tension between ethical judgements and the call for toleration between cultures. A civilization that had become the breeding ground for the First World (with, as we now know, more horrors to come) was seen to have destructive tendencies. This in itself put into question the appropriateness of measuring other cultures against its scale of values, even if it were possible.

Benedict's readers were to be found mainly in Europe and North America. The clear implication of her writing, like that of other anthropologists, was that the lived experience of another culture, alien though it might be to her readers, could be translated and made comprehensible to them. The very possibility of border crossings between cultures is thereby indicated, although in Benedict's time this tended to be a one-way track rather than a criss-crossing: that is, 'we' understand 'them'. Even so, despite the holistic theorizing of 'patterns', the cultures were not hermetically sealed. In that sense there was already a gap between the paradigm and the reality. Today we can see that the gap is wider, such that a contemporary anthropologist can write: 'Social analysis must now grapple with the realisation that its objects of analysis are also analysing subjects who critically interrogate ethnographers – their writings, their ethics and their politics' (Rosaldo 1993: 21).

Clifford Geertz has also reminded us that there was a time when the concept of culture had a firm design and a definite edge (Geertz 1995). But like most powerful ideas in the human sciences it came under attack. Questions were raised about the very idea of a cultural scheme; about the idea of connected wholes; of homogeneity; about the discreteness of particular cultures. There are a panopoly of considerations: 'Questions about continuity and change, objectivity and proof, determinism and relativism, uniqueness and generalisation, description and explanation, consensus and conflict, otherness and commensurability – and about the sheer possibility of anyone, insider or outsider, grasping so vast a thing as an entire way of life and finding words to describe it. Anthropology, or anyway the sort that studies cultures, proceeds amid charges of irrelevance, bias, illusion, and impracticability' (Geertz 1995: 43). So let us consider one anthropologist who has taken on some of these questions with considerable intellectual toughness.

Ernest Gellner epigrammatically wrote of relativism as a spectre haunting human thought (Gellner 1986). For him, writing as anthropologist and philosopher, relativism had to be seen as a problem not a solution. Throughout his considerable corpus of writing he relentlessly pursued questions of truth, knowledge and power. In doing so, rather like E.P. Thompson in the Marxist case, he has sometimes given the impression of taking on all-comers: Wittgenstein, Winch, Feyerabend, Rorty and Geertz are among the prominent examples. We find him attacking the philosophical relativism of the linguistic analysts, the solipsism of ethnomethodology, the truth claims of Marxism, the sociological idealism of the functionalists and the cultural hermeneutics of the interpretative anthropologists. Before he was done he attacked much that came under the label of postmodernism (Gellner 1964, 1973, 1979, 1987, 1992, 1998).

Much of Gellner's work pivots on what he sometimes termed the Big Ditch approach to knowledge, which was based on the premise that different cultures may have different access to, and experience of, cognitive power. In this important sense all cultures are not equal. The pre- and post-scientific periods of existence are closely associated with the rise of industrial societies, first in the west and then more extensively. It is science which enables us to detect falsity in the world of events, even if it cannot establish final, absolute truths about the nature or essence of things. For Gellner, any epistemology or methodology which fails to come to terms with this divide does not get off first base.

As an anthropologist, Gellner understood the importance of attending to the hermeneutic task. But, he argued, to do so exclusively is to slip into the idealist fallacy. There are meanings but there are also causes. There are realities which a hermeneutic analysis alone cannot capture: 'Hermeneutists do not seem very interested in political and economic structures; it is domination by symbols and discourse which really secures and retains their attention. They are enormously sensitive to the way in which concepts constrain and less attentive to other, and perhaps more important, means of coercion. Their attitude engenders a selective sensitivity which in effect ignores those constraints, or even by implication denies their existence. If we live in a world of meanings, and meanings exhaust the world, where is there any room for coercion through the whip, gun or hunger. The cosy world of the well-heeled scholar is allowed to stand in for the harsh world outside' (Gellner 1992: 63).

As with Thompson's attack on idealism there is a similar sense of wanting to give weight to the cultural without becoming a culturalist. This, it is worth recalling, is something Gellner and Thompson both share with Bourdieu, whose work on cultural theory has been impressively addressed by Fowler (1997). For Gellner, there is culture and something else that has to be taken into account: 'Human societies are a complex interaction of external factors – coercion, production – and of internal meanings. That much is not in doubt. The precise nature of that interaction cannot be prejudged prior to inquiry, in favour of the predomination of semantic or "cultural" elements. The major fact about the world as it is now con-stituted is that it is going through a crucial and fundamental transition, as a result of a profound and not properly understood asymmetry between one distinct cultural style and all others' (Gellner 1992: 70). He proceeds to link this with a criticism of postmodernism as a movement or general tendency which, he argued, not only has a penchant for relativism and a blindness to the non-semantic aspects of society, but most significantly ignores the 'immensely important, absolutely pervasive asymmetry in cognitive and economic power in the world situation' (Gellner 1992: 70).

This kind of critical intervention presents a clear challenge to much that passes for cultural studies today with its overemphasis on texts and codes and underemphasis on the conditions in which the texts are produced. Even to recognize that there are limits to interpretation and dangers of overinterpretation, as Eco has convincingly argued, would be a start (Eco 1990, 1992).

Gellner is emphatically not arguing that societies which have achieved a high level of cognitive power are morally superior. But he does put back on the agenda the culture-transcending possibilities of reason (Gellner 1992, 1998). Consequently, when it comes to questions of moral-ity, this local culture or that local culture do not have the last absolutist word on what 'ought' to be done. This, surely, is one of the implications of Bauman's study of the Holocaust (Bauman 1989). It challenges any notion that equates morality with social discipline and the programmatic rela-tivism that entails. The sharpness of this question is underlined now that issues of nationalism and 'ethnic cleansing' have become central to European experience and conduct. It is, after all, the dialectic between culture(s) and reason that allows us to work on questions of human rights and environmental issues.

It is nearly time to take leave of the bazaar, but we cannot in all conscience pass by the Raymond Williams stall. It is like a one-man cottage industry, although he is not without his helpers. It was Joy Williams who drew his attention to the work of Ruth Benedict. For him it was with the discovery of patterns of a characteristic kind that any useful analysis begins and, 'it is with the relationships between these patterns, which sometimes revealed unexpected identities and correspondences in hitherto separately considered activities, sometimes again reveal discontinuities of an unexpected kind, that general cultural analysis is concerned' (Williams 1965: 63). He was later to develop his own distinctive theoretical perspective of cultural materialism arising in part with his dissatisfaction with base-superstructure models in Marxist theory (Williams 1980). His approach to cultural analysis and his commitment to democratic socialism were conjoined to make a telling critique of early and late capitalism (Eldridge and Eldridge 1994).

Characteristically, Williams opposed those, whether on the political right or left, who worked from the premise that there are 'masses' to save, capture or direct by challenging the very concept: 'There are in fact no masses; there are only ways of seeing people as masses. In an urban industrial society there are many opportunities for such ways of seeing . . . The fact is, surely, that a way of seeing other people which has become characteristic of our kind of society, has been capitalised for the purpose of political or cultural exploitation. What we see, neutrally, is other people, many others, people unknown to us. In practice, we mass them, and interpret them according to some convenient formula. Within its terms the formula will hold. Yet it is the formula, not the mass, which it is our real business to examine' (Williams 1961: 289).

The ramifications of this perspective are seen throughout Williams' work. Take, for example, his essay 'Advertising: the magic system' (Williams 1980). He traces the development of the modern distributive systems of large-scale capitalism to the point where selling has become central and public relations more and more professionalized, such that it is not only goods that are sold in a particular kind of economy but people who are 'sold' in a particular kind of culture: 'It is impossible to look at modern advertising without realising that the material object being sold is never enough; indeed this is the crucial quality of its modern forms. If we are sensibly materialistic, in that part of our lives in which we use things, we should find most advertising to be of insane irrelevance . . . We have a cultural pattern in which the projects are not enough but must be validated, if only in fantasy, by association with social and personal meanings which in a different cultural pattern might be more directly available (Williams 1980: 185).

All this has had direct consequences for the ways in which the mass media have developed in modern societies. Advertising revenue is at the root of it (Eldridge *et al.* 1997). Moreover, the media not only serve as channels for other people's markets, they become a market themselves. The communications society and the consumer society chase one another as public space becomes ever more privatized (Mattelart 1991). When Williams developed the concept of 'flow' in his work on television, it was not only a way of describing and analyzing what is distinctive about that medium. Flow is embedded in economic and commercial considerations which, in permeating the cultural formation, can also affect our capacity for reason and critique within this system of communication (Williams 1974).

Williams' approach to questions of modernism and postmodernism was a wary one. He observed the ways in which these potentially oppositional tendencies have been incorporated within the economic formations of late capitalism. This paradox of unintended consequences is evident when he writes of the irony of the process. Those who wish to claim Williams as a postmodernist because of his awareness of the changing connections between the local and the global, or as a relativist because he challenged received notions of the literary canon (and even the concept of the literary), would do well to read the sharpness of the following comment:

> The climax of the pretensions by which this situation was hidden was the widely accepted proposition of the 'global village'. What was being addressed was the real development of universal distribution and of unprecedented opportunities for genuine and diverse cultural exchange. What was ideologically inserted was a model of homogenised humanity consciously serving from two or three centres, the monopolising corporations and the elite metropolitan intellectuals. One practised homogenisation, the other theorised it. Each found its false grounds in the technologies which had 'changed and opened up the world and brought it together'. But nothing in the technologies led to this theory or practice. The real forces which produced both, not only in culture but in political life, belonged to the dominant capitalist order in its paranational phase. But this was the enemy which could not be named because its money was being taken. (Williams 1985: 143)

These kinds of concern were extensively pursued in Jameson's analysis of the cultural logic of late capitalism (Jameson 1992). For Jameson, the global division of labour represents a cultural revolution, wherein the

cultural and the economic are continuously involved in reciprocal interaction and feedback loops. And the preoccupation with the 'postmodern',
with its connotations of fragmentation and preoccupation with surface manifestations, can create a cultural resonance through which we are distracted
from understanding the real structural and organizational changes that are
taking place in marketing, advertising and business organization. Hence
we are inside the culture of the market and that is why it is difficult to
imagine anything else and, for that matter, why the countries of eastern
Europe are driven towards a culture of consumption. For Jameson, therefore, it is the problem of the market that is central to the task of theorizing or re-thinking socialism.

And so it was with Williams:

> The originally precarious and often desperate images – typically of frag-
> mentation, loss of identity, loss of the very grounds of human com-
> munication – have been transferred from the dynamic compositions of
> artists who had been, in the majority, literally exiles, having little or
> no common ground with the societies in which they were stranded to
> become an eaective surface, a 'modernist' or 'postmodernist' establishment.
> This, near the centres of corporate power, takes human inadequacy, self-
> deception, role-playing, the confusion and substitution of individuals in
> temporary relationships, and even the lying paradox of the communica-
> tion of the fact of non-communication, as the self-evident routine data.
>
> (Williams 1985: 141)

We may think that Williams is going into overdrive here but it is
central to his argument that notions concerning the fictionality of all actions,
the arbitrariness of language, can become part of the cultural formation
so that it is difficult to understand what is going on in the world. It is, in
anticipation so to speak, saying no to Baudrillard. Williams sees his task
as first to identify the interpenetration of the cultural and the economic
and recognize the strength of what is defined as 'normal' in order to
imagine alternative possibilities. This represents a refusal to abandon the
field of cultural studies to those who think it is enough to offer endless
descriptions and limitless interpretations, who act as though relativism
is the solution not the problem. That is why he both recognized and opposed
the conjunction of technological determinism – these technologies must
produce these contents and effects – and cultural pessimism – there is
nothing to be done about it.

It is time to leave the bazaar with its crowds and its clamour. Every
student of rhetoric knows how important the last word can be. I offer it
to an anthropologist who has dared to write a book called *Culture and Truth*.

It is too long for a soundbite but why dwell in unnecessary intellectual poverty? So here it is:

> In the present post-colonial world, the notion of an authentic culture as an autonomous internally coherent universe no longer seems tenable, except perhaps as a 'useful fiction' or a revealing distortion. In retrospect, it appears that only a concerted disciplinary effort could maintain the tenuous fiction of a self-contained cultural whole. Rapidly increasing global interdependence has made it more and more clear that neither 'we' nor 'they' are as neatly bounded and homogeneous as once seemed to be the case. The stock market crash of October, 1987, for example, was global not local. News from Tokyo and Hong Kong mattered as much as word from New York and London. Similarly, Latin American and African fiction influence and are influenced by French and North American literary production. All of us inhabit an interdependent . . . world marked by borrowing and lending across national and cultural boundaries that are saturated with inequality, power and domination.   (Rosaldo 1993: 217)

References

Adorno, T. and Horkheimer, M. (1979) *Dialectic of Enlightenment*, London: Verso.

Alexander, J. and Seidman, S. (eds) (1990) *Culture and Society. Contemporary Debates*, Cambridge: Cambridge University Press.

Barker, M. (1992) 'Stuart Hall. Policing the crisis', in M. Barker and A. Beezer *Reading into Cultural Studies*, London: Routledge.

Baudrillard, J. (1995) *The Gulf War Did Not Take Place*, Sydney: Tower Publications.

Bauman, Z. (1989) *Modernity and the Holocaust*, Cambridge: Polity.

Benedict, R. (1961) *Patterns of Culture*, London: Routledge and Kegan Paul.

Bratlinger, P. (1990) *Crusoe's Footprints: Cultural Studies in Britain and America*, London: Routledge.

Cannadine, D. (2000) *Class in Britain*, Harmondsworth: Penguin.

Chaney, D. (1994) *The Cultural Turn. Scene-Setting Essays on Contemporary Cultural History*, London: Routledge.

Cohen, S. (1987) *Folk Devils and Moral Panics*, Oxford: Blackwell.

Danton, R. (1984) *The Great Cat Massacre and Other Episodes in French Cultural History*, New York: Basic Books.

Davis, M. (1990) *City of Quartz*, London: Verso.

During, S. (ed.) (2000) *The Cultural Studies Reader*, London: Routledge.

Dyer, G. (1991) *But Beautiful*, London: Vintage.

Eagleton, T. (2000) *The Idea of Culture*, Oxford: Blackwell.

Eco, U. (1990) *The Limits of Interpretation*, Bloomington: University of Indiana Press.

Eco, U. (1992) *Interpretation and Overinterpretation*, Cambridge: Cambridge University Press.

Eldridge, J. and Eldridge, L. (1994) *Raymond Williams: Making Connections*, London: Routledge.

Eldridge, J., Kitzinger, J. and Williams, K. (1997) *Mass Media and Power in Modern Britain*, Oxford: Oxford University Press.

Fowler, B. (1997) *Pierre Bourdieu and Cultural Theory. Critical Investigations*, London: Sage.

Frisby, D. (1987) *Sociological Impressionism. A Reassessment of Georg Simmel's Social Theory*, London: Heinemann.

Frisby, D. (1991) 'The aesthetics of modern life: Simmel's interpretation', *Theory, Culture and Society* 3.3: 73–98.

Geertz, C. (1995) *After the Fact. Two Countries, Four Decades, One Anthropologist*, Cambridge MA: Harvard University Press.

Gellner, E. (1959) *Words and Things*, London: Gollancz.

Gellner, E. (1964) *Thought and Change*, London: Weidenfeld and Nicolson.

Gellner, E. (1973) *Cause and Meaning in Social Science*, London: Routledge and Kegan Paul.

Gellner, E. (1979) *Spectacles and Predicaments. Essays in Social Theory*, Cambridge: Cambridge University Press.

Gellner, E. (1986) *Relativism and the Social Sciences*, Cambridge: Cambridge University Press.

Gellner, E. (1987) *Culture, Identity and Politics*, Cambridge: Cambridge University Press.

Gellner, E. (1992) *Postmodernism, Reason and Religion*, London: Routledge.

Gellner, E. (1998) *Language and Solitude*, Cambridge: Cambridge University Press.

Gitlin, T. (1995) *The Twilight of Common Dreams. Why America is Wracked by Culture Wars*, New York: Henry Holt.

Gramsci, A. (1985) *Selections from Cultural Writings*, London: Lawrence and Wishart.

Hall, S. (1986) 'Cultural studies: two paradigms', in R. Collins, J. Curran, N. Garnham, P. Scannell, P. Schlesinger and C. Sparks (eds) *Media, Culture and Society. A Critical Reader*, London: Sage.

Hall, S., Critcher, C., Jefferson, T., Clarke, J. and Roberts, B. (1978) *Policing the Crisis: Mugging, the State, and Law and Order*, London: Macmillan.

Harris, D. (1992) *From Class Struggle to the Politics of Pleasure. The Effects of Gramscianism on Cultural Studies*, London: Routledge.

Hill, C. (1989) *A Turbulent, Seditious and Factious People. John Bunyan and his Church*, Harmondsworth: Penguin.

Hobsbawm, E. (1989) *The Jazz Scene*, London: Weidenfeld and Nicolson.

Jameson, F. (1992) *Postmodernism: or the Cultural Logic of Late Capitalism*, London: Verso.

Johnson, R. (1981) 'Against absolutism', in R. Samuel (ed.) *People's History and Socialist Theory*, London: Routledge and Kegan Paul.

Le Roy Ladurie, E. (1980) *Montaillou: Cathars and Catholics in a French Village, 1294–1324*, Harmondsworth: Penguin.

Le Roy Ladurie, E. (1981) *Carnival in Romans: A People's Uprising at Romans, 1579–1580*, Harmondsworth: Penguin.

Le Roy Ladurie, E. (1990) *Jasmin's Witch*, Harmondsworth: Penguin.

Lovell, T. (ed.) (1995) *Feminist Cultural Studies* (2 vols.), London: Edward Elgar.

McGuigan, J. (1992) *Cultural Populism*, London: Routledge.

McGuigan, J. (2000) *Modernity and Postmodern Culture*, Milton Keynes: Open University Press.

Marcuse, H. (1964) *One Dimensional Man*, London: Routledge, and Kegan Paul.

Mattelart, A. (1991) *Advertising International*, London: Routledge.

Philo, G. and Miller, D. (2000) 'Cultural compliance', in G. Philo and D. Miller *Market Killing. What the Free Market Does and what Social Science can Do About It*, London: Longman.

Rojek, C. and Turner, B. (eds) (1993) *Forget Baudrillard?*, London: Routledge.

Rosaldo, R. (1993) *Culture and Truth*, London: Routledge.

Rose, G. (1978) *The Melancholy Science*, London: Macmillan.

Said, E. (1978) *Orientalism*, New York: Pantheon.

Salomon, A. (1935) 'Max Weber's sociology', *Social Research* 3.

Samuel, R. (ed.) (1981) *People's History and Socialist Theory*, London: Routledge and Kegan Paul.

Schama, S. (1989) *Citizens*, Harmondsworth: Penguin.

Schroeder, R. (1992) *Max Weber and the Sociology of Culture*, London: Sage.

Simmel, G. (1991) *Money in Modern Culture, in Theory, Culture and Society*: 17–31.

Sokal, A. and Bricmont, J. (1998) *Intellectual Impostures*, London: Profile Books.

Thompson, E.P. (1955) *William Morris: Romantic to Revolutionary*, London: Lawrence and Wishart.

Thompson, E.P. (1963) *The Making of the English Working Class*, London: Gollancz.

Thompson, E.P. (1978) *The Poverty of Theory*, London: Merlin.

Thompson, E.P. (1981) 'The politics of theory', in R. Samuel (ed.) *People's History and Socialist Theory*, London: Routledge and Kegan Paul.

Thompson, E.P. (1991) *Customs in Common*, London: Merlin.

Thompson, E.P. (1993) *Witness Against the Beast. William Blake and the Moral Law*, Cambridge: Cambridge University Press.

Tudor, A. (2000) *Decoding Culture: Theory and Method in Cultural Studies*, London: Sage.

Turner, G. (1990) *British Cultural Studies: An Introduction*, London: Unwin and Hyman.

Weber, M. (1949) *The Methodology of the Social Sciences*, Glencoe IL: Free Press.

Weber, M. (1958) *The Rational and Social Foundations of Music*, Carbondale IL: Southern Illinois University Press.

Williams, R. (1961) *Culture and Society 1750–1950*, Harmondsworth: Penguin.

Williams, R. (1965) *The Long Revolution*, Harmondsworth: Penguin.

Williams, R. (1974) *Television: Technology and Cultural Form*, Glasgow: Fontana.

Williams, R. (1976) *Keywords: A Vocabulary of Culture and Society*, Glasgow: Fontana.

Williams, R. (1980) *Problems in Materialism and Culture*, London: Verso.

Williams, R. (1981) *Culture*, Glasgow: Fontana.

Williams, R. (1985) *Towards 2000*, Harmondsworth: Penguin.

Witkin, R. (1998) *Adorno on Music*, London: Routledge.

chapter 5

Feminism and postmodernism in social theory

Mary Maynard

Introduction

Concern has been expressed about the increasing fragmentation of social theory. Defined as a crisis by some, commentators point to a prevailing ambivalence as to the purpose and kinds of social theory which are required for the beginning of the twenty-first century (Holmwood 1995; Mouzelis 1995; Seidman and Wagner 1992). Feminism and postmodernism are both identified, positively as well as negatively, as having responsibilities for the loss of old certainties. For instance, feminist sociology has been heralded as having 'come of age' (Roseneil 1995: 191) and as having given the discipline 'its most needed – and substantial – jolt in twenty years' (McLennan 1995: 126). Similarly, the ideas of postmodernism also court controversy. Postmodernism, it is suggested, elicits 'highly charged reactions across intellectual disciplines and associated theoretical and political constituencies' (Smart 1993: 11). However it is conceptualized, whether by supporters or detractors, there seems to be considerable agreement that 'things are no longer quite as they might once have seemed' (Smart 1990: 411).

This chapter focuses on the place of feminism and postmodernism in social theory and, in particular, the influence of the latter on the former. It begins by looking at the changing nature of feminist social theory. This is followed by a discussion of postmodern ideas, indicating that they might usefully be viewed in terms of five formulations. The chapter then considers the implications of postmodernism for social theory, feminists' responses to this and their attempts to grapple with aspects of postmodernism within feminist theory itself. It ends by questioning the extent to which postmodernism should be regarded as synonymous with social theory.

The changing nature of feminist social theory

Second-wave feminist theory was initially concerned with the structured nature of relationships between men and women. Arising from anxieties about the invisibility of women in existing social theory, it explored and explained the systematic patterning of inequality which constructed men as the dominant group and women as subordinate. The intention was to challenge the masculinist concepts and frameworks which dominated social thought. Feminists aimed to counter the sexist, biased and exclusionary nature of much of what counted for knowledge.

This early phase in feminist thinking has typically been described in terms of three differing positions: liberal feminism, Marxist feminism and radical feminism. Liberal feminism is portrayed as focusing on individual rights and the choices which are denied women. It is seen as concentrating on the concepts of equality, justice and equal opportunities, emphasizing the legal and policy changes necessary for engineering women's greater equality with men. Marxist feminism is seen as being concerned with women's oppression in relation to capitalism's exploitation of labour, analyzing women's paid and unpaid work in terms of its function within the capitalist economy. Radical feminism is viewed as 'radical' because of its aim of formulating new ways of theorizing women's relationship to men. Men's control of women through various mechanisms is regarded as central, particularly violence, heterosexuality and reproduction, with men as a group being seen as responsible for women's continued oppression. Instead of explaining gender relationships as a product of capitalism, radical feminism argues that they arose out of a separate system of male domination, patriarchy.

There are a number of problems with categorizing feminist theory in this way (Maynard 1995; Stacey 1997; Jackson 1998). For instance, many textbooks suggest that Marxist and radical feminists were unproblematically divided into two opposing camps. Yet, although antagonisms did arise at many meetings and in some publications, the theoretical divisions which emerged during the 1970s were, as Jackson suggests, far more complex, with a continuum between those emphasizing capitalism or patriarchy as the main factor in explaining women's subordination (Jackson 1998). Further, the 'perspectives' approach to feminist theory reinforces unhelpful stereotypes, such as the fact that Marxist feminists are not concerned about violence, or radical feminists are not aware of class. It overlooks the fact that both of these groups have joined with liberal feminists in order to campaign for such things as abortion rights and anti-harassment policies. There are also significant differences between writers classified under the same label. For example, some Marxist feminists, as in the domestic labour debate (Kaluzynska 1980), tried rather slavishly to apply Marx's economic analysis of capitalism to women's subordination. Others, such as Barrett, were less inclined to explain women's unequal position in class terms, focusing, instead, on reworking Marxism and giving more emphasis to cultural and ideological factors (Barrett 1980). Similarly, in radical feminism there are considerable differences between the approach of Millett (1969), who underplays the use of direct force in maintaining patriarchy, arguing, instead, that this is largely achieved through cultural legitimation, acceptance and consent, and other writers who emphasize the role of different kinds of violence and their threat in intimidating and controlling women. For all these reasons, then, there is a need for caution when delineating the parameters of feminist thinking.

In recent years, the nature of feminist social theory has become even more complex. There has been a move away from using a 'perspectives' approach, with its implication that theory can simply be 'mugged up', learnt and applied parrot-fashion. This has been partly brought about by a proliferation in the number of available standpoints, for example black feminism, lesbian feminism, material feminism and queer positions and the clear implication that labelling is not mutually exclusive. Further, the search for, and likelihood of being able to establish, the fundamental cause(s) of women's subordination, together with the location of specific sites of their oppression, has also been contested. This is related to criticism of approaches that position women as a group within some overarching structure or system, whether this be identified as patriarchy, capitalism or a male-defined liberal democracy. It is now acknowledged by many that the language of systems theory creates problems for feminism because of its connotations of passivity, determinism and mechanization. These deny women agency and the ability to resist, struggle and act. Currently, there is much more emphasis on women's subjectivity and capacities for experiencing and creating desires, pleasures and satisfactions.

Another challenge to feminist theory has come, in particular from black and Third World women but from other groups as well, to the undifferentiated and homogenized use of the category 'woman'. This has led to an increased emphasis on diversity in women's experiences, the existence of hierarchical power relations between women and the inherent racism of a lot of white feminist work. As a result the concept of 'difference' has become central to feminist thinking, thereby replacing earlier concerns about equality with men to a considerable degree. In addition, the waning of communism and of Marxism has led, as with other forms of social thought, to theories based on material analyses going somewhat out of fashion. As Jackson points out, whereas social science approaches were at the forefront of feminist analyses during the 1970s, these have since been displaced from their central position by literary and cultural theory (Jackson 1998). Barrett has described such a shift as as a 'turn to culture' and as a movement away from a preoccupation with 'things', such as housework or inequalities in the labour market, towards 'words' and an interest in symbolization and representation (Barrett 1992: 204–5). This concern with culture has led many feminists to focus on developing a better understanding of subjectivity, identity and the self. In this they have drawn on, and critically engaged with, post-colonial theory, which deals with the continuous effects of colonial occupation on cultures, societies and identities, both in colonized, diasporic and colonizer settings. They have also been influenced by, and have themselves attempted to influence, postmodern ways of thinking. Feminists have been attracted to postmodernism by, among other things, its anti-essentialism, which challenges the idea that women and men are given, natural and essential beings, and its stance against meta-narratives or grand theory, together with its insistence on fragmentation and plurality. The following sections explore the nature and variety of postmodern thought, before moving to consider its implications for feminism.

What is postmodernism?

Any attempt to unravel the plethora of ideas, perspectives and stances which might be said to constitute postmodernism is clearly fraught with difficulties. 'Postmodernism' is a highly contested term, concerning which not even those who identify with it agree. Some would suggest that the very act of trying to characterize or categorize postmodern thinking falls foul of exactly the kinds of modernist obsessions with grouping, naming and classifying of which postmodernists are so critical. Doubt has been expressed as to whether the term itself is useful, given that, whatever nuanced rendering is offered, the end result is to unify a wide range of different writers and aspects of theory (Butler 1992). As Ahmed notes, the very question 'what is postmodernism?' assumes, a priori, that there is something already in existence which might adequately be named as postmodern (Ahmed 1998). Yet, this 'something' is also portrayed in terms of 'indeterminacy', a lack of boundaries and 'the muliplicity of its con-figurations'. Ahmed concludes that the latter all mean that postmodernism 'refers to its own impossibility as a referent and hence comes to mean *potentially anything*' (1998: 5).

Despite the above kinds of argument, however, many commentators have found it both possible and useful to map the main elements of, and relations between, different aspects of what might comprise postmodernism. Along with Boyne and Rattansi, they delight in the irony present in 'the paradox of a set of cultural projects united by a self-proclaimed commit-ment to heterogeneity, fragmentation and difference' (Boyne and Rattansi 1990: 9). These projects also share commonalities in that they are a reaction to the modern world, broadly conceived as emerging in the west from the seventeenth century onwards and as forming a disjunction with traditional societies. Modern societies were characterized as: heavily industrialized; based on mass production for mass markets; structured hierarchically on the basis of socially differentiated groups; politically and administratively organized on the basis of the nation-state; rooted in reason, rationality and rational procedures; and increasingly dominated by science, technology, the secular and a concern for objectivity and truth. It is whether this adequately captures the nature of the contemporary world which postmodernism calls into question. The 'post' in postmodernism indicates that it can only be addressed in terms of its relation to the modern. This implies a process of ongoing transformation and change, rather than an overturning of, or sharp break with, the past.

There are many different ways of endeavouring to engage with post-modernism. The term has been used to describe changes in areas such as architecture, fashion, music, literature, art, experiences of space and time, and notions of identities, along with sociological, philosophical and polit-ical ways of thinking about social life. Boyne and Rattansi, for instance, refer to a 'series of crises of representation' across a range of epistemolog-ical, artistic and social scientific senses (1990: 12–13). Not only have pre-vious ways of defining and portraying the objects of these forms of thought been challenged, but the boundaries between language and the objects it seeks to represent have been dissolved, giving rise to a plurality of perspectives and a blurring of the lines between disciplines such as sociology, history, philosophy and literary criticism. Other commentators focus on the political, economic and social changes which are trans-forming both the social world and the ways in which we make sense of it (Crook *et al.* 1992).

Broadly, there are five main linked and interrelated ways in which ideas about postmodernism might be discussed. These are: in relation to architecture and art; the constitution of new social formations; an emphasis on culture; poststructuralism; and postmodern philosophy. The following sections provide an overview of these five positions.

Mapping the postmodern

Architecture and art

The first and earliest formulation of postmodernism is to be found in the fields of architecture and art, where it refers to the ways in which elements of past styles are borrowed and reassembled to create new designs and forms (Harvey 1989). Similarly, it has also been used to describe a range of literary strategies, such as the use of irony, parody, pastiche, juxtaposition and fragmentation, arising out of but moving beyond cultural modernism (Waugh 1998). Such forms of postmodernism have often been regarded as progressive because they locate themselves outside the dominant and, some would say, moribund conventions of high modernist aesthetics. Further, it is argued, they involve blurring the boundaries between high art and popular culture and, by taking advantage of new developments in technology, produce potentially democratic and anti-elitist cultural forms (Wolff 1990; Hutcheon 1993). These kinds of cultural transformations are strongly linked to the rise of cultural studies as a field of analysis and enquiry. They are also related to issues to do with postmodern theorizing which aims 'to deconstruct apparent truths, dismantle dominant ideas and cultural forms and to engage in the guerrilla tactics of undermining closed and hegemonic systems of thought' (Wolff 1990: 190).

The constitution of new social formations

The second way in which postmodernism can be discussed is in terms of the constitution of new social formations. It is argued that the role of production was central to the development and organization of the modern capitalist world. Production formed the basis of structured social relationships and was reflected in the social stratification system and nature of social divisions. It influenced whom individuals and groups were likely to identify and associate with, socially, politically and culturally. However, it is claimed, capitalism has changed from being driven by mechanical production for mass markets and is increasingly geared to consumption. Moreover, consumption these days is less concerned with satisfying material needs and directed more towards considerations of taste, style and signification. In other words 'you are what you consume' and lifestyle (type and locality of house, mode and label of dress, make and model of car, leisure pursuits) has become a symbol of identity and position in the place, for example, of old class distinctions. Variously described as a move from an industrial to a post-industrial society (Touraine 1971; Bell 1973), from Fordism to post-Fordism (Murray 1989), from 'organized' to 'disorganized' capitalism (Lash and Urry 1987), as 'New Times' (Hebdidge 1989; Laclau 1990) or as 'the cultural logic of late capitalism' (Jameson 1991), the result is the introduction of flexible and niche marketing using extensive advertising, the media and information technology in order continually to sell new consumer commodities. Further, and ironically, all of this exists within an economic network which is increasingly global at the same time as it is becoming more and more decentralized into production units which subcontract out highly differentiated production activities (Thomas and Walsh 1998).

These socio-economic changes, it is suggested, not only alter work relationships, they also have other significant effects. In particular, the corporate state of late modernity is being eroded in the face of both multinational and local organizations. There has been a decline in allegiance to traditional political parties and the emergence of new social movements (for example, environmental groups and anti-poll tax demonstrations), based on non-material values and single-issue concerns. The development of flexible manufacturing systems has also led to the decline of the union movement, together with the reprofessionalization of labour and a reduction in the scale of bureaucracies. These, then, are the elements which are seen as integral to the empirical condition of postmodernity. Postmodernization refers to the processes through which the changes from modernity to postmodernity are taking place (Crook *et al.* 1992).

An emphasis on culture

A third way in which the postmodern has been influential is in relation to the elevation of the cultural to a key analytic category in social thought. Although sociologists have always been interested in culture, they have tended, with the exception of groups such as the Chicago school, to subordinate its significance to social processes and institutions (Long 1997). Talcott Parsons, one of the most culturally sensitive mid-twentieth-century sociologists, treated culture either as an overarching and independent variable in his analysis of social action or as subjectivized and individually held attitudes. In the general attempt to establish sociology as a discipline with sufficient authority and methodological rigour to analyze the 'social', cultural matters were often regarded as the prerogative of the humanities. Religion and mass communication, the most obvious culturally relevant sub-areas, have had, until comparatively recently, an existence somewhat at the margins of the accepted disciplinary core (Long 1997).

In the last twenty or so years, however, there has been an extensive 'turn to culture' in social thought, along with massive interest in interdisciplinary cultural studies. This has also influenced feminist thinking, as previously discussed. Partially originating in the political maelstrom of the 1960s and 1970s, this emphasis on culture has increasingly been influenced by postmodern thinking in two significant ways. On the one hand, the focus has been transformed from mainly studying the content and nature of different cultural forms and ideas in terms of sub-cultures and their potential for resistance to hegemonic capitalism (Kellner 1997). The emphasis today is on the fragmentation of different cultural styles and practices, with a concern for pleasure, consumption and the individual construction of identities. Culture in this sense is concerned with what people 'do' when they perform such acts as choosing clothes, shopping, selecting television programmes or music. Attention is paid to the signification of such acts, as well as to how cultural forms themselves might be 'read', emphasizing the possibility of diverse and multiple meanings.

On the other hand, this has also involved the appropriation of deconstruction as an approach. Developed from literary criticism, this involves taking apart the internal characteristics of a phenomenon in order to analyze how it is made up and regulated. It means treating cultural forms as texts and narratives in order to interrogate, evaluate and even overturn and disrupt their meanings. Such a strategy aims to tease out any implied presuppositions and points to any inherent contradictions which are present. The idea is to remove power from any particular author or creator, investing it with those engaging with the text instead. Such dismantling signals that cultural forms and practices are not to be passively consumed and cannot be restricted to a single and authoritative reading. Rather, they are open to plural meanings and contain the radical possibility of dismantling dominant ideas and challenging conventional ways of thinking: hence, for example, the claim that it was possible to see Madonna as offering young women representations of an active, rather than a passive, female sexuality (Fiske 1987).

Poststructuralism

A fourth variety of postmodernism includes a form of thinking that others have referred to as poststructuralism. Indeed, there is a debate in the literature as to how far poststructuralism can, in fact, be distinguished from other forms of postmodern philosophy which are discussed next (Boyne and Rattansi 1990). Here they are differentiated on the grounds that post-structuralism takes its departure from a critical reading of structuralist work and, thus, predates the work of other postmodernist writers. A structuralist position assumes that there are relatively fixed structures underlying all social relationships, cultures and language. Poststructuralist theory takes its starting point, in particular, from Saussure's structuralist lingustic model. Saussure argued that language has a pre-given structure prior to its realization in speech or writing. He regarded language as an abstract system comprising chains of signs. Each sign consists of the signifiers (sounds) and the signified (meanings). However, the relationship between the two is arbitrary, extra-individual and set according to social convention. As Weedon explains, 'Each sign derives its meaning from its difference from all the other signs in the language chain. It is not anything intrinsic to the signifier "whore", for example, that gives it its meaning, but rather its difference from other signifiers of womanhood such as "virgin" and "mother"' (Weedon 1987: 23).

Poststructuralists reject Saussure's notion that language is a closed system and the elements of the sign relatively fixed. If this were the case it would be impossible to account for conflicting meanings and change over time. Instead, they argue that the signifieds in language are never fixed once and for all but are constantly deferred, broken down and form-ing new combinations. Derrida, for instance, is critical of the idea that signs have fixed meanings which are easily recognized by individual subjects (Derrida 1973). He suggests that the meaning of signifiers depends on the discursive relations within which they are located and that they are con-tinually being challenged, redefined and reinterpreted. Similarly, Foucault also emphasizes the plurality of meaning and how it is constantly deferred. He focuses on discourse, not just as language but as the structured ways of knowing which are both produced in, and the shapers of, culture (Foucault 1979, 1981). For Foucault, discourse is also the purveyor of power. Power is not something possessed by people or groups. Rather, it is enshrined in, and used through, discourse. What is meant by madness or sexuality, for example, depends on the historically specific discourses within which they are located and which constitute them in a certain way. He also concentrates on the institutional effects of discourse – what it implies for how madness and punishment are dealt with, for instance – together with its role in the construction and regulation of individuals. Overall, then, poststructuralists hold that meaning is constituted within discourse and is not guaranteed by the speaking subject. Ideas about true, fixed or real meanings are, thereby, called into question. Deconstructive techniques analyze how discourse works rhetorically to create the illusions of coherence and credibility. The aim is to challenge the pretensions of previously unproblematized discourses, with a view to replacing them by strategies of enquiry and debate.

Although Foucault does allow for the possibility of resistance through his notion of reverse discourse, the above arguments are sometimes referred to via the aphorism, 'the death of the subject', due to their attack on the idea that people are the authors of their own thoughts and actions. This is also linked to another aspect of poststructuralist thinking, the decentring of the subject and the deconstruction of the self.

Since the Enlightenment, western thought has been dominated by an emphasis on reason and the role of the rational thinking subject in producing knowledge. This is known as the mind/body dualism. Rationality is juxtaposed to emotions, objectivity to subjectivity, and culture to nature, with the implication that it is the first of these binary opposites which are to valorized. For poststructuralists, however, the self is no longer conceived as rational, unified and fixed. Instead, it is portrayed as fragmented, pluralistic, eroticized and continually changing. The subject is presented as being divided against itself and as the product of conflicts and contradictions between its various parts and its positioning in various discourses. One consequence of such arguments is the corollary that there is, therefore, no 'I', no unifed subject who can be an ultimate knower. Rather, subjectivity is constituted and reconstituted in and through language whenever a person speaks. The subject in poststructuralist theory is continually being constructed, holding out the possibility of multiple subjectivities and identities. Overall, poststructuralist claims about fragmented subjectivities and fluctuating meanings raise serious issues about what it is possible to achieve in terms of the generation of social theory.

Postmodern philosophy

Finally, the idea of postmodernism also includes the philosophical interventions in social theory which characterize the work of writers such as Lyotard and Baudrillard. For Lyotard, the advent of postmodernism is marked by a shift from a search for truth to an emphasis on fiction and narrative (Lyotard 1984). This is accompanied by movement from a concern with experience to that of language. It involves the demise of the three major meta-narratives of modernism, those of science, religion and politics, and their replacement by local 'language games'. For Lyotard, we each live at the intersection of many language games and may have to resort to quite different sets of codes, depending on the situation in which we find ourselves. We, therefore, do not necessarily establish stable language combinations and, thus, have only fragmentary subjectivities, since no coherent or codifiable sense of identity is possible. Lyotard argues that the development of scientific narratives to support reason and progress is no longer legitimate. To endeavour to do so is to become part of a self-serving game in which it is 'performativity', rather than knowledge and truth, which is important. The postmodern condition makes rational systems and subjects into fictions, so that research is more about the augmentation of power than about the search for truth and knowledge. Given that it is nostalgic to claim otherwise, Lyotard calls for a 'war on totality' in which social theory's search for meta-narratives and true stories should finally be laid to rest (1984: 82).

Similarly, Baudrillard contends that we are living in a postmodern age of hyper-reality (1990). Here, there is a world of pervasive unreality. It is one where perceptions are increasingly shaped by mass imagery, political rhetoric and techniques of wholesale disinformation which become substitutes for reasoned political debate. Any notion that people are free to think for themselves is simply belied by the ways in which their ideas, attitudes and voting behaviour are programmed in advance. Baudrillard talks of 'hyperchondriacal madness', the 'obscenity' whereby human needs, desires and interests are continually manufactured for them. However, Baudrillard's stance on this is, essentially, neutral. He is in no position to take a critical view, having repeatedly argued against the idea of objective truth. Thus, there are no means of deciding what people's real needs and interests might be. There is no way of progressing beyond false appearances because nothing 'real' exists behind them. We are, therefore, forever condemned to the realm of illusory images that constitute the postmodern world. As Hebdige puts it: 'signs begin increasingly to take on a life of their own referring not to a real world outside themselves but to their own reality – the system that produces the signs' (Hebdige 1989: 151).

Postmodernism and social theory

The five aspects of postmodernism discussed above suggest that the postmodern world is seen as representing an increasing disjuncture with the modern one. Located in the globalized and post-industrial context of media, communication and information systems, it is organized on the basis of consumption rather than work and production and comprises fragmented and pluralistic groups with diverse cultures and lifestyles. Identity is no longer conditioned by an individual's or group's hierarchical place in the social structure, as with class. It is, instead, discursively located and continually being reconstructed and restyled. Thomas and Walsh describe the result thus: 'it is a world of culture in which tradition, consensual values, normative control, absolutist forms of knowledge and universal beliefs and standards have been challenged, undermined and rejected for heterogenity, differentiation and difference' (1998: 364). As a consequence, it is argued, the practice of social theory, itself a modernist project, has been undermined. The concepts, methods, assumptions and ambitions of social theory, which lie in modernist attempts to intervene in and control social forces and relations, are no longer either relevant or useful. The need for systematic and consistent social theory is called into question. This is both because the world which is its referent is itself no longer systematically structured and because postmodern epistemology indicates that the 'fragmentation of social theory into a series of mutually inconsistent, partial accounts is something to be acceded to as the irremediable condition of social inquiry' (Holmwood 1995: 414). In short, there is no point in seeking certainties in an uncertain world. Social theorists should, therefore, relinquish any search for generality and coherence. In their most extreme form, postmodern writers, such as Baudrillard, describe the social world as a 'chaotic constellation' which is 'unrepresentable' (Baudrillard 1983). There is no such thing as 'the social' which might be the object of any coherent theoretical analysis.

There are three ways in which social theorists can respond to this postmodern challenge (Bauman 1992; McLennan 1995; May 1996; Thomas and Walsh 1998). One is to dismiss it as offering a false and exaggerated account of social change and as operating with an epistemology which is inherently flawed. Another is to embrace postmodernism wholeheartedly, with a view to constructing new postmodern forms of analysis. It needs to be understood, however, that such a position is really a contradiction in terms and that what might constitute 'social' or 'theory' in this context will be very different from how these things have been conventionally regarded. The first approach means overlooking some of postmodernism's most important insights concerning the nature of the contemporary social world, while also ignoring its significant epistemological questions about the nature and role of theory. The second involves the dismantling of the social sciences and their replacement with hybrid and highly contingent accounts, which only fleetingly relate to anything of substance and whose meaning is located in the very process of their writing and utterance. The third way of responding to the postmodern challenge is to adopt a stance which, while sceptical of strong postmodernism, is prepared to accept that some of the issues it raises are both productive and exciting (McLennan 1995). In contrast to the other two, this is not a complacent strategy, since it is prepared to take on board the negative aspects of social thought, while also accepting the potential in new approaches to what constitutes understanding and the generation of knowledge (May 1996). What is the feminist position in relation to these kinds of arguments? The next section explores the ways in which feminist social theory has engaged with postmodernism.

Feminism/postmodernism

As a number of commentators have pointed out, feminism has, to some extent, always been 'postmodern' (Nicholson 1990; Waugh 1998). Feminist critiques of claims about universal truths and objective knowledge have revealed their partiality and gender-blindness. They have challenged accepted Enlightenment ways of thinking, with their emphases on reason, rationality and the disembodied self, to reveal a way of knowing dubbed 'the male epistemological stance' (McKinnon 1982). Enlightenment discourses, it is argued, universalize white, western middle-class male experience, which is then represented as the absolute truth. As MacKinnon observes, 'men create the world from their own point of view, which then *becomes* the truth to be described' (1982: 23–4). Feminists have long acknowledged the need to understand the relationship between power and knowledge, emphasizing the constructed and situated nature of knowledge creation, together with the complicity of the knower in this process. They have argued that, rather than suppressing the social basis of knowledge, more reliable understandings will be produced by being reflexively aware of the hidden agendas necessarily implicated in social reseach and social thought. Postmodern ideas about difference and diversity also offer feminists ways of countering tendencies to generalize across the boundaries of culture and region. In short, at first glance, postmodernism would appear to be a natural ally of feminism.

Yet, in addition to containing elements of opposition to Enlightenment thinking, feminist ideas also arise from Enlightenment thinking (Waugh 1998). The emergence of feminist theory and practice is clearly related to modernist notions of reason, justice and autonomous subjectivity and allied to this have been political claims for women to be treated as human subjects, alongside men, and to be granted full citizenship and civil rights. In other words, feminism has always had a practical and political agenda as well as a related, theoretical one. In relation to post-modernism, then, there seem to be two crucial questions for feminists. First, how far is it possible to retain the emancipatory ideals of modernity, which have been almost definitional of the feminist project, whilst simultaneously rejecting its apparently absolutist epistemological foundations? Second, to what extent might those epistemological foundations be modified, rather than totally abandoned, in an attempt to 'reconcile context-specific difference or situatedness with universal political aims' (Waugh 1998: 181)?

Like other social theorists, feminists are very divided about post-modernism. Some are completely dismissive, regarding it either as academic pretentiousness or as reinventing the wheel, by using the work of male theorists to support ideas which are already present in feminism (Jackson 1992; Bell and Klein 1996; Oakley 1998). For instance, Walby has suggested that it is not necessary to abandon ideas of causality, nor to move from analyses of structure to a focus on discourse, in order to capture the complexities of women's lives, and she argues that the postmodern tendency to fragment categories, such as those of gender, 'race' and class, is misplaced (Walby 1992). Bodribb, in her book, *Nothing Mat[t]ers*, whose title encapsulates her views about the valuelessness of the current academic fad of postmodernism, sees the latter as nothing more than a cultural product of late patriarchy (Bodribb 1992).

Other writers regard postmodernism as the only possible way forward for feminism. For instance, Hekman, whose arguments are often quoted in the context of support for a 'strong' postmodern position, writes: 'feminism and postmodernism are the only contemporary theories that present a truly radical critique of the Enlightenment legacy of modernism. No other approaches on the contemporary intellectual scene offer a means of displacing and transforming the masculinist epistemology of modernity' (Hekman 1990: 189). More recently, Brooks has suggested that, despite some successes, second-wave feminism has been constrained by the limitations of both its political agenda and its modernist inclinations (Brooks 1997). She argues that feminism is now transcending these difficulties, bringing together postmodernist and post-colonial thinking in ways which constitute evidence of maturity, rather than the inevitable fragmentation which detractors claim. For Brooks, the combination of these two intellectual approaches is leading to dynamic and vigorous debate about theoretical, philosophical and politically relevant issues. Somewhat controversially heralding this as the dawn of 'postfeminism', Brooks insists that there has been a paradigm change in feminism which challenges what she refers to disparagingly as 'hegemonic' feminism. Feminist theory now seeks to 'rupture the coherence of address', 'dislocate meaning' and destabilize theory, revisiting the whole idea of the representation of women and resisting closure of definition (1997: 10).

Feminism in postmodernism and postmodernism in feminism

As with other forms of social theory, however, some feminists have been attempting to follow a more middle-of-the-road stance compared to the positions described above. It is acknowledged that there are some elements of postmodern approaches which are important for feminist theory's future development, while also attempting to avoid what are perceived by many as postmodernism's worst excesses. There is some agreement, for instance, that the western philosophical notion of a transcendent self, a universal subject devoid of differences, is to be rejected (Flax 1990; Benhabib 1995). Subjectivity is recognized, instead, as being deeply embedded within culture and history. Also widely accepted are arguments against unitary and linear models of historical change and explanatory grand narratives which are monocausal and essentialist (Nicholson 1993). Deconstruction of the idea of 'woman' and an emphasis on 'difference' have also been important (Brah 1996). Feminists have welcomed too the acknowledgement of the role of cultural forms and of signification and representation in analyzing gender (Skeggs 1995). They are well aware that language and discourse are not transparent means of communication and that they construct, rather than reflect, meanings and social reality (Jackson 1998). Feminists have utilized these ideas in their work in a range of areas, such as the body/embodiment, sexualities, identities, (auto)biography, ethnicities, disapora and power. As one, not particularly sympathetic, commentator has put it: 'the foregrounding of social complexity and the problematization of the concepts experience, subjectivity and identity for which feminist postmodernism is largely (though not uniquely) responsible' (Roseneil 1995: 199) have been important developments for feminist social theory.

None the less, there are still difficulties, the most significant of which relate to epistemological issues and questions concerning the nature and status of knowledge. First, strong versions of postmodernism eliminate the idea of subjectivity all together (Nicholson 1995). Selves are so

fragmented, partial and fleeting that it is difficult to conceptualize individual agency, let alone notions of autonomy, reflexivity and accountability.
This raises the problem as to whether there is anything sufficiently stable
to constitute a 'knower' and the contingency of the knowledge which is
'known'. Flax, however, argues that the notion of the subject should not
be abandoned altogether (1990). She points out that there is an immense
difference between refuting the idea that the self is homogeneous and positing that it is, therefore, nothing but persistent and ephemeral fluctuations.
Drawing on her work as a therapist, Flax indicates that, while the self may
change, it still retains some consistent elements. It is, thus, capable of
using logic and engaging in reasoned thinking, although the outcomes of
this, of course, may be contested or modified.

A second issue, related to the first, is to do with postmodernism's
treatment of knowledge creation as both pluralistic and fallibilistic. The
impossibilities associated with constructing any kind of objective truth leads
to the opposite relativistic position of 'anything goes'. As Benhabib notes,
however, such a position is resonant with claims about value-free social
science, the very approach which it is designed to undermine (Benhabib
1995). This is because a disinterested stance, or one which makes no attempt
to evaluate different accounts, simply provides hidden justification to
the invisible assumptions of the status quo. Further, it eliminates the
possibility of emancipation or political intervention from social analysis.
The feminist standpoint approach has been developed to counter such
epistemiological and practical problems (Harding 1991). Although there
are debates and variations as to precisely what this involves, standpoint
theory is irreconcilable with much postmodernist thinking because it
presupposes a 'real' world which exists outside and prior to discourse. While
not disputing the difficulties in interpreting and analyzing this, taking a
feminist standpoint combines a commitment to a realist acceptance of
the existence of social processes which are potentially 'knowable', with
the general feminist axiom of the importance of experience in producing
more representative accounts of women's lives. Drawing on the Marxist
idea concerning the epistemic privilege of oppressed groups, Harding has
argued, for example, that understanding women's lives from a committed feminist exploration of their experiences constructs knowledge with
'strong' as opposed to 'weak' objectivity (Harding 1991). Conventional
notions of objectivity are 'weak' because they hide the analyst's own cultural agendas and assumptions. By contrast, the knowledge produced
by the feminist standpoint is 'strong' precisely because it includes the
systematic examination of such background beliefs and explores the relationship between subject and object, without simply separating the

knower from the known (May 1998). It, thus, escapes scientistic notions of objectivity, while also avoiding damaging forms of relativism (Harding 1991).

A third matter, also connected to the relativism issue, concerns the need to distinguish between universalizations and generalizations. Of course, it is highly important, as feminists would be the first to agree, to recognize the impossibility of constructing theories dealing with totalities and closed explanations which are universally applicable. But this is not the same as denying that it is possible to make general statements. These address, albeit in qualified terms, general properties and, through comparison, highlight similarities and differences. For feminism, Frye has described this in terms of pattern perception (1990). She suggests that patterns are important because they enable us to sketch a schema within which certain meanings are sustained. Their significance is in rendering intelligible those repetitions in social life which may be invisible or perceived in isolated and personal terms by the individual. Yet, this does not mean that they are either statistical or universal generalizations. Patterns may change as new fields of meaning open up. They are important because (as with a traveller in unknown territory) they offer a map, however partial, of knowledge so far attained and further directions which it might be prudent to pursue. Such generalizations do not provide a summing up, thereby foreclosing further discussion (Frye 1990). Rather, they can open up new fields of meaning and generate new understandings and political possibilities.

Feminists have also taken issue with postmodern hype concerning the privileging of culture, language and representation over other social processes, implying that this renders material concepts redundant. Adkins and Lury have argued that the 'social' has been attacked, 'demonized' and largely rejected as an outmoded form of analysis (1995). This has huge implications, for it ignores the ways in which material processes influence the cultural practices which are available to individuals. It implies, for instance, that there is some kind of free market in terms of culture and identity from which women and men can freely choose, overlooking any intervening factors, access to resources or networks, for example, which might inhibit or restrain them. In this context, it is salutary to note that feminists have demonstrated much less interest in that form of postmodernism which is concerned with shifts in social formations than they have in issues addressed by cultural studies or by poststructuralism and postmodern philosophy. While some feminists have written about the effects of such changes as globalization, new employment practices and transformations in the nation-state on women, little of this seems to have found its way into what might be regarded as mainstream feminist social theorizing (Pettman 1996).

Recently, however, Jackson has suggested that there are signs that some feminists are retreating from the more extreme anti-materialist implications of postmodernism and are moving back to accepting the existence and importance of structural inequalities and social divisions for gender relations (Jackson 1998). She points out that American theorists (for instance, Hennessy 1993; Landry and MacLean 1993; Hennessy and Ingraham 1997) have revived the term 'material feminism' and that this has been influenced by a concern to avoid what she describes as 'the politically disabling consequences of postmodernism consequent upon the denial of any material reality outside language and discourse' (Jackson 1998: 25–6). Jackson, herself, has played an important role in publicizing the work of the materialist feminist, Christine Delphy, who developed her approach during the 1970s and early 1980s (Jackson 1996). Along with Ramazanoglu, she has been at the forefront of attempts to include a material dimension to aspects of women's lives and identities which have tended to be analyzed in cultural and discursive terms, for example sexuality and the body (Jackson 1995; Ramazanoglu 1995). This kind of work presents a kind of feminist material analysis different from the previous Marxist feminist forms. It has been made possible by rethinking the nature of materialism through a postmodern lens. Arguing that such an approach, which pays attention to structured inequalities, is as relevant today as it ever was, Jackson suggests that the challenge for feminist social theory is, 'to analyse the localised contexts of women's everyday existence and the meanings women give to their everyday lives without losing sight of structural patterns of dominance and subordination' (1998: 28).

Feminism and postmodernism – epistemology or theory?

It is clear that postmodernism has had a significant impact on feminist social thought and the nature of its influence has been hotly debated. The problem for feminists (and for other social thinkers) is that the 'posts' tend to ask questions about the ways in which knowledge is constructed and how this operates, rather than about what is actually known. A lot of feminist postmodern writing focuses, therefore, on epistemological issues rather than strictly theoretical ones. It rightly problematizes such issues as subjectivity, objectivity, truth claims and the status of knowledge. But this becomes something of an unravelling procedure in which the process of knowledge creation is continually deconstructed but little time is spent on the creation of knowledge itself. In such circumstances feminist social theory runs the risk of ceasing to be theory about the gendered nature of the social world, becoming instead theory about theory. While all social theorizing entails epistemological assumptions which should be made clear, it also requires referrents in the form of subject matter other than itself. Mouzelis, for example, has drawn attention to the fact that epistemology and social theory cannot be collapsed into each other (Mouzelis 1991). While there are continuities between them, there are marked discontinuities as well. Mouzelis argues that the current conflation and abolition of the distinction between what constitutes epistemology and what constitutes theory 'destroys the latter's specificity and relative autonomy' (1991: 3). While resulting analyses may offer important insights and clever comments, they 'often lead to misleading or inadequate conclusions' (Mouzelis, 1991: 4). Feminist social theory which wishes to retain a commitment to knowledge creation and political intervention needs to take such comments seriously into account.

References

Adkins, L. and Lury, C. (1995) 'Das "Soziale" in feministischen Theorien: eine nutzliche Analysekategorie?' in L.C. Armbruster, U. Muller and M. Stein-Hilbers (eds) *Neue Horizonte?*, Opladen: Leske und Budrich.

Ahmed, S. (1998) *Differences That Matter. Feminist Theory and Postmodernism*, Cambridge: Cambridge University Press.

Barrett, M. (1980) *Women's Oppression Today*, London: Verso.

Barrett, M. (1992) 'Words and things', in M. Barrett and A. Phillips (eds) *Destabilizing Theory*, Cambridge: Polity Press.

Baudrillard, J. (1983) *In the Shadow of the Silent Majorities, Or, the End of the Social and Other Essays*, New York: Semiotext[e].

Baudrillard, J. (1990) *Revenge of the Crystal: A Baudrillard Reader*, London: Pluto.

Bauman, Z. (1992) *Intimations of Postmodernity*, London: Routledge.

Bell, D. (1973) *The Coming of Post-Industrial Society*, New York: Basic Books.

Bell, D. and Klein, R. (1996) (eds) *Radically Speaking. Feminism Reclaimed*, London: Zed.

Benhabib, S. (1995) 'Feminism and postmodernism', in S. Benhabib, J. Butler, D. Cornell and N. Fraser, *Feminist Contentions*, London: Routledge.

Boyne, R. and Rattansi, A. (1990) (eds) *Postmodernism and Society*, London: Macmillan.

Brah, A. (1996) *Cartographies of Diaspora*, London: Routledge.

Brodribb, S. (1992) *Nothing Mat[t]ers*, Melbourne: Spinifex Press.

Brooks, A. (1997) *Postfeminisms*, London: Routledge.

Butler, J. (1992) 'Contingent foundations: feminism and the question of "post-modernism"' in J. Butler and J.W. Scott (eds) *Feminists Theorize the Political*, London: Routledge.

Crook, S., Pakulski, J. and Waters, M. (1992) *Postmodernization*, London: Sage.

Derrida, J. (1973) *Speech and Phenomenon*, Evanston: Northwestern University Press.

Fiske, J. (1987) *Television Culture*, London: Routledge.

Flax, J. (1990) *Thinking Fragments*, Berkeley: University of California Press.

Foucault, M. (1979) *Discipline and Punish*, Harmondsworth: Penguin.

Foucault, M. (1981) *The History of Sexuality*, vol. 1, Harmondsworth: Pelican.

Frye, M. (1990) 'The possibility of feminist theory', in D.L. Rhode (ed.) *Theoretical Perspectives on Sexual Difference*, New Haven CT: Yale University Press.

Harding, S. (1991) *Whose Science? Whose Knowledge?*, Buckingham: Open University Press.

Harvey, D. (1989) *The Condition of Postmodernity*, Oxford: Blackwell.

Hebdige, D. (1989) 'After the masses', in S. Hall and M. Jacques (eds) *New Times*, London: Lawrence and Wishart.

Hekman, S. (1990) *Gender and Knowledge: Elements of a Postmodern Feminism*, Cambridge: Polity Press.

Hennessy, R. (1993) *Materialist Feminism and the Politics of Discourse*, London: Routledge.

Hennessy, R. and Ingraham, C. (1997) (eds) *Materialist Feminism*, London: Routledge.

Holmwood, J. (1995) 'Feminism and epistemology: what kind of successor science?' *Sociology* 29 (3): 411–28.

Hutcheon, L. (1993) *The Politics of Postmodernism*, London: Routledge.

Jackson, S. (1992) 'The amazing deconstructing woman', *Trouble and Strife*, 25: 25–31.

Jackson, S. (1995) 'Gender and heterosexuality: a materialist feminist analysis', in M. Maynard and J. Purvis (eds) *(Hetero)sexual Politics*, London: Taylor and Francis.

Jackson, S. (1996) *Christine Delphy*, London: Sage.

Jackson, S. (1998) 'Feminist social theory', in S. Jackson and J. Jones (eds) *Contemporary Feminist Theories*, Edinburgh: Edinburgh University Press.

Jameson, F. (1991) *Postmodernism or the Cultural Logic of Late Capitalism*, London: Verso.

Kaluzynska, E. (1980) 'Wiping the floor with theory – a survey of writings on housework', *Feminist Review* 6: 27–54.

Kellner, D. (1997) 'Critical theory and cultural studies: the missed articulation', in J. McGuigan (ed.) *Cultural Methodologies*, London: Sage.

Laclau, E. (1990) *New Reflections on the Revolution of our Time*, London: Verso.

Landry, D. and MacLean, G. (1993) *Materialist Feminisms*, Oxford: Blackwell.

Lash, S. and Urry, J. (1987) *The End of Organized Capitalism*, Cambridge: Polity Press.

Long, E. (1997) 'Introduction: engaging sociology and cultural studies: disciplinarity and social change', in E. Long (ed.) *From Sociology to Cultural Studies*, Oxford: Blackwell.

Lyotard, J.F. (1984) *The Postmodern Condition*, Manchester: Manchester University Press.

MacKinnon, C. (1982) 'Feminism, marxism, method and the state: an agenda for theory', in N.O. Keohane, M. Rosaldo and B. Gelpi (eds) *Feminist Theory*, Brighton: Harvester.

McLennan, G. (1995) 'After postmodernism – back to sociological theory', *Sociology* 29 (1): 117–32.

May, T. (1996) *Situating Social Theory*, Buckingham: Open University Press.

May, T. (1998) 'Reflections and reflexivity', in T. May and M. Williams (eds) *Knowing the Social World*, Buckingham: Open University Press.

Maynard, M. (1995) 'Beyond the "Big Three": the development of feminist theory into the 1990s', *Women's History Review* 4 (3): 259–81.

Millett, K. (1969) *Sexual Politics*, London: Rupert Hart-Davis.

Mouzelis, N. (1991) *Back to Sociological Theory*, London: Macmillan.

Mouzelis, N. (1995) *Sociological Theory: What Went Wrong?*, London: Routledge.

Murray, R. (1989) 'Fordism and post-Fordism', in S. Hall and M. Jacques (eds) *New Times*, London: Lawrence and Wishart.

Nicholson, L. (1990) 'Introduction', in L. Nicholson (ed.) *Feminism/Postmodernism*, London: Routledge.

Nicholson, L. (1993) 'On the postmodern barricades: feminism, politics and theory', in S. Seidman and D.G. Wagner (eds) *Postmodernism and Social Theory*, Oxford: Blackwell.

Nicholson, L. (1995) 'Introduction', in S. Benhabib, J. Butler, D. Cornell and N. Fraser (eds) *Feminist Contentions*, London: Routledge.

Oakley, A. (1998) 'Science, gender and women's liberation: an argument against postmodernism', *Women's Studies International Forum* 21 (2): 133–46.

Pettman, J.J. (1996) *Worlding Women*, London: Routledge.

Ramazanoglu, C. (1995) 'Back to basics: heterosexuality, biology and why men stay on top', in M. Maynard and J. Purvis (eds) *(Hetero)sexual Politics*, London: Taylor and Francis.

Roseneil, S. (1995) 'The coming of age of feminist sociology: some issues of practice and theory for the next twenty years', *British Journal of Sociology* 46 (2): 191–205.

Seidman, S. and Wagner, D.G. (1992) (eds) *Postmodernism and Social Theory*, Oxford: Blackwell.

Skeggs. B. (1995) (ed.) *Feminist Cultural Theory*, Manchester: Manchester University Press.

Smart, B. (1990) 'On the disorder of things', *Sociology* 24 (3): 397–416.

Smart, B. (1993) *Postmodernity*, London: Routledge.

Stacey, J. (1997) 'Feminist theory: capital F, capital T', in D. Richardson and V. Robinson (eds) *Introducing Women's Studies*, London: Macmillan.

Thomas, H. and Walsh, D.F. (1998) 'Modernity/postmodernity', in C. Jenks (ed.) *Core Sociological Dichotomies*, London: Sage.

Touraine, A. (1971) *The Post-Industrial Society*, New York: Random House.

Walby, S. (1992) 'Post-post-modernism? Theorizing social complexity' in M. Barrett and A. Phillips (eds) *Destabilizing Theory*, Oxford: Blackwell.

Waugh, P. (1998) 'Postmodernism and feminism', in S. Jackson and J. Jones (eds) *Contemporary Feminist Theories*, Edinburgh: Edinburgh University Press.

Weedon, C. (1987) *Feminist Practice and Poststructuralist Theory*, Oxford: Blackwell.

Wolff, J. (1990) 'Postmodern theory and feminist art practice', in R. Boyne and A. Rattansi (eds) *Postmodernism and Society*, London: Macmillan.

chapter 6

Developments in the sociology of gender and women's studies

Sylvia Walby

Introduction

The analysis of gender relations has been developing in Britain since the mid-1970s and is now an established area within British sociology. The theoretical debates are at the cutting edge of sociology, the substantive areas wide-ranging, and the range of methodologies diverse. The field is either integrated within mainline sociology departments and programmes or exists autonomously with its own centres and programmes. There are women's studies/gender studies programmes at either undergraduate or graduate levels in most institutions of higher education. The 1990s saw the establishment of several new academic journals, and of national and international professional associations.

Some aspect of gender relations is now usually included within most fields of sociology, going way beyond any narrowly defined 'woman question' – few, if any, areas of social life are now considered to be entirely ungendered. This increase in breadth of scope has, in recent years, been tempered by a greater realization of the importance of other forms of social relations in the construction of specific forms of gender relations, so that gender is less frequently considered in isolation from ethnicity, 'race', class and other social divisions.

This paper focuses on developments within sociology in the UK which have been variously called the sociology of gender, women's studies, gender studies or feminist research. Women's studies/gender studies/feminist research refers to an inter-disciplinary field of study about gender relations and the position and representation of women; the sociology of gender is that part of this field which is within sociology. Sometimes, as here, the terms women's studies and gender studies are used to signify the same field of study. Elsewhere, they have been differentiated in order to draw attention to the priority given to women's accounts of women's issues in some analyses (see Evans 1991). The position in this paper is that, while the naming of the field can be the subject of controversy, in current practice the use of the different terms does not usually imply a different substantive field or theoretical or epistemological perspective.

In the early establishment of women's studies in the UK, sociology was the most important contributing discipline. More recently women's studies has drawn on the humanities, especially literary theory. This 'cultural turn' associated with a 'postmodernist' theoretical turn is similar to that which has occurred in many, but not all, other branches of sociology.

Women's studies has developed as an international field of study with much interchange of ideas and materials between different countries. The US, in particular, has been the source of many influential ideas, though the increasing integration of the UK into the EU has also generated new questions and perspectives. Perspectives from the south have long been welcomed as providing important insights beyond First World concerns. While the focus in this chapter is work written in the UK, the international debates are an integral part of local developments. These will be included where necessary to make sense of debates among women's studies practitioners in the UK.

Theoretical developments

Feminist analysis has been part of the major movements in social theory; indeed in some instances it might claim to have been a key element in some of the changes, especially in relation to the challenge to the 'meta-narratives' of Marxist and class analysis. These developments include a shift from the analysis of the economic aspects of social relations and the significance of class, towards culture, a move which has been associated with a change from analysis of structures to the analysis of discourses, a postmodernist mode of theorizing, and an increased interest in the significance of diversity.

The traditional centre to British sociology has often been represented as the analysis of social inequality in which class was seen as the central concept. During the 1980s a strong critique was developed to the presumption that class could be analyzed without taking account of the significance of gender, leading to the revision of the conventional view

(Goldthorpe 1983; Stanworth 1984; Crompton and Mann 1986). Since then, new analyses of class almost always address the question of the significance of gender, although disagreement continues on its importance (Marshall *et al.* 1988; Erikson and Goldthorpe 1992).

The loss of pre-eminence of the concept of class as the focus of research projects in British sociology has coincided with an increase of interest in culture, discourse analysis and postmodernism The sociology of gender has been at the forefront of these developments; indeed the development of cultural studies and women's studies have been closely intertwined. The old meta-narratives of Marx and class are replaced by a vision of complexity and fluidity (Barrett and Phillips 1992).

This postmodernist turn in the sociology of gender and women's studies in the 1990s was given impetus by the developing concern to address questions of ethnocentrism and diversity in feminist theory. There are many forms of gender relations to explain, not only that of the majority white ethnic group; generalization from white women to all women is a mistake. The diversity of women's experiences relating to ethnicity, 'race', nationality, sexual orientation, 'disability', have become key issues within feminist analysis (see the collections from the annual women's studies conferences: Aaron and Walby (1991); Hinds *et al.* (1992); Kennedy *et al.* (1993)).

The analysis of 'difference' became one of the pressing theoretical debates of the 1990s. In what way were gender relations different in different ethnic groups (hooks 1984; Bhopal 1997)? In what way were different nations gendered (Yuval-Davis 1997)? How are perspectives from the south to be understood and integrated (Mohanty 1991)? How should the standard for justice be determined if different social groups have different conceptions of justice (Young 1990)? What was the relationship between routes seeking social justice on the basis of difference and those seeking it on the basis of equality (Meehan and Sevenhuijsen 1991)? How can the tension between difference and equality be resolved (Scott 1988; Fraser 1995)? Did the focus on difference itself tend to reify the differences (Squires 1999)? What should be the ontological status of difference (Felski 1997)? Does sensitivity to different value systems have to lead to social relativism (Alcoff 1988; Fraser and Nicolson 1988)? How should a feminist analysis of fundamentalism proceed (Afshar 1998)? How should social complexity at the intersection of different social divisions be theorized (Walby 1992)?

A related theoretical debate of the 1990s was that around 'essentialism'. Did feminist analysis assume too many commonalities amongst women? Was radical feminist analysis, in its focus on the oppression of women by men, necessarily essentialist, reducing complex social processes to simple biological dichotomies (Segal 1987), or was this simply a caricature (Bell and Klein 1996)? Was indeed some analytic strategy of 'essentializing' always necessary in order to build categories sufficiently stable for practical analysis (Fuss 1989)? Could the concept of patriarchy be developed so as to be sensitive to historical change and cultural difference (Kandiyoti 1988; Walby 1990)?

The reconsideration of the issues of agency and structure in mainstream sociology (Giddens 1984) had a lively resonance in feminist debates. Did macro accounts of women's oppression by men give too much weight to structure and insufficient to women's active agency? While feminists in economics criticized their discipline for an overly individualistic account of human economic action, the revisionists in sociology were criticizing their discipline for an overly social structural account which gave insufficient weight to human agency.

Gender and employment

The analysis of women's position in employment is a continuing theme in the sociology of gender, though perhaps not as high profile in the theoretical debates today as it was twenty years ago. In this area of gendered employment relations, there has been a flowering of theoretically informed, detailed, empirical studies. The question remains that of understanding the changes in the complex forms of inequality and difference between men and women in the labour market and their connection to other social divisions and changes.

The increase in women's paid employment was a continuing feature of the latter part of the twentieth century. Yet, while some aspects of inequality have reduced, others are tenacious. The wages gap between women and men has reduced for those who work full-time so that these women are now paid four-fifths of men's rates, yet those who work part-time are still only paid three-fifths. Occupational segregation has declined a little, but new forms have developed.

The debates on difference and ethnicity are enriched by studies of the complexity of the interrelationship between gender and ethnicity among women workers, where paid work has varying locations in the lives of women from different social locations (Westwood 1984; Phizacklea 1990; Brah and Shaw 1992). The increasing significance of the European Union has produced interest in the comparative analysis of gendered labour markets in the member states of the European Union, the explanation of the differences found and of the role of the EU in regulating these labour markets (Rubery *et al.* 1999). The influence of the cultural turn in gender studies may be seen in the interest in the role of sexuality in the workplace (Hearn and Parkin 1987; Adkins 1994), and the role of culture in restricting women's success in management.

The debates in mainline industrial sociology on the nature of new forms of flexibility at work informed various studies, including those of part-time work (O'Reilly and Fagan 1998); and of home-working (Phizacklea and Wolkowitz 1995). This addresses the extent to which the extension of women's employment has been in forms of employment which are casualized, insecure and low-paid, or whether women can benefit from the new flexibility. Much of this work suggests that while the flexibility has been important in facilitating the return of women with domestic responsibilities to paid work, this has been at a high cost in terms of job conditions for many female workers.

There is debate as to the extent to which equal opportunities policies can be effective in reducing gender inequality. This is explored in studies which examine attempts to introduce equal opportunities policies into the workplace (Cockburn 1991), the impact and nature of the changing legal framework (Gregory 1987, 1999) and the assessment of the implementation of policy and law (England 1992). Increasing integration into the European Union has been shown to lead to the greater importance of EU-based regulations promoting equal opportunities, since EU law takes precedence over domestic UK law in this area (Pillinger 1992; Hoskyns 1996; Rees 1998; Walby 1999b).

Occupational segregation has been seen as one of the more tenacious features of the gendered labour market, though even here there are changes (Scott 1994). There have been studies of the extent of the changing dimensions and patterns of occupational segregation (Cockburn 1983; Hakim 1992; Witz 1992) and a new sophistication in its measurement (Hakim 1992; Blackburn *et al.* 1993). As some forms of occupational segregation have been reduced, as educated young women increasingly enter the professions, especially as younger women enter the professions and management, and some heavily male-dominated industries, such as coal, steel and cars, decline in significance, new forms of segregation have developed, most notably in the development of an insecure and poorly paid part-time sector for women (Walby 1997).

The sociology of gender relations in employment has produced a theoretically informed and increasingly sophisticated set of empirical studies over the last few years. The changes in gender are complex, with some forms of inequality between women and men reducing as others emerge into significance. Gender is implicated in most of the current changes in the workforce and analyses of gender articulate with all mainstream debates on the future of work.

Violence

The significance of male violence in women's lives was severely underestimated until recently. Feminist scholarship in this area has over-turned traditional assumptions that such violence was caused by a few sick men or that it can be understood in terms of some evolutionary male imperative. The social shaping of patterns of violence and social responses to this violence have brought this field firmly within a sociological frame of enquiry. The relationship between violence and socially structured gendered power relations has been key to this field, though not uncontroversially so.

Early small-scale studies on special or local samples (Dobash and Dobash 1979; Hanmer and Saunders 1984), were followed by large-scale surveys which confirmed the finding that violence against women was widespread (Johnson 1996; Mirrlees-Black 1999). Feminist research in this field has contributed to the rapidly changing political and policy debates, as well as revised conceptions of male violence in women's magazines and popular culture. Early academic work in Britain tended to be based on small-scale qualitative studies, for reasons of giving voice to the women who have suffered and survived the violence, theories of feminist methodology and lack of funding (Kelly 1988). Current work is more methodologically pluralist, including embracing large quantitative surveys of the prevalence of male violence in a way which has led to a revision of theories of feminist methodology. Such surveys are no longer seen to inevitably distort the process of recording experiences of violence, since some may prefer the anonymity of a questionnaire to a face-to-face inter-view when dealing with such problematic memories (see Kelly *et al.* 1992). Such surveys may have an additional impact by providing information to policy makers in a form that they find most useful.

There has been a steady uncovering and naming of more diverse forms of violence against women. This includes not only rape, sexual assault and domestic violence, but also child sex abuse, sexual harassment, and stalking, all part of a continuum of violence against women (Hanmer and Maynard 1987; Kelly 1988). There is a recurring dilemma in feminist research on women's oppression as to how to avoid feeding a view of women as passive victims of patriarchal structures, overwhelmed by men's brutal power, while yet giving full accounts of the extent of the oppression. In contrast, if there is too great a focus on women's agency, of women actively making choices, then there is a symmetrical danger of perhaps appearing to present women as collaborators in their own oppression. This is a particularly acute issue in the analysis of male violence, and has produced a number of innovative resolutions, such as the deliberate avoidance of the use of the term 'victim' and a preference for the term 'survivor' (Kelly 1988).

The theorization of the different patterns in gendered violence has been hampered by the lack of reliable survey data in the UK; for instance, there is as yet no reliable national survey data on the prevalence of rape and sexual assault (Walby and Myhill 2000). Debates here thus depend upon data gathered in other countries especially the US and Canada. Straus and Gelles' (1990) two surveys confirmed the widespread nature of domestic violence, but controversially suggested that men were also significant victims. This research has been subject to blistering methodological critiques, for instance its failure to distinguish between women's actions in self-defence and the initiation of an attack and for the more general neglect of the context of the actions (Saunders 1988; Dobash *et al.* 1992). Johnson (1996), reporting on the Statistics Canada survey on violence against women in Canada, and Mirrlees-Black (1999) on domestic violence in the UK, both find that domestic violence is more prevalent in poorer households, though the interpretation of this finding is controversial.

The critical analysis of the response of the criminal justice system and relevant agencies to gendered violence has proved a fruitful area of enquiry, again demonstrating the importance of social context and of the social response to the violence in structuring its impact. The criminal justice system has been shown to be often, but not always, problematic for women who have suffered violence, and the detail of police and legal procedures is often not to their advantage. There is evidence that further changes in state policies would reduce domestic violence and sexual assault (Taylor-Browne 2000).

The implications of these analyses of men's violence against women for sociological theory is as yet much underdeveloped. The feminist interventions have expanded the field of sociology, showing the strength of an analysis which places this behaviour within a sociological rather than a biological or psychological frame of reference. Yet, the concepts traditionally used to grasp social inequality by British sociology which have focused on socio-economic matters, continue to marginalize these concerns about violence. This violence is thus still conceptualized primarily in the context of deviant behaviour, rather than, say, social stratification or the state. It is only within women's studies that violence against women is conceptualized systematically as an issue of social power: in particular, as gendered social power related to a wider gendered social structure.

Politics and the state

The gendered sociological analysis of politics and the state has tended to focus on specific areas, rather than a re-theorization of politics and the state as a whole. These areas include: citizenship, welfare, and feminist politics.

The gendering of sociological debates on welfare and on citizenship has taken as its starting point the critique of the neglect of the care work which is so often performed by women to a greater extent than men. This is an example of an area where sociological theory has proved reluctant to integrate the domestic position of women into ostensibly general accounts of society. The debates on citizenship took as their starting point a public conception of the citizen. The feminist critique demonstrated that such a theorization effectively marginalized the contribution of women to society, especially their contributions in the home as mothers (Lister 1997). This was similar to the debates about welfare, where an influential new typology in the 1990s was also criticized for marginalizing the contribution that women made to welfare. Esping-Andersen's (1990) influential threefold typology of welfare regimes into liberal, social democratic and corporatist was criticized for not taking sufficient account of gender and the family and for his contradictory specification of de-commodification as in general emancipatory, while yet suggesting that women's entry to employment as in the social democratic model (i.e. commodification of their labour) was emancipatory (Orloff 1993). The debate spurred the development of alternative models and the gathering of data to test them (Sainsbury 1996; O'Connor et al. 1999).

The entry of women into the formal arena of the state has been given less attention in sociological work in the UK than in other countries. Perhaps not surprisingly it was the Scandinavians who first developed sociological accounts of the entry of women into electoral politics, since it was there that this first developed (Showstack Sassoon 1987). In US sociology there has been a continuing tradition of examining the implications of modernity for democracy and here we have seen the gendering of this debate, as in the argument by Ramirez et al. (1997) that links gender and democracy to globalization. In the UK it was political scientists who asked the questions as to whether women MPs would make a difference to policy questions (Norris and Lovenduski 1995).

The increasing significance of the European Union problematizes the notion of a single state being relevant in a specific country. The gender dimension of this is especially significant; in particular, key aspects of the regulation of the labour market are now within the primary remit of the European Union rather than the UK, especially in relation to policies for equal opportunities (Hoskyns 1996; Rees 1998; Walby 1999b).

Curiously, despite a strong tradition of social movement analysis in UK sociology, there have been remarkably few attempts to understand the contours of the British feminist movement, and here again it is political science which has tended to lead (Lovenduski and Randall 1993). The main exceptions here are around ethnicity and around culture. The intersection of ethnic and gender politics has been subject to many important analyses, grounding theoretical debates on difference in detailed empirical studies (see Mirza's 1997 collection of classic and contemporary writings here). The analysis of culture as politics is also highly developed in UK sociology, reflecting the cultural turn in British sociology and women's studies (Franklin *et al.* 1991).

Sexuality

The debates on the place of sexuality within the analysis of gender relations have drawn on a range of sources of theoretical inspiration including: Freud (Mitchell 1975); symbolic interactionism (Plummer 1975); radical feminism (Jeffreys 1990); and Foucault (Weeks 1985). Despite the lack in Foucault's own work of much in an explicit and direct way about gender, his conceptualization of sexuality and power became very influential in the 1990s in theories of gender and sexuality, though not uncontroversially so (Ramazanoglu 1991). The sociological analysis of gender and sexuality might be considered to have been 'mainstreamed' by Giddens' (1992) work on changes in the patterns of intimacy associated with changing patterns of gender relations.

Substantive research topics have included that of the subordination of women and girls within sexual practices; the use of demeaning sexualized stereotypes to attempt to control women's and girls' conduct, for instance as 'slags' or 'drags' (Lees 1993); the construction of heterosexuality (Jackson 1999); the diversity of sexual moralities (Weeks 1995); pornography (Kappeler 1986); and the exploitation of women's sexuality at work (Adkins 1994). Not all research has seen sexuality unambiguously as a terrain of male power, some seeing it as a site of negotiation, such as Pringle's (1989) work on sexuality at work, while there has been much attention to powerful female icons such as Madonna.

Culture

Feminist cultural studies has been one of the areas within the sociology of gender and women's studies which has developed most extensively, with the establishment of several journals, as well as many books, at the point of intersection of women's studies, sociology, and cultural and literary theory. The initial interest in the content analysis of images presented by advertising, television and the media has been replaced by sophisticated textual analysis informed by the discourse analysis of Foucault and the deconstructionism of Derrida (Kuhn 1982; Franklin *et al.* 1991; McNay 1992). A key feature of these recent analyses has been the breaking down of any remaining monolithic notions of femininity, or indeed, masculinity (Hearn 1992; Morgan 1992), and the exploration of the diversity found, especially that associated with ethnicity (Mirza 1997). There has been a tendency to celebrate women's agency, including that of non-feminist female icons such as Princess Diana and Madonna. There are debates as to whether this celebration of women's agency extends to women's involvement in sexual discourses that are not conventionally seen by 'traditional' feminists as emancipatory (Coward 1984; McRobbie and Nava 1984; Winship 1985).

Feminist cultural analysis had a tremendous influence on the forms of theorizing in women's studies during the 1980s and early 1990s, leading a shift away from analysis in terms of social structures to those of discourses and of agency. Further, there has been the problematization of the notion of a coherent monolithic subject, for instance, in Butler's (1990) work on 'performativity'. Here gender is merely what exists at the moment of performance; that is, the notion of a stable gender identity is rejected by Butler because it is considered to be overly essentializing. However, Butler's analysis has tended to lead away from the sociological analysis of the social institutions which provide the framing for any such performance.

Today the analysis of culture is largely integrated into analyses of gender, rather than constituting a separate field. The term 'gender' itself has been subject to extensive reconsideration in the light of so much deconstructionist analysis (Hawkesworth 1997).

Caring and the household

The sociology of the family was traditionally a strong area of sociology, but in the early development of women's studies this field tended to be side-lined in favour of newer substantive fields of enquiry. However, there has been a strong strand of research into the various forms and changes in care giving. This includes analysis of kinship and marital obligations for caring between generations (Finch 1992), and between spouses (Gershuny 1983; Delphy and Leonard 1992). This care work includes not only the care of children, but increasingly the care of the frail elderly, as the population lives longer. The significance of this unpaid care work and the burdens that are placed on women in this regard which tend to be unrecognized in social theory, as elsewhere, is a continuing theme in this work (Folbre 1994; Gardiner 1997).

During the 1990s the increased diversity of household forms has been the subject of sociological enquiry, especially the increasing proportion of lone mothers (Phoenix 1991; Ford and Millar 1998); and gay and lesbian households (Weeks 1995). The changes in household forms have generated interest in how young people actually manage the transitions between different household forms and stages (Irwin 1995), especially the diverse transitions by young women to either employment or to motherhood, which varies significantly by ethnicity and by education (Bhopal 1997; Proctor 1999).

Within the analysis of caring runs an underlying theoretical question as to why so many women actively choose to care when it reduces their access to many conventional forms of social power. Housewives and their choices are one of the substantive issues which drive the feminist interest in the agency/structure debate. What does it mean to say that housewives have agency? If women have more 'choices', do they choose to be 'housewives' less often? Do lone mothers have more 'freedom' or merely more poverty? Does this mean that they had less agency in times when more women were housewives? However, these questions are still framed by a concern with the wider social context in which women and carers make their decisions.

Nature and science

The relationship between the biological and the social has always been an area of debate in the sociology of gender. Early attempts by radical feminists to incorporate a conception of the body into their work on patriarchal domination (Firestone 1974) were often initially condemned as essentialist, and as leading inevitably to the reduction of gender to biology and hence to ahistoric and falsely universalistic analysis (Segal 1987). However, today it is widely accepted in mainstream sociology that it is necessary to have a conception of the body in sociology (Turner 1984). While the early radical feminist texts might have been sometimes unsubtle in their conceptualization, their critics' assertions that their concern with bodies and biology was necessarily essentialist have been found to be profoundly incorrect.

Contemporary debates are about the two-way traffic between concepts originating in the social and the biological fields of enquiry (Haraway 1989, 1997), rather than assuming that any reference to biology will dominate or in some way inappropriately contaminate a sociological analysis. Biology, in the age of the genome project which has mapped the shape of the human genes, is no longer seen as a fixed entity, but as a fluid area of discovery. Haraway's work shows how metaphors migrate in both directions between the social and the biological fields, taking some of their meaning from one and transposing it into the other. In so doing, the concepts with which we think about gender are changing.

There have been debates as to whether the new reproductive technologies, such as in vitro fertilization, empower women or take away women's last source of power and place it in the hands of male doctors, and whether they are actually helpful to infertile women, or merely medical experimentation. These analyses of the new reproductive technologies have explored the interconnections and tensions between scientific developments and 'natural' social relations (Stanworth 1987). Science and the environment have been analyzed as gendered issues (Shiva 1989), demonstrating how far the range of the field of gender studies can extend.

Science itself has been taken as an object of study and been found to be gendered (Rose 1994). The implications of this for feminist methodology (Reinharz 1993) and feminist epistemology (Harding 1986) are profoundly contested (McLennon 1995). While Harding (1986, 1991) considers that a standpoint epistemology, based on women's experiences, is a route to improved objectivity, Nelson (1990) argues for a revised feminist empiricism based on Quine. However, since science is neither a mirror of nature nor a mirror of culture, neither absolutist position is tenable. Rather, it is necessary to utilize the methods of science, piecing together evidence and theories in socially located networks.

Globalization and development

There has long been a gender analysis in development studies (Moser 1993). This is now frequently framed by the debates on globalization. The analysis of the international and development as gendered processes includes: the relationship between women in the First and Third Worlds (Mies 1986; Mitter 1986); whether economic development is necessarily or likely to improve or make worse the position of women (Moghadam 1996); women's relationship to national projects, world religions and states (Kandiyoti 1991); and women's engagement with the rise of fundamentalism (Afshar 1998). The way that increasingly powerful international bodies, such as the World Bank, the World Trade Organization, and the United Nations, affect the gendered strategies available in specific locations is a newly developing area of gender studies. These bodies both enhance the power of global capital and yet also facilitate global feminist networking (Walby 2000). These developments add a new twist to the debates on diversity within feminist theory, since no community can be hermetically sealed; all are connected and thus ultimately comparable. In such a new context the local is always already framed by the global, and a retreat to local specificity can never be a full answer.

Institutional development

The sociology of gender and women's studies are key areas of research, teaching and publishing in the UK. Gender issues are now seen as important in most current theoretical debates, from class analysis to cultural studies to the new debates on globalization. Few social phenomena are now seen as entirely ungendered.

There has been a rapid development of diverse institutional forms in this area. Its mode of academic institutionalization ranges from separate centres to integration into mainstream programmes. Women's studies has a history of experimentation, diversity and change. The analysis of gender relations has taken place both as an integrated part of sociology and as sub-units or entirely independent centres of women's studies. During the early 1990s there was a major development of stand-alone programmes of women's studies/gender studies. In the later 1990s some of these programmes were withdrawn. At the same time the gender questions have been much more routinely mainstreamed into the general sociology curriculum.

The developments in the UK were initially led from the bottom, with high-level support a rarity (though the support of the British Sociological Association may be regarded as an important exception to this). This contrasts sharply with developments in several other countries where governments and research foundations have funded developments, such as the Ford Foundation's support for women's research centres in the US;

the Canadian, Norwegian and Dutch governments' creation of chairs in women's studies; and the Swedish research council for social sciences and humanities' creation of women's studies fellowships. The sociology of gender has made rapid advances in the UK, despite the variable institutional response. The publishing industry took up the new area with alacrity, creating specialist lists within existing publishers, setting up new journals and establishing new publishers.

The increasing methodological pluralism within the sociology of gender is a welcome development. While small-scale qualitative studies abound, large datasets which contain material useful to the analysis of gender are few. Most existing large datasets contain information on gender which is at best primitive in relation to the sophistication of the theories and questions in the field. This lack of basic data can be found in most areas: for instance, the extent of job segregation at the level of the workplace (despite the collection of workplace-level data by the Employment Department); the spread and range of equal opportunities policies (despite the existence of the Workplace Industrial Relations Survey); and the prevalence of the various forms of male violence (despite the British Crime Survey).

Gender analysis is being mainstreamed into the sociology curriculum and research programmes. The existence of gender analysis depends less significantly upon specialized units for its existence. This is a sign of the success and maturity of the field, even though the loss of some of the dedicated programmes might be regretted. However, large-scale research funds have yet to be allocated to this area in the UK, unlike in some other countries, and despite the significance of gender in the curriculum. This is especially problematic in those areas for which the collection of large-scale data is needed. Gender mainstreaming is far from complete.

References

Aaron, Jane and Walby, Sylvia (eds) (1991) *Out of the Margins: Women's Studies in the Nineties*, London: Falmer Press.

Adkins, Lisa (1994) *Gender Families and Work*, Milton Keynes: Open University Press.

Afshar, Haleh (1998) *Islam and Feminisms: An Iranian Case-Study*, Basingstoke: Macmillan.

Alcoff, Linda (1988) 'Cultural feminism versus post-structuralism: the identity crisis in feminist theory', *Signs* 13: 405–36.

Barrett, Michele and Phillips, Ann (eds) (1992) *Destabilizing Theory*, Cambridge: Polity Press.

Bell, Diane and Klein, Renate (eds) (1996) *Radically Speaking: Feminism Reclaimed*, London: Zed.

Bhopal, Kalwant (1997) *Gender, 'Race' and Patriarchy: A Study of South Asian Women* Aldershot: Ashgate.

Blackburn, Robert, Jarman, Jennifer and Siltanen, Janet (1993) 'The analysis of occupational gender segregation over time and place: considerations of measurement and some new evidence', *Work, Employment and Society* 7 (3): 335–62.

Brah, Avtar and Shaw, Sobia (1992) *Working Choices: South Asian Young Muslim Women and the Labour Market*, Department of Employment research paper no. 91, London: Department of Employment.

Butler, Judith (1990) *Gender Trouble*, London: Routledge.

Cockburn, Cynthia (1983) *Brothers: Male Dominance and Technological Change*, London: Pluto Press.

Cockburn, Cynthia (1991) *In the Way of Women: Men's Resistance to Sex Equality in Organisations*, London: Macmillan.

Coward, Rosalind (1984) *Female Desire*, London: Granada.

Crompton, Rosemary and Mann, Michael (eds) (1986) *Gender and Stratification*, Cambridge: Polity Press.

Delphy, Christine and Leonard, Diana (1992) *Familial Exploitation*, Cambridge: Polity Press.

Dobash, R.E. and Dobash, R.P. (1979) *Violence Against Wives: A Case Against the Patriarchy*, Shepton Mallet: Open Books.

Dobash, R.P., Dobash, R.E., Wilson, M. and Daly, M. (1992) 'The myth of sexual symmetry in marital violence', *Social Problems* 39 (1): 71–91.

England, Paula (1992) *Comparable Worth: Theories and Evidence*, New York: Aldine de Gruyter.

Erikson, Robert and Goldthorpe, John H. (1992) *The Constant Flux: A Study of Class Mobility in Industrial Societies*, Oxford: Clarendon Press.

Esping-Andersen, Gosta (1990) *The Three Worlds of Welfare Capitalism*, Cambridge: Polity Press.

Evans, Mary (1991) 'The problem of gender for Women's Studies', in Jane Aaron and Sylvia Walby (eds) *Out of the Margins: Women's Studies in the Nineties*, London: Falmer Press.

Felski, Rita (1997) 'The doxa of difference', *Signs* 23 (1): 1–22.

Finch, Janet (1992) *Family Obligations*, Cambridge: Polity Press.

Firestone, Shulamith (1974) *The Dialectic of Sex: The Case for Feminist Revolution*, New York: Morrow.

Folbre, Nancy (1994) *Who Pays for the Kids? Gender and the Structures of Constraint*, London: Routledge.

Ford, R. and Millar, J. (eds) (1998) *Public Lives and Private Responses – Lone Parenthood and Future Policy in the UK*, London: Policy Studies Institute.

Franklin, Sarah, Lury, Celia and Stacey, Jackie (eds) (1991) *Off-Centre: Feminism and Cultural Studies*, London: HarperCollins.

Fraser, Nancy (1995) 'From redistribution to recognition? Dilemmas of justice in a 'post-socialist' age', *New Left Review* 212: 68–93.

Fraser, Nancy and Nicolson, Linda (1988) 'Social criticism without philosophy: an encounter between feminism and postmodernism', *Theory, Culture and Society* 5: 373–94.

Fuss, Joanna (1989) *Essentially Speaking: Feminism, Nature and Difference*, New York: Routledge.

Gardiner, Jean (1997) *Gender, Care and Economics*, Basingstoke: Macmillan.

Gershuny, Jonathan (1983) *Social Innovation and the Division of Labour*, Oxford: Oxford University Press.

Giddens, Anthony (1984) *The Constitution of Society*, Cambridge: Polity Press.

Giddens, Anthony (1992) *The Transformation of Intimacy: Sexuality, Love and Eroticism in Modern Societies*, Cambridge: Polity Press.

Goldthorpe, John (1983) 'Women and class analysis: a defence of the conventional view', *Sociology* 17 (4): 465–88.

Gregory, Jeanne (1987) *Sex, Race and the Law: Legislating for Equality*, London: Sage.

Gregory, Jeanne (1999) 'Revisiting the sex equality laws', in Sylvia Walby (ed.) *New Agendas for Women*, Basingstoke: Macmillan.

Hakim, Catherine (1992) 'Explaining trends in occupational segregation: the measurement, causes and consequences of the sexual division of labour', *European Sociological Review* 8 (2): 127–52.

Hanmer, Jalna and Maynard, Mary (eds) (1987) *Women. Violence and Social Control*, London: Macmillan.

Hanmer, Jalna and Saunders, Sheila (1984) *Well-Founded Fear: A Community Study of Violence to Women*, London: Hutchinson.

Haraway, Donna (1989) *Primate Visions*, New York: Routledge.

Haraway, Donna (1997) *Modest_Witness@Second_Millennium.FemaleMan_Meets-Oncomouse: Feminism and Technoscience*, New York: Routledge.

Harding, Sandra (1986) *The Science Question in Feminism*, Ithaca: Cornell University Press.

Harding, Sandra (1991) *Whose Science? Whose Knowledge? Thinking from Women's Lives*, Milton Keynes: Open University Press.

Hawkesworth, Mary (1997) 'Confounding gender', *Signs* 22 (3): 649–85.

Hearn, Jeff (1992) *Men in the Public Eye: The Construction and Deconstruction of Public Men and Public Patriarchies*, London: Routledge.

Hearn, Jeff and Parkin, Wendy (1987) *'Sex' at 'Work': The Power and Paradox of Organisation Sexuality*, Brighton: Wheatsheaf.

Hinds, Hilary, Phoenix, Ann and Stacey, Jackie (eds) (1992) *Working Out: New Directions for Women's Studies*, London: Falmer Press.

hooks, bell (1984) *Feminist Theory: From Margin to Center*, Boston: South End Press.

Hoskyns, Catherine (1996) *Integrating Gender: Women, Law and Politics in the European Union*, London: Verso.

Irwin, S. (1995) *Rights of Passage – Social Change and the Transition from Youth to Adulthood*, London: UCL Press.

Jackson, Stevi (1999) *Heterosexuality in Question*, London: Sage.

Jeffreys, Sheila (1990) *Anticlimax: a Feminist Perspective on the Sexual Revolution*, London: Women's Press.

Johnson, Holly (1996) *Dangerous Domains – Violence Against Women in Canada*, Toronto: Nelson Canada.

Kandiyoti, Deniz (1988) 'Bargaining with patriarchy', *Gender and Society* 2 (3): 274–90.

Kandiyoti, Deniz (ed.) (1991) *Women, Islam and the State*, Basingstoke: Macmillan.

Kappeler, Suzanne (1986) *The Pornography of Representation*, Cambridge: Polity Press.

Kelly, Liz (1988) *Surviving Sexual Violence*, Cambridge: Polity Press.

Kelly, Liz, Regan, Linda and Burton, Sheila (1992) 'Defending the indefensible? Quantitative methods and feminist research', in Hilary Hinds, Ann Phoenix and Jackie Stacey (eds) *Working Out: New Directions for Women's Studies*, London: Falmer Press.

Kennedy, Mary, Lubelska, Cathy and Walsh, Val (eds) (1993) *Making Connections*, London: Taylor and Francis.

Kuhn, Annette (1982) *Women's Pictures: Feminism and Cinema*, London, Routledge.

Lees, Sue (1993) *Sugar and Spice: Sexuality and Adolescent Girls*, Harmondsworth: Penguin.

Lister, Ruth (1997) *Citizenship: Feminist Perspectives*, Basingstoke: Macmillan.

Lovenduski, Joni and Randall, Vicky (1993) *Contemporary Feminist Politics: Women and Power in Britain*, Oxford: Oxford University Press.

Marshall, Gordon, Newby, Howard; Rose, David and Vogler, Carolyn (1988) *Social Class in Modern Britain*, London: Hutchinson.

McLennan, Greg (1995) 'Feminism, epistemology and postmodernism: Reflections on current ambivalence', *Sociology* 29 (2): 391–409.

McNay, Lois (1992) *Foucault and Feminism: Power, Gender and the Self*, Cambridge: Polity Press.

McRobbie, Angela and Nava, Mica (eds) (1984) *Gender and Generation*, Basingstoke: Macmillan.

Meehan, Elizabeth and Sevenhuijsen, Selma (eds) (1991) *Equality Politics and Gender*, London: Sage.

Mies, Maria (1986) *Patriarchy and Accumulation on a World Scale*, London: Zed.

Mirrlees-Black, C. (1999) *Domestic Violence: Findings from a New British Crime Survey Self-completion Questionnaire*. Home Office research study 191, London: Home Office.

Mirza, Heidi Safia (ed.) (1997) *Black British Feminism: A Reader*, London: Routledge.

Mitchell, Juliet (1975) *Psychoanalysis and Feminism*, Harmondsworth: Penguin.

Mitter, Swasti (1986) *Common Fate: Common Bond*, London: Pluto Press.

Moghadam, Valentine M. (ed.) (1996) *Patriarchy and Development: Women's Positions at the End of the Twentieth Century*, Oxford: Clarendon Press.

Mohanty, Chandra Talpade (1991) 'Under western eyes: feminist scholarship and colonial discourses', in Chandra Talpade Mohanty, Ann Russo and Lourdes Torres (eds) *Third World Women and the Politics of Feminism*, Bloomington: Indiana University Press.

Morgan, David H.J. (1992) *Discovering Men*, London: Routledge.

Moser, Caroline, O.N. (1993) *Gender Planning and Development: Theory, Practice and Training*, London: Routledge.

Nelson, Lynn Hankinson (1990) *Who Knows: From Quine to a Feminist Empiricism*, Philadelphia: Temple University Press.

Norris, Pippa and Lovenduski, Joni (1995) *Political Recruitment: Gender, Race and Class in the British Parliament*, Cambridge: Cambridge University Press.

O'Connor, Julia S., Orloff, Ann Shola and Shaver, Sheila (1999) *States, Markets, Families: Gender, Liberalism and Social Policy in Australia, Canada, Great Britain and the United States*, Cambridge: Cambridge University Press.

O'Reilly, Jacqueline and Fagan, Colette (eds) (1998) *Part-Time Prospects: An International Comparison of Part-Time Work in Europe, North America and the Pacific Rim*, London: Routledge.

Orloff, Ann Shola (1993) 'Gender and the social rights of citizenship: State policies and gender relations in comparative perspective', *American Sociological Review* 58 (3): 303–28.

Phizacklea, Annie (1990) *Unpacking the Fashion Industry*, London: Routledge.

Phizacklea, Annie and Wolkowitz, Carol (1995) *Homeworking Women: Gender Racism and Class at Work*, London: Sage.

Phoenix, Ann (1991) *Young Mothers?* Cambridge: Polity Press.

Pillinger, Jane (1992) *Feminising the Market: Women's Pay and Employment in the European Community*, Basingstoke: Macmillan.

Plummer, Ken (1975) *Sexual Stigma: An Interactionist Account*, London: Routledge.

Pringle, Rosemary (1989) *Secretaries Talk: Sexuality, Power and Work*, London: Verso.

Proctor, I. (1999) *Life Course Variation Among Young Adult Women: Workers and/or Mothers?* www.warwick.ac.uk/fac/soc/sociology.html.

Ramanzanoglu, Caroline (ed.) (1991) *Up Against Foucault: Explorations of Some Tensions Between Foucault and Feminism*, London: Routledge.

Ramirez, F.O., Soysal, Y. and Shanahan, S. (1997) 'The changing logic of political citizenship: cross-national acquisition of women's suffrage rights, 1890–1990', *American Sociological Review* 62: 735–45.

Rees, Teresa (1998) *Mainstreaming Equality in the European Union: Education, Training and Labour Market Policies*, London: Routledge.

Reinharz, Shulamit (1993) *Feminist Methods in Social Research*, New York: Oxford University Press.

Rose, Hilary (1994) *Love, Power and Knowledge: Towards a Feminist Transformation of the Sciences*, Cambridge: Polity Press.

Rubery, Jill, Smith, Mark and Fagan, Colette (1999) *Women's Employment in Europe: Trends and Prospects*, London: Routledge.

Sainsbury, Diane (1996) *Gender Equality and Welfare States*, Cambridge: Cambridge University Press.

Saunders, D.G. (1988) 'Wife abuse, husband abuse, or mutual combat? In K. Yllo and M. Bograd (eds) *Feminist Perspectives on Wife Abuse*, California: Sage.

Scott, Alison (ed.) (1994) *Gender Segregation and Social Change*, Oxford: Oxford University Press.

Scott, Joan W. (1988) 'Deconstructing equality-versus-difference: or, the uses of post-structuralist theory for feminism', *Feminist Studies* 14 (1): 33–49.

Segal, Lynne (1987) *Is the Future Female? Troubled Thoughts on Contemporary Feminism*, London: Virago.

Shiva, Vandana (1989) *Staying Alive: Women, Ecology and Development*, London: Zed.

Showstack Sassoon, Anne (ed.) (1987) *Women and the State: The Shifting Boundaries of Public and Private*, London: Hutchinson.

Squires, Judith (1999) 'Re-thinking the boundaries of political representation', in Sylvia Walby (ed.) *New Agendas for Women*, Basingstoke: Macmillan.

Stanworth, Michelle (1984) 'Women and class analysis: a reply to John Goldthorpe', *Sociology* 18 (2): 159–70.

Stanworth, Michelle (ed.) (1987) *Reproductive Technologies: Gender, Motherhood and Medicine*, Cambridge: Polity Press.

Straus, Murray A. and Gelles, R.J. (eds) (1990) *Physical Violence in American Families*, New Brunswick NJ: Transaction Publishers.

Taylor-Browne, Julie (ed.) (2000) *Reducing Domestic Violence: What Works?* London: The Stationery Office.

Turner, Bryan (1984) *The Body and Society: Explorations in Social Theory*, Oxford: Blackwell.

Walby, Sylvia (1990) *Theorizing Patriarchy*, Oxford: Blackwell.

Walby, Sylvia (1992) 'Post-postmodernism: theorizing social complexity', in Michele Barrett and Anne Phillips (eds) *Destabilizing Theory: Contemporary Feminist Debates*, Cambridge: Polity Press.

Walby, Sylvia (1997) *Gender Transformations*, London: Routledge.

Walby, Sylvia (ed.) (1999a) *New Agendas for Women*, Basingstoke: Macmillan.

Walby, Sylvia (1999b) 'The new regulatory state: the social powers of the European Union', *British Journal of Sociology* 50 (1): 118–40.

Walby, Sylvia (2000) 'Gender, globalization and democracy', *Gender and Development* 8 (1): 20–8.

Walby, Sylvia and Myhill, Andrew (2000) 'Assessing and managing the risk of domestic violence', in Julie Taylor-Browne (ed.) *Reducing Domestic Violence: What Works?* London: The Stationery Office.

Weeks, Jeffrey (1985) *Sexuality and its Discontents: Meanings, Myths and Modern Sexualities*, London: Routledge.

Weeks, Jeffrey (1995) *Invented Moralities: Sexual Values in an Age of Uncertainty*, Cambridge: Polity Press.

Westwood, Sallie (1984) *All Day Everyday: Factory and Family in the Making of Women's Lives*, London: Pluto Press.

Winship, Janice (1985) ' "A girl needs to be streetwise": magazines for the 1980', *Feminist Review* 21: 25–46.

Witz, Anne (1992) *Professions and Patriarchy*, London: Routledge.

Young, Iris (1990) *Justice and the Politics of Difference*, Princeton NJ: Princeton University Press.

Yuval-Davis, Nira (1997) *Gender and Nation*, London: Sage.

part 2

Substantive areas

chapter 7

Developments in the sociology of religion

James A. Beckford

Introduction

It seemed to me in the mid-1980s that the sociology of religion in advanced industrial societies had become isolated from, and insulated against, the issues that were of interest to most social scientists (Beckford 1985). It was mainly preoccupied with such things as the dynamics of religious organizations, the concepts of church, sect and cult, and the specificity of religious conversion experiences. The theoretical backdrop to these issues was dominated by assumptions about the demise, decline or marginalization of religion in conditions of modernity. By the end of the 1980s, however, my view (Beckford 1989) was that theoretical and empirical developments among sociologists of religion and others were beginning to bring the study of religion closer to the mainstream of social science. I want to argue in this chapter that the last decade of the twentieth century has seen an acceleration of the process of rapprochement between the study of religion and other fields of sociology. In other words, religion has regained a place of importance on the sociological agenda partly because sociologists of religion have moved beyond their 'in-house' preoccupations and partly because other social scientists have come to find religion more intriguing as an object of analysis.

In order to substantiate my claim that the study of religion has become more important for sociologists in recent years I intend firstly to discuss a series of conceptual shifts which tend to frame religion in new or more challenging ways. They include fresh thinking about identity, gender, the body and 'global' society. My second aim is to chart the latest developments of critical thinking about the notion of secularization. My necessarily selective review of these developments will focus on applications of rational choice theory and on the notion of the 'restructuring of religion'.

Identity

Disputes about the definition of religion are a constant feature of attempts to account for religious phenomena in sociological terms (Platvoet and Molendijk 1999). Yet, a common thread running through most definitions is the acknowledgement that religion is one of the sources of human identity in the sense that many human beings locate themselves in relation to absolute notions of time, history and ultimately sovereign powers such as gods, spirits and supernatural forces.

One strand of thinking among sociologists of religion has tended to limit the notion of identity to questions about individuals' commitment to particular groups or belief systems (Luckmann 1967; Mol 1976). A different strand of thinking about identity in relation to religion has oriented research towards cultural and collective aspects of the topic. It is this strand that has generated the most significant developments in the sociology of religion in recent years. Following the 'cultural turn' in sociology, interest has grown in the diversity of religious resources on which social collectivities can draw in the continuous negotiation of their identity in relation to other collectivities. Ethnographic studies of a black-led Pentecostal church in Birmingham (Toulis 1997) and of young Muslim adults in London (Jacobson 1998) are representative of this approach. They support Hetherington's (1998: 6) claim that 'the relationship between expressivism, belonging and identity is a major feature of the quest for identity that runs throughout modern societies'.

The range of explanations for the salience of issues concerning religious identity at the end of the twentieth century is wide. One possibility is to explain it in terms of the 'return of the repressed' (Giddens 1991) in conditions of late modernity. A second possibility is to attribute it to defensive reactions against the global forces that favour the individualization of identity (Castells 1997). Strong communities of religious believers are therefore said to defend their values or meanings by huddling together in 'cultural communes' or safe havens where religious identity functions as a refuge from, and a protection against, global disorder and rapid social change. Muslim 'fundamentalism' supposedly serves as the clearest example of processes whereby

[a] new identity is being constructed, not by returning to tradition, but by working on traditional materials in the formation of a new godly, communal world, where deprived masses and disaffected intellectuals may reconstruct meaning in a global alternative to the exclusionary social order.

(Castells 1997: 20)

Contrary to superficial appearances, however, many so-called fundamentalist religious groups do not represent a restoration of tradition. Instead, they represent a characteristically modern project of stripping away the layers of tradition in the belief that they can establish a way of life based on the pristine principles underlying their particular faith (Bruce 1984; Parekh 1991).

This view is not easily compatible, however, with the third possibility of explaining religious identity in conditions of modernity, which is encapsulated in Danièle Hervieu-Léger's (1993a, 1999) thesis that religion necessarily involves reference to long chains of collective memory. Indeed, she places belief in the continuity of lineages of believers at the very centre of the religious life. And, although she recognizes that modernity threatens this continuity, her claim is nevertheless that new ways of making connections with religious traditions are gaining in popularity. For example, new styles of pilgrimage and fresh notions of religious conversion are taken as evidence of the persistence and the adaptation of religion to ostensibly unpromising circumstances. Religion may be in decline as an obligatory, communal way of living, but this is counterbalanced by the increase in ways of being religious as the result of deliberate, voluntary, personal commitment to religious values and beliefs still rooted in collective memory (Hervieu-Léger 1999).

The range of issues on which collective religious identity has a direct bearing is extremely wide, but outstanding research has cast fresh light on, for example, 'culture wars' in the US between conservative and liberal opinion on the family, education, the media and the law (Hunter 1991), sectarian tensions in Northern Ireland (Bruce and Wallis 1992), communal relations in Singapore (Hill and Lian 1995), and competition between Protestants and Catholics in Latin America (Martin 1990; Lehmann 1996). Among the most significant developments has been a concern to map the subtle relations between religion and ethnic identity in countries where immigration in the latter half of the twentieth century has increased religious diversity and led to the consolidation of extensive faith communities of Buddhists, Hindus, Muslims and Sikhs among others. The different political, legal, economic, religious and social institutions in Britain (Vertovec 1996; Bhatt 1997; Beckford and Gilliat 1998), France (Kepel 1987, 1994;

Khosrokhavar 1997; Saint-Blancat 1997; Boyer 1998; Césari 1998) and Germany (Tibi 1998, 1999) have made the religious identity of minority communities salient in different ways. Extensive immigration from developing countries into western Europe (Nielsen 1992) and the change of regimes in countries formerly under the sway of the Soviet Union (Weigel 1992) have both underlined the necessity for sociologists to take seriously the contribution of collective religious identity towards the struggles for communal autonomy, cultural influence and public respect (Davie and Hervieu-Léger 1996).

Research in the US has tended to pay less attention to the broadly political relevance of religious identity among settled communities of migrants and more attention towards processes of cultural adaptation and institution building. For example, research on 'ethnic congregations' among Christians, Jews, Muslims and Hindus (Warner and Wittner 1997) has clearly demonstrated the importance of local congregations as communal vehicles not only for religious identity but also for integration into civil society. Questions remain unanswered, however, about the members of minority communities who do not want to associate with these ethnic congregations and about the potential for competition and conflict between them.

Contrary to simplistic versions of the secularization thesis, questions about religious identity at the individual and collective levels loom increasingly large in discussions of many societies in the late twentieth century. This is especially true of societies in which ethnic and religious identities are superimposed (Modood *et al.* 1994). Consequently, the 'politics of identity' cannot be adequately comprehended unless due account is taken of the extent to which religion serves as a marker of collective identity (Hanf 1994).

Gender

In common with many other branches of sociology, the sociological study of religion was slow to grasp the significance of gender as a factor affecting virtually all aspects of the phenomenon. Moreover, although the gendered aspects of religion are now the focus of extensive research, especially in North America, the sociology of religion shows relatively few signs of influence from feminist perspectives (King 1994). For my purposes, feminist perspectives share assumptions about men's systematic exploitation of women (with the consequence that gender inequalities are considered endemic in societies) and about the capacity of women to change their collective situation by fostering solidarity and empowering themselves.

The first impact of these ideas on sociological studies of religion was to raise the question of why so little attention had been given to women in analyses of, for example, religious organizations, church and sect typologies, conversion processes and secularization (Hargrove 1985; Neitz 1993; Wallace 1996, 1997). For the tendency had been to equate men with all human beings and to assume that separate analysis of women's interests and experience was unnecessary. Subsequent studies have examined, for example, the degree to which women are religious (Walter and Davie 1998) and enjoy opportunities for full participation in mainstream churches (Aldridge 1989, 1992; Wallace 1992) and orthodox Judaism (Davidman 1991; Davidman and Greil 1993) as well as the ordination of women (Lehman 1985, 1993; Chaves 1997) and the impact of women's ordination on churches (Nesbitt 1997).

Secondly, the practice has developed of routinely asking questions about the gendered character of religion – not only as a set of practices and relationships but also as distinctive experiences, beliefs and feelings (Plaskow and Christ 1989; King 1994; Madsen 1994; Winter et al. 1994). A case has also been made for the distinctiveness of women-only or women-centred religious groups in which female spirits or goddesses are worshipped (Gunn 1986; Neitz 1990) or in which healing rituals draw upon varieties of ancient, pagan or witchcraft wisdom (McGuire 1988; Jacobs 1989, 1990; Neitz 1994; Berger 1999). There are strong connections between these interests in women's spirituality and broader analysis of the 'New Age' (Bednarowski 1992; Puttick 1999). This is a convenient but contested label for the richly diverse and loosely structured complex of values, beliefs, practices and businesses which all turn around optimistic claims that human beings can discover ways of feeling 'whole' and fulfilled by establishing the correct balance between the social world, the natural world and their own 'inner' being (York 1995; Heelas 1996).

A concern with the gendered aspects of new religious movements (NRMs) has also begun to burgeon (Davidman and Jacobs 1993; Palmer 1993). Interest is strong, for example, in women's reasons for joining NRMs (Palmer 1994), in the unequal distribution of power and authority between male and female members (Jacobs 1984, 1989, 1991; Wessinger 1993; Puttick 1996, 1999) and in sex-role segregation (Aidala 1985; Nason-Clark 1987; Puttick and Clarke 1993; Knott 1995).

A fourth dimension of sociological studies of gender and religion concerns the fact that some women feel drawn to participate in conservative religious organizations where their position seems inherently subordinate to men's. Women's participation has been analyzed in conservative Christian churches (Ammerman 1987; Rose 1987; Poloma 1989; Hawley 1994; Toulis 1997), conservative Jewish organizations (Davidman 1991; Kaufman 1991) and Islam (Khosrokhavar 1997; Jacobson 1998). The findings seem to support Somerville's (1997) argument that, while many feminists and anti-feminists come from similar social and cultural backgrounds, religion discriminates between them. Being active in religion is characteristic of anti-feminists who, in most other respects, have similar backgrounds to those of feminists.

The body

It became fashionable in the 1980s to argue that sociology's preoccupation with the cognitive, social or cultural bases of social life had produced two unfortunate implications for any attempt to appreciate the significance of the fact that human beings had physical bodies. It either neglected the relevance of human corporeality for social action; or it denied that corporeality was relevant to explanations of social and cultural life. Yet, studies of religion had examined, for example, bodily manifestations of spirit possession or altered states of consciousness, and of relations between religion and diet, sexuality, eroticism, well-being, healing, illness, ageing, asceticism, suicide and sport. In fact, the sociology of religion was actually in advance of other branches of sociology to some extent (Turner 1981), but the framing of religion and the human body as a specific topic for research certainly began to acquire a higher profile when it became fashionable to analyze many other areas of cultural and social life in terms of embodiment.

The most ambitious theoretical framework for highlighting the centrality of human bodies to religion is the claim, advanced separately and together, by Mellor and Shilling that the historical development of Christianity has had a decisive effect on changes in the dominant image of human bodies (Shilling 1993, 1997; Mellor and Shilling 1994, 1997). Their argument is that medieval Catholicism yielded in the early modern period to Protestant forms of sociality based on contractual commitments and that in late modernity these purely cognitive commitments became banal and self-referential. Western societies are now said to be at a stage of development when the sensual effervescent, bodily, expressive forms of association are threatening to rebel against banality and to interfere with the 'controlled, ordered lives of the middle classes' (Mellor and Shilling 1997: 199). If modernity continues to ignore or repress sensuality, a sense of the sacred may allegedly erupt in the kind of volatile, carnal forms which characterized life in the European Middle Ages.

It is difficult to reconcile this interpretation with Giddens' (1991) argument that the popularity of old-time religion and New Age spirituality can be explained in terms of, respectively, the search for moral certainties in an age when certainties are in very short supply and the fashion for self-monitoring in an age dominated by expert systems. Indeed, the 'sequestration' of emotion is cited by Giddens as a feature of late modernity: not Dionysian, carnal effervescence (Maffesoli 1988).

Healing practices have a prominent place in most religious traditions, and sociologists have paid special attention to healing in Pentecostalism (McGuire 1982; Cohen 1995), 'wicca' or witchcraft (Warwick 1995; Berger 1999, 2000), the New Age (Beckford 1984; McGuire 1988; Beckford and Suzara 1994; Foltz 1994; Hedges and Beckford 1999), spiritism (Pereira de Queiroz 1989) and sectarian movements (Dericquebourg 1988). Relatively few scholars have focused primarily on the bodily techniques of religious and spiritual healers, but their analyses of the belief systems underlying the healing practices testify to the rich diversity of ideas about the complex relations between the body, health and illness.

Just as the sociology of religion has always had an implicit interest in human bodies as sites of transcendent experiences and as objects of transformative rituals, so it has also had a longstanding, if slight, concern with emotions (Hervieu-Léger 1993b). Indeed, strong feelings of effervescence, awe, mystery, fear, adoration and powerfulness are widely regarded either as the raw material from which institutionalized religions were originally fashioned or as the deep wellsprings from which individuals draw their religious inspiration. This is reflected in studies of 'religious experience' that tend to isolate 'peak' or special feelings as a distinct category, thereby perhaps giving the misleading impression that this is the only aspect of religion in which emotion is involved. For example, the social production and management of emotions involved in Pentecostal and charismatic experiences have been studied in the setting of American Catholicism (McGuire 1982) and British Protestantism (Walker and Atherton 1971). Research on the patterns of emotions associated with the full range of religious actions and events is relatively rare, however. Nevertheless, studies of death, dying, grieving and funerals have begun to analyze the associated patterns of emotion, some of which have religious resonance (Williams 1990; Hockey 1993).

Yet, there is scope for further sociological examination of the patterned emotions associated with the routine aspects of mainstream religions. For example, the social management of feelings of solemnity, joy, peace, cleanliness and love in routine religious practices and ceremonies is no less interesting than are altered states of consciousness and ecstatic experiences. Agnès Rochefort-Turquin's (1990) exploration of how emotions were managed in a wing of the Action Catholique movement in France is a model of research on the social production of emotions congruent with the ideology of a mainstream religious organization.

Globalization

In so far as sociologists have explored the implications of identity, gender and the body for religion, they have been following the contour lines of mainstream sociology in advanced industrial societies. This is also true of work on globalization and religion, but with one important difference. The very notion of globalization has its origins in reflections on the status of religion in modernity. Roland Robertson's earliest sketches of the concept (Robertson 1985, 1989; Robertson and Chirico 1985), especially the attempt to emphasize its distinctiveness from notions of a world system, were intended to show that globalization had a specifically religious significance. Why? The answer was that, as the world was experienced as a progressively smaller place in the wake of accelerated communication and interaction between states and trans-national corporations, debate about the meaning of 'humanity' intensified. The world's religious traditions are primary sources of symbols with which to capture the meaning of humanity but they are said to need adapting to a new situation in which ethnic, religious and national boundaries are all put under pressure by higher-level concerns with 'the human' as the ultimate mark of identity. Religious responses may be particularistic (for example, fundamentalisms) or universalistic (for example, New Age spiritualities or eco-theologies) or, conceivably, both simultaneously (for example, religious movements such as the Baha'is with a mission to create globe-wide communities of the faithful (Warburg 1999)). In other words, even particularistic or local religious ideologies are obliged to respond to pressures from the 'global circumstance' if only to deflect or refract them into an image of their own distinctiveness in an increasingly globalized world.

The global dimension of religion has been highlighted in research on, for example, the Islamic revolution in Iran (Beyer 1994), fundamentalisms in various parts of the world (Lechner 1993; Brouwer *et al.* 1996; Castells 1997; Kürti 1997) and communal tensions in India (Bhatt 1997). Many of the findings are convincing, but, as with so many other aspects of the sociology of religion, they relate mainly to marginal and/or extreme phenomena. The impact of global forces on mainstream religious organizations is not yet central to the research agenda, although there is ample scope for investigations of global flows of theological and pastoral ideas, religious professionals and organizational practices.

Evidence of a rapprochement between the sociology of religion and mainstream sociology is emerging from studies of identity, the body, gender and globalization. The findings of research on these topics show that there is much to be gained from exploring their mutual relations with religion. These particular developments in the sociology of religion indicate that religion cannot be safely ignored in attempts to understand social and cultural change at the dawn of the twenty-first century. The next section will ask whether recent theoretical developments in the sociology of religion are equally innovative and consonant with developments in other branches of sociology.

Developments in theoretical ideas

It is commonplace to claim that debates about secularization have virtually dominated the sociology of religion. The debates have subsequently gone through all manner of twists and turns, but the central issue has not changed. It is whether the advent of modernity set in train processes that would remove religion's capacity to shape important societal values, social institutions and individual life courses. Ideas about secularization are diverse and complex but they amount to the 'master frame' or ruling paradigm within which most research in the sociology of religion has been generated. Since the 1960s, however, numerous attempts have been made to dismantle or bypass the secularization framework in favour of theoretical ideas that claim that it is a mistake to think of religion as necessarily in decline.[1] In the space available here I shall outline only two such attempts to move beyond the secularization problematic.

Rational choice theory

The advocates of rational choice theory (RCT) define religion as rational in so far as its practitioners believe that the associated benefits outweigh the associated costs. But whereas many of the rewards that humans pursue in their everyday life are specific and practical benefits in the here-and-now, others are so general and intangible that they have to be postponed to the distant future. Thus, 'So long as humans intensely seek certain rewards of great magnitude that remain unavailable through direct actions, they will be able to obtain credible compensators only from sources predicated on the supernatural' (Stark and Bainbridge 1985: 7–8). Religions are therefore understood as human organizations for 'providing general compensators based on supernatural assumptions' (Stark and Bainbridge 1985: 8). This relatively new theoretical perspective on religion has made two distinctive contributions to the sociology of religion possible. The first concerns new ways of thinking about old issues. The second concerns new insights into the conditions favouring the persistence of religious activity.

1.   We have known since the early 1970s that the rate of adherence to liberal Christian denominations in the US and elsewhere was declining and that relatively demanding, conservative denominations were growing. Iannaccone (1988, 1990, 1992, 1994) has been able to provide a clear, theoretically based explanation for these phenomena by invoking RCT. Adapting the logic of the free-rider principle, he reasoned that levels of participation in a church are likely to vary positively with the demands that are made on members' time, resources and commitments. By contrast, churches that permit members to participate without investing heavily in these respects are likely to deter potential members who would be put off by the thought that the non-committed would get away with a free ride.

Rational choice theorists have also deconstructed and reconstructed such well-known devices as the church–sect typology, thereby helping to clarify in theoretical terms some of the sociology of religion's stock of existing knowledge. Churches, for example, are said to impose low costs on members and to offer correspondingly low rewards for participation. Sects, on the other hand, are portrayed as organizations that insist that members pay high costs in return for the highly distinctive rewards on offer. This basic typology becomes even more finely calibrated when it comes to cults. Stark and Bainbridge (1985: 30 emphasis original) argue that 'audience cults offer compensators of modest value at a correspondingly modest price . . . Client cults offer valuable, but relatively *specific* compensators . . . Only cult movements offer the most *general* compensators . . . Thus, only cult movements are fully developed religious movements.'

2. RCT perspectives on the historical trajectory of churches and denominations are based on the premise that individual religious actors choose their religious groups in roughly the same way as consumers in an economic market make decisions about goods and services. That is, they optimize the balance between the costs and benefits associated with each option. This means that the collective fortunes of religious organizations competing with each other in the religious market depend largely on the aggregate of choices made by individual, rational actors. Stark (1996: 70) is content to describe this approach as 'reductionism' because it seeks 'to explain as much of the world as possible by reference to as little as possible'.

The historical data that Finke and Stark (1986, 1988, 1989, 1992), Stark and Finke (1988), Finke (1990, 1992) and Stark (1991) have assembled show some surprising tendencies. They suggest, for example, that the proportion of the US population that is affiliated to Christian churches and denominations increased steadily from no more than 30 per cent in the eighteenth century to about 60 per cent at present. This inference from data, which have admittedly aroused some scepticism (Breault 1989; Land *et al.* 1991), casts doubt on some versions of secularization theory. A second finding which challenges received wisdom about a central aspect of modernization is that the rate of membership growth in American churches has been higher in urban than in rural areas. Thirdly, the rate of membership growth is higher in areas where there is greater heterogeneity than homogeneity in religious groups (controlling for the proportion of Catholics). But the most far-reaching claim is that the strength of American churches and denominations derives from the relative lack of governmental regulation of the religious marketplace. Moreover, the theory also anticipates 'not the extinction of religion, but the weakening of some particular religious organisations. The counterbalancing processes of revival and innovation keep religion, in general, alive' (Stark and Bainbridge 1987: 117).

Criticisms of RCT perspectives on religion fall into two broad categories. Firstly, reservations have been expressed about the special way in which RCT construes rationality. There are two main aspects of this critical response. On the one hand, this approach is criticized for going too far beyond Max Weber's strategy of employing rational ideal-types as mere yardsticks for assessing the extent to which actual conduct conforms with, or departs from, hypothetical models of fully rational actors. The accusation is that RCT turns a thoroughly acceptable heuristic device into an unacceptably rigid claim about the allegedly real motives and processes of human action. Critics have also complained that RCT is based on an idea of rationality that is too exclusively instrumental. In other words, different forms of rationality are believed to exist alongside, but separate from, the purely maximizing or optimizing strategy that underlies the assumptions of RCT. There is, for example, a rationality of caring (Waerness 1984) and a rationality of sacrifice (Voyé 1992).

A second cluster of criticisms revolves around the tendency of rational choice theorists to focus their explanations of decision making on the level of *individual* actors and in such a way that the individuals appear to be isolated and purely autonomous. Again, it is admitted that the assumption of individual autonomy *can* serve as a useful heuristic device for aiding the design of testable hypotheses. But rational choice theorists are said to run the risk of appearing to assume that real-life agents actually perform as socially isolated cost–benefit accountants. Critics therefore complain that RCT gives insufficient consideration to the social and cultural forces that shape the agents' perception of costs and benefits.[2]

It is also difficult for some critics to see how the theory can begin to identify or assess the impact of religious organizations on their host societies and culture. Yet, this kind of analysis is surely needed if questions about the waxing or waning significance of religion are to be tackled. In other words, rational choice theorists may be able to account for religiosity at the level of individuals, but it is less clear how they can explain the differential importance of religious organizations in society.

RCT, as applied to the sociology of religion, has not yet reached the status of 'normal science', but at least a dialogue about its status and claims has begun (Robertson 1992a, 1992b; Bruce 1993; Warner 1993, 1997; Young 1997). The new perspective has unsettled some shibboleths and has raised some awkward questions about American religious history. The most pragmatic assessment is Michael Hechter's belief that 'the approach will motivate studies on religion that otherwise never would have been carried out, for it will suggest questions that had never been considered by scholars of religion' (Hechter 1997: 157).

Restructuring of religion

The most extended project to reframe the concept of modernity in order to find a more satisfactory explanation of religious change than theories of secularization provide is the work of Danièle Hervieu-Léger (1986, 1989, 1990, 1992, 1993a, 1993b, 1999) and her associates in France. Their highly distinctive depiction of modernity lends no support to the commonly held view that rationalization will squeeze religion out of social life. On the contrary, their view is that the application of instrumental rationality to more and more spheres of life actually generates new questions, dilemmas and options that call for a religious response. This means that modernity brings about new conditions requiring metaphysical, spiritual or religious responses that go beyond mere technical reason just as surely as it undermines faith in moral absolutes and fixed religious beliefs. The clearest examples concern cultural responses to new reproductive technologies, organ transplants and definitions of life and death. Equally perplexing dilemmas also surround issues of human rights, animal rights, environmental conservation and the uses of nuclear power.

The main theoretical implication of Hervieu-Léger's innovative work is that many of the issues central to secularization theories should either evaporate as non-issues or lose their apparent significance for large-scale social change. She frames her own ideas in terms of the constant *restructuring* of religion. She argues that religion's work is to fill the gap between reality and utopia as the horizon of modernity keeps inexorably receding. Hervieu-Léger's account of religion in modernity is not therefore vulnerable to evidence of decline in religious organizations or in personal religious beliefs because, in her view, there is no reason to expect that religious organizations must be the only agencies for doing the work of religion. She believes that the restructuring of religious symbols, values and motivations can occur independently of religious organizations.

Instead of adopting the rational choice theorists' view that sectarian or cultic innovations will take market share from 'lazy' mainstream churches, Hervieu-Léger's more radical perspective on the restructuring of religion has led her to attach special significance to the allegedly growing popularity of emotional styles of religious practice in various French religious communities. Her collaborative research (Champion and Hervieu-Léger 1990) has identified a return to what they claim to be the pure sources of religion in emotion among Catholic, Jewish (Cohen 1990), mystical (Champion 1990), Islamic (Andezian 1990) and Buddhist (Hourmant 1990) communities in the 1980s. Yet, true to the overarching conception of modernity as contradictory, this wave of emotional religion is interpreted as a subjective re-appropriation of religious traditions. In other words, the authority that used to inhere in 'lineages of belief' (Hervieu-Léger 1993a, 1999) is allegedly being reworked as the basis for a new type of subjectivity that stresses individual autonomy *and* the freedom to choose to be traditional.

This focus on the variety of possibilities for restructuring religion in modernity has the advantage of bypassing most of the discourses of secularization but is also open to two criticisms. The first is that its relevance may be confined to countries that are still emerging from the dominance of a monolithic church. The significance that Hervieu-Léger attaches to emotion and voluntariness, for example, may be less a matter of a return to a primordial basis for all religion and more a matter of a release from a relatively authoritarian, collectivist and hierarchical form of Christianity. In other words, it is not modernity as such which generates emotional religion but, rather, the distinctive character of French Catholicism's tussle with modernity. The second criticism is that a hint of teleological functionalism may attach to Hervieu-Léger's belief that the work of religion can or must continue even when the Roman Catholic Church is in decline. She sometimes appears to believe that the restructuring of the 'field' of religion takes place independently of particular groups or organizations in conformity with high-level societal forces producing social order. What is needed, as a response to both criticisms, is further empirical examination in more than one country of Hervieu-Léger's general arguments.

Conclusion

This survey of recent developments in the sociology of religion has been selective. It is a deliberate selection of contributions that represent relatively new ideas and fresh departures. In particular, I have given priority to developments that offered the prospect of closer ties between the sociology of religion and other fields of sociology. It goes without saying, therefore, that many other contributions have had to be omitted from my survey for the sole reason that they did not feed directly into the areas that I had identified as innovative ways of making the study of religion relevant to important strands of sociological thinking about social change and continuity. There is no doubt that my selection is partial and contestable. I have good grounds for believing, however, that the sociology of religion's prospects for remaining a lively field of debate and investigation will depend heavily on the strength of its intellectual ties to broader discussions about the changing character of social and cultural life. This means not only that sociologists of religion can enhance the quality of their work by keeping broad debates about socio-logic in mind, but also that attempts to explain the developments of socio-cultural systems need to take proper account of the state of religion. This is why the focus of this chapter has deliberately been on intellectual developments at the intersection of general sociology and the sociology of religion.

Notes

1. For a spirited statement of the case against the secularization paradigm, see Warner (1993, 1997). See Wilson (1992) for an equally spirited defence of the 'orthodox' paradigm.
2. Bruce (1993) pays special attention to the lack of a cultural dimension in rational choice perspectives on religions.

References

Aidala, Angela (1985) 'Social change, gender roles, and new religious movements', *Sociological Analysis* 46: 287–314.

Aldridge, Alan (1989) 'Men, women and clergymen: opinion and authority in a sacred congregation', *Sociological Review* 37: 42–63.

Aldridge, Alan (1992) 'Discourse on women in the clerical profession: the diaconate and language-games in the Church of England', *Sociology* 28: 45–57.

Ammerman, Nancy T. (1987) *Bible Believers. Fundamentalists in the Modern World*, New Brunswick NJ: Rutgers University Press.

Andezian, S. (1990) 'La Confrérie des "*Issâwa*"', in F. Champion and D. Hervieu-Léger (eds) *De l'emotion en religion*, Paris: Centurion.

Beckford, James A. (1984) 'Holistic imagery and ethics in new religious and healing movements', *Social Compass* 31: 259–72.

Beckford, James A. (1985) 'The insulation and isolation of the sociology of religion', *Sociological Analysis* 46: 347–54.

Beckford, James A. (1989) *Religion and Advanced Industrial Society*, London: Unwin Hyman.

Beckford, James A. and Gilliat, Sophie (1998) *Religion in Prison. Equal Rites in a Multi-Faith Society*, Cambridge: Cambridge University Press.

Beckford, James A. and Suzara, Araceli (1994) 'A new religious and healing movement in the Philippines', *Religion* 24: 117–42.

Bednarowski, Mary F. (1992) 'The New Age and feminist spirituality', in J.R. Lewis and J.G. Melton (eds) *Perspectives on the New Age*, Albany NY: SUNY Press.

Berger, Helen A. (1999) *Community of Witches*, Columbia: University of South Carolina Press.

Berger, Helen A. (2000) 'High priestess. Mother, leader, teacher', in Wendy Griffin (ed.) *Daughters of the Goddess. Studies of Healing, Identity, and Empowerment*, Walnut Creek CA: Alta Mira.

Beyer, Peter (1994) *Religion and Globalization*, London: Sage.

Bhatt, Chetan (1997) *Liberation and Purity. Race, New Religious Movements and the Ethics of Postmodernity*, London: UCL Press.

Boyer, Alain (1998) *L'Islam en France*, Paris: Presses Universitaires de France.

Breault, K. (1989) 'New evidence on religious pluralism, urbanism and religious participation', *American Sociological Review* 54: 1048–53.

Brouwer, S., Gifford P. and Rose, S.D. (1996) *Exporting the American Gospel. Global Christian Fundamentalism*, New York: Routledge.

Bruce, Steve (1984) *Firm in the Faith*, Aldershot: Gower.

Bruce, Steve (1993) 'Religion and rational choice: a critique of economic explanations of religious behaviour', *Sociology of Religion* 54: 193–205.

Bruce, Steve and Wallis, Roy (1992) 'Paisleyism, politics, and ethnic honor in Northern Ireland', in William H. Swatos Jr (ed.) *Twentieth-Century World Religious Movements in Neo-Weberian Perspective*, Lewiston NY: Edwin Mellen.

Castells, Manuel (1997) *The Power of Identity*, Oxford: Blackwell.

Césari, J. (1998) *Musulmans et républicains. Les Jeunes, l'Islam et la France*, Paris: Complexe.

Champion, F. (1990) 'La Nébuleuse mystique-ésotérique', in F. Champion and D. Hervieu-Léger (eds) *De l'emotion en religion*, Paris: Centurion.

Champion, Françoise and Hervieu-Léger, Danièle (eds) (1990) *De l'emotion en religion*, Paris: Centurion.

Chaves, Mark (1997) *Ordaining Women: Culture and Conflict in Religious Organizations*, Cambridge MA: Harvard University Press.

Cohen, Martine (1990) 'Les Renouveaux catholique et juif en France', in F. Champion and D. Hervieu-Léger (eds) *De l'emotion en religion*, Paris: Centurion.

Cohen, Martine (1995) 'Les Charismatiques et la santé. Offres religieuses de salut ou nouvelles médicines parallèles?', in F. Lautman and J. Maître (eds) *Gestions religieuses de la santé*, Paris: L'Harmattan.

Davidman, Lyn (1991) *Tradition in a Rootless World*, Berkeley CA: University of California Press.

Davidman, Lynn and Greil, Arthur (1993) 'Gender and the experience of conversion: the case of "returnees" to modern Orthodox Judaism', *Sociology of Religion* 54: 83–100.

Davidman, Lyn and Jacobs, Janet (1993) 'Feminist perspectives on new religious movements', in D. Bromley and J. Hadden (eds) *A Handbook of Sects and Cults in America*, Greenwich CT: JAI Press.

Davie, Grace and Hervieu-Léger, Danièle (eds) (1996) *Identités religieuses en Europe*, Paris: La Découverte.

Dericquebourg, Regis (1988) *Religions de guérison*, Paris: Cerf.

Finke, Roger (1990) 'Religious deregulation: origins and consequences', *Journal of Church and State* 32: 609–26.

Finke, Roger (1992) 'An unsecular America', in S. Bruce (ed.) *Religion and Modernization*, Oxford: Clarendon Press.

Finke, R. and Stark, R. (1986) 'Turning pews into people: estimating 19th century church membership', *Journal for the Scientific Study of Religion* 25: 180–92.

Finke, R. and Stark, R. (1988) 'Religious economies and sacred canopies: religious mobilization in American cities', *American Sociological Review* 53: 41–9.

Finke, R. and Stark, R. (1989) 'How the upstart sects won America', *Journal for the Scientific Study of Religion* 28: 27–44.

Finke, R. and Stark, R. (1992) *The Churching of America, 1776–1990: Winners and Losers in our Religious Economy*, New Brunswick NJ: Rutgers University Press.

Foltz, Tanice G. (1994) *Kahuna Healer. Learning to See with Ki*, New York: Garland.

Giddens, Anthony (1991) *Modernity and Self-Identity. Self and Society in the Late Modern Age*, Cambridge: Polity Press.

Gunn, Paula (1986) *The Sacred Hoop: Recovering the Feminine in American Indian Tradition*, Boston: Beacon Press.

Hanf, Theodor (1994) 'The sacred marker: religion, communalism and nationalism', *Social Compass* 41: 9–20.

Hargrove, Barbara (1985) 'Gender, the family and the sacred', in Phillip E. Hammond (ed.) *The Sacred in a Secular Age*, Berkeley CA: University of California Press.

Hawley, John Stratton (ed.) (1994) *Fundamentalism and Gender*, New York: Oxford University Press.

Hechter, Michael (1997) 'Religion and rational choice theory', in L. Young (ed.) *Rational Choice Theory and Religion*, New York: Routledge.

Hedges, Ellie and Beckford, James A. (1999) 'Holism, healing and the New Age', in Steven Sutcliffe and Marion Bowman (eds) *Beyond New Age: Exploring Alternative Spirituality*, Edinburgh: Edinburgh University Press.

Heelas, Paul (1996) *The New Age Movement*, Oxford: Blackwell.

Hervieu-Léger, Danièle (1986) *Vers un nouveau christianisme?* Paris: Cerf.

Hervieu-Léger, Danièle (1989) 'Tradition, innovation and modernity: research notes', *Social Compass* 36: 71–81.

Hervieu-Léger, Danièle (1990) 'Religion and modernity in the French context', *Sociological Analysis* 51: 15–25.

Hervieu-Léger, Danièle (1992) 'Società e atteggiamenti religiosi in Francia', in aa.vv. *La religione degli europei*, Turin: Fondazione Giovanni Agnelli.

Hervieu-Léger, Danièle (1993a) *La Religion pour mémoire*, Paris: Cerf.

Hervieu-Léger, Danièle (1993b) 'Present-day emotional renewals. The end of secularization or the end of religion?', in William H. Swatos Jr (ed.) *A Future for Religion?* Newbury Park CA: Sage.

Hervieu-Léger, Danièle (1999) *Le Pèlerin et le converti. La Religion en mouvement.* Paris: Flammarion.

Hetherington, Kevin (1998) *Expressions of Identity. Space, Performance, Politics*, London: Sage.

Hill, Michael and Lian Kwen Fee (1995) *The Politics of Nation Building and Citizenship in Singapore*, London: Routledge.

Hockey, Jenny (1993) 'The acceptable face of human grieving? The clergy's role in managing emotional expression during funerals', in David Clark (ed.) *The Sociology of Death*, Oxford: Blackwell.

Hourmant, L. (1990) ' "Transformer le poison en élixir". L'Alchimie du désir dans un culte néo-bouddhique, la Soka Gakkai française', in F. Champion and D. Hervieu-Léger (eds) *De l'emotion en religion*, Paris: Centurion.

Hunter, James Davison (1991) *Culture Wars. The Struggle to Define America*, New York: Basic Books.

Iannaccone, L. (1988) 'A formal model of church and sect', *American Journal of Sociology* 94: 241–68.

Iannaccone, L. (1990) 'Religious practice: a human capital approach', *Journal for the Scientific Study of Religion* 29: 297–314.

Iannaccone, L. (1992) 'Religious markets and the economics of religion', *Social Compass* 39: 123–31.

Iannaccone, L. (1994) 'Why strict churches are strong', *American Journal of Sociology* 99: 1180–211.

Jacobs, Janet L. (1984) 'The economy of love in religious commitments: the deconversion of women from nontraditional religious movements', *Journal for the Scientific Study of Religion* 23: 155–71.

Jacobs, Janet L. (1989) 'The effects of ritual healing on female victims of abuse: a study of empowerment and transformation', *Sociological Analysis* 50: 265–79.

Jacobs, Janet L. (1990) 'Women-centered healing rites', in T. Robbins and D. Anthony (eds) *In Gods We Trust: New Patterns of Religious Pluralism in America*, New Brunswick NJ: Transaction.

Jacobs, Janet L. (1991) 'Gender and power in new religious movements. A feminist discourse on the scientific study of religion', *Religion* 21: 345–56.

Jacobson, Jessica (1998) *Islam in Transition: Religion and Identity among British Pakistani Youth*, London: Routledge.

Kaufman, Debra (1991) *Rachel's Daughters*, New Brunswick NJ: Rutgers University Press.

Kepel, Gilles (1987) *Les Banlieues de l'Islam*, Paris: Le Seuil.

Kepel, Gilles (1994) *The Revenge of God*, Oxford: Blackwell.

Khosrokhavar, Farhad (1997) *L'Islam des jeunes*, Paris: Flammarion.

King, Ursula (1994) 'Voices of protest and promise: women's studies in religion, the impact of the feminist critique on the study of religion', *Studies in Religion* 23: 315–29.

Knott, Kim (1995) 'The debate about women in the Hare Krishna movement', *Journal of Vaishnava Studies* 3: 85–109.

Kürti, N. (1997) 'Globalisation and the discourse of otherness in the "new" Eastern and Central Europe', in T. Modood and P. Werbner (eds) *The Politics of Multiculturalism in the New Europe*, London: Zed.

Land, K., Deane, G. and Blau, J. (1991) 'Religious pluralism and church membership: a spatial diffusion model', *American Sociological Review* 56: 237–49.

Lechner, Frank (1993) 'Global fundamentalisms', in William H. Swatos, Jr (ed.) *A Future for Religion?* London: Sage.

Lehman, Edward C. (1985) *Women Clergy: Breaking Through Gender Barriers*, New Brunswick NJ: Transaction.

Lehman, Edward C. (1993) *Gender and Work: The Case of the Clergy*, Albany NY: SUNY Press.

Lehmann, David (1996) *Struggle for the Spirit: Religious Transformation and Popular Culture in Brazil and Latin America*, Cambridge: Polity Press.

Luckmann, Thomas (1967) *The Invisible Religion*, London: Macmillan.

Madsen, C. (1994) 'A God of one's own: recent work by and about women in religion', *Signs* 19: 480–98.

McGuire, Meredith B. (1982) *Pentecostal Catholics. Power, Charisma and Order in a Religious Movement*, Philadelphia: Temple University Press.

McGuire, Meredith B. (1988) *Ritual Healing in Suburban America*, New Brunswick NJ: Rutgers University Press.

Maffesoli, Michel (1988) *Le Temps des tribus. Le Déclin de l'individualisme dans les sociétés de masse*, Paris: Klincksieck.

Martin, David A. (1990) *Tongues of Fire*, Oxford: Blackwell.

Mellor, Philip and Shilling, Chris (1994) 'Reflexive modernity and the religious body', *Religion* 24: 23–42.

Mellor, Philip and Shilling, Chris (1997) *Re-Forming the Body. Religion, Community and Modernity*, London: Sage.

Modood, T., Beishon, S. and Virdee, S. (1994) *Changing Ethnic Identities*, London: Policy Studies Institute.

Mol, J.J. (1976) *Identity and the Sacred*, Agincourt: Book Society of Canada.

Nason-Clark, Nancy (1987) 'Are women changing the image of the ministry?' *Review of Religious Research* 28: 330–40.

Neitz, Mary Jo (1990) 'In goddess we trust', in Thomas Robbins and Dick Anthony (eds) *In Gods We Trust*, New Brunswick NJ: Transaction.

Neitz, Mary Jo (1993) 'Inequality and difference. Feminist research in the sociology of religion', in William H. Swatos, Jr (ed.) *A Future for Religion?* London: Sage.

Neitz, Mary Jo (1994) 'Quasi-religions and cultural movements: contemporary witchcraft as a churchless religion', in A.L. Greil and T. Robbins (eds) *Between Sacred and Secular: Research and Theory on Quasi-Religion*, Greenwich CT: JAI Press.

Nesbitt, Paula D. (1997) *The Feminization of the Clergy in America*, Oxford: Oxford University Press.

Nielsen, Jørgen S. (1992) *Muslims in Western Europe*, Edinburgh: Edinburgh University Press.

Palmer, Susan J. (1993) 'Women's "cocoon work" in new religious movements: sexual experimentation and feminine rites of passage', *Journal for the Scientific Study of Religion* 32: 343–55.

Palmer, Susan (1994) *Moon Sisters, Krishna Mothers, Rajneesh Lovers*, Syracuse NY: Syracuse University Press.

Parekh, Bhiku (1991) 'The concept of fundamentalism', Coventry: University of Warwick Centre for Research in Asian Migration.

Pereira de Queiroz, Maria Isaura (1989) 'Afro-Brazilian cults and religious change in Brazil', in James A. Beckford and Thomas Luckmann (eds) *The Changing Face of Religion*, London: Sage.

Plaskow, Judith and Christ, Carol (1989) *Weaving the Visions: New Patterns in Feminist Spirituality*, San Francisco: Harper.

Platvoet, J.G. and Molendijk, A.L. (eds) (1999) *The Pragmatics of Defining Religion: Contexts, Concepts and Contests*, Leiden: Brill.

Poloma, Margaret (1989) *Assemblies of God at the Crossroads*, Knoxville TN: University of Tennessee Press.

Puttick, Elizabeth (1996) *Women in New Religions*, London: Macmillan.

Puttick, Elizabeth (1999) 'Women in new religious movements', in B.R. Wilson and J. Cresswell (eds) *New Religious Movements. Challenge and Response*, London: Routledge.

Puttick, Elizabeth and Clarke, Peter B. (eds) (1993) *Women as Teachers and Disciples in Traditional and New Religions*, Lewiston NY: Edwin Mellen Press.

Robertson, Roland (1985) 'The sacred and the world system', in P.E. Hammond (ed.) *The Sacred in a Secular Age*, Berkeley CA: University of California Press.

Robertson, Roland (1989) 'Globalization, politics and religion', in James A. Beckford and Thomas Luckmann (eds) *The Changing Face of Religion*, London: Sage.

Robertson, Roland (1992a) 'The economization of religion? Reflections on the promise and limitations of the economic approach', *Social Compass* 39: 147–57.

Robertson, Roland (1992b) *Globalization: Social Theory and Global Culture*, London: Sage.

Robertson, Roland and Chirico, JoAnn (1985) 'Humanity, globalization and worldwide religious resurgence: a theoretical exploration', *Sociological Analysis* 46: 219–42.

Rochefort-Turquin, Agnès (1990) 'La JECF des années 30 à 60. Spiritualité et gestion des affects dans un mouvement d'Action catholique: l'expérience de la conviction', in F. Champion and D. Hervieu-Léger (eds) *De l'emotion en religion*, Paris: Centurion.

Rose, Susan (1987) 'Women warriors: the negotiation of gender in a charismatic community', *Sociological Analysis* 48: 245–58.

Saint-Blancat, C. (1997) *L'Islam de la diaspora*, Paris: Bayard.

Shilling, Chris (1993) *The Body and Social Theory*, London: Sage.

Shilling, Chris (1997) 'Emotions, embodiment and the sensation of society', *Sociological Review* 45: 195–21.

Somerville, Jennifer (1997) 'Social movement theory, women and the question of interests', *Sociology* 31: 673–95.

Stark, Rodney (1991) 'Normal revelations: a rational model of "mystical" experiences', in D.G. Bromley (ed.) *Religion and Social Order*, vol. 1, Greenwich CT: JAI Press.

Stark, Rodney (1996) *The Rise of Christianity. A Sociologist Reconsiders History*, Princeton NJ: Princeton University Press.

Stark, Rodney and Bainbridge, W.S. (1985) *The Future of Religion*, Berkeley CA:. University of California Press.

Stark, Rodney and Bainbridge, W.S. (1987) *The Theory of Religion*, New York:. Peter Lang.

Stark, Rodney and Finke, Roger (1988) 'American religion in 1776: a statistical report', *Sociological Analysis* 49: 39–51.

Tibi, Bassam (1998) *Europa ohne Identität? Die Krise der multikulturellen Gesellschaft*, Munich: Bertelsmann.

Tibi, Bassam (1999) 'Organisierte Religion wie in der katholischen und protestantischen Kirche: ein Vorbild für die Islam-Diaspora', in G. Besier and E. Scheuch (eds) *Die neuen Inquisitoren. Religionsfreiheit und Glaubensneid*, Zurich: Edition Interform.

Toulis, Nicole Rodriguez (1997) *Believing Identity. Pentecostalism and the Mediation of Jamaican Ethnicity and Gender in England*, Oxford: Berg.

Turner, Bryan S. (1981) 'The body and religion: towards an alliance of medical sociology and sociology of religion', *Annual Review of the Social Sciences of Religion* 4: 247–86.

Vertovec, Steven (1996) 'Multiculturalism, culturalism and public incorporation', *Ethnic and Racial Studies* 19: 49–69.

Voyé, L. (1992) 'Religion et économie: apports et limites de l'analyse du religieux à partir de cadres théoriques empruntés à l'économie', *Social Compass* 39: 159–69.

Waerness, K. (1984) 'The rationality of caring', *Economic and Industrial Democracy* 5: 185–211.

Walker, A.G. and Atherton, J.S. (1971) 'An Easter Pentecostal convention: the successful management of a "time of blessing"', *Sociological Review* 19: 367–87.

Wallace, Ruth A. (1992) *They Call Her Pastor: A New Role for Catholic Women*, Albany NY: SUNY Press.

Wallace, Ruth A. (1996) 'Feminist theory in North America: new insights into the sociology of religion', *Social Compass* 43: 467–79.

Wallace, Ruth A. (1997) 'The mosaic of research on religion: where are the women?' *Journal for the Scientific Study of Religion* 36: 1–12.

Walter, Tony and Davie, Grace (1998) 'The religiosity of women in the modern West', *British Journal of Sociology* 49: 640–60.

Warburg, Margit (1999) 'Baha'i: a religious approach to globalisation', *Social Compass* 46: 47–56.

Warner, R. Stephen (1993) 'Work in progress toward a new paradigm for the sociological study of religion in the United States', *American Journal of Sociology* 98: 1044–93.

Warner, R. Stephen (1997) 'Convergence toward the new paradigm. A case of induction', in L. Young (ed.) *Rational Choice Theory and Religion*, New York: Routledge.

Warner, R. Stephen and Judith Wittner (eds) (1997) *Gatherings in Diaspora. Religious Communities and the New Immigration*, Philadelphia: Temple University Press.

Warwick, L. (1995) 'Feminist wicca – paths to enlightenment', *Women and Therapy* 16: 121–33.

Weigel, George (1992) *The Final Revolution*, New York: Oxford University Press.

Wessinger, Catherine (ed.) (1993) *Women's Leadership in Marginal Religions: Explorations outside the Mainstream*, Urbana IL: University of Illinois Press.

Williams, Rory (1990) *A Protestant Legacy: Attitudes to Death among Older Aberdonians*, Oxford: Oxford University Press.

Wilson, Bryan R. (1992) 'Reflections on a many sided controversy', in Steve Bruce (ed.) *Religion and Modernization*, Oxford: Oxford University Press.

Winter, M.T., Lummis, A. and Stokes, A. (1994) *Defecting in Place: Women Claiming Responsibility for their own Spiritual Lives*, New York: Crossroad.

York, Michael (1995) *The Emerging Network. A Sociology of the New Age and Neo-Pagan Movements*, Lanham MD: Rowman and Littlefield.

Young, Lawrence A. (ed.) (1997) *Rational Choice Theory and Religion*, New York: Routledge.

chapter 8

Developments in the sociology of education since 1950: from structural functionalism to 'policy sociology'

Kevin J. Brehony

Introduction

It is now widely accepted that the sociology of education, in England at least, is officially dead. Obituaries for it first began to appear in the early 1990s. Among the first was one written by Shilling (1993b) who announced sociology of education's demise during a review of a collection of essays in the sociology of education edited by Arnot and Barton (1992). Since then, the death of sociology has become something of a conventionalist truth. In such a theory of truth, Sayer explains, what is true is simply something that is inter-subjectively agreed upon (Sayer 2000: 41). The most recent of the mourners at sociology of education's deathbed is Delamont (2000) but she is only the latest in a line that also includes Dale (1992) and Hammersley (1996). There are, however, still a few who dispute this diagnosis. Among them may be counted Whitty (1997) who implies that there is still some life left in sociology of education. If there is near unanimous agreement over the condition of sociology of education currently, there are nevertheless numerous differences in explaining how its moribund state came about.

In order to assist my cartographical ambitions in what is necessarily rather an impressionistic attempt to map developments in the sociology of education since the 1950s, I shall first attempt to define and delimit the field. This will be followed by a brief historical account of the rise of the field and its subsequent decline. My interpretation will rely heavily, but also selectively, on the concept of a field as proposed by Bourdieu (Bourdieu and Wacquant 1992; Bourdieu 1993). A field in this sense is a network of objective positions occupied by agents who accept the rules of the game, the objective of which is competition for the various kinds of capital available within it. The concept of field permits facts of the development of the sociology of education to be interpreted in ways different to traditional notions of 'discipline' or 'subject'. These categories tend to be used rather unreflexively in accounts of the sociology of education (Walford 1987) but not perhaps as unreflexively as some sociologists who refer to sociology as a profession (Westergaard and Pahl 1989).

Starting from a perspective that privileges the material rather than the ideational, my account will deal first with the 'objective structure' of the field through a consideration of the institutional development of the sociology of education and then with the succession of perspectives that have at one time or another been dominant in the field. I shall conclude with a brief account of the rise of what has been termed 'policy sociology' before returning to the evidence for and accounts of the decline of the sociology of education.

What is sociology of education?

The first aspect of this definitional problem I wish to address concerns the spatial or geographical location of the field. Most of the obituarists cited above and also some other diagnosticians (Ball 1995) imply, or are sometimes quite explicit that what they are talking about is 'British' sociology of education. The problem with this is that it can be argued that sociology of education is a series of global fields whose composition is related to the languages spoken by their participants and that its geographical location is dispersed. I shall return later to this issue but the designation 'British' is also flawed, as in these post-devolution times the term has become more and more problematic (Nairn 2000a). My own preference leans more towards 'English' rather than 'British' because of the differences, which are now increasing, between the education systems of the four national regions of the United Kingdom and also because most of the empirical research conducted by sociologists of education has been conducted in England and not Britain. Nevertheless, 'British' must suffice, for as Nairn has argued, England is subsumed, or smothered, by England's Britain (Nairn 2000b). Moreover, as the focus of much sociology of education has been on state-provided education, the state has loomed large in many of their writings (Dale 1989) and invariably the state referred to is the British state.

The search for transcendent definitions of the sociology of education that are both timeless and universal in their application is futile. Academic fields are constantly in a process of composition and recomposition; of expansion and contraction. What is required here is merely some test of practical adequacy that furnishes criteria for distinguishing what might be included within the field and what might not. For some of those who are, or have been, agents in the field, the relationship of the sociology of education to sociology is paramount. For Davies, the sociology of education meant sociology applied to education (Davies 1982). In this view, as in the distinction which Burgess makes between the 'parent discipline' and 'the sub discipline' (Burgess 1984), sociology is regarded as the primary discipline. Delamont also takes a similar view (Delamont 2000: 95). Other agents, on the other hand, write occasionally as if the sociology of education was entirely independent of sociology (Ball 1995; Hammersley 1996).

For those who regard sociology of education as a sub-discipline of sociology, matters would be easier if the field of sociology had at its theoretical and methodological core, a generally accepted canon. However, this has not been so since the decline of structural functionalism as its dominant perspective. Thus relations between sociology and sociology of education are not as clear-cut as the figure of parent discipline and sub-discipline would suggest. In Bernstein's terms, both sociology and sociology of education exhibit weak classification of knowledge (Bernstein 1971). Not only is it difficult to define what is referred to as the discipline and its sub-disciplines, it is equally hard to adopt an empirical approach and define sociology of education as that which is produced by sociologists of education. Leaving aside the problem of objectively determining who is a sociological practitioner, few these days define themselves as such. It is my argument that this is to a large extent due to the destruction of its institutional base which forced sociologists of education to seek new identities.

If the link to sociology and the presence of sociologists in the field is insufficient to define, even in a broad manner, the sociology of education, then recourse must be made to the subject and methods of research in the sociology of education. This is an easier matter, as there is an overwhelming consensus within sociology of education that the questions researched in the field are concerned with, on the one hand, the relation between social divisions and social relations and on the other with the formal organization of education or schooling. This latter category I extend to include further and higher and any other kind of formal post-school education and training. This is not to denigrate the place of other forms of education but simply to point out what has been the case. For much of sociology of education's existence as a field, it is social class that has received the most attention, usually in the form of questions about access to formal education or the outcomes of schooling in adolescence and adulthood.

Regarding the methods used in research by sociologists of education, the field is characterized by methodological pluralism. Viewed historically, there has occurred a shift from overwhelmingly quantitative studies to qualitative ones, but in this the field parallels that of sociology in general. Methodological commitment therefore is not useful as a criterion by means of which to designate the field.

Sociology of education's institutional base

Sociology of education in England has a prehistory that begins around 1900 (Szreter 1984). For a while it contended with psychology to become the basis of the theories of education that were being taught in the new university departments of education. Armed with the apparatus and techniques of mental testing, the psychologists became hegemonic and sociology of education was all but extinguished. In the early 1950s, however, it began to expand again as the policies of selection legitimated by mental testing began to be subjected to sociological critique. This in turn added weight to social democratic criticisms of selection and the role of schooling in sustaining class divisions. Significantly, the sociology of education that emerged in the postwar period was a field of study created by sociologists who were mostly located in sociology departments. Of these, the department at the London School of Economics was the most significant (Karabel and Halsey 1977). This is reflected in the contributions its staff made to sociology journals. A cursory examination of the articles on education and schooling published in the *British Journal of Sociology*, for example, reveals that most, during this period, were written by staff and research students based in sociology departments. As sociology rapidly expanded within the universities during the 1960s (Westergaard and Pahl 1989) it also entered the institutes and colleges of education, where it was taught to students on initial teacher training courses. From this period onwards, the fortunes of the sociology of education were harnessed to the study of education rather than to sociology. In turn, the study of education has mainly depended for its institutional base upon those departments and colleges responsible for initial training of teachers. Policies relating to the place of the study of education in initial teacher training have therefore been of fundamental importance in shaping developments in the sociology of education. Sociology of education is best viewed, from this point onwards, not as a part of the field constituted by sociology but a part of the field of education.

The 1960s' expansion

During the 1960s, sociology came to be regarded as the fourth foundation discipline of education. This period, after the 1960 Robbins Report expansion of higher education with the foundation of the so-called new universities, was one of considerable growth in student numbers and an era in which teacher training courses attained degree status, albeit somewhat grudgingly, from the universities that validated them (Dent 1977). As sociology was recruited to help fill up the expanded teacher training courses, it was given a less than enthusiastic welcome by many who taught the other disciplines that had previously made up the courses in education, namely psychology, philosophy and history of education. Sociologists of education were, in Bourdieu's terms, engaged in struggles and competition for the capital of the education field. Fearful of sociology's imperialist expansion, historians of education, for example, reacted by setting up the History of Education Society which was intended in part at least to try to defend their territory against the newcomers (Gordon and Szreter 1989).

In addition to the fears of lecturers in the other foundation disciplines of education, sociology of education was also regarded with suspicion, and in some instances hostility, by those whose main concern was with the professional training of students and who were mainly concerned with subjects of the school curriculum and the supervision of teaching practice (Taylor 1966; Thorburn 1987). These tensions, plus others arising between those in the sociology of education whose primary subject identity was as sociologists and those who saw themselves more as educationalists, exerted pressures on the sociology of education to conform to what Davies has described as, 'the normative, practical bent of the field' of education (Davies 1982). Institutional counterweights to this tendency were provided by the University of London Institute of Education and the Open University. In the former, the first taught master's degree in the sociology of education was offered in 1964. In the latter institution, path-breaking multi-perspective undergraduate courses in the sociology of education were offered to a student body that contained a high proportion of teachers eager for degrees, as an all-graduate teaching profession began to take shape. In both, the figure of Basil Bernstein was central. If the field can be said to have produced an organic intellectual, to pilfer Gramsci's category, it was surely Bernstein (Davies 1994; Atkinson *et al.* 1995; Sadovnik Alan 1995).

Contraction of the base

Despite latent antagonism towards sociology and the tendency towards sociology of education becoming incorporated into the concerns of practitioners, during the late 1960s and early 1970s, it had a fairly well-established institutional base in both university sociology departments and in departments and institutions concerned with initial teacher training. In the mid-1970s this latter base began to shrink as the demand for teachers fell and the rationalization of teacher education colleges led to closures, mergers and amalgamations. After the election of a Conservative government in 1979, the position of sociology of education worsened considerably. During the first four terms of the Conservative administration, sociology of education and its theoretical role within teacher education was singled out for particular vilification by the right (sociology itself and also social sciences were the subject of similar attacks, as for example in the renaming of the Social Science Research Council as the Economic and Social Research Council, in order to exclude the term science). While sociology of education could withstand ideological attacks, it could not, along with the rest of education, survive accompanying measures designed to reduce its place, firstly to a minimum and latterly to nothing, within courses of initial teaching training (Reid and Parker 1995). In this, the sociology of education shared the fate of all the foundation subjects of education so ably chronicled in the case of history of education by Richardson (1999). Like the historians, the reaction of sociologists of education, as Dale has observed, was to emphasize the 'applied' aspects of the field and thus sociologists of education now teach a wide range of topics and courses which, superficially at least, indicate very little connection to sociology (Dale 1992). Recently, new courses, such as those with a focus on how to teach the literacy and numeracy hours which primary school teachers are now obliged to hold, have tended to replace courses with a sociological content for undergraduates.

Those teachers of sociology of education who survive have moved into the spaces created by an expansion in taught higher degree programmes; either to provide sociology of education courses, which is rare, or courses to do with, for example, education policy and management. As sociologists of education became less distinguishable from others teaching and researching in education, they increasingly came into competition for high-status posts not with other sociologists but with agents of newly established fields like school leadership and school improvement. Migration to sociology departments, in the way that some women historians of education did to history departments, was hardly an option as education had long ceased to be of interest to most academic sociologists.

Other forms of institutionalization

Within the community of sociologists of education, institutional support in the form of conferences and two journals have helped to maintain a sense of identity and purpose as well as provide support for debate. The annual International Sociology of Education Conference, held formerly at Westhill College in Birmingham, and more recently at Sheffield, is perhaps the largest annual conference for sociologists of education. The conference for ethnographic researchers in education, which began meeting at St Hilda's College, Oxford, in the 1980s, and which after a sojourn elsewhere and a brief disappearance, has now returned to Oxford, is another important forum, especially for those new to the sociology of education. More important perhaps than these in providing an identity for sociologists of education and in defining the field is the *British Journal of Sociology of Education*. Begun in 1980 just as the institutional decline commenced, this journal has done much to sustain sociology of education. Intended to be an international journal based in Britain, many of its articles originate in the Antipodes. This may be taken as another morbid symptom of the decline of English sociology of education or alternatively explained as a consequence of the fact that within the English-speaking world, it is very difficult to locate the field in a single geographical centre.

In their first editorial, the editors of the *British Journal of Sociology of Education* noted the tendency towards the 'perpetuation of a golden circle of practitioners' (Banks *et al.* 1980) who were invited to contribute to the collections of articles in the field that had appeared from time to time. Thus it was hoped that the journal would encourage those outside the circle to publish. The strategy of representing themselves as outsiders appears to have succeeded, as most of the surviving editors now hold chairs in education. The absolute increase in the number of holders of chairs, partly due to, and notwithstanding, the transmogrification of the polytechnics into universities in 1992, indicates the maturation in career terms of many of those in the generation that came into the field during the 1970s. It is also indicative of the large contribution made by sociologists to the field of education not just as researchers and teachers but also as leaders and managers in organizations of higher education. Latterly this has become even more marked by Bob Burgess becoming the

Vice-Chancellor of Leicester University and Geoff Whitty being appointed Director of the Institute of Education in London. In a move that takes him perhaps even closer to the field of power, David Hargreaves is to be the new chief executive of the government's examination and curriculum quango, the Qualifications and Curriculum Authority (QCA) which came into being on 1 October 1997.

The *International Studies in Sociology of Education* journal, which like the *British Journal of Sociology of Education* has been edited from its beginning by Len Barton at the University of Sheffield, has an editorial board that exhibits a remarkable similarity to that of the *British Journal of Sociology of Education*. This may be taken to indicate that a new golden circle of practitioners has formed which has changed little over more than a decade. If so, this would seem to support Shilling's (1993b) criticism that sociology of education is suffering from intellectual stagnation. An additional factor that distinguishes the current period from the past, and might also account for the stagnation, is that there are very few sociologists of education who are in the early phases of their academic careers. As is the case in other branches of sociology, the number entering the field, because of institutional contraction and the lack of posts, is below the replacement rate. The effects of this lack of new blood are incalculable but they must include a slowing down in the pace of new developments, as there are no challengers to the dominant agents in the field.

The appearance of these journals dedicated to the sociology of education does not seem to have had much effect upon the number of articles on education being published in mainstream sociology journals, which was never large. Unlike the early days, contemporary contributors to these journals tend to be in education departments but regard themselves primarily as sociologists. At least one sociology journal, *Sociological Review*, has what seems to be a disproportionate number of sociologists of education on the editorial board, but scrutiny of its content does not reveal a predisposition to grant more space to the sociology of education than do other sociology journals. This is, however, perhaps partly a function of the nature of the papers submitted. The presence of sociologists of education on the editorial board of *Sociological Review* also raises the point that in some, admittedly relatively rare instances, sociologists actively engaged in the sociology of education may also be active in other branches of sociology. It is also significant that two of the three sociology of education members of this editorial board are women, and education is a field in which women are more likely to attain dominant positions than in many others.

As well as being involved in mainstream sociology journals, sociologists of education have been active, perhaps disproportionately so, in the

British Sociological Association. It may be that working in what is widely regarded as a low-status field (Bernstein 1972) causes these sociologists to reaffirm their sociological identity through activity associated with the main field. Alternatively, the low regard with which the sociology of education is held may be an effect not of the work produced in the field but of a general disdain for education and schooling.

The relations between sociologists of education and other sociologists are important for the identity of sociologists of education and the legitimation of their work. Shilling (1993b) contended that sociology of education and sociology were drifting apart. Delamont goes further and asserts that 'the sociology of education is an anomalous beast for the parent discipline, whose practitioners reject and fear it' (Delamont 2000: 95).

The founding of journals and the institutionalization of sociology of education in colleges and departments of education represent the moment when the field of sociology and that of sociology of education began to drift apart. In their practice, many in the dwindling band who identify themselves as sociologists of education have tried to stay in touch with developments in sociology but, as will be seen below, this has not meant that theoretical developments in the main field have always found a response in the sociology of education.

Perspectives

Walford argues against visualizing the development of the sociology of education in Britain as a linear process in which one perspective replaced another (Walford 1987: 2). He accepts the narrative in which functionalism was replaced by the 'new' sociology of education which soon split into the two camps of Marxism and interpretativism. Feminism then challenged the former but, at more or less the same time as its emergence in the field, a turn was made towards policy. When it emerged as an organized field of knowledge during the 1950s, sociology of education was, like many other sociological fields (Clegg and Hardy 1999), dominated by structural functionalism. With its concern with the process of socialization and the relations between the various structures of society, structural functionalism provided an especially propitious framework in which sociological work on education could be legitimated. What it did not provide directly was a research programme. This came instead from the 'political arithmetic' tradition based mainly at the London School of Economics. As Karabel and Halsey put it, this approach was concerned principally with 'calculating the chances of reaching various stages in the educational process for children of different class origins' (Karabel and Halsey 1977: 11). The scale of activity at the time was rather small. There were, according to Bernstein, only two 'major sociologists', Jean Floud and A.H. Halsey, engaged in research or systematic teaching in the sociology of education (Bernstein 1972).

Connection to policy

Nevertheless, the impact on policy making was high and the relation between policy makers and these sociologists of education has been described as 'intimate' (Karabel and Halsey 1977). That this position no longer held after 1979 was noted by Shilling as further evidence for the decline of sociology of education. As is well known, the dominance of structural functionalism came under attack during the 1960s when interpretative perspectives began to gain adherents. These perspectives, some of which were subsumed for a while under the label of the 'new' sociology, have been seen as being associated with new generations of sociologists of education (Bernstein 1972; Karabel and Halsey 1977). Provided that 'generation' is not taken too literally and so that it refers not to age but to length of time spent in an academic career, this explanation is quite plausible. In any academic field there are always those beginning their careers who are willing to épater les bourgeois with fashionable theoretical positions and methodologies. It is also characteristic of newcomers trying to shift the dominant paradigms that they wish to supersede and dispose of previous approaches. Thus Bernstein, writing critically of the first phase of sociology of education, was dismissive of it on the grounds that it 'bore the hallmarks of British applied sociology, atheoretical, pragmatic, descriptive and policy focussed' (Bernstein 1972: 102).

The golden age?

The 1970s, as Randall Collins, has claimed, were something of a golden age for the sociology of education (Collins 1981). Its position in relation to other branches of sociology was never stronger. One indication of this was the decision by the British Sociological Association to hold its annual conference in 1970 on the theme of education. In his introduction to the volume of papers from the 1970 conference, Richard Brown observed how for some years, sociology of education had been 'an obvious candidate as a theme for the Annual Conference' (Brown 1973). But despite this prominent position relative to other branches of sociology, there were some like Olive Banks who feared that 'centrifugal tendencies' threatened to tear the subject apart (Banks 1982). McLennan has written of sociology's 'seemingly endless regime of internal doubt and contestation' (McLennan 1998), but competition between proponents of differing perspectives is the normal condition of academic fields, so the debates between Marxists and interactionists or proponents of macro and micro analyses, for example, that were characteristic of the 1970s and early 1980s were perhaps not nearly as life threatening to sociology of education as Banks implied.

Expansion and fragmentation

Conflicts over theoretical perspectives or research methods are not the only ways in which the unity and coherence of a field of knowledge may be threatened. Extension of a field to new areas together with increasing specialization and the continual division and fragmentation of intellectual labour may also engender a feeling that a common language is no longer possible. An indication of how far these processes had progressed by the early 1980s is provided by the edited collection entitled *The Social Sciences in Educational Studies* (Hartnett 1982). While the title of the book denoted that the social sciences were its field, many of the essays addressed themes and issues in the sociology of education. In fact fifteen of the twenty-one contributions may be construed as sociological in orientation. Among these were articles on 'race' and gender and their relation to education and, as the decade progressed, work in these areas of substantial inequality began to replace the former preoccupation with social class. Other newly emergent interests for research and theorization in the sociology of education in the 1980s included classroom interaction and special needs.

Traditionally, divergent perspectives and interests were surveyed in texts produced mainly to serve as course readers to be used on sociology of education courses. Among the many over time that fulfilled that role, those by Meighan (1986), Burgess (1986) and Reid (1986), which were all either new or in a new edition in 1986 have been the most prominent. The relative absence of new texts of this nature is symptomatic of a decline in the number of taught courses at undergraduate level rather than of more tendencies in the field towards fission.

The 1988 Education Reform Act and after: making the policy turn

Writing in 1986, Burgess noted that a focus on policy making and politics was relatively underdeveloped among sociologists of education (Burgess 1986). Later, Shilling adduced as evidence of the decline of the sociology of education the widespread interest in policy making and the politics of education among sociologists of education consequent upon the Education Reform Act of 1988 and other aspects of the attempts by the Conservative government to restructure the administration, organization, curriculum, assessment and pedagogy of the state school system. Although the perspectives adopted by researchers into the origins and effects of the Conservative reforms have differed, most have been united methodologically by a general orientation to qualitative data collection and analysis. Another unifying strand within this work was a concern with some of the older themes of the sociology of education such as the inequalities consequent upon social divisions; only now, with the adoption by sociologists of education of what Moore terms the 'equal opportunities' paradigm (Moore 1996), had the number of social groups considered to be disadvantaged expanded. Under scrutiny in much of this work is the extent to which the education reforms have either reduced or exacerbated inequalities of 'race', gender and class within the education system (Ball 1994; Bowe *et al.* 1994; David *et al.* 1994, 1996, 1999; Gewirtz *et al.* 1995; Gillborn and Youdell 1999).

Policy sociology

A number of those engaged in research into the effects of the Conservative education reforms have adopted the label 'policy sociology' to describe their enterprise. This usage derives almost invariably from a formulation by Ozga which states that policy sociology is 'rooted in the social science tradition, historically informed and drawing on qualitative and illuminative techniques' (Ozga 1987: 144; see also Ozga 2000). Ozga's definition became much amplified through citation and in 1993 an advertisement appeared for a master's course in 'policy sociology' at a midlands university. And yet it is doubtful whether this is a new field or simply a way to distinguish this sociologically informed work from that on similar phenomena but which has been more closely aligned with management and administration. One of the more dismal aspects of the recent period has been the burgeoning of management courses in education which, when on those rare occasions that theory is invoked, typically ransack sociology's back catalogue in order to legitimate what is often little more than a species of commonsense. That the management literature having pillaged, say, Weber on authority, then displays an almost total lack of understanding of what he was trying to say while at the same time disparaging sociology in general, is one of the more depressing outcomes of the fad for management and leadership. These 'modes of objectification', as Ball (1995: 260) describes management theories, have obtained a significant boost under New Labour which has enthusiastically embraced 'corporate populism' (Barnett 2000) to the extent that it may be regarded as the political representative of new managerialism (Clarke *et al.* 1994; Clarke and Newman 1997). Both terms signify the attraction of business ideologies for New Labour. So delegitimized is the field of education and so in thrall is New Labour with business consultancy that business consultants Hay McBer, not education researchers, were given the task of researching teacher effectiveness (McBer 2000).

Returning to 'policy sociology', what is immediately noticeable about the work conducted under this label is the relative absence of subject boundaries around it. Weak classification persists as a characteristic of the sociology of education, and work on the Conservative reforms in education draws theoretical succour from such diverse sources as social policy and cultural studies almost as often as from mainstream sociology. Unfortunately, while sociologists of education have tended to adopt interdisciplinary approaches, workers in adjacent fields such as health or local government, have so far shown little awareness of what sociologists of education have been doing. At the annual conference of the British Sociological Association, for instance, papers on education policy are almost invariably placed with other papers on education and not with papers on policy in general. This ghettoization of work in and on education is evidence of the low esteem accorded to education by agents who themselves are inescapably within it.

Social/sociological theory

While the activities subsumed under the label of policy sociology involve 'the empirical investigation of social reality', some feel that this is at some cost to the other plank in the sociological platform, 'apprehending the nature of society theoretically'. Thus Shilling writes of the neglect by sociologists of education of theories and concepts of modernity, postmodernity, structuration, self-identity, the civilizing process, consumption and the body. To that list of concerns which, to judge from his own writing, are ones that most interest him (Shilling 1992, 1993a), may be added a series of recent perspectives that have had relatively little impact on the sociology of education in Britain. Such a list would include structuralism (with the possible exception of its Marxist variant), poststructuralism and critical realism. Stephen Ball, whose research in policy sociology has been exemplary, is one of the few British sociologists of education to make a turn to poststructuralism (Ball 1990, 1994). Does this mean therefore that, like the earlier generation criticized by Bernstein, current sociologists of education are 'atheoretical'? Dale, for one, thinks that while sociology of education has developed concepts with which to interrogate the reforms of the right, theoretical development has not kept pace (Dale 1992). From the other side of the macro/micro divide, Hammersley has consistently reiterated his message that the work of Hargreaves, Lacey and Ball on differentiation and polarization 'is one of the clearest examples of theory development and testing in ethnographic research, and indeed in sociology generally' (Hammersley 1992: 195).

In an ideal world, theoretical development and empirical investigation would proceed more or less in parallel as theories were tested, inducted or abducted through research. Unfortunately, researchers do not inhabit such a world. Currently the sheer scale of reform and the pace of change consequent upon recent legislation has militated in a variety of ways against what I suspect either Dale or Hammersley would recognize as theory production and development. Even without these pressures, researchers engaged in empirical work are sometimes, as Walford (1987) has pointed out, overwhelmed by the daily round of research problems. In these circumstances the questions posed by researchers in education and the analyses applied to their data are much more likely to be adopted or adapted from mainstream sociological theory or that of other cognate social sciences than they are to be developed *ab initio*. Arguably, social theory, more so perhaps than sociological theory (Mouzelis 1991, 1993), occupies a higher status in the world of sociology than does empirical work. Like the classics in the view of the nineteenth-century sociologist, Herbert Spencer, it serves as a badge of elite status (Spencer 1929: 2) and distinction. If this is the case, then the sociology of education must forever remain a poor relation in the family of sociology which has social theory at its head.

This observation invites a return to the theme of the relation between sociology of education and sociology in general. If contributions to methodology are examined, then some sociologists of education like Burgess and Hammersley, to name but two, have made an extremely important contribution to our knowledge and understanding of qualitative methods of data collection and analysis. The ethnographic study of schools and classrooms has been a considerable jewel in the crown of sociology in general and not just that of the sociology of education. The sociology of education in various ways has also provided all sociologists with theories and concepts with which to be reflexive about what it is they do when they seek to develop and reproduce the sociological field. Such work includes debates on the professions, work on curriculum, on pedagogy and on assessment and evaluation. It would be a welcome development if other sociologists familiarized themselves with this work, as it appears to be the case that at present most have not.

Explaining decline

The explanations for the demise of sociology of education advanced by its obituarists may be arranged in the form of a binary opposition consisting, on the one hand, of processes external to the field and, on the other, processes internal to it. Few things are ever as neat as that simple division, as Shilling's account demonstrates. First, he pointed to the declining influence sociologists exercise over policy makers in education; alongside this he placed the loss of sociology of education's institutional base in teacher education. Finally, Shilling noted the occurrence in recent years of a migration of many sociologists from sociology of education to policy studies (Shilling 1993b). Walford's was a more internalist account that saw changes within the field as 'changes in fashion' (Walford 1987: 3). External accounts are insufficient for Hammersley who argues that the sociology of education suffered from internal intellectual problems (Hammersley 1996). While not explicitly stating it, Delamont seems to lay the blame on other sociologists and the British Sociological Association. She identifies four

> types of disdain apparent in mainstream sociology's relationship with the sociology of education: a failure to defend the sociology of education; a failure to provide a platform for the sociology of education; a failure to address the subspecialism adequately; the paradox around culture. There is also the United Kingdom versus England problem.
>
> (Delamont 2000: 102)

From what I have said already about the relations between sociologists of education and other sociologists, these charges may misrecognize the situation. Arguably, it is not sociology of education that the sociologists who have most of the capital in the sociology field disdain, but any sociologists who are engaged in teaching and research in fields that have practical application. More perhaps could have been done by all the 'professional' associations to defend the study of education, but they themselves had little access to the field of power. Delamont talks of a changed situation under New Labour and particularly of the role of Anthony Giddens, presumably due to his adoption of the role of theorist of the 'third way' (Giddens 1998, 2000), but arguably New Labour long ago ceased to be a social democratic party and therefore the hope that it should follow an equality agenda seems misplaced.

My own preference is for most explanatory weight to be placed on an external reading, such as that of Dale, who has produced an account (Dale 2000) that bears certain similarities, in that both emphasize processes of selection, to the neo-Darwinist work of Runciman (1999). Whatever problems sociology of education has had internally regarding the generation of appropriate theory, internal conflicts over the macro and the micro and so on, they are as nothing when compared to the destruction of its institutional base, the foundations of which had barely been laid. Relentless ideological pressure combined with the elimination of courses on which it could be taught by the agencies responsible for the training of teachers could not have evoked any better response than dispersion into other fields.

Conclusion

I indicated at the outset that my map of developments was to be a personal one. It is also, due to constraints of space, more than a little reductionist in its stress on the structural location of the sociology of education within a field. Explaining new trends in these terms does not of course deal with their truth claims. Moreover, by focusing only on Britain, much of the vitality of the field which comes from its international range has been lost. If British sociologists of education borrow from social theory they borrow most from social theory generated abroad. A favourite borrowing is from Parisian fashions usually refracted through a North American or Australian lens (Ladwig 1996).

This chapter has been concerned with developments in the field. It is hard not to conclude that Shilling and the other obituarists are right with regard to the institutional base of the sociology of education and its divorce from the current policy-making process. While the shrinking institutional base threatens to severely attenuate future developments, the lack of impact on policy formation is hardly the fault of the many sociologists of education who immersed themselves in research on policy. As Miller (1988) has so clearly demonstrated, life for sociologists of education is possible outside education departments, but this situation is far from the ideal in which sociologists have something useful to say and to learn from education practitioners. As some sociologists have always recognized, the material world in the form of social being has this curious way of setting limits to developments. Yet, as recent political debates over social class and university entrance illustrate, issues that for long have been at the centre of the field have not gone away despite claims that they are modernist preoccupations that have been overtaken by postmodernity. That there is still an urgent necessity for empirical research in education informed by sociological theories and methodology, and for sociological theory informed by empirical research seems self-evident. But if sociologists are no longer interested in one of the principal ways in which society, social divisions and social relations are produced and reproduced then it would seem that there is little future for sociology.

References

Arnot, M. and Barton, L. (eds) (1992) *Voicing Concerns*, Wallingford: Triangle.

Atkinson, P., Davies, B. and Delamont, S. (eds) (1995) *Discourse and Reproduction*, Cresskill NJ: Hampton Press.

Ball, S. (1990) *Foucault and Education: Disciplines and Knowledge*, London: Routledge.

Ball, S. (1994) *Education Reform: A Critical and Post-Structural Approach*, Milton Keynes and Philadelphia: Open University Press.

Ball, S.J. (1995) 'Intellectuals or technicians? the urgent role of theory in educational studies', *British Journal of Educational Studies* XXXXIII (3): 255–71.

Banks, O. (1982) 'Sociology of education', in L. Cohen, J. Thomas and L. Manion (eds) *Educational Research and Development in Britain 1970–1980*, Windsor: NFER-Nelson, 43–54.

Banks, O., Barton, L., Dale, R. *et al.* (1980) 'Editorial', *British Journal of Sociology of Education* 1 (1): 3–5.

Barnett, A. (2000) 'Corporate populism and partyless democracy', *New Left Review* (3): 80–9.

Bernstein, B. (1971) 'On the classification and framing of educational knowledge', in M.F.D. Young (ed.) *Knowledge and Control*, London: Collier Macmillan, 47–69.

Bernstein, B. (1972) 'Sociology and the sociology of education: some aspects', in F. Swift Donald, A. McPherson, B. Bernstein, Open University School and Society Course Team (eds) *Eighteen-Plus: The Final Selection*, Bletchley, Bucks: Open University Press, 99–109.

Bourdieu, P. (1993) *Sociology in Question*, London: Sage.

Bourdieu, P. and Wacquant, L.J.D. (1992) *An Invitation to Reflexive Sociology*, Cambridge: Polity Press.

Bowe, R., Ball, S.J. and Gewirtz, S. (1994) 'Parental choice, consumption and social theory: the operation of micro markets in education', *British Journal of Educational Studies* 42 (1): 38–52.

Brown, R. (ed.) (1973) *Knowledge, Education and Cultural Change*, London: Tavistock.

Burgess, R.G. (1984) 'Exploring frontiers and settling territory: shaping the sociology of education', *British Journal of Sociology* XXXV (1): 122–37.

Burgess, R.G. (1986) *Sociology, Education and Schools: An Introduction to the Sociology of Education*, London: Batsford.

Clarke, J. and Newman, J. (1997) *The Managerial State*, London: Sage.

Clarke, J., Cochrane, A. and McLaughlin, E. (eds) (1994) *Managing Social Policy*, London: Sage.

Clegg, S. and Hardy, C. (1999) 'Introduction', in S. Clegg and C. Hardy (eds) *Studying Organization: Theory and Method*, London: Sage, 1–22.

Collins, R. (1981) *Sociology Since Mid-Century*, New York: Basic Books.

Dale, R. (1989) *The State and Educational Policy*, Milton Keynes: Open University Press.

Dale, R. (1992) 'Recovering from a pyrrhic victory? Quality, relevance and impact in the sociology of education', in M. Arnot and L. Barton (eds) *Voicing Concerns*, Wallingford: Triangle Books, 201–17.

Dale, R. (2000) 'Forming sociology of education 1945–95', in J. Demaine (ed.) *Sociology of Education Today*, London: Palgrave.

David, M.E., West, A. and Ribbens, J. (1994) *Mother's Intuition? Choosing Secondary Schools*, London: Falmer.

David, M.E., Arnot, M. and Weiner, G. (1996) *Educational Reforms and Gender Equality in Schools*, Manchester: Equal Opportunities Commission.

David, M.E., Arnot, M. and Weiner, G. (1999) *Closing the Gender Gap: Post-war Education and Social Change*, Cambridge, Polity Press.

Davies, B. (1982) 'Sociology and the sociology of education', in A. Hartnett (ed.) *The Social Sciences in Educational Studies*, London: Heinemann Educational, 35–42.

Davies, B. (1994) 'Durkheim and the sociology of education in Britain', *British Journal of Sociology of Education* 15 (1): 3–25.

Delamont, S. (2000) 'The anomalous beasts: hooligans and the sociology of education', *Sociology* 34 (1): 95–111.

Dent, H.C. (1977) *The Training of Teachers in England and Wales*, London: Hodder and Stoughton.

Gewirtz, S., Ball, S. and Bowe, R. (1995) *Markets, Choice, and Equity in Education*, Buckingham: Open University Press.

Giddens, A. (1998) *The Third Way: The Renewal of Social Democracy*, Malden MA and Cambridge: Polity Press.

Giddens, A. (2000) *The Third Way and its Critics*, Malden MA: Polity Press.

Gillborn, D. and Youdell, D. (1999) *Rationing Education: Policy, Practice, Reform, and Equity*, Buckingham and Philadelphia: Open University Press.

Gordon, P. and Szreter, R. (eds) (1989) *History of Education: The Making of a Discipline*, London: Woburn Press.

Hammersley, M. (1992) *What's Wrong with Ethnography?* London: Routledge.

Hammersley, M. (1996) 'Post mortem or post modern? Some reflections on British sociology of education', *British Journal of Educational Studies* 44 (4): 395–408.

Hartnett, A. (1982) *The Social Sciences in Educational Studies: A Selective Guide to the Literature*, London: Heinemann Educational.

Karabel, J. and Halsey, A.H. (1977) 'Educational research: a review and interpretation', in J. Karabel and A.H. Halsey (eds) *Power and Ideology in Education*, Oxford: Oxford University Press, 1–85.

Ladwig, J.G. (1996) *Academic Distinctions*, London: Routledge.

McBer, H. (2000) 'A model of teacher effectiveness', report by Hay McBer to the Department for Education and Employment, http://www.dfee.gov.uk/teachingreforms/mcber/

McLennan, G. (1998) 'Fin de sociologie? The dilemmas of multidimensional social theory', *New Left Review* 230: 58–90.

Meighan, R. (1986) *A Sociology of Educating*, Eastbourne: Holt, Rinehart and Winston.

Miller, H. (1988) 'Social analysis of education: after the new sociology', *British Journal of Sociology of Education* 9 (4): 485–9.

Moore, R. (1996) 'Bad to the future: the problem of change and the possibilities of advance in the sociology of education', *British Journal of Sociology of Education* 17 (2): 145–61.

Mouzelis, N.P. (1991) *Back to Sociological Theory*, London: Macmillan.

Mouzelis, N.P. (1993) 'The poverty of sociological theory', *Sociology* 27 (4): 675–95.

Nairn, T. (2000a) *After Britain: New Labour and the Return of Scotland*, London: Granta.

Nairn, T. (2000b) 'Ukania under Blair', *New Left Review* 1 (second series): 69–103.

Ozga, J. (1987) 'Studying educational policy through the lives of policy makers: an attempt to close the macro–micro gap', in S. Walker and L. Barton (eds) *Changing Policies, Changing Teachers: New Directions for Schooling?* Milton Keynes and Philadelphia: Open University Press.

Ozga, J. (2000) *Policy Research in Educational Settings: Contested Terrain.* Buckingham and Philadelphia: Open University Press.

Reid, I. (1986) *The Sociology of School and Education*, London: Fontana.

Reid, I. and Parker, F. (1995) 'Whatever happened to the sociology of education in teacher education?' *Educational Studies* 21 (3): 395–413.

Richardson, W. (1999) 'Historians and educationists: the history of education as a field of study in post-war England, Part II: 1945–72', *History of Education* 28 (2): 109–41.

Runciman, W.G. (1999) 'Social evolutionism: a reply to Michael Rustin', *New Left Review* 236: 145–53.

Sadovnik Alan, R. (1995) *Knowledge and Pedagogy: The Sociology of Basil Bernstein*, Norwood NJ: Ablex Pub. Corp.

Sayer, A. (2000) *Realism and Social Science*, Thousand Oaks CA and London: Sage.

Shilling, C. (1992) 'Reconceptualizing structure and agency in the sociology of education – structuration theory and schooling', *British Journal of Sociology of Education* 13 (1): 69–87.

Shilling, C. (1993a) *The Body and Social Theory*, London: Sage.

Shilling, C. (1993b) 'The demise of sociology of education in Britain?' *British Journal of Sociology of Education* 14 (1): 105–12.

Spencer, H. (1929) *Education: Intellectual, Moral and Physical*, London: John Watts.

Szreter, R. (1984) 'Some forerunners of Sociology of Education in Britain: an account of the literature and influences *c.* 1900–1950', *Westminster Studies in Education* 7: 13–43.

Taylor, W. (1966) 'The sociology of education', in W. Taylor (ed.) *The Study of Education*, London: Routledge and Kegan Paul, 179–213.

Thorburn, D. (1987) 'Sociology and teacher training: some reflections on colleges in transition', *Journal of Further and Higher Education* 11 (1): 80–8.

Walford, G. (ed.) (1987) *Doing Sociology of Education*, Social Research and Educational Studies Series 6, London: Falmer Press.

Westergaard, J. and Pahl, R. (1989) 'Looking backwards and forwards: the University Grants Committee's review of sociology', *British Journal of Sociology of Education* 40 (3): 374–92.

Whitty, G. (1997) 'Education policy and the sociology of education', *International Studies in Sociology of Education* 7 (2): 121–35.

chapter 9

The sociology of work and employment: new perspectives on new issues

Richard K. Brown

Introduction

The sociology of industry, under that or a similar title, has been a central element in British sociology at least since the subject began to emerge in its modern form following the Second World War. The study of industrial organizations and industrial conflict, of social relations on the shop and office floor, and of related topics such as trade unionism, and the professions and other occupations, has been a core feature of the undergraduate curriculum in sociology in a majority of university and other departments, and a central research interest for a substantial minority of British sociologists. In the last two or three decades, industrial and organizational sociology has also been a core element, though not always with that title, in the courses offered by management centres and business schools.

There have been suggestions in recent years that this claim to centrality within sociology can no longer be justified. Commentators have argued that paid work is of declining significance in contemporary society and have drawn attention to the supposed concomitant loss of interest amongst students, teachers and researchers in sociology in this area of the subject. In his important and stimulating review of the subject, Castillo (1999: 23), for example, reported arguments that, 'Just as work is no longer a central sociological category, so too the study of it has come to occupy a less prominent place in the discipline', though he did go on to assert the continuing importance of the sociological analysis of work and employment. In Britain, Chaney (1998: 533), reviewing books on consumption, suggested that 'an emphasis on industrialisation as the engine of modernity has inappropriately privileged processes of production' and went on to argue for the importance of consumption and consumer culture for an understanding of contemporary society, an argument which has been made by many others. These issues will recur later in this chapter but at this point it might be relevant to consider briefly some evidence for the continuing importance, despite a relative decline, of industrial sociology/the sociology of work and employment in the work and interests of British sociologists.

Data from the membership registers of the British Sociological Association, and from surveys, indicate that about a fifth or more of BSA members have had research interests in 'industrial sociology and the sociology of work' since the early 1960s or even earlier (see Carter 1968: 18; Brown 1992: 8). The BSA members' register for 1988 recorded that 9 per cent of the 636 members who listed their current research interests had an interest in 'industrial sociology', whilst a further 21 per cent had interests in 'organizations and bureaucracy', 'trade unions', 'unemployment' and/or 'work, occupations, professions, labour markets'. There does appear to have been a decline in the last ten years in the proportion of BSA members with such research interests, but even so, the numbers and percentages remain substantial: the most recent details of their research interests received from members show 303 (almost 15 per cent) of the 2025 members who declared a research interest listing 'employment and unemployment', 'industrial sociology', 'industrial relations', 'organizations and bureaucracy', 'trade unions' and/or 'work, occupations, professions, labour markets'. Further indications of the continuing salience of the sociology of work and employment for British sociologists include the fact that, in 1999, 424 (15.7 per cent) of the total membership of 2708 subscribed to the BSA journal *Work, Employment and Society*, as either their first or second choice journal.[1] In relation to teaching, Gubbay's survey of the sociology undergraduate degree curriculum at the start of this decade showed that at the sixty-two institutions surveyed, forty-seven mounted a total of eighty-two courses in what may be broadly described as sociology of work and employment (Gubbay 1991: 1).

Such a persistent if not entirely unchanging pattern should be no surprise. Work, paid and unpaid, remains a major and essential aspect of social life. How it is organized, allocated and rewarded is of crucial importance for the individual experience and social relations of those directly engaged in these activities and for the social situations and life chances of those associated with or dependent on them.

The precise wording of the terms used to categorize this area of study should perhaps be treated more carefully. Otherwise one risks losing sight of one of the major developments in this field of study in the past twenty years: the change of focus from the study of 'industry', often virtually synonymous with male manual workers' employment in manufacturing and extractive industry, to the at least potentially much more extensive and varied study of 'work'. This change is central to the developments to be discussed in this chapter. It has implications for the theoretical frameworks which sociologists have used, for the substantive issues they have tried to investigate, and for the strategies and methods they have adopted in carrying out empirical research.

Theoretical perspectives: the organization of industrial work

Much research and writing within industrial sociology has been apparently atheoretical. The preoccupation has been with providing largely descriptive accounts of 'the world of work' which were seen as being of interest in their own right, as contributing to an overall picture of social conditions in contemporary society, and/or as being of policy relevance. However, even the most avowedly empiricist or descriptive work will reflect some theoretical presuppositions. These latent theoretical concerns can be examined alongside more explicit explorations of theoretical themes to show that industrial sociology has reflected, and to some extent contributed to, the main debates within sociology more generally (see the rather different accounts of these contributions in Burrell and Morgan 1979; Morgan 1986; Rose 1988; Brown 1992).

There has been a series of attempts, for example, to characterize the employing organization as a 'system' (see Jaques 1951; Scott *et al.* 1956; Rice 1963), and such broadly 'functionalist' analysis also characterized research which saw the structure of work organizations, and roles and social relations within them, as largely contingent on the aims they were pursuing and/or the context within which they were operating (see Woodward 1965; Pugh and Hickson 1976). In contrast, others have advocated an 'action approach' to the understanding of workers' attitudes and behaviour (e.g. Goldthorpe *et al.* 1968) or of organizations more generally (e.g. Silverman 1970). For a decade or more from the late 1970s, however, the dominant perspective was derived from the work of Marx, and the 'labour process debate' was at the centre of research and writing, though not to the entire exclusion of other concerns.

Though Marx's ideas had always had some influence within industrial sociology, particularly in relation to the study of industrial conflict, the publication of Braverman's *Labor and Monopoly Capital* in 1974 pro-vided a powerful encouragement to treat Marx's approach to the analysis of employment within capitalist industrial societies as the starting point for the analysis of industrial organizations and employment relations. Braverman focused on employers' need to control their employees in order to secure a surplus in competitive market economies and, through his emphasis on the influence of scientific management, and the ideas of F.W. Taylor and his followers, provided a persuasive account of how this had been done during the twentieth century by means of a progressive 'deskilling' and 'degradation' of work (Braverman 1974).

The labour process debate gave new or renewed emphasis to a num-ber of questions which are central to any understanding of employment in industrial societies (see Thompson 1983). The central issue of control raised questions as to the range of strategies available to employers in managing their employees, how far choice between them is available and consciously made, and what, if any, possibilities exist for employees to resist such controls (see, for example, the discussion in Hyman 1987). The emphasis on 'deskilling' raised questions about the ways in which work has been and is organized and tasks allocated, and Braverman's thesis in this regard stimulated some valuable historical and contemporary research (see, for example, Wood 1982, 1989). The focus on the employ-ment relationship also directed attention outside the employing organi-zation to consider the necessary conditions in the wider society for the establishment and maintenance of employment in capitalist enterprises; to consider the place, for example, of the family, the education system and the local community in providing and sustaining an appropriately social-ized workforce, and the role of the state in providing the political and legal conditions for the growth and economic success of capitalist enterprises.

In the course of exploring these and other issues it became apparent that Braverman's arguments had significant limitations. Though there has been plenty of evidence of such changes in the nature of people's jobs, the 'degradation' of work has been neither an unambiguously appropri-ate way in which to characterize trends in the organization of work in the twentieth century nor always the most effective, if at all effective, way to control employees. Workers could and did resist employers' controls, their resistance influenced the resultant pattern of social relations, and, partly as a consequence, securing consent to managerial authority could be as important as using more coercive means of control. Indeed, secur-ing *some* consent could be seen as a necessary part of the employment relationship (Cressey and MacInnes 1980). Growing awareness of the very different ways in which employees were controlled and the very different levels at which that control might be exercised made Braverman's powerful account seem too simple and deterministic.

As these debates continued, a number of rather different developments took place. In many people's work, including some of the publications arising from the annual Labour Process Conferences (first held in 1983), the notion of 'the labour process' lost much if not all of its original context in a Marxian political economy and became more or less synonymous with 'work organization'. The origins of the approach in a 'primary concern with capital accumulation and class struggle' were lost to view, as was the need to view it with a 'wide-angle lens' so as to include awareness of 'the labour-market context together with state regulation' which constrain and set conditions for social relations and processes in the workplace (Nichols 1999: 115–17). In the context of this weakening of the notion of 'labour process', other concerns than those central to Marx's or Braverman's accounts of it were pursued, drawing on theories which were distinct from if not entirely antipathetic to those which had given rise to the labour process debate in the first place.

In the latter part of the 1980s these concerns included the influential arguments about 'flexible specialization' and 'the flexible firm'. These concepts were linked to assertions that capitalist economies had moved from 'Fordism' (the mass production and sale of standardized goods and services) to a new stage of 'post-Fordism' (using multi-skilled – 'polyvalent' – workers and computer technology to allow the production by networks of flexible specialized producers of smaller quantities of a greater variety of goods and services aimed at specific markets). This provided a very different perspective on the development of industrial organizations and industrial work from the one provided by Braverman (see Piore and Sabel 1984; Atkinson and Meager 1986; Allen and Massey 1988), but one which did not go unchallenged (see Pollert 1988, 1991). Indeed, some very widespread developments in the service sector towards the fragmentation, intensification, control and 'rationalization' of work, to which Ritzer (1993) gave the term 'McDonaldization', ran directly counter to the concept of flexible specialization and all that it implied.

The late 1980s and 1990s also saw a concern among sociologists to understand the content and impact of new managerial practices and discourses (human relations management (HRM), total quality control/management (TQC/TQM), just-in-time production (JIT), and so on), their implications for worker subjectivity and identity, and the role of culture in the workplace (see, for example, Casey 1995; du Gay and Salaman 1992; du Gay 1996; Roberts 1997). Some, though not all, of these ideas were associated with the process of 'Japanization' – the influence attributed to and the imitation of the managerial philosophies, policies and practices of Japanese 'transplants' in the United Kingdom and other western societies (see, for example, Garrahan and Stewart 1992; Elger and Smith 1994; Elger 1999).

In this context, some sociologists, probably a minority, found the ideas of Foucault particularly fruitful and influential. His theories did appear to offer new purchase on two issues which have long been at the centre of the sociology of work: power, or control, and identity; and to do so in an admirably parsimonious way. As we have seen, issues of the control of work and of organizations were at the core of the labour process debate. Foucault offered an account of the way in which a 'discourse' can produce knowledge which constitutes power over those who are known by and through it.[2] In these terms, control within work organizations and over the employment relationship is derived from the power located in a particular discourse. The 'discourses' of 'enterprise', and of 'just-in-time manufacturing and total quality control (JIT/TQC)' have been described as operating in this way (see, for example, du Gay 1996; Sewell and Wilkinson 1992).

Foucault also emphasized the ways in which modern organizations, including work organizations, used detailed monitoring and surveillance of employees' activities to control their behaviour (Sewell and Wilkinson 1992; Webster and Robins 1993). Modern electronic technologies make such surveillance much easier and more complete, especially in contexts such as telephone call centres where the activities of employees can be automatically and continuously recorded in minute detail (see Taylor 1997). Although Foucault argued that power and resistance are inseparable, Thompson and Ackroyd (1995), in a persuasive critique of these theoretical trends in industrial sociology which took issue with this claimed monopoly of control within organizations, have argued that resistance, and labour as an active agent, tend to disappear from view in analyses within a Foucauldian framework.

Issues of identity have an equally long-established, though not as prominent a position in the sociology of work as issues of control. They have, however, often been discussed within different theoretical traditions and without reference to questions of power and control. Thus, whilst Braverman (1974: 26–8) explicitly omitted 'subjective' aspects of class from his discussion of the labour process, the rich materials on identity within the tradition of symbolic interactionism contain equally sparse references to questions of power (for example, the work of Hughes 1958; of Becker 1971; and of Strauss 1969). Drawing on the work of Foucault, however, Knights and Willmott (1989: 538) have argued that 'subjects come to recognise themselves as discrete and autonomous individuals whose sense of a clear identity is sustained through participation in social practices which are a condition and consequence of the exercise of power and the production of specific knowledges. A more adequate appreciation of subjectivity . . . requires us to theorise it both as a medium and outcome of power relations and as a response to problems which are compounded by the individualisation of subjects in modern society.' Power is exercised in part by the ways in which a discourse defines the subjectivities of those who are subject to it, and identities cannot be considered in isolation from this exercise of power.

Those, like Knights and Willmott, who have used Foucault's ideas in their analyses of organizations and occupations, see them as providing a resolution of the dualism of 'structure' and 'action' which characterizes so much of social theory. In contrast to this claim it could be suggested that what they provide is merely a new rhetoric, a different way of talking about familiar problems, and one which, as Thompson and Ackroyd (1995) and other critics maintain, produces its own distortions. Certainly, the approach offered by Foucault's work has not been as widely influential as the earlier and still continuing labour process debate.

An important sub-theme in Braverman's account was the growth of a 'universal market': the ways in which individuals and families were increasingly deprived of the means to provide directly for themselves and all goods and services became commodities to be bought and sold in the market. This argument in its most comprehensive form was challenged by the work of Pahl (1984), whose research on the Isle of Sheppey suggested that many families had a variety of alternative ways in which they could meet their material needs, including 'self-provisioning'. The logic of Pahl's position was that, rather than starting with an analysis of the nature of employment within contemporary capitalism, the prior requirement was to ask how people sought to meet their needs for goods and services and then explore the implications of the means chosen for the work they had to do.

Employment in the capitalist firm, or the public sector enterprise, and purchasing goods and services in the market could then be seen as only one, albeit the most important in contemporary society, of the ways in which households could provide for their needs. Productive work could and did also occur outside the 'formal' economy, for example in the household, in the form of mutually supportive community work, as voluntary work, and as illegal and criminal activities. The relative importance of these different contexts for work remains contentious, but employment and self-employment have to be seen as only two of the ways in which needs for goods and services can be met. Subsequent research (e.g. Morris 1989, 1990) has questioned how far there are, or indeed can be, 'household work strategies' in a highly industrialized society like Britain, where many people have relatively little if any choice in face of all the vagaries of a capitalist market economy. Nevertheless, Pahl's arguments have played a significant part in bringing about a very necessary expansion of the horizons for the sociology of work and employment. Such an expansion was also necessitated by concurrent changes in the nature and organization of work.

Substantive concerns: exploring contemporary work and employment

British industrial sociology developed during the period of the long post-Second World War boom. This era of rising prosperity, relatively low inflation and full employment is conventionally regarded as having been brought to a fairly abrupt end in 1973 when the first of two massive increases in oil prices triggered inflation worldwide. The attempts by governments to control this inflation meant the abandonment of Keynesian economic policies and led to high rates of unemployment, largely successful attempts to restrict the power of trade unions, and a range of measures which had the (often intended, though not always admitted) effect of making increased demands on employees in exchange for reduced and more uncertain rewards.

Over the same quarter of a century since the end of the long boom there have been several other, not altogether unrelated, major long-term shifts in patterns of employment in Britain and, with some differences of detail and emphasis, in most other highly industrialized capitalist societies. They have included the decline in the proportion of the workforce engaged in manufacturing industry and an absolute and relative growth in the size of the service sector. The number and proportion of women in employment has continued to increase, with a concomitant growth in part-time employment especially of married women. 'Standard' forms of employment in full-time jobs of indefinite duration have diminished in importance and there has been a growth on the one hand of self-employment and on the other of a variety of 'non-regular' forms of employment in part-time, temporary or fixed-term contract jobs, or as homeworkers. In Britain under the influence of Conservative governments between 1979 and 1997, changes in the culture of work and the workplace have been advocated to emphasize 'enterprise', the priority to be given to market forces and to the privatization and commercialization of areas of economic activity previously under public control, and these emphases have not been changed in major ways since 1997. The power and influence of collective organization and representation among employees have been restricted. The period also saw a considerable extension and intensification of the processes of globalization. Facilitated by the development of much faster and cheaper means of communication, large corporations and financial and commodity markets operate on a worldwide basis increasingly unconstrained by any regulation by national governments.

These developments have been accompanied by significant changes in the conditions of employment of most employees and the characteristics of the jobs they are required to do, changes which have occurred in both the public and the private sectors. The pressure to control costs in the face of increasing competition in global markets, or of cash limits and cuts in public expenditure, has led employers to seek numerical flexibility – the ability to reduce the size of their workforce at short notice. This has meant increasing insecurity of employment for many employees, with jobs being filled on a temporary or fixed-term contract basis, and few of them being 'jobs for life' in the way that could often be realistically assumed to be the case in the past. Similarly in the workplace many employers have sought increasing control over their employees, sometimes by the fragmentation of jobs in the way Braverman argued, sometimes by the sorts of surveillance discussed earlier, and have demanded a greater intensity of work, greater levels of effort and longer hours. In contexts where employees interact with customers, either face-to-face or by phone, the contribution demanded from them can include 'emotional labour', 'the management of human feeling within paid employment in order to "create a publicly observable facial and bodily display"' (Hochschild 1983: 7; Taylor 1997: 177). In these and other contexts they may be expected to be 'intrapreneurial': constantly contributing, for example through 'quality circles', to the improvement of the production process.

Sociologists of work and employment have responded to these changes in economy and society, albeit partially and unevenly, and there have been significant changes in their agendas, some of them also induced by other developments. Until the late 1960s, for example, the labour market had been largely seen as a problem for economists. The rising levels of unemployment, and continuing concerns with the part low pay, discrimination and inadequate job opportunities played in perpetuating poverty, led to a growing interest among sociologists in the ways in which labour markets are structured and in how they operate (see, for example, Blackburn and Mann 1979; Gallie 1988a; Fevre 1992). These concerns were reinforced by the interest in the labour market stimulated on the one hand by the 'action approach', which saw patterns of recruitment as an important influence on workers' orientations to work (see, for example, Ingham 1970), and by the labour process debate, within which selective recruitment could be seen as an important source of control (e.g. Friedman 1977; Nichols 1980: Part III; Gordon *et al.* 1982).

The concern with unemployment, which spawned a large literature on its own (see Marsh 1988), gave rise to a number of debates. It revitalized longstanding questions about the meaning and significance of employment in people's lives and whether other forms of work outside the employment relationship, as discussed by Pahl and his colleagues, or other sorts of activities (e.g. DIY, leisure activities) could provide an adequate alternative, economically or psychologically, for some or all of those without paid work (see, for example, Jahoda 1982; Kelvin and Jarrett 1985; Ashton 1986). Concern with the causes of unemployment, and an unwillingness on the part of those in power to see them as being in any way due to the economic policies of the state, focused attention on the characteristics and supposed deficiencies of the unemployed and contributed to a wider debate about 'the underclass' (see, for example, Murray 1990; Morris 1994).

Questions about the importance of gender differences and about the situations and actions of women in employment and at work in other contexts were being raised by feminists in the 1960s and 1970s at the same time as women's participation in paid work was increasing rapidly and equal pay and sexual discrimination legislation was coming into force. The realization that gender was a significant issue for the sociology of work found early expression in contributions to the BSA annual conference in 1974 (see Barker and Allen 1976) and then much more substantial realization in a series of studies. These ranged from a major national survey (Martin and Roberts 1984; Dex 1987), and a number of important historical studies (e.g. Bradley 1989; Glucksmann 1990) to research on particular workplaces (e.g. Pollert 1981; Westwood 1984), on women's attitudes to work and employment (Dex 1988) and on recruitment and the labour market (e.g. Collinson *et al.* 1990; Rees 1992). Gender has become an essential factor to consider in the analysis of work and employment (and race or ethnicity is, deservedly, beginning to be accorded the same status, though much more remains to be done in this respect); and the still contentious notion of patriarchy has been developed to try to remedy the deficiencies of, if not to replace, accounts of women's employment based solely on an analysis of capitalism (Cockburn 1983; Walby 1990; but see also Pollert 1996).

Research on women's participation in paid work has necessarily meant studying employment outside the manufacturing and extractive industries, and under other than 'regular' employment contracts. Progress in these areas has been somewhat slower, partly because of difficulties of definition, identification and access. However, office, retail and other forms of service sector employment have been the subject of research, sometimes because it is there that one can best observe the impact of technological change (one of the classic concerns of industrial sociologists); in recent years 'new technology' has more often than not meant the computerization of clerical or retail operations (see, for example, Crompton and Jones 1984; Lane 1988). There have been some important studies of part-time work (e.g. Beechey and Perkins 1987), of homeworking (e.g. Allen and Wolkowitz 1987), of franchising (Felstead 1991; O'Connell Davidson 1994), and of self-employment and small business (e.g. Scase and Goffee 1982, 1987; Allen and Truman 1993). Research on manufacturing has been augmented by studies in a range of other settings such as the betting shop (Filby 1992), contract cleaning and catering (Rees and Fielder 1992), cleansing services (McIntosh and Broderick 1996), the health and welfare services (e.g. Cousins 1988) and elsewhere in the public sector (e.g. Halford and Savage 1995; Sinclair *et al.* 1996). Such changes in forms of employment have also been observed and noted in studies with another primary focus, for example in a series of surveys of workplace industrial relations (Daniel and Millward 1983; Millward and Stevens 1986; Millward *et al.* 1992) whose main intent has been to chart changes in industrial relations and trade union organization in the 'Thatcher' years and thereafter.

In the mid-1980s there was a major attempt to provide an overview of the changes then occurring in the world of work, including unpaid work, in Britain. This had originated in a review by Gallie of research requirements with regard to the social implications of current patterns of economic change (Gallie 1985). He listed a considerable number of questions under seven main headings: the structuring of employment opportunities; worker involvement in the labour market; the labour market and gender; ethnicity and the labour market; the informal economy; the social implications of unemployment; and labour market experience, unemployment and social stratification. On the basis of this review the Economic and Social Research Council (ESRC) established a major research programme, the 'Social Change and Economic Life Initiative' (SCELI) which involved teams of researchers from fourteen different universities working in six different local labour markets in Britain and coordinating their basic enquiries. The programme was concerned with four major substantive areas: 'the nature and determinants of employer labour force strategies, the changing character of people's experiences of employment and the labour market, the dynamics of household relations and their implications for both paid and unpaid work, and the impact of changes in the employment structure on social integration and social stratification in the community' (Gallie 1988a: 1). It represented perhaps the best example of an approach to the study of work and employment which had taken note of the new agenda. The findings appeared in a series of volumes which explored unemployment, gender segregation, skill and occupations, employer labour market strategies, and the social and political economy of the household (Gallie *et al.* 1993; Anderson *et al.* 1994; Penn *et al.* 1994; Rubery and Wilkinson 1994; Scott 1994).

SCELI did address many of the questions Gallie identified, and did so in a systematic way which made possible important connections and comparisons: for example, connections between the demand side and the supply side of the labour market in particular localities, between employers' organization of work and recruitment strategies, and actual and potential employees' orientations to work and job search behaviour; and comparisons between respondents' orientations to work and attitudes on economic and employment-related matters in different local labour markets. Nevertheless there remains a need for further research in almost all the areas he listed, and not only because the situations investigated by the SCELI teams have now changed in important ways during the last decade; and in some of them (ethnicity and the labour market, and the informal economy, for example) the work has only just begun.

Work and employment: new research objectives in a new century?

The sociology of work and employment is concerned with a subject matter which is constantly changing and thereby creating new and unfamiliar situations and, by implication at least, the need for further research. As Marx stressed a century and a half ago, capitalism is 'constantly revolutionising the instruments of production, and thereby the relations of production, and with them the whole relations of society' (Marx and Engels 1973: 70), and this assertion can be seen to apply as fully as ever to the closing years of the twentieth century and at the start of the twenty-first. In such circumstances it is difficult if not impossible to set out a programme for sociological research on work and employment which will not rapidly prove outdated. Indeed, it is significant that, judging by the details so far available, the current ESRC programme of research on 'The Future of Work' is largely concerned with what might be termed 'the unfolding present' (i.e. the sorts of developments which have been discussed already in this chapter) rather than a longer-term perspective (see Brown 1999). However, it is possible to outline some considerations which might helpfully guide the development of the sociology of work and employment as it enters the new century.

In the first place, if the arguments of Pahl (1984) and others are accepted, that work within the 'formal' framework of employment and self-employment in return for a salary, wage or other payment is only one way in which the demand for goods and services can be met, then much more research is needed on other forms of and social settings for work. The 'informal' economy remains underexplored and the same is true to an even greater extent for unpaid work. Oakley showed many years ago that housework could usefully be considered using the same concepts as in the study of employment, for example orientation to work, job satisfaction, work organization and division of labour (Oakley 1974). Recognition of the importance of domestic labour, and of the relationship between the domestic division of labour and labour market participation, makes such research even more important. A full exploration of the sociology of (all forms) of work will require the imaginative development of both new concepts and new modes of enquiry. Glucksmann's use of the concept of the 'total social organisation of labour', and its exploration in relation to women's paid and domestic work in Lancashire in the twentieth century, is a fine example of the sort of research which needs to be done (Glucksmann 2000).

Secondly, the implications for work within the employment relationship of the important changes occurring in the British, and world, economies need to be investigated. Such changes include the growing division of employment opportunities between a declining proportion of 'permanent', 'regular' jobs and a growing proportion of jobs which are non-regular, insecure and in many cases peripheral. Questions need to be asked about the implications of these developments for social relations at work and in the community, for employees' sense of class and status group identity and their willingness and ability to engage in collective action, for individual and household work 'strategies', and for individual careers and occupational identity, to mention only some of the more obvious issues. Such changes have implications too for the distribution of employment opportunities in relation to differences of gender, ethnicity and age. They also need to be examined in relation to the industrial sector, to changing patterns of ownership and control (privatization; multinationals) and to changes in the location of economic activities on a regional, national or worldwide scale.

Thirdly, there is a place for lines of enquiry which do not result directly from either of these starting points, but rather attempt to address other deficiencies in the existing approaches and coverage of the sociology of work. One example can be given. Much research in this area has taken either an organizational, a labour market or an individual focus; the problem has been to analyze social relations and social processes in a firm or a trade union, to chart the allocation of jobs to people and people to jobs in a local labour market and assess its impact on life chances and opportunities, or to explain the orientations and attitudes of individuals, or of individuals aggregated into socially relevant categories in terms of 'fact sheet' variables like sex, age, educational qualifications or occupation. Occupations as such have much more rarely been a subject for investigation (but see, for example, Lane 1986). Processes of occupational formation and the growth of occupational identity, and of closure, exclusion and professionalization, would seem likely to provide another insight into the world of employment and one which could have important implications for organizations, labour markets and individuals. The ways in which tasks are allocated and controlled, and in which employees are recruited and selected for the resultant jobs, and the careers available to individuals, are all affected if not determined by the ways in which and the extent to which the division of labour in society is influenced by the actions of occupational groupings.

Finally, it would be mistaken to lose sight of some issues which have been the subject of research in the past but which those in power have defined as irrelevant in recent years: worker participation and industrial democracy; workers' control; and more radically still the possibility and potential of alternative forms of work organization, of changes in the division of labour, and of collegial forms of authority and decision making. The task of sociology should include exploration of what might be, as well as of what is.

In tackling these and other issues there is also a need to jettison or at least rethink some of the core assumptions which characterized the sociology of industry in the earlier postwar period. These include the, not necessarily articulated, assumption that full employment meant full-time paid work for all men who were available for work between the ages of 16 and 65, and for single and some widowed and divorced women. Since the 1960s the collapse of the labour market for young people under the age of 25, and the withdrawal of many men from the labour market after the age of 55 or 60, or even earlier, together with the expansion of numbers in further and higher education, and in youth training, have greatly reduced the number of men who are economically active and therefore defined as 'unemployed' if they are not in paid work. The typical age range of economically active men has been drastically cut at both ends, though the argument has been put more recently that in an ageing population it will no longer be desirable, or even possible, for many people to retire so early. Over the same period the number and proportions of women in employment, much but by no means all of it part-time, have grown massively, and being employed can no longer be considered an optional extra for most women, if it ever was. It has also become accepted that one person's earnings – in the past it was the male 'breadwinner's' – are insufficient to support a family; the two-earner household is the norm, though it is a norm which many cannot achieve. What 'full employment' means or should mean is very different from what it meant a generation or so ago.

A second case for a conceptual rethink is the notion of 'regular' or 'standard' conditions of employment, conditions which provide a norm against which flexibility and insecurity can be assessed: full-time employment of indefinite duration, with 'normal' fringe benefits (holidays, sick pay, pension provision, etc.) and, for many, the prospects of incremental increases in earnings and/or of promotion. Without accepting that the increased levels of flexibility and insecurity characteristic of much contemporary employment are inevitable, the usefulness of the traditional point of reference must at least be questioned. Historically, such 'standard' conditions of employment were far from the norm for perhaps a majority of the workforce, and they are no longer available to many men and, especially, women at the present time. Yet they still represent the underlying assumptions on which much of the provision of social welfare is based, and are a target for employment policy more generally. It may be possible and desirable to resist the erosion of such an ideal, for example by adopting and enforcing European measures like the Social Chapter and the Working Time Directive; or it may be more realistic to recognize that many, perhaps most, jobs will lack the full security and benefits of 'standard' employment and to look for alternative ways of meeting employees' and their families' needs. Certainly the traditional notion of 'standard' employment can no longer be taken for granted.

Discussions of the changing character of paid work as jobs are fragmented and more closely controlled and employees are subject to demands to work harder and longer (the 'intensification' of work) tend to draw on a notion of 'good', 'rewarding' and 'fulfilling' work against which to compare these changes. In the British case the occupations which have been traditionally seen as coming closest to such an ideal of 'non-alienating'/satisfying work were probably those of the skilled craftsman or artisan, and the skilled professional, especially in independent practice. Both these types of occupation demanded relatively lengthy training leading to the possession of a distinctive skill which became the source of power and job security in the labour market, the ground for satisfaction and autonomy at work, and the basis for a clear occupational identity and a respected standing in the wider society. Neither type of occupation has been immune from the processes of 'degradation' which Braverman and others have enumerated. A key question must be whether it is useful any longer to continue to use such notions of a 'good job' as points of reference in evaluating the character of work, and, if not, whether any alternatives can be found and what they would be.

Conclusion

In the first decades after the end of the Second World War, research in industrial sociology in Britain contributed a great deal to the development of sociology generally and to our understanding of central aspects of economy and society. It was primarily focused, however, on large organizations and workforces, particularly in manufacturing, where one could find the more obvious and acute problems of industrial conflict, productivity, technical change and management organization. The widespread replacement of 'industrial sociology' by 'the sociology of work and employment' is a response to the changes which have taken place in the structure, organization and distribution of paid work in the past quarter century or more. It also reflects sociologists' concern to identify a more coherent field of study, one which does not privilege research on certain sorts of (paid) work in certain sorts of enterprise. It is perhaps not surprising that work within the employment relationship continues to attract most attention. Indeed, it can be argued that the particular and problematic features of that relationship provide the best starting point for an exploration of all the social relations and social processes surrounding paid work (Brown 1988). However, our understanding of the particular features of employment relations, and how such relations are shaped and changed, will be greatly increased if such research is carried out as part of a broader concern with all sorts of work. Placing employment within such a context and making comparisons with other types of work in other settings illuminates the significance of employment within society. A concern with all the contexts within which work is carried out provides a more coherent and comprehensive field of study. It also focuses on the basic questions of how members of a society provide the goods and services they need and what are the consequences for society of the ways in which they make such provision.

A methodological epilogue

The core literature of industrial sociology has been a series of case studies of one or a small number of organizations, sometimes limited to a particular workshop, sometimes covering the whole workplace or the whole enterprise. The work of Jaques (1951), Scott *et al.* (1956), Lupton (1963), Beynon (1973), Nichols and Beynon (1977), Pollert (1981) and Roberts (1992) in this country, and of Roy (1952), Gouldner (1955) and Burawoy (1979) in the United States, to quote only a few, mostly classic studies, has provided a rich tradition of research which has given us many of the key concepts and ideas in this area of sociology and could be quarried for further insights on a wide range of issues. Others (for example, Burns and Stalker 1961; Woodward 1965; Pugh and Hickson 1976) have extended their coverage to a larger number of cases in order to establish more firmly the relationship between the aspects of the workplace or enterprise in which they were interested and the wider range of contextual or environmental factors which influenced it. Inevitably such studies have used a variety of methods: interviews of various sorts, observation, documentary sources and so on. Whatever other types and styles of investigation are now required it is to be hoped that the empirically grounded, contextually located, historically aware and theoretically sophisticated case study of an industry, organization, workplace, occupational milieu or locality will continue to have an important place.

The new agenda of the sociology of work and employment, and remedying some of the deficiencies of industrial sociology (e.g. its concentration on manufacturing and extractive industry), demand rather different approaches. Domestic work, homeworking, voluntary work, and much service-sector employment cannot easily be captured within a case study framework. Consequently, there is an important place for systematic social surveys either on a national basis (e.g. Martin and Roberts 1984; Millward *et al.* 1992) or within geographically confined areas as in the case of the Social Change and Economic Life Initiative (Gallie 1988a), even though such research is generally more expensive and its findings sometimes less immediately accessible than case studies. In a world in which easily identifiable and, if access can be gained, easily studied large-scale workplaces are less frequently the location of employment, and work, paid and unpaid, is often being carried out in isolation from others, considerable ingenuity will be needed to design and carry out sociological research which adequately encompasses its subject. As with questions of theory and substance there remains plenty of room for the exercise of the sociological imagination.

Notes

1 I am grateful to Nicola Boyne, former Executive Secretary of the British Sociological Association, for this information.
2 In basic terms a discourse 'is a group of statements which provide a language for talking about – i.e. a way of representing – a particular kind of knowledge about a topic. When statements about a topic are made within a particular discourse, the discourse makes it possible to construct the topic in a certain way. It also limits the other ways in which the topic can be constructed' (Hall 1992: 291).

References

Allen, J. and Massey, D. (eds) (1988) *The Economy in Question*, London: Sage.
Allen, S. and Truman, C. (eds) (1993) *Women in Business. Perspectives on Women Entrepreneurs*, London: Routledge.
Allen, S. and Wolkowitz, C. (1987) *Homeworking – Myths and Realities*, London: Macmillan.
Anderson, M., Bechhofer, F. and Gershuny, J. (eds) (1994) *The Social and Political Economy of the Household*, Oxford: Oxford University Press.
Ashton, D.N. (1986) *Unemployment under Capitalism. The Sociology of British and American Labour Markets*, Brighton: Wheatsheaf.
Atkinson, J. and Meager, N. (1986) *Changing Working Patterns. How Companies Achieve Flexibility to Meet New Demands*, London: National Economic Development Office.
Barker, D.L. and Allen, S. (eds) (1976) *Dependence and Exploitation in Work and Marriage*, London: Longman.
Becker, H.S. (1971) *Sociological Work*, London: Allen Lane.
Beechey, V. and Perkins, T. (1987) *A Matter of Hours. Women, Part-time Work and the Labour Market*, Oxford: Polity Press.
Beynon, H. (1973) *Working for Ford*, Harmondsworth: Penguin.
Blackburn, R.M. and Mann, M. (1979) *The Working Class in the Labour Market*, London: Macmillan.
Bradley, H. (1989) *Men's Work, Women's Work*, Oxford: Polity Press.
Braverman, H. (1974) *Labor and Monopoly Capital*, New York: Monthly Review Press.
Brown, R.K. (1988) 'The employment relationship in sociological theory', in D. Gallie (ed.) *Employment in Britain*, Oxford: Blackwell.
Brown, R.K. (1992) *Understanding Industrial Organisations. Theoretical Perspectives in Industrial Sociology*, London: Routledge.

Brown, R.K. (1999) 'El reto del trabajo del futuro para Ciencias Sociales del Trabajo' (The challenge of the work of the future for the social sciences of work), in J.J. Castillo (ed.) *El trabajo del futuro*, Madrid: Editorial Complutense.

Burawoy, M. (1979) *Manufacturing Consent*, Chicago: University of Chicago Press.

Burns, T. and Stalker, G.M. (1961) *The Management of Innovation*, London: Tavistock.

Burrell, G. and Morgan, G. (1979) *Sociological Paradigms and Organisational Analysis*, London: Heinemann.

Carter, M.P. (1968) 'Report on a survey of sociological research in Britain', *Sociological Review* 16: 5–40.

Casey, C. (1995) *Work, Self and Society after Industrialism*, London: Routledge.

Castillo, J.J. (1999) 'Sociology of work at the crossroads', *Current Sociology* 47 (2): 21–46.

Chaney, D. (1998) 'The new materialism? The challenge of consumption', *Work, Employment and Society* 12: 533–44.

Cockburn, C. (1983) *Brothers. Male Dominance and Technological Change*, London: Pluto Press.

Collinson, D.L., Knights, D. and Collinson, M. (1990) *Managing to Discriminate*, London: Routledge.

Cousins, C. (1988) 'The restructuring of welfare work: the introduction of general management and the contracting out of ancillary services in the NHS', *Work, Employment and Society* 2: 210–28.

Cressey, P. and MacInnes, J. (1980) 'Voting for Ford: industrial democracy and the control of labour', *Capital and Class* 11: 5–33.

Crompton, R. and Jones, G. (1984) *White Collar Proletariat. Deskilling and Gender in Clerical Work*, London: Macmillan.

Daniel, W.W. and Millward, N. (1983) *Workplace Industrial Relations in Britain: The DE/PSI/ESRC Survey*, Aldershot: Gower.

Dex, S. (1987) *Women's Occupational Mobility. A Lifetime Perspective*, Basingstoke: Macmillan.

Dex, S. (1988) *Women's Attitudes towards Work*, Basingstoke: Macmillan.

du Gay, P.L.J. (1996) *Consumption and Identity at Work*, London: Sage.

du Gay, P.L.J. and Salaman, G. (1992) 'The cult(ure) of the customer', *Journal of Management Studies* 29: 616–33.

Elger, T. (1999) 'Manufacturing myths and miracles: work reorganization in British manufacturing since 1979', in H. Beynon and P. Glavanis (eds) *Patterns of Social Inequality*, London: Longman.

Elger, T. and Smith, C. (eds) (1994) *Global Japanization? The Transnational Transformation of the Labour Process*, London: Routledge.

Felstead, A. (1991) 'The social organization of the franchise: a case of "controlled self-employment"' *Work, Employment and Society* 5: 37–57.

Fevre, R. (1992) *The Sociology of Labour Markets*, Hemel Hempstead: Harvester Wheatsheaf.

Filby, M.P. (1992) '"The figures, the personality and the bums": service work and sexuality', *Work, Employment and Society* 6: 23–42.

Friedman, A. (1977) *Industry and Labour. Class Struggle at Work and Monopoly Capitalism*, London: Macmillan.

Gallie, D. (1985) 'Directions for the future', in B. Roberts, R. Finnegan and D. Gallie (eds) *New Approaches to Economic Life*, Manchester: Manchester University Press.

Gallie, D. (1988a) *The Social Change and Economic Life Initiative: An Overview*, working paper 1, Swindon: Economic and Social Research Council.

Gallie, D. (ed.) (1988b) *Employment in Britain*, Oxford: Blackwell.

Gallie, D., Marsh, C. and Vogler, C. (eds) (1993) *Social Change and the Experience of Unemployment*, Oxford: Oxford University Press.

Garrahan, P. and Stewart, P. (1992) *The Nissan Enigma*, London: Mansell.

Glucksmann, M. (1990) *Women Assemble. Women Workers and the New Industries in Inter-war Britain*, London: Routledge.

Glucksmann, M. (2000) *Cottons and Casuals. The Gendered Organisation of Labour in Time and Space*, Durham: Sociologypress.

Goldthorpe, J.H., Lockwood, D., Bechhofer, F. and Platt, J. (1968) *The Affluent Worker: Industrial Attitudes and Behaviour*, Cambridge: Cambridge University Press.

Gordon, D.M., Edwards, R. and Reich, M. (1982) *Segmented Work, Divided Workers*, Cambridge: Cambridge University Press.

Gouldner, A.W. (1955) *Patterns of Industrial Bureaucracy*, London: Routledge and Kegan Paul.

Gubbay, J. (1991) 'Teaching sociology of work and employment, report on a conference', University of Manchester, 12 October 1991 (unpublished).

Halford, S. and Savage, M. (1995) 'Restructuring organizations, changing people: gender and restructuring in banking and local government', *Work, Employment and Society* 9: 97–122.

Hall, S. (1992) 'The West and the rest: discourse and power', in S. Hall and B. Gieben (eds) *Formations of Modernity*, Cambridge: Polity Press in association with the Open University.

Hochschild, A.R. (1983) *The Managed Heart: The Commercialisation of Human Feeling*, Berkeley CA: University of California Press.

Hughes, E.C. (1958) *Men and their Work*, Glencoe IL: Free Press.

Hyman, R. (1987) 'Strategy or structure: capital, labour and control', *Work, Employment and Society* 1: 25–55.

Ingham, G.K. (1970) *Size of Industrial Organization and Worker Behaviour*, Cambridge: Cambridge University Press.

Jahoda, M. (1982) *Employment and Unemployment. A Social-Psychological Analysis*, Cambridge: Cambridge University Press.

Jaques, E. (1951) *The Changing Culture of a Factory*, London: Tavistock.

Kelvin, P. and Jarrett, J.E. (1985) *Unemployment. Its Social Psychological Effects*, Cambridge: Cambridge University Press.

Knights, D. and Willmott, H. (1989) 'Power and subjectivity at work: from degradation to subjugation in social relations', *Sociology* 23: 535–58.

Lane, C. (1988) 'New technology and clerical work', in D. Gallie (ed.) *Employment in Britain*, Oxford: Blackwell.

Lane T. (1986) *Grey Dawn Breaking. British Merchant Seafarers in the Late Twentieth Century*, Manchester: Manchester University Press.

Lupton, T. (1963) *On the Shop Floor*, Oxford: Pergamon Press.

Marsh, C. (1988) 'Unemployment in Britain', in D. Gallie (ed.) *Employment in Britain*, Oxford: Blackwell.

Martin, J. and Roberts, C. (1984) *Women and Employment. A Lifetime Perspective*, London: HMSO.

Marx, K. and Engels, F. (1973) *Manifesto of the Communist Party*, in D. Fernbach (ed.) *Political Writings*, vol. 1: *Karl Marx. The Revolutions of 1848*, Harmondsworth: Penguin.

McIntosh, I. and Broderick, J. (1996) ' "Neither one thing nor the other": compulsory competitive tendering and Southburgh cleansing services', *Work, Employment and Society* 10: 413–30.

Millward, N. and Stevens, M. (1986) *British Workplace Industrial Relations 1980–1984: The DE/ESRC/PSI/ACAS Surveys*, Aldershot: Gower.

Millward, N., Stevens, M., Smart, D. and Hawes, W.R. (1992) *Workplace Industrial Relations in Transition: The ED/ESRC/PSI/ACAS Surveys*, Aldershot: Dartmouth.

Morgan, G. (1986) *Images of Organization*, London: Sage.

Morris, L. (1989) 'Household strategies: the individual, the collectivity and the labour market – the case of married couples', *Work, Employment and Society* 3: 447–64.

Morris, L. (1990) *The Workings of the Household*, Cambridge: Polity Press.

Morris, L. (1994) *Dangerous Classes. The Underclass and Social Citizenship*, London: Routledge.

Murray, C. (1990) *The Emerging British Underclass*, Choice in Welfare Series no. 2, London: Institute of Economic Affairs.

Nichols, T. (ed.) (1980) *Capital and Labour. A Marxist Primer*, Glasgow: Fontana.

Nichols, T. (1999) 'Industrial sociology and the labour process', in H. Beynon and P. Glavanis (eds) *Patterns of Social Inequality*, London: Longman, 109–19.

Nichols, T. and Beynon, H. (1977) *Living with Capitalism. Class Relations and the Modern Factory*, London: Routledge and Kegan Paul.

Oakley, A. (1974) *The Sociology of Housework*, London: Martin Robertson.

O'Connell Davidson, J. (1994) 'What do franchisors do? Control and commercialisation in milk distribution', *Work, Employment and Society* 8: 23–44.

Pahl, R.E. (1984) *Divisions of Labour*, Oxford: Blackwell.

Penn, R., Rose, M. and Rubery, J. (eds) (1994) *Skill and Occupational Change*, Oxford: Oxford University Press.

Piore, M.J. and Sabel, C.F. (1984) *The Second Industrial Divide*, New York: Basic Books.

Pollert, A. (1981) *Girls, Wives, Factory Lives*, London: Macmillan.

Pollert, A. (1988) 'The "flexible firm": fixation or fact', *Work, Employment and Society* 2: 281–316.

Pollert, A. (ed.) (1991) *Farewell to Flexibility?* Oxford: Blackwell.

Pollert, A. (1996) 'Gender and class revisited; or, the poverty of "patriarchy" ', *Sociology* 30: 639–59.

Pugh, D.S. and Hickson, D.J. (eds) (1976) *Organizational Structure in its Context*, Farnborough: Saxon House.

Rees, G. and Fielder, S. (1992) 'The services economy, subcontracting and the new employment relations: contract catering and cleaning', *Work, Employment and Society* 6: 347–68.

Rees, T. (1992) *Women and the Labour Market*, London: Routledge.

Rice, A.K. (1963) *The Enterprise and its Environment*, London: Tavistock.

Ritzer, G. (1993) *The McDonaldization of Society*, Thousand Oaks CA: Pine Forge Press.

Roberts, I.P. (1992) *Craft, Class and Control: The Sociology of a Shipbuilding Community*, Edinburgh: Edinburgh University Press.

Roberts, I.P. (1997) 'The culture of ownership and the ownership of culture', in R.K. Brown (ed.) *The Changing Shape of Work*, Basingstoke: Macmillan.

Rose, M. (1988) *Industrial Behaviour. Research and Control*, Harmondsworth: Penguin.

Roy, D. (1952) 'Quota restriction and goldbricking in a machine shop', *American Journal of Sociology* 57: 427–42.

Rubery, J. and Wilkinson, F. (eds) (1994) *Employer Strategy and the Labour Market*, Oxford: Oxford University Press.

Scase, R. and Goffee, R. (1982) *The Entrepreneurial Middle Class*, London: Croom Helm.

Scase, R. and Goffee, R. (1987) *The Real World of the Small Business Owner*, London: Croom Helm.

Scott, A.M. (ed.) (1994) *Gender Segregation and Social Change*, Oxford: Oxford University Press.

Scott, W.H., Banks, J.A., Halsey, A.H. and Lupton, T. (1956) *Technical Change and Industrial Relations*, Liverpool: Liverpool University Press.

Sewell, G. and Wilkinson, B. (1992) ' "Someone to watch over me": surveillance, discipline and the just-in-time labour process', *Sociology* 26: 271–89.

Silverman, D. (1970) *The Theory of Organizations*, London: Heinemann.

Sinclair, J., Ironside, M. and Seifert, R. (1996) 'Classroom struggle? market oriented education reforms and their impact on the teacher labour process', *Work, Employment and Society* 10: 641–61.

Strauss, A. (1969) *Mirrors and Masks*, San Francisco: Sociology Press.

Taylor, S. (1997) ' "Empowerment" or "degradation"? Total quality management and the service sector', in R.K. Brown (ed.) *The Changing Shape of Work*, Basingstoke: Macmillan.

Thompson, P. (1983) *The Nature of Work. An Introduction to Debates on the Labour Process*, London: Macmillan.

Thompson, P. and Ackroyd, S. (1995) 'All quiet on the workplace front? A critique of recent trends in British industrial sociology', *Sociology* 29: 615–33.

Walby, S. (1990) *Theorizing Patriarchy*, Oxford: Blackwell.

Webster, F. and Robins, K. (1993) ' "I'll be watching you": comment on Sewell and Wilkinson', *Sociology* 27: 243–52.

Westwood, S. (1984) *All Day every Day. Factory and Family in the Making of Women's Lives*, London: Pluto Press.

Wood, S. (ed.) (1982) *The Degradation of Work? Skill Deskilling and the Labour Process*, London: Hutchinson.

Wood, S. (ed.) (1989) *The Transformation of Work? Skill, Flexibility and the Labour Process*, London: Unwin Hyman.

Woodward, J. (1965) *Industrial Organization: Theory and Practice*, London: Oxford University Press.

chapter 10

Science and technology studies – the environmentally friendly cottage industry

Peter Glasner

Introduction

By the early 1970s, STS, representing science, technology and *society*, was already identifiable as a separate, institutional area of study, with its own specialized teaching and research institutions, books, journals and related publications, and national and international organizations (see Spiegel-Rosing in Spiegel-Rosing and de Solla Price 1977: 9). However, by the mid-1990s, it was best described as a complex and developing field, still showing adolescent qualities, which had not yet come of age (Bowden 1994; Edge 1994). It had, however, become science and technology *studies*, with a continuing split between the social study of science, engineering and technology (sometimes referred to as SET) and science policy studies (Glasner and Rothman 1994) each of which appears to have developed its own separate community (Edge 1994: 12). There were, though, calls for recognizing the necessary, interrelated and co-constructed nature of these enterprises, in the context of managing the changing character of science and technology through policy development (see, for example, Webster 1991). This need has been highlighted by the impact of accounts of what has been variously described as the onset of 'late modernity' or the advent of the 'risk society' (Giddens 1990; Beck 1992). The particular focus has been on the new scientific and technological developments as evidenced in a range of environmentally related issues such as nuclear meltdown, chemical disaster, global warming and genetic modification (Lash *et al.* 1996).

The authoritative *Handbook of Science and Technology Studies* published by the Society for the Social Studies of Science in 1994 runs to twenty-eight chapters and over eight hundred pages without trying to map the whole of the field (see the Introduction to Jasanoff *et al.* 1994). This chapter recognizes the difficulty in attempting to provide a complete overview of any sub-discipline in a restricted space, given the problems of boundary maintenance and politics inherent in such an enterprise. Instead, the chapter will focus on the issue of genetic modification and show how the resources of science and technology studies can be brought to bear on illuminating what, for many, is very much a technological 'black box'. In doing so, it will begin by discussing how the area has become framed by the debate about risks and hazards in late modernity, and follow this with an exploration of the effects of policy developments, the role of scientific experts, and the involvement of the ordinary citizen in decision making. Using the example of genetically modified foods, this chapter will illustrate the extent to which, in comparison with the great factories of sociology, this 'cottage industry', as Law (1991) described it, can seriously be described as 'environmentally friendly'.

Barbarism modernized: the age of risk

Natural hazards have always made society a dangerous place whether in ancient times, or later, in predominantly agricultural economies (Giddens 1998: 27). These were also widespread, though their causes were often attributed to God or Fate. However, following industrialization in the nineteenth century, and the rise of science and technology, society in the mid-twentieth century has become characterized by the ubiquity of its crises: apocalypse has now become banal (Giddens 1991: 183–4). According to Ulrich Beck (1992), a major reason for this perception comes from the fact that, while in previous epochs science and technology were part of society's attempt at mastery over Nature so as to control hazards, experiments were generally confined to the laboratory bench. Now, society itself has become part of a global laboratory, and the risks have replaced hazards as the global threat. Whereas, initially those responsible for creating hazards could be identified, especially since the unquestioning authority of science was embedded in the wider culture, today's risks escape direct perception as they appear in toxins in foodstuffs, or in fallout from nuclear accidents, and there is no one to take responsibility. Their victims often do not detect them until it is to late, and some of their consequences become visible only in future generations (Beck 1998).

The result is that the claims of science to a monopoly of expertise have become more difficult to sustain in the face of competing claims, interests and viewpoints from the 'agents of modernity' (the producers of risk) and the injured parties. An obvious, recent example is the link between new variant Creutzfeld–Jakob Disease (CJD) and so-called 'Mad Cow Disease' or BSE. Here we do not see a simple scientific problem resolvable at the laboratory bench. Instead, as Wynne (1996a) observes, the issues are co-constructed by British relationships with the European Union and its regulations, the apparent proximity of government to private industrial interests, fast-eroding public confidence in official bodies, and a 'distinct whiff' of political control of science, alongside painstaking medical and scientific research. Society also faces the uncertainty of whether or not the thousands of innocent victims of 'beefgate' (*The Independent* quoted in Beck 1998: 10), who enjoyed a diet of beefburgers in recent years, are already infected with a life-threatening disease for which as yet there is no cure. They are part of a living laboratory, waiting to see over the next generation if this unwanted experiment will end in disaster (Cousens *et al.* 1997: 197). While these threats are real, the perception of risks is as much to do with a breakdown of trust resulting from an increased dependency in modern society on expert-led institutions, as it is to any direct link between CJD and BSE.

In the Introduction to the English edition of Beck's *Risk Society* (1992: 1–8), Lash and Wynne relate his discussion to recent advances in the sociology of science and technology, and in particular to the results of studies undertaken under the Economic and Social Research Council initiative on the Public Understanding of Science (for full details see Irwin and Wynne 1996). They suggest that society operates with an idealized model of the risk system, which gives undue weight to laboratory knowledge without recognizing the contextually narrow nature of its production, and then proceeds to give it the force of prescription. The example they use is of the reaction by the British government to the alleged health hazards associated with herbicides by farm workers. The government turned to the Pesticides Advisory Committee (PAC), which reviewed the scientific literature on the laboratory toxicology of the chemicals in question, and concluded that no risk existed. An even fatter dossier of cases of medical harm was dismissed as 'merely anecdotal, uncontrolled non-knowledge'. When pushed further, with even more examples, the PAC admitted that there was no risk as long as the herbicide was produced and used under the correct (laboratory) conditions. However, they failed to recognize what all farm workers knew: that instructions for use were frequently obliterated or lost, the proper spraying equipment was often unavailable, protective clothing was often inadequate, and weather conditions were frequently ignored in the pressure to get the spraying done.

Experts are given the role of defining agendas in the risk arena but, as has been seen time and again, and increasingly, they fail to recognize what sociologists and others have discovered by their research. Lash and Wynne summarize this in three points. Firstly, risks, however real, are socially located; secondly, their magnitude is a direct function of social as well as physical processes; and thirdly, the primary risks are often 'alien, obscure and inaccessible' to those most likely to experience them. The relationship between scientific expertise, generated through laboratory knowledge, and the contextually generated lay understanding of the application of knowledge is perhaps nowhere more chillingly illustrated than in the case of supposed Gulf War Syndrome. Here, organophosphate pesticides, similar to sheep dips and chemically related to nerve gas, were widely used by British troops in the Gulf. They were apparently kept in ignorance of the potential consequences, as indeed was Parliament, afterwards, by the Ministry of Defence (Fairhall 1997: 6). Malathion, used in very small quantities to kill hair infestations in children, was applied in large quantities and without the benefit of protective clothing, to delouse prisoners of war. The resulting symptoms of this pesticide misuse bear close similarities to those experienced by the farm workers using agricultural organophosphates described by Lash and Wynne. The effects have already resulted in disability and death, and some suggestion of transmission across generations to the children of war veterans. The case of genetically modified (GM) food has not developed against a backdrop of severe illness and loss of life in the way that the controversies over CJD–BSE and Gulf War Syndrome have. However, the potentially hazardous nature of introducing genetically modified organisms (GMOs) into the world has begun to create a debate with similar sociological characteristics. It may, therefore, be helpful to begin with a brief outline of the key events as they occurred in Britain. Complementary accounts of these events to the one that follows can be found in Adam (2000), Levidow (1999) and, by various authors, in a special issue of *Sociological Research Online* (SRO 1999).

The genetically modified food controversy

Following a long history of directed plant breeding, deriving from Mendel's experiments on peas in the nineteenth century, the first genetically modified plants – tobaccos – were developed as early as 1983, and the first foods – cereals – in 1990. The use of GMOs for the development of herbicide-resistant crop strains such as soya, and their introduction into the food chain, began to arouse controversy in the 1990s in the context of massive public concern after the identification of a possible CJD–BSE link, and alongside a series of other food-related safety concerns surrounding outbreaks of (sometimes lethal) *E. coli* O157. Together with the introduction by a major supermarket of genetically modified tomato paste, which was on sale and labelled as such for some eighteen months without causing undue concern, came calls from consumer organizations, and non-governmental organizations (NGOs) such as Friends of the Earth and Greenpeace, for better labelling of foods to improve and facilitate consumer choice (see, *inter alia*, Hamilton 1998). Organizations such as schools and supermarkets even banned the use of foods identified as containing GM ingredients around six months or so after concerns had been expressed by NGOs, when it became clear that legislation both in Britain and Europe concerning labelling was inadequate to deal with *processed* foods such as biscuits or pies, where the GM input had occurred at the very start of the food chain through, for example, the mixing of GM and non-GM products such as soya prior to their processing and export from the primary producer, the USA.

This complex set of interrelated difficulties was further compounded by a report from the prestigious Rowett Research Institute in October 1998. Dr Arpad Pusztai, a senior member of its staff, appeared to have shown that potatoes, genetically modified to contain a snowdrop gene, adversely affected the organs and metabolism of rats to which they were fed. While his unpublished results did no more than raise questions of safety for future research, their announcement, made in a television documentary, caused a political storm (see, for example, Driscoll and Carr-Brown, 1999) and Dr Pusztai was dismissed following an internal audit. His research became part of the media debate over the dangers to the public of eating any GM food, and finally the Royal Society produced a report on his experiments, peer-reviewed by half a dozen eminent statesmen of science, which concluded that no reliable or convincing evidence for his claims had been provided (Royal Society 1999).

The controversy then widened from a clear public concern about foods to reservations about the possible detrimental effects of growing GM herbicide-resistant crops in proximity to those not so modified. In particular, government-approved trials in several farms across Britain were found to be only several hundred yards from neighbouring farms producing officially recognized organically grown crops. The danger of cross-pollination meant that these farmers were in danger of losing their recognition, and having their livelihoods seriously jeopardized. A US study by researchers at Cornell University, reported by Kleiner (1999) in the *New Scientist*, suggested that, in their experiment, one half of monarch butterfly caterpillars fed on leaves of milkweed (their only food), dusted with pollen from GM corn, died within four days. However, their research had also not been peer-reviewed, and was instantly dismissed by experts from industry and the US Environmental Protection Agency. In Britain, English Nature vociferously expressed its concern about the possible ill effects of any large-scale trials of GM herbicide-resistant crops on adjacent flora which provide the habitat for a rich diversity of birds and insects. These concerns were dismissed by the Nuffield Council for Bioethics (1999), while the need for caution was expressed in an interim statement issued by the BMA (1999). The questions raised by the various parties were summarized in a most public fashion by the Prince of Wales in an article in the *Daily Mail* on 1 June 1999, generating even wider debate about the respective roles and responsibilities of science, government and industry.

The study of scientific controversies has a long history in the social studies of science and technology, and a good overview is provided by Nelkin (1994; see also Nelkin 1982), while a more general account is to be found in Englehart and Caplan (1987), and the distinctively British tradition of the 'Bath school' approach can be found in Collins (1981). Nelkin (1994) suggests that controversies arise in a variety of contexts, for example, when questions of social equity clash with those of economic efficiency as in the siting of nuclear waste facilities – the Not In My Back Yard (NIMBY) 'syndrome'. They may also stem from fears of risks associated with contamination such as resulted from the disaster at Chernobyl. However, they can equally arise from the apparent curtailment of individual freedoms as in the case of the hazards of smoking to health, or the violation of traditional values as with the development of *in vitro* fertilization techniques. Controversies, according to Mazur (1981), typically developed in three stages: a warning stage, a public stage, and a mass movement. In the case of the introduction of GM crops and food in the UK, the warning stage is best illustrated by the actions of a whistle blower (Arpad Pusztai), and an interest group (English Nature). The mass clearance of GM-based foods from supermarket shelves, and the issuing of reports by the BMA and the Nuffield Council on Bioethics, constitutes a good example of the second, public stage, while the extent to which the British public entertain doubts about the safety of GM foods in the long term will determine whether a mass movement with lasting effects is created. The study of controversies facilitates insight into the policy-making process, helps promote a greater understanding of the roles of experts, illuminates ways in which non-scientists can become involved in decision making, and clarifies the social and political nature of the scientific enterprise.

Science policy and the regulation of risk

A key element of the policy-making process is the development of appropriate laws and regulatory agencies to ensure that new scientific and technological advances do not pose unnecessary risks to the public. The adoption in the late 1970s, by the statutory Genetic Manipulation Advisory Group (GMAG), of a hazard-tree rather than a phyllogenic-based scheme for reconceptualizing the risks associated with the regulation of genetic manipulation techniques in Britain (Bennett *et al.* 1986) followed a worldwide moratorium in 1974 arising from public concern in the USA and Europe (Krimsky 1982; Wright 1994). Initially, scientists were able to identify degrees of risk only in terms of the closeness of any manipulated genetic material to humankind. Hence manipulating the genes in a plant was likely to be less hazardous than, for example, using a mammal. However, the net result was seen by scientists as too inhibiting of research and, following the relaxation of the moratorium in the USA, it became necessary to find an alternative method of calculating the hypothetically possible risks concerned. The solution was to adopt a hazard-tree approach which allowed calculation of risks to be made at each stage of a project. This opened the way to relating the 'riskiness' of any experiment to a suitable laboratory environment, and allowed even the most potentially hazardous of research projects to take place, for example, in facilities such as Porton Down in the UK. In this way, the assessment of uncertainty was transformed into merely following a bureaucratic routine, with the eventual abolition of the GMAG as a regulatory body, and the incorporation of many of its functions into the Health and Safety Executive.

This routinization of the risk analysis process is seen by Jasanoff (1995) as part of the repertoire of rhetorical devices used by science advisers to ensure that political decisions are not made which could be detrimental to their desire for unfettered pursuit of knowledge. In Britain, the Advisory Committee on Releases to the Environment (ACRE) which is made up predominantly of senior scientific experts, was asked in 1990 to rule on the release of genetically modified organisms into the atmosphere. The committee was to review all applications for release, whether they were drugs, crops, foods, or pesticides, and develop guidelines. However, as Jasanoff (1995: 321) notes, the risk assessment procedure was based on a method originally developed in the chemical industry, something which aligned biotechnology with a less novel form of hazardous activity. In addition, the procedure required that scientific experts would be able to imagine all possible future hazards. However, as Beck (1992) and Giddens (1990) have suggested, it is precisely because the potential hazards are *beyond* imagining in late modernity that places us in a 'risk' society.

Controversies can, however, also be seen as sites of 'social learning' through an informal process of technological risk assessment (Mazur 1981; Rip 1986), in contrast to the formalized processes developed by official regulatory agencies. Cambrosio and Limoges (1991) go further to suggest that controversies are indeed the *central* element of any social assessment of technological risk. Wynne (1995), using the example of the ways in which the European Commission facilitated the development of the European biotechnology industry, argues that the failure of draft legislation on the regulation of animal growth hormones to get Commission approval in 1985 (in spite of significant backing from the scientific establishment) stemmed from a lack of recognition that the required socio-technical conditions for its implementation were never likely to be realized in all member states. The resulting controversy stemmed not from a debate between science and anti-science, but from two different, but equally legitimate, views on how a risk assessment culture operated in the real world. For the scientists, all that was required was a set of formal procedures to be carried out in a pre-arranged manner. For the interest groups, whose influence scuppered the legislation, it was clear that the social policing necessary to ensure that the regulations were correctly applied at all times, by farmers in all the member states from Greece to Italy, was never likely to be put in place. The development of a controversy over animal growth hormones in cattle has, therefore, had the effect of illuminating a significant area of real concern in Europe.

These STS resources can be used in the context of the continuing debate about genetically modified food and crops. For example, there has been growing public concern about the lack of information available about contents on food packaging. The Food Advisory Committee in 1993 established guidelines for labelling which were accepted by the British Medical Association and the National Farmers Union on the grounds that the precautionary principle must be the right way to proceed. Supermarkets were dismayed, mainly because of the likely cost, of which not all would necessarily pass to the customer. Consumer organizations and other interest groups felt that the guidelines did not go far enough, and without the force of law were unlikely to be consistently applied. So, the controversy began. The decision to pass legislation requiring labelling of food ingredients was confirmed in 1995/6, and in the spring of 1999 a new and more thoroughgoing law was announced which recognized, in particular, the need to identify any ingredients (over 1 per cent) which had been genetically modified. While the new proposals still did not go far enough to satisfy some radical environmental groups, they were seen as politically and socially acceptable since they appeared to act in the best interests of the consumer by facilitating choice.

However, it was slowly becoming apparent that, since a major ingredient of supermarket food in Britain was genetically engineered soya and maize grown primarily in the USA, the apparently straightforward matter of identifying whether it was genetically modified was to be problematic. The difficulty revolved around the fact that, working under a more liberal regulatory regime, American farmers had for almost a decade mixed the genetically modified beans or maize with those grown without the benefit of scientific intervention, prior to processing them for export around the world. Soya is an ingredient of about two-thirds of processed foods, such as ready-to-eat meals, consumed in Britain. It is also a constituent of cooking oil and, with starch from maize, of the emulsifier, lecithin. As a result, the requirement to label a food as including genetically modified ingredients has proved impossible to fulfil; the processing undergone prior to export results in a new product which provides no recognizable evidence of the modification of its constituent parts. In addition, the proposed legislation completely ignored another fatal complication, since even foodstuffs sourced from non-USA outlets could include a proportion of US-grown, and therefore probably modified, ingredients.

Hence this case study illustrates how regulatory agencies and laws are developed in order to help establish and control risks enabling the public to make informed choices. But new regulatory regimes involving labelling appear to have benefited from the application by industrial science advisers of just those rhetorical devices identified by Jasanoff (1995) as facilitating rather than inhibiting further research on GM food ingredients since the modifications take place prior to processing. The labelling debate has also helped identify the major protagonists – industry, government, the NGOs – and shown the importance of social and political concerns in the decision on what, on the surface, appears simply to be scientific advice on regulatory policy. Science alone, it seems, is unable to establish the *definitive* basis for improving consumer choice. The case study also shows how, in spite of expert scientific advice, the framing of new laws and regulations in a 'risk society' cannot guarantee that the unimaginable will not arise. In this way, it clarifies the importance of controversies in facilitating the process of social learning in technological risk assessment.

The tragedy of expertise

Scientists have throughout history used their status as 'experts' to both draw a line between their own work and that produced by quacks and charlatans (Collins and Pinch 1982), and to defend themselves against the consequences of uncritical consumption of their research by non-scientists such as people in business and government – the 'lay public' (Gieryn 1983). In a period of 'reflexive modernisation' (Beck *et al.* 1994), the institutions of risk society are opened to criticism as never before, and scientists' own pronouncements about the nature of the dangers science itself creates are increasingly revealed as lacking legitimation. Sociologists have noted for some time that disagreements between experts provide useful insights into how scientific knowledge is constructed and evaluated (Irwin 1995). Barnes and Edge (1982: 237) in their review of the early literature, suggest that the credibility of scientific expertise rests as much with the contexts in which it is offered as it does with the rationality of the arguments. They describe the recognition of this ubiquitous contingency as the 'tragedy of expertise'.

In their study of medical and scientific professionals in the new genetics, Kerr, Cunningham-Burley and Amos (1997) suggest that this tragedy is still unfolding. Their respondents held the view that rational scientific knowledge was a 'gold standard' clearly demarcating good, and value-free, research from illogical or politically distorted opinion, which they paternalistically attributed to an undifferentiated lay public. However, these experts went further in appearing to promote objective advice about the risks of the new genetics, while simultaneously disguising the extent of their own social location and vested interests. This has recently become part of the GM controversy as well with the publication in the national press of the links between membership of government advisory committees, including ACRE and the Advisory Committee on Novel Foods and Processes (NCNFP), and major biotechnology companies such as Monsanto, Zeneca and Novartis. In the case of ACRE and NCNFP, it was suggested that one half the members have such links (Nuki 1999). These were not made clear to the public when the committees initially proffered their advice to government on the regulation of GM foods and crops.

Gilbert and Mulkay (1984) identified a difference, based upon public and private pronouncements by scientists, which helps to explain how experts' contrasting linguistic repertoires are themselves socially located. They suggested that two distinct repertoires exist, and scientists are clear when one or the other is to be used. The first recognizes the contextual nature of knowledge production, is used informally, for example in conversation between scientists in the laboratory, and is called the 'contingent repertoire'. However, when communicating formally, as in published reports and papers in academic journals, or communicating with the public, scientists invariably resort to using an 'empiricist repertoire'. Here events, actions, and beliefs become a neutralized medium through which the empirical truth emerges, and science is reconstructed as a rational and value-free activity. This implicit presupposition of the politically and morally neutral value of science contributes to constructing a particular identity of 'science-in-general' (Michael 1996: 105) which then becomes a vital resource in enrolling the public into accepting the validity of scientific expertise. It can also be argued that those most prominent experts are scientists who are also furthest from day-to-day research at the laboratory bench (Glasner and Rothman 1999). Hence their pronouncements are made with a degree of confidence which those much closer to its contingent nature might find more difficult to sustain; distance may effectively legitimate certainty (Collins 1988: 726).

One reason for studying controversies is that they force protagonists to clarify the often tacit and unarticulated assumptions that underpin their arguments. The Pusztai case mentioned earlier, and widely publicized in the media (see, for example, Radford 1999), throws light on the significance of using appropriate repertoires to legitimate expertise, and clearly highlights for the wider public the tacit assumptions underlying what constitutes certified scientific knowledge. Dr Pusztai stood accused by many leading experts of having made his research findings public without first going through the normal channels and publishing them in a peer-reviewed specialist journal. As a result, it was argued, the validity of his findings could not be properly evaluated, and, given their controversial nature, the publicity had thrown his employers, the prestigious Rowett Research Institute, into disrepute. The issue was further clouded by the need for Pusztai to seek further funding for his work, suggesting a mix of motives similar to those found in a previous case, that of cold fusion research, where the results of a potentially ground-breaking experiment were also made public at a televised press conference (Close 1992). This violation of scientific protocol had the effect both of making more complex the accepted linear method of scientific communication, and of adding to rather than simplifying the confusion about how valid the experiments really were (Lewenstein 1995).

Dr Pusztai was suspended, pending an internal audit of his work. Following its failure to confirm his findings, the Institute allowed Dr Pusztai to publish an alternative report on the internet. During this time he was given very public support by a group of twenty international scientists, who suggested that it was too early to wholly dismiss his claims, and that further research might well establish the validity of his conclusions. When his report became publicly available, one national newspaper requested a 'peer review' from a respected expert toxicologist, and subsequently printed his critical findings (Sanders, in Conner 1999). The matter came to a head with Dr Pusztai's data being submitted to a distinguished panel of experts from the Royal Society, who concluded that the results of any further tests for GM food safety should not be published until they had been appropriately peer reviewed (Royal Society 1999). *The Lancet*, while issuing an editorial disclaimer, felt it appropriate to publish at least some of his findings later in the year. The reaction from the leaders of the scientific community remained dismissive. This effectively closed the debate and re-established, at least in the short term, the hegemony of the scientific establishment over the certification of scientific knowledge (Collins 1985: 142 *et seq.*).

These events also vividly illustrate the important differences between linguistic repertoires in the legitimation process, showing how both the initial televisual 'publication' of the results and the subsequent media-inspired 'peer-review' process were couched in a discourse characterized by the contingent repertoire identified by Gilbert and Mulkay. This had the effect of denying scientific validity to either side, and served only to further fuel the flames, and muddy the waters, of the controversy about the potential risks of GM foods. Closure to the debate only became possible through the intervention of the Royal Society, the British scientific institution with the highest status. Its report, based on the use of orthodox review procedures, and couched in careful and unambiguous language, thereby using the empiricist repertoire which distanced the authors from its conclusions, rejected Dr Pusztai's data as inadequate. However, it was also an example of how actor-networks (Callon 1986; Latour 1987) function to enrol and mobilize expert opinion and identify as dependent a lay public in mending ruptures to its legitimating fabric. For the scientific establishment, at least, the 'tragedy' had been averted through this 'simplifying' intervention into an increasingly complex controversy involving television, the press, the scientific media including official journals, and the world wide web.

Involving the public

The need for greater citizen involvement in policy decision making is not solely limited to developments in science and technology (Pateman

1970; Young 1990; Cochrane 1996) although the results of studies under the overall rubric of 'the public understanding of science' (PUS) have brought them, according to Irwin (1995), into the foreground for STS (see, for example, Eden 1996). Dorothy Nelkin (1975) noted that to define decisions as technical, as normally occurs with each new advance in science and technology, rather than political, effectively disenfranchises the public at large. Recent studies of PUS (for example, Irwin and Wynne 1996) have established that scientists utilize what Wynne (1991, 1994) describes as a 'deficit' model of scientific knowledge when evaluating lay contributions to technical debates. This assumes that public reservations about science and technology are predicated upon ignorance, so that better science education will necessarily lead the public to a greater understanding and more objective appreciation of its contribution to social progress. However, by default, it also implies that the only legitimate carriers of such knowledge are those already trained as scientists themselves, and that what constitutes knowledge is itself universal and uncontentious (Michael 1996).

The deficit model of scientific knowledge highlights the recognition that 'framing' what constitutes legitimate science is a socially constructed process involving numerous groups and institutions in society. Until the recent past, responsibility for reproducing the hegemonic view has rested with a scientific establishment enjoying the active support of society at large (Beck 1992). In the sociology of science, this has been represented by the systems approach of Robert Merton, a key social theorist and founding parent of the sub-discipline, who famously regarded the scientific norms of communalism, universalism, disinterestedness and organized scepticism (known as the CUDOS syndrome) as a vital ingredient of the democratic process (Merton 1973). The constructivist 'turn', building on the sociology of knowledge, social interactionism, and ethnomethodology in the 1970s (Mulkay 1979), paved the way for STS to make a significant contribution to the wider theoretical debates in sociology as a whole (see, for example, Velody and Williams 1998).

The opportunities for acceptable participation in the policy-making processes of science and technology are now seen as severely circumscribed by the institutions within which they occur. Much work has been done on alternative ways to involve the public in overcoming this democratic deficit. Early attempts, particularly those based on survey research, suffered from confusing the citizen with the consumer, and confounding the discourse of market competition with that of rights and responsibilities (Irwin 1995). More imaginative ways of avoiding this confusion have included focus groups, public meetings and conferences, citizens' panels and juries, and deliberative polls (Seargeant and Steele 1998), although each have their strengths and weaknesses (Coote and Lenaghan 1997).

In November 1994, the Science Museum organized a Consensus Conference on Plant Biotechnology, the first of its kind in Britain (Joss and Durant 1995; Barns 1996; Fixdal 1997; Purdue 1999). A lay panel was constituted to question witnesses from science, industry and NGOs, in order to arrive at a view about the future of this contentious technology. However, according to one observer, the conference suffered from a deep ambivalence about whether it was there to facilitate the decision-making process, or to simply be part of an ongoing consultation exercise (Purdue 1999: 96). As a result, the expert–lay divide became further entrenched, and what on the surface was delivered as a consensual outcome, was actually unconnected to the policy process and therefore of little practical value. These limitations were reflected in a later attempt to involve the public in ameliorating the democratic deficit, a citizens' jury on genetic testing for common disorders in Wales (Dunkerley and Glasner 1998; Glasner and Dunkerley 1999) where the jury model, like the Consensus Conference, served only to accentuate the legitimacy of the scientific and technical experts. In addition, the jury's recommendations were not binding on the ultimate sponsors, a multinational pharmaceutical corporation, but instead were reported to the government's Advisory Commission on Human Genetics, along with many other views.

The Citizen Foresight project was an attempt to involve the public while addressing some of the issues raised by using the jury model by the London Centre for Governance, Innovation and Science and the Genetics Forum (LCGIS 1998). It focused on the future of agriculture and the food system, including questions on sustainable agriculture, organic food, genetically modified organisms and public confidence. Unlike in the jury model, the twelve randomly selected 'panelists' (as they were deliberately called) from the Brighton area themselves set out the issues they wanted to explore. Witnesses were assessed by a stakeholder panel of key interest groups to ensure a balanced view, and the conclusions were drawn up by the panelists themselves. The report was launched at the Parliamentary Environment Group at the House of Commons in an attempt to directly influence policy makers. In this way the organizers hoped to both contribute to offsetting the democratic deficit, albeit for only a small number, ensure that expert credibility was co-constructed rather than imposed, and forefront the importance of public involvement in framing the questions as well as suggesting the way forward.

The various experiments in involving the citizen in the decision-making processes of scientific and technological advance have therefore had mixed success. While only a few are privileged to be closely involved, the experiments have provided rare opportunities for public debate, and helped encourage debate and openness in areas where, for commercial or other reasons, secrecy sometimes obtains (Rothman, *et al.* 1996). Irwin (1995: 173) acknowledges that there is no single model or blueprint to meet the challenge of inclusive involvement in satisfactorily bringing together the social, environmental and technical issues.

Conclusion

This chapter has not attempted to map the full range of issues, insights and debates that form the core of science and technology studies in Britain at the turn of the century. However, by focusing on an important case study at the interface between humankind and the natural world, the controversy over genetically modified foods and organisms, it has shown how the resources of STS can be harnessed to better understanding of the complex social and natural processes involved in the introduction of this new technology. This understanding informs a better appreciation of the policy-making processes which assess potential risks and develop appropriate regulatory mechanisms to deal with them. It also promotes greater participation and involvement in these processes through insights into how risks are framed by experts, and the role of lay expertise in the management of new technology. It effectively illustrates how developments in science and technology cannot be divorced from society at any level, through clarifying the socially and politically co-constructed nature of social life. Clearly gaps exist, but the increasingly central nature of the scientific enterprise to the future of social life suggests that STS still has a lot to contribute.

The social study of science and technology has, over the last twenty-five years, established itself as a flourishing sub-discipline within sociology in Britain: a vigorous and successful 'cottage industry'. Events appear to have overtaken those who initially suggested that its theoretical and practical concerns might appear parochial. STS now contributes significantly to informing wider debates in theory and empirical research, and has placed itself at the forefront of the arguments about modernity and the 'risk society'. In addition, significant advances in methodology have been made, for example in reflexivity and actor-network theory. As the environment has become a key issue on the agenda of other sociological factories and cottage industries, the contribution of STS to theory and practice has become more central (see, for example, ESRC 1999).

It would be wrong to say that environmentalist issues are the terrain on which STS is to become fully assimilated into the mainstream of either sociology or science policy studies. In 1991, Howard Newby, then running the Economic and Social Research Council, made it clear, in his address to the British Sociological Association on its fortieth anniversary, that there was a continuing two-cultures approach to environmental issues in Britain. He felt that, to a large extent, it was the fault of sociology that its insights had not been taken into account by environmentalists and other experts (Newby 1991). STS has, however, over the last few years, avoided the 'social fix' approach and begun to explore the interface between the human and the natural. Indeed, it could be argued that this is precisely what makes STS more 'environmentally friendly' than other sociological factories and cottage industries.

References

Adam, B. (2000) 'The temporal gaze: the challenge for social theory in the context of GM food', *British Journal of Sociology* 51 (1) (January/March): 125–42.

Barns, I. (1996) 'Manufacturing consensus? Reflections on the UK national Consensus Conference on Plant Biotechnology', *Science as Culture* 23: 200–17.

Barnes, B. and Edge, D. (eds) (1982) *Science in Context. Readings in the Sociology of Science*, Milton Keynes: Open University Press.

Beck, U. (1992) *Risk Society: Towards a New Modernity*, London: Sage.

Beck, U. (1995) *Ecological Politics in an Age of Risk*, Cambridge: Polity Press.

Beck, U. (1998) 'Politics of risk society', in J. Franklin (ed.) *The Politics of Risk Society*, Cambridge: Polity Press.

Beck, U., Giddens, A. and Lash, S. (1994) *Reflexive Modernisation*, Cambridge: Polity Press.

Bennett, D., Glasner, P. and Travis, D. (1986) *The Politics of Expertise: Regulating rDNA Research in Britain*, London: Routledge and Kegan Paul.

BMA (1999) *The Impact of Genetic Modification on Agriculture, Food and Health – an Interim Statement*, London: British Medical Association, May (http://www.bma.org.uk/public/science/genmod.htm)

Bowden, G. (1994) 'Coming of Age in STS. Some methodological musings', in S. Jasanoff *et al.* (eds) *Handbook of Science and Technology Studies*, London: Sage.

Callon, M. (1986) 'Some elements in the sociology of translation: domestication of the scallops and the fishermen of St Brieux Bay', in J. Law (ed.) *Power, Action and Belief: A New Sociology of Knowledge?* London: Routledge and Kegan Paul.

Cambrosio, A. and Limoges, C. (1991) 'Controversies as governing processes in technology assessment', *Technology Analysis and Strategic Management* 3 (4): 377–96.

Close, F. (1992) *Too Hot to Handle: The Race for Cold Fusion*, London: W.H. Allen.

Cochrane, A (1996) 'From theories to practices: looking for local democracy in Britain', in D. King and G. Stoker (eds) *Rethinking Local Democracy*, Basingstoke: Macmillan.

Collins, H.M. (ed.) (1981) 'Special issue knowledge and controversy: studies of modern natural science', *Social Studies of Science* 11: 1–158.

Collins, H.M. (1985) *Changing Order: Replication and Induction in Scientific Practice*, London: Sage.

Collins, H.M. (1988) 'Public experiments and displays of virtuosity: the core set revisited', *Social Studies of Science* 18: 725–48.

Collins, H.M. and Pinch, T. (1982) *Frames of Meaning. The Social Construction of Extraordinary Science*, London: Routledge and Kegan Paul.

Conner, S. (1999) 'Pusztai: the verdict', *Independent*, Friday Review, 19 February: 9.

Coote, A. and Lenaghan, J. (1997) *Citizens' Juries: Theory into Practice*, London: Institute for Public Policy Research.

Cousens, S.N., Vynnycky, E., Zeidler, M., Will, R.G. and Smith, P.G. (1997) 'Predicting the CJD epidemic in humans', *Nature* 385 (16) (January): 197–8.

Driscoll, M. and Carr-Brown, J. (1999) 'What's eating us?' *The Sunday Times*, News Review, 21 February: 6.

Dunkerley, D. and Glasner, P. (1998) 'Empowering the public? Citizens' juries and the new genetic technologies', *Critical Public Health* 8: 181–92.

Eden, S. (1996) 'Public participation in environmental policy: considering scientific, counter-scientific and non-scientific contributions', *Public Understanding of Science* 5: 183–204.

Edge, D. (1994) 'Reinventing the wheel', in S. Jasanoff *et al.* (eds) *Handbook of Science and Technology Studies*, London: Sage.

Englehardt, T.H. and Caplan, A.L. (eds) (1987) *Scientific Controversies: Case Studies in the Resolution and Closure of Disputes in Science and Technology*, Cambridge: Cambridge University Press.

ESRC (1999) *The Politics of GM Food. Risk, Science and Public Trust*, ESRC Global Environmental Change Programme special report no. 5, Brighton: University of Sussex.

Fairhall, D. (1997) 'Ministers misled over Gulf', *The Guardian*, 27 February: 6.

Fixdal, J. (1997) 'Consensus conferences as extended peer groups', *Science and Public Policy* 24 (6): 366–76.

Funtowicz, S.O. and Ravetz, J. (1993) 'Science for the post-normal age', *Futures* 25 (7): 739–55.

Giddens, A. (1990) *The Consequences of Modernity*, Cambridge: Polity Press.

Giddens, A. (1991) *Modernity and Self-identity: Self and Society in the Late Modern Age*, Cambridge: Polity Press.

Giddens, A. (1998) 'Risk society: the context of British politics', in J. Franklin (ed.) *The Politics of Risk Society*, Cambridge: Polity Press.

Gieryn, T.F. (1983) 'Boundary work and the demarcation of science from non-science: strains and interests in professional ideologies of scientists', *American Sociological Review* 48: 781–95.

Gieryn, T.F. (1994) 'Boundaries of science', in S. Jasanoff *et al.* (eds) *Handbook of Science and Technology Studies*, London: Sage.

Gilbert, G.N. and Mulkay, M. (1984) *Opening Pandora's Box. A Sociological Analysis of Scientists' Discourse*, Cambridge: Cambridge University Press.

Glasner, P. and Dunkerley, D. (1999) 'The new genetics, public involvement and citizens' juries: a Welsh case study', *Health, Risk and Society* 1 (3): 233–40.

Glasner, P. and Rothman, H. (1994) 'Science studies: a guide for strategic management', *Technology Analysis and Strategic Management* 6 (4): 505–25.

Glasner, P. and Rothman, H. (1999) 'Does familiarity breed concern? Bench scientists and the human genome mapping project', *Science and Public Policy* 26: 313–24.

Hamilton, N. (1998) *Attack of the Genetically Engineered Tomatoes. The Ethical Dilemma of the '90s*, Stowmarket: Whittet Books/Nemesis Press.

Irwin, A. (1995) *Citizen Science. A Study of People, Expertise and Sustainable Development*, London: Routledge.

Irwin, A. and Wynne, B. (eds) (1996) *Misunderstanding Science? The Public Reconstruction of Science and Technology*, Cambridge: Cambridge University Press.

Jasanoff, S. (1995) 'Product, process or programme: three cultures and the regulation of biotechnology', in M. Bauer (ed.) *Resistance to New Technology: Nuclear Power, Information Technology and Biotechnology*, Cambridge: Cambridge University Press.

Jasanoff, S., Markle, G.E., Petersen, J.C. and Pinch, T. (eds) (1994) *Handbook of Science and Technology Studies*, London: Sage.

Joss, S. and Durant, J. (eds) (1995) *Public Participation in Science. The Role of Consensus Conferences in Europe*, London: Science Museum.

Kerr, A., Cunningham-Burley, S. and Amos, A. (1997) 'The new genetics: professionals' discursive boundaries', *Public Understanding of Science* 4: 243–53.

Kleiner, K. (1999) 'Monarchs under siege', *New Scientist*, 22 May: 4.

Krimsky, S. (1982) *Genetic Alchemy*, Cambridge MA: MIT Press.

Lash, S., Szerszynski, B. and Wynne, B. (1996) *Risk, Environment and Modernity: Towards a New Ecology*, London: Sage.

Latour, B. (1987) *Science in Action*, Milton Keynes: Open University Press.

Law, J. (1991) 'Introduction: monsters, machines and socio-technical relations', in J. Law (ed.) *Sociology of Monsters: Essays on Power, Technology and Domination*, London: Routledge.

LCGIS (1998) *Citizen Foresight: A Tool to Enhance Democratic Policy-making*, vol. 1: *The Future of Food and Agriculture*, London: London Centre for Governance, Innovation and Science, and the Genetics Forum.

Levidow, L. (1999) 'Britain's biotechnology controversy: elusive science, contested expertise', *New Genetics and Society* 18: 47–64.

Lewenstein, B.V. (1995) 'From fax to facts: communication in the cold fusion saga', *Social Studies of Science* 25: 403–36.

Mazur, A. (1981) *The Dynamics of Technical Controversy*, Washington DC: Communications Press.

Merton, R.K. (1973) *The Sociology of Science. Theoretical and Empirical Investigations*, Chicago: University of Chicago Press.

Michael, M. (1996) *Constructing Identities*, London: Sage.

Mulkay, M. (1979) *Science and the Sociology of Knowledge*, London: George Allen and Unwin.

Nelkin, D. (1975) 'The political impact of technical expertise', *Social Studies of Science* 5: 35–44.

Nelkin, D. (1982) 'Controversy as a political challenge', in B. Barnes and D. Edge (eds) *Science in Context: Readings in the Sociology of Science*, Milton Keynes: Open University Press.

Nelkin, D. (1994) 'Science controversies: the dynamics of public disputes in the United States', in S. Jasanoff *et al.* (eds) *Handbook of Science and Technology Studies*, London: Sage.

Newby, H. (1991) 'One world, two cultures: sociology and the environment', *Network* 50, May.

Nuffield Council for Bioethics (1999) *Genetically Modified Crops: The Ethical and Social Issues*, London: Nuffield Council for Bioethics.

Nuki, P. (1999) 'GM food advisers have links to biotech companies', *The Sunday Times* 13 June: 5.

Pateman, C. (1970) *Participation and Democratic Theory*, Cambridge: Cambridge University Press.

Purdue, D. (1999) 'Experiments in the governance of science and technology: a case study of the UK National Consensus Conference', *New Genetics and Society* 18: 79–99.

Radford, T. (1999) 'They don't know, you know', *The Guardian*, 23 February: 17.

Rip, A. (1986) 'Controversies as informal technology assessment', *Knowledge* 8 (December): 349–71.

Rothman, H., Glasner, P. and Adams, C. (1996) 'Proteins, plants and currents: rediscovering science in Britain', in A. Irwin and B. Wynne (eds) *Misunderstanding Science? The Public Reconstruction of Science and Technology*, Cambridge: Cambridge University Press.

Royal Society (1999) *Review of Data on Possible Toxicity of GM Potatoes* (http://www.royalsoc.ac.uk/st_pol54.htm)

Seargeant, J. and Steele, J. (eds) (1998) *Consulting the Public. Guidelines and Good Practice*, London: Policy Studies Institute.

Speigel-Rosing, I. and de Solla Price, D. (eds) (1977) *Science, Technology and Society. A Cross-Disciplinary Perspective*, London: Sage.

SRO (1999) 'Rapid response – the genetic modification of food', *Sociological Research Online* 4 (3) (http://socresonline.org.uk)

Velody, I. and Williams, R. (eds) (1998) *The Politics of Constructionism*, London: Sage.

Webster, A. (1991) *Science, Technology and Society: New Directions*, Basingstoke: Macmillan.

Wright, S. (1994) *Molecular Politics: Developing American and British Regulatory Policies for Genetic Engineering 1972–1982*, Chicago: University of Chicago Press.

Wynne, B. (1991) 'Knowledges in context', *Science, Technology and Human Values* 16: 111–21.

Wynne, B. (1994) 'Public understanding of science', in S. Jasanoff *et al.* (eds) *Handbook of Science and Technology Studies*, London: Sage.

Wynne, B. (1995) 'Technology assessment and reflexive social learning: observations from the risk field', in A. Rip, T.J. Misa and J. Schot (eds) *Managing Technology in Society: The Approach of Constructive Technology Assessment*, London: Pinter.

Wynne, B. (1996a) 'Patronising Joe Public', *The Times Higher Educational Supplement* 12 April: 13.

Wynne, B. (1996b) 'May the sheep safely graze? A reflexive view of the expert–lay knowledge divide', in S. Lash, B. Szerszynski and B. Wynne (eds) *Risk, Environment and Modernity. Towards a New Ecology*, London: Sage.

Young, I.M. (1990) *Justice and the Politics of Difference*, Princeton NJ: Princeton University Press.

chapter 11

Family sociology in from the fringe: the three 'economies' of family life

David H.J. Morgan

Introduction

In the 1960s it might have seemed that there was a solid basis developing for the study of British family life. Studies of working-class (Dennis *et al.* 1956; Young and Willmott 1962) or rural families (Frankenberg 1957; Littlejohn 1964) were being complemented by studies of middle-class family life (Bell 1968) while a later textbook by Harris (1983) provided a clear overview of some of the central issues of the family in a modern industrial society. A more polemical, if well-documented, study of the British family proved to be a godsend to sociology tutors (Fletcher 1966). Overviews of family and community studies drew attention to a rich range of works (Klein 1965; Frankenberg 1966) and pointed to some key conceptual tools. Amongst these, Elizabeth Bott's highly influential study provided insights into the ways in which marital relationships could be understood in wider contexts and placed the idea of social networks at the centre, not only of family analysis, but also of many studies that were attempting to come to grips with the complexities of relationships in a modern society (Bott 1957).

Yet, despite this promise, it cannot be said that family studies immediately went on to become a major stream within British sociology as a whole. Whatever may have happened in more recent years, there was little evidence of a cumulative development of family studies in Britain during much of the 1970s and early 1980s. For a long time it appeared that Marxian and neo-Weberian issues to do with class, power and the state provided the dominant debates while family studies appeared to be a relatively minor and trivial area of concern. Within sociology teaching, courses in social inequalities and sociological theory were seen as essential elements in the training of sociologists; the same could not be said of courses in family sociology.

In a sense this apparent marginalization of family studies would seem to be curious, not simply because so many of the classic British studies dealt with the bracketed areas of 'family and community'. Whatever might have been happening at the level of sociological debates, there can be little doubt that family life constitutes a major part of many people's individual experiences and remains, in one form or another, a popular topic of conversation. How was it that something that, in all its variety, constituted an important area of everyday experience failed to occupy a central area of concern within sociological analysis?

Perhaps it was the apparent obviousness of family life that contributed to the marginalization of these studies within sociology; in a sense we all 'know' about families. Perhaps, also, family life is too close to our experience and its pains and pleasures may be thought to get in the way of dispassionate analysis. However, there may have also been some more specific reasons. Within sociology, family studies appeared to be relatively atheoretical or, in the case of the much stronger American family research, reflecting theoretical traditions and interests that did not seem to have many followers within the British sociology of the time. Where the study of the family was related to wider societal processes this appeared to reflect versions of functionalism which were themselves being discredited. Debates, for example, around whether the family had 'lost' or was changing its functions tended to seem less relevant as the very ideas of 'function' and functionalism were being strongly criticized.

Almost certainly, the main reason for the apparent weakness of family studies within Britain was the growth of the feminist critique of sociological research, theorizing and practice. Developing from the late 1960s and early 1970s, feminist scholarship quickly identified the family as a major, if not the key, source of women's oppression, implicating sociological studies of the family within this wider critique. Family studies were seen as conservative or shot through with patriarchal assumptions and much contaminated by functionalist or positivist modes of thinking and analysis.

The overall impact of this critique was somewhat mixed. On the one hand, it led to a range of studies exploring many aspects of family life such as the daily work of housewives (Oakley 1974), motherhood and parenthood (Backett 1982; Boulton 1982) and the interaction between work, employment and the family especially as it affected women (Hunt 1980; Finch 1983; Porter 1983; Yeandle 1984). Later developments included more theoretical or general assessments of the part played by the family in the oppression of women (Barrett and McIntosh 1982; Delphy and Leonard 1992). On the other hand, the study of the family was seen to be important only in so far as such studies provided insight into the origins and reproductions of gender subordinations and the ways in which these might be transcended. To put the matter over-simply, family studies appeared to be in danger of being subsumed under feminist or gender studies. What needs to be stated firmly is that there is more to family living than relationships between men and women.

This is not to say that interest in family matters declined completely in the 1970s and 1980s. Some important textbooks were produced (Allan 1985; Elliott 1986) while my own work received a fair measure of attention (Morgan 1975, 1985). But it could not be said that the sociology of the family or family studies more generally were the main foci of sociological interest in either research or teaching.

New developments, new opportunities

From the standpoint of the 1960s/1970s, it might have appeared that family studies were on the way out. However, it is likely that the combined effect of the feminist critique of much family sociology together with growing concerns about the limits of the welfare state contributed to a 'new realism' in relation to family studies (Finch and Morgan 1991). The family as an institution was not about to disappear, yet it was increasingly realized that family life was not simply a fundamental institution based upon mutual support and altruism. Violence and abuse, as well as love and care, were part of the family story, and family life continued to be shaped by economic and political considerations as much as by sentiments.

Certainly, public interest in family life showed no signs of declining. The Conservative administrations of Thatcher and Major produced a number of public statements and claims as well as some actual initiatives in relation to the family (Jones and Millar 1996). Perhaps the most discussed and the most controversial of these was the Child Support Act of 1991 which, together with the accompanying debates, linked concerns about the care of children, lone mothers, absent fathers and the rising cost of social services. These concerns continued with the return of a Labour government and the publication of a widely discussed consultative document on family life (Ministerial Group on the Family 1998). The Labour government has also turned its attention to the continuing problems of the Child Support Agency and its apparent failure either to provide adequate support for lone mothers and their children or to ensure payment on the part of absent fathers.

These public debates both drew upon and inspired sociological research into many aspects of family life, with particular focus on the interaction between poverty and social exclusion, childcare and household structures (for some examples see: Bradshaw and Millar 1991; Henricson 1994; Jones 1995; Speak *et al.* 1995; Clarke *et al.* 1996; Humphrey 1996; McGlone *et al.* 1998). Up to a point it might be argued that some of the more policy-orientated research as well as the wider political and public debate that made use of and encouraged such research tended to reproduce a rather limited understanding of what family life was all about. A familiar list of concerns was repeatedly reproduced: rising divorce rates; rising numbers of lone parents, especially lone mothers; increasing rates of cohabitation; increasing numbers of individuals living alone, and so on. This may have had the effect of producing a restricted perspective on family life, one not only limited to a series of issues defined as 'social problems' but also some-what detached from wider concerns about changes in work, social divi-sions, consumption and leisure. Family matters appeared to continue to be about what happened in or around domestic settings, households, and between adults as spouses or cohabitees and between parents and children. While, clearly, most people would regard family life as addressing these matters, such relationships are not necessarily confined to households; fam-ily life is implicated in schools and education, systems of transport and urban planning, trends in consumption and shopping and developments in information technology and the mass media.

It may be further argued that the, by now familiar, annual lists of divorce rates, numbers of lone-parent households, cohabitation rates and so on tend to be at some distance from the everyday experiences of family life. Some decades ago, C. Wright Mills drew attention to the gulf between divorce *rates* and the individual experiences of the pains of separation and rebuilding a life, and argued that it was the responsibility of the sociol-ogist to bring together these two levels of social life (Mills 1959). Statistical and demographic analysis is vital for mapping some of the key changes within our society and for producing a basis for historical and inter-national comparisons. But such figures tell us nothing about experiences and a simple repetition of 'the facts' does little to enhance real social understanding. Figures about the numbers of reconstituted households, for example, say little in themselves about the many different routes to step-parenthood or to the complexities and rich variety of step-parent experiences (Barnes *et al.* 1998).

However, sociological analysis has not confined itself to the provision of more detailed statistical information and neither has it limited its framework to the 'social problems' defined through the public debates. Thus, Finch and Mason's study of family responsibilities, while clearly reflecting and contributing to wider public debates about informal care between family members, also raises questions of the nature and character of the ties and obligations between family members across different households and the everyday use and negotiation of social rules as opposed to conformity to more abstract moral codes (Finch and Mason 1993). Smart and Neale's study of step-parenting similarly looks at matters of public concern while being equally concerned with issues of gender and the working out of everyday moralities (Smart and Neale 1999). Sara Irwin's study, *Rites of Passage* (1995), is not simply concerned with young people's transitions to adulthood but with the location of these understandings within a wider framework of social and economic inequalities.

References to such recent empirical studies could be multiplied. Further, they have been accompanied by more general discussions which consider a wide range of issues associated with family life but going beyond the agendas set by public policy debates. These include edited collections (McKie *et al.* 1999; Silva and Smart 1999) and more general texts or theoretical discussions (Cheal 1991; Morgan 1996; Bernardes 1997; Jamieson 1998) and readers (Allan 1999). Work is beginning to break beyond the confines of any one nation (e.g. Gullestad and Segalen 1997) although there is clearly scope for much more comparative work of this kind. Further, the contributions from social anthropologists (e.g. Strathern 1992) and social historians (Gillis 1997; Davidoff *et al.* 1999) are increasingly influential and acknowledged.

What we may see emerging from these discussions is the development of a broader and deeper understanding of family life. It is broader in that it encourages the reader to look beyond the particular problems which constitute the core of public debates or much statistical analysis and to locate discussions within a wider framework that includes social divisions, economic, social and cultural change and more global developments. Particularly influential here has been the recent work of Giddens (1992), Beck (1992) and Beck and Beck-Gernsheim (1995) on individuality, risk and modernity. It may be fairly argued that this wider understanding was beginning to develop with feminist studies which saw the need to consider family practices within a framework which included all kinds of relationships within the gender order or patriarchy.

This emerging new understanding of family life is also deeper in that it seeks to be closer to everyday experience and understanding of family life. Again, feminist scholarship has played a major part in foregrounding the experiences of women within domestic situations and these experiences have been augmented by including the experiences of children and of men within families. It is likely that such accounts have been enriched by more rigorous and systematic developments within qualitative research and, possibly, by newer developments such as the growth in interest in auto/biographical studies.

An abiding concern within family studies in recent years has been the very term 'family' itself (Gubrium and Holstein 1990). There is a strong consensus that the term 'the family' as a noun should be used rarely, if at all, since it conveys a misleading impression of a readily identifiable and clearly bounded unit. Such units were supposed to be very similar to each other in structure and function. In other words, use of the term 'family' in this way tended to smooth over the diversity of experiences and practices associated with family living. Yet people do continue to use the word 'family' in order to make sense of their daily lives, so to abandon the term altogether would seem to fly in the face of everyday practices. The answer would seem to be to consider the word 'family' more as an adjective, to describe a particular set of activities or relationships. My discussion of 'family practices' attempted to develop this idea (Morgan 1996). Other approaches would argue for a detailed consideration of the ways in which individuals use the term 'family' and what they seek to convey when the term is used in different contexts or circumstances.

One consequence of these shifts in the way in which the term 'family' is used and understood is the realization that family practices do not stand alone but overlap with all kinds of other practices to do with gender, work (paid, domestic, voluntary), class, ethnicity, consumption, leisure and so on. Discussions of policy issues, for example, draw attention to the development of 'family-friendly' policies on the part of governments or organizations, pointing to the continuities and possible tensions between the worlds of family and of paid employment.

In the remainder of this chapter, I shall look at some of these areas of sociological enquiry and show how understandings of family and household might be important in developing a more rounded understanding of these topics. In the first place, I shall consider a collection of rather standard, if central, topics to do with work and employment, class and stratification and gender. Taken together these topics might be seen as loosely constituting part of the 'political economy' of family life in that they deal with the allocation of resources (including time and effort) within the household and within the wider society and the way in which questions to do with class and gender impact on these.

We may also consider two other 'economies' which overlap with the political economy of family life. In the first place, we may talk about the 'moral economy' of 'the' family, that is the ways in which family members reflect upon and account for the decisions that they have made in the course of day-to-day family living. Second, I talk of the 'emotional economy' to do with the part played by feelings and emotions within family living. In both these additional 'economies', gender and other divisions continue to play an important part.

Of course, the term 'economy', in common with many other terms used in social science, is a metaphor and, as such, has its limitations. It might suggest too much of calculation and measurement: that rational weighing up of alternative courses of action. However, the use of the term is not intended to imply any whole-hearted commitment to 'rational choice' theory although this may well be a part of the way in which family life is understood. It is worth recalling that the original meaning of the term 'economy' referred to 'household management'. What is intended is the realization that choices are constantly being made within family settings and that reference is frequently made to ideas of family in the course of making such choices. What is being suggested here is that in some senses people behave within families in much the same sort of way as they behave in other social settings (work, leisure, community, etc.) but that, in addition, there is some sense that family decisions are different from other decisions. Part of the aim of this chapter is to explore what these differences might be. If this can be achieved, it will support the argument that 'family' is an important dimension in many areas of social life not often associated with family practices.

The political economy of family living

One major development within a wide range of social sciences has been the focus on the household and the analysis of the way in which the household, as well as or instead of individuals, is an important element in the analysis of economic life as a whole and of systems of social stratification. There are some difficulties and complexities involved in the definition of the household but, at its simplest, it refers to residential units – houses, flats and so on – whose members share certain core facilities especially those to do with cooking and eating. Households, according to this understanding, could, and increasingly do, consist of single individuals, although they still more frequently contain more than one person. Household members might be related to each other through birth or marriage although this is not necessarily part of the definition. Thus a group of students sharing communal facilities within a particular dwelling could constitute a household.

Households came to be seen as important elements within the wider economic and social structure. Households constituted a place where employees could feed, rest and enjoy or participate in other non-employment activities and hence were important, as Marxist theorists would argue, in the reproduction of labour. Further, much of the unpaid work that takes place within a modern society – cooking, cleaning, repairing clothes or other items – takes place within households. A particularly important aspect of this is to do with childcare and socialization. As within the wider economy, there are divisions of labour within households and these may be highly variable and quite complex despite the relative smallness of the unit.

Households could also be seen as key elements in the analysis of consumption, for individuals may purchase particular goods or services on behalf of the households of which they are a part rather than simply on their own account. Such an analysis does not stop at the boundaries of the household but looks at divisions, equal or otherwise, between individual household members.

Households, as well as individuals, may also be seen as important elements in the wider class and status systems. Where the notion of 'head of household' continues to be a relevant consideration, it can be argued that other individuals within the household, conventionally women and children, may be said to derive their class or status identities indirectly from the head rather than in their own right. While this model, as we shall see, has been increasingly challenged in recent years, the idea of the household as an element within the wider social structure remains an important one. Similarly, in so far as households may be units within which individuals share resources, then participation within the wider system of social status may again be made on the basis of household membership rather than simply individual ownership of money or other relevant resources.

Housing may be seen as an illustration of where several strands of modern economic and social life converge. Houses, apartments and other dwellings constitute the physical locations of households and household activities. Much consumption is directed towards the upkeep and decorating of dwellings, and an individual's prestige in part depends on his or her address and the type of housing that is occupied. While the notion of 'housing classes' may not tell the whole story about class in modern society (Saunders 1990), where one lives is clearly an important element in locating an individual within the class and status structure. Importantly, such dwellings, whether or not they are legally owned by individuals or by couples, are often shared by members of a household. Thus there is a triangular relationship between household, dwelling and social status.

These are just some indications of the way in which the household is becoming an increasingly important element in the analysis of wider economic and social processes. While such an analysis may not fully replace one based upon individuals it certainly deserves to be considered along-side it. However, there are some difficulties which have been identified with this developing household approach. First, it remains important to retain a distinction between households and families. This is not just academic hair-splitting but a recognition that both terms, distinct yet often overlapping, raise different sets of analytical problems. Very roughly, families have something to do with relationships established through parenthood and marriage or cohabitation. Thus while households may contain indi-viduals who are related in this way they need not necessarily do so. Further, family relationships of necessity cut across households. Thus the isolated individual may constitute a household while retaining family relationships with others located in different households. A further important point of distinction lies in the fact that individuals frequently change their household but only change their existing kinship and family ties under exceptional circumstances.

The importance of this distinction may be seen in numerous ways. A sense of family obligations may well affect patterns of consumption, as when parents buy items of clothing or special foods for their children or through the numerous gifts that are exchanged between family members on ritual occasions such as weddings or birthdays (Cheal 1988). Whether unrelated individuals sharing a household respond or behave in the same way as related individuals is an open question but it is fairly certain that, in addition, these individuals will also acknowledge ties and obligations outside their particular households. Further, in considering the ways in which family relationships are important in the reproduction of class and status relationships over time one need only consider the continuing import-ance of patterns of inheritance which frequently go along family lines or through family connections (Finch 1997). Yet again, the values and life styles associated with particular classes, however defined, are frequently learnt by children in their interactions with parents. In numerous ways, therefore, family relationships interact with and cut across household relationships.

Another critical issue associated with the development of household studies was the fear that such an emphasis might obscure issues of gender. Thus, if the household rather than the individual should be taken as the key unit within the economy or system of social stratification, then there might be a danger that other divisions between men and women within the household will become obscured. The same could also be said of differences between adults and children. Some writers began to speak of the 'black box' of the household and the need to open this up to further, more detailed, scrutiny (Brannen and Wilson 1987).

The importance of considering differences and divisions within the household may be illustrated by two examples. First, consider the household as a unit in the economy, supplying labour for participation in paid employment and consuming goods and services. To take employment first, considerable research has demonstrated the intimate connections between gender divisions of labour in the labour market and within the home. Within the home such divisions, based upon customary expectations, patriarchal power or deep-rooted understandings of what it is to be a man or a woman, may influence participation in the labour market. A strongly marked gender division of labour, for example, might restrict women's participation in the labour market while more shared participation in child-rearing or domestic labour might enhance it. Conversely, the divisions between men and women in the labour market and the differences in earning power often associated with these differences may provide legitimations for the maintenance of what is frequently regarded as the 'traditional' breadwinner/ housewife distinction. The complex interplays between the public and the private, gendered differences in earning power and constructions of femininity and masculinity have been explored in numerous research-based studies (Morris 1990; McKie *et al.* 1999). Much recent work has benefited from detailed studies of money management within the household (Pahl 1989; Vogler 1994) and the use of time budgets (Gershuny *et al.* 1994; Horrell 1994). These latter works also point to changes in the gendered divisions of labour in the direction of greater sharing between partners within the household.

There are similar divisions when it comes to consumption. It is not simply the case that the household 'consumes' goods and services produced outside it. Resources may be unequally distributed within the household or there may be differences between the management of money and consumption, differences that follow gender distinctions. Husbands and wives, within households, may not participate equally or identically in consumption because they may not have equal access to or management of the necessary financial resources. Again, there are complex relationships between gendered divisions within the home and decisions about consumption and the sharing of resources.

Another area where gender may make a difference is in the study of social stratification. Statements to the effect that the household is a unit in the class structure have been the subject of considerable, and sometimes heated, debate. Such an approach often seemed to assume a simple model where there is a single, usually male, head of the household and where it might be assumed that the status of other members of the household derive from his occupational status (Goldthorpe 1983; Crompton 1993; Roberts 1993). Such understandings came to be seen as increasingly unrealistic in times of increasing numbers of dual-earner households and cross-class marriages. The growing recognition that both individuals and households may, in different ways, be seen as elements in the wider social structure may increase the levels of complexity of class analysis but will undoubtedly be more realistic and, probably, closer to the experiences of men and women.

These critical points stressing the differences between households and families and the continued importance of gender divisions may cause some modification in household-based analysis but they do not lessen its importance. Indeed, taking these themes together has provided for the potentiality for some powerful models of the political economy of family living. Such an approach recognizes the gendered divisions of labour within households and within the wider society and the ways in which these impact upon each other. Family life is woven into economic life, mediated through and modified by households and gender. More recent analyses of the economic significance of children within households and economic life reinforce this need to explore the political economy of families and households (James and Prout 1997; James et al. 1998). Such an approach, further, requires a richer, more expanded understanding of the meaning of work, seeing it as both paid and unpaid, formal and informal (Wallman 1979).

These converging and developing understandings which see family and household life as continuous with other spheres of economic and social life have the effect of weakening the divisions between family sociology and other areas of social enquiry. Thus it is not simply the case that ideas and research derived from the study of economic or political life, such as discussions of rational choice or of power, may be fruitfully applied to the analysis of the family. It is also the case that these other areas of social enquiry into stratification or economic life have to be more conscious of family and household and the ways in which gender and age differences cut across these. But in order to explore the contributions that family analysis may make to other areas of social research we need to explore further dimensions of family life.

The moral economy of family living

Recent sociological discussion of family living has taken issues of morality m[...]   [...] is these issues that I wish to explore
unde[...]   [...]ral economy of family living'. The
term[...]   [...]ttle strange, involving the yoking
togetl[...]   [...]d of economics with the more absolute c[...]   [...]onventionally associated with morality. F[...]   [...]ey the idea that family members
routir[...]   [...]matters of considerable importance
dealir[...]   [...]e, human need and sometimes of
life a[...]   [...]se a language of morality in order
to ev[...]   [...]ions.

Questions of 'care' serve as a good illustration of this general idea. There
is now a large body of research which has explored the many and complex dimensions of the care, mostly unpaid and informal, that takes place
within domestic settings and between family members (Leira 1983;
Waerness 1987; Finch 1989). This may be between parents and children
or between adults where one party is elderly, infirm or sick. Feminist
researchers have pointed out that much of this care is undertaken by women.
Distinctions have been made between 'caring for', the routine practical tasks
involved in the caring process, and 'caring about', the emotional feelings
which family members are supposed to have for one another. In popular
discourse, 'care' is treated as a more or less unqualified good as, for example, when the term 'caring society' is used. Thus, the work of caring,
especially as it becomes identified with family practices, comes to be woven
around ideas of morality.

Finch and Mason, in their study of the negotiation of family responsibilities, write:

> In other questions about children looking after elderly parents, people
> tended to agree that children had a responsibility to do *something*, but views
> varied on *what* they should do.
>
> (Finch and Mason 1993: 19 original emphasis)

This gets to the heart of the idea of a moral economy. There is a sense of
obligation and responsibility coupled with a recognition that choices
need to be made within a range of variable options. Their understanding
of the way in which moral ideas enter into everyday family decisions rules
out a picture of family members simply following rules of obligation. Rather,
what is to be done is a matter for negotiation between family members in
which a whole host of factors are taken into account including physical

availability, the presence of already existing obligations to children, spouses or kin, employment commitments and so on. Woven into these negotiations, which may be open and direct or concealed and indirect, are ideas of exchange and reciprocity.

Again, these notions of exchange and negotiation seem to belong to the rational worlds of accounting and calculation rather than morality. However, morality is involved firstly because the issues at stake are frequently to do with human need and care. Further, questions of morality enter into the ways in which people talk about these decisions and the ways in which questions of self and identity are frequently a part of these family processes. Thus Finch and Mason talk about 'legitimate excuses', the reasons which individuals may offer for not providing care or help of a particular kind (e.g. in terms of taking in a sick relative or providing extended financial help) and the extent to which these are regarded as reasonable or legitimate. Further, they write about the way in which these decisions, and the negotiations surrounding them, are bound up with ideas of reputation and moral identity. If, within a family setting, I have a reputation as a caring or supportive individual then it is often difficult to distance myself from this reputation without some loss to my own sense of moral identity.

of care and responsibility between family members are
ure of moral concerns and the careful weighing up of altern-
 area where the idea of the moral economy of family
seen is in relationships within 'reconstituted' households
step-parents and children. The break-up of a family unit
ce and the subsequent reconstitution of family life through
duces considerable complexities in the analysis of such rela-
cially between parents, previous children and step-children,
ent or non-resident. These are occasions when the nature of
nsibilities, and the extent to which these may differ as between
biolog... d social parents, come to be matters of critical importance
and where, again, issues of morality, of how we 'ought' to behave, often come to the fore.

Following the divorce or separation of a couple with children, a variety of outcomes is possible (Smart and Neale 1999). Co-parents may reach some agreement about the sharing of both parental authority and parental care; custodial parenting may involve the sharing of the care but with no sharing of the authority, while solo parenting will mean the absence of either shared care or shared authority. Whatever the particular outcomes, questions of morality are involved. These are not, as Smart and Neale point out, questions of absolute morality condemning the very act of divorce or separation itself or of blaming a 'guilty' party. It is more a question of carefully reflecting upon the decisions that need to be made and of providing accounts to explain or justify the decisions that have been reached. Contrary to some popular beliefs, they argue, individuals do not lightly abandon partners or set up new relationships, especially where children are concerned. There is frequently a careful consideration of what are understood to be the needs of the children, in terms of both discipline and authority and care and support and how these needs are to be balanced against other personal needs or obligations. Further, bound up with these ongoing processes of moral reasoning in family contexts, there are evaluations of the different claims of biological as against step-parents (Edwards *et al.* 1999) as to whether certain kinds of responsibilities are 'naturally' based.

There are, therefore, numerous occasions within family living where moral decisions are made and reflected upon. We could also consider, for example, decisions about when and whether to have children, including decisions not to have children (Marshall 1993; McAllister and Clarke 1998). All these are moral in that they sometimes use the language of morality and frequently involve serious reflection and discussion. They are also to do with the 'economy' in that they deal with the allocation of time and resources and the making of future commitments. The term 'moral economy' would seem to be justified in that these would seem to represent two intersecting sides of the same coin.

Other important issues arise out of these considerations. Is it, as it is sometimes argued, a question that there are different moral frameworks for men and women? Clearly, as all these studies show, gender enters into the processes of negotiation and moral debate and it is likely that, within our culture, there are different styles of moral argument between the two sexes. But it is important also to recognize that both men and women do enter into these moral negotiations and find their identities, gendered and moral, bound up with the decisions that are made and the ways in which they conduct themselves.

Another complex question deals with the extent to which there is something especially moral about family life. In so far as family matters frequently deal with questions of health and sickness, life and death and sexuality, it may be argued that there are particularly strong linkages between family practices and questions of morality. But the same may often be true about professional medical practice, relationships between friends, the conduct of war and many other areas of social life. Nevertheless, it can be suggested that in modern society the idea of 'the family' has come to be particularly strongly identified with questions of right and wrong and the nature of care and our responsibilities to others. Such an identification may not be inevitable or exclusive but it remains strong.

The emotional economy of family living

It is both curious and understandable that issues of emotions have been somewhat marginal to sociological analysis. It is curious in that emotions and feelings are intimately bound up with what it is to be human; it is understandable in that the mainstream of sociological debate has been around ideas of rationality and rational behaviour. Emotions seem to be on the fringe of many theories of social behaviour.

However, the sociology of emotions is now developing partly, one might suppose, in response to the feminist critique of sociological practice (Bendelow and Williams 1998). Further, there can be no doubt that emotions are especially closely bound up with family living and the way in which it is talked about and experienced. The very ideas of 'care', mentioned in the previous section, highlight complex mixtures of practical tasks – feeding, washing, providing medication, etc. – and feelings, both positive and negative. People frequently talk about family life and other family members and such talk is rarely free of expressions of feeling or emotion.

Terms such as 'emotional labour' or 'emotional work' have been developed and elaborated in recent years, and while their usage has not been confined to the family they clearly have considerable reference when it comes to looking at domestic life. The reasons for this are complex and various but would include the experiences of dependencies that are established across generations (i.e. arising out of relationships between parents and children) and the close and often continuous or frequent proximity of individuals within clearly defined, and often limited, areas of space. Thus the idea of 'the home' comes to take on deep and complex, sometimes ambivalent, symbolic and emotional significance.

These terms 'emotional labour' or 'emotional work' have come to encompass a range of meanings and practices. They may include the emotions that are bound up with everyday caring work. They may be to do with the control or expression of one's own emotions or the control of the emotions of others. Thus a parent confronted with the tantrums of a child has to handle not only the emotions and tears of the child concerned but also personal emotions of anger or sympathy or distress in the face of such an outburst. Marital or cohabiting partners come to anticipate the emotional responses of the other and to take account of these in everyday negotiations. Family contexts are often, therefore, the sites for the expression and control of emotions. These emotions may be positive or negative and the attempts to control them may be successful or unsuccessful. While much of this may seem to be the province of the psychologist, sociological analysis enters at several points in considering, for example, the ways in which people talk about, understand and construct emotions within everyday family situations.

Issues of emotion are frequently associated with another rapidly developing area of sociological enquiry, namely the sociology of the body (Shilling 1993). The connections between the two are numerous. The body is frequently understood to be the key site for the expression of emotions; happiness, grief and anger have, allowing for cultural variations, strong bodily connotations. The use of the word 'feelings' almost inevitably conjures up the idea of bodily sensations even where the term may be used metaphorically. Second, bodily concerns are often the occasion for the expression of emotions, whether they be feelings of desire or tenderness for a loved one or feelings of disgust or repulsion for certain bodily functions. As has already been mentioned, the practices associated with care involve a complex mixture of embodied feelings and bodily practices. Further, feelings for another may be closely associated with the bodily closeness or co-presence of another or others and this closeness in terms of time and space is a prominent, if not exclusive, feature of family life.

As with the discussions of the moral economy, discussions of emotions often involve questions of gender differences. Thus it is frequently argued that, in a whole range of settings, women are defined as 'emotional specialists', individuals who as a result of nature or nurture are particularly skilled at managing their own emotions and the emotions of others. Clearly this understanding carries considerable ideological weight and, in the context of the household, may lead to a 'division of emotional labour' (Duncombe and Marsden 1993). Examples of this are frequently found in social science literature. Men, for example, are more likely to view marital conversations in practical, problem-solving terms rather than as something valuable in their own right (Mansfield and Collard 1988) and this understanding may spill over into the expectations that husbands have in marital counselling sessions (Brannen and Collard 1982). Whether or not men really have difficulties in 'getting in touch with their feelings', it seems reasonably clear that these gender differences frequently enter into the way in which men and women talk about, or account for, their relationships and hence these understandings take on a reality of their own. 'Isn't that just typical of a man/woman' may be frequently heard in marital arguments.

Again, we need to ask the question about the use of the word 'economy' in this section. Clues are already provided in the growing use of the terms 'emotional labour' and 'emotional work' since they imply the expenditure of effort in a particular direction (e.g. towards someone in need of care), effort which might well be used elsewhere. While there is a tendency to speak of emotions as natural and spontaneous, it would seem reasonable to suppose that these are not inexhaustible and that individuals make some kind of decision about where to devote their feelings. We do, after all, talk about concentrating one's feelings in one direction or another or, alternatively, of being emotionally drained. The key point here is that in family, and other contexts, individuals are concerned not simply with the control or expression of their own emotions but also with the emotions of others. The use of the term 'economy', while it may seem over-rationalistic, does recognize that the everyday expression and control of emotions involves the allocation of time to others and that time is a finite resource.

Conclusion

The aim of this chapter has been to show how family studies have moved more centre-stage over the last two or three decades. Increasing governmental and political interest in family life has been one, but not the sole or even the most important, influence. Further, while there has been a growth in studies which might be clearly identified as family studies there has also, it has been argued, been a growth in the recognition of the part that family or household studies might play in the analysis of other areas of social life. In part this is a recognition of a more fluid way of understanding social life, one which recognizes overlaps and interconnections rather than, as in the older functional models, of establishing distance between distinct areas of social life such as the family, the economy, political life and so on. It is interesting to note that in a recent book which examines *Sociological Research Methods in Context* (Devine and Heath 1999) one chapter deals quite explicitly with a family study (Finch and Mason 1993) but several of the other chapters could also be said to deal more or less indirectly with family matters such as nannies and waged domestic labour, housing and home-working women.

In conducting this exploration, I looked firstly at a set of related issues to do with employment, the household, class and gender described generally as 'the political economy of family life'. This referred to questions of the allocation of time and resources to different sets of people or activities and the ways in which these were shaped by and impacted upon issues of gender. Much mainstream and family sociology continues to revolve around these core issues. But I also argued that this did not conclude the investigation of family practices and that in order to do this more fully we needed to examine two other 'economies': the moral and the emotional.

These three broad headings each pointed to continuities between family studies and other areas of social enquiry. With the first, the continuities are with studies of economic life and stratification. With the second, there are overlaps with the studies of morality seen here at the level of more practical day-to-day ethics rather than with philosophical or abstract discussions. The third overlaps with the recent studies of the sociologies of the emotions and of the body. All of these overlap with considerations of gender and all, incidentally, with disciplines outside sociology.

These three areas also overlap with each other. Perhaps the clearest example is in the organization of care. Under the first heading we can see this in terms of the relationships between formal and informal, paid and unpaid systems of care and the associated gendered divisions of labour. Under the second heading we can see the ways in which ethics of care shape and emerge out of the gendered practices of care within the home and elsewhere. In the third area we have seen the way in which care is concerned with questions of emotions and the body, again both of which are gendered. While I have treated these headings separately, the three economies interact and out of these interactions emerges something of the distinctive quality of family life in modern society. This is not to say that similar mixes cannot be found in other areas of social life within, for example, some of the professions or service-based occupations. Nevertheless, in terms of popular understandings of family life as being something distinct, it is likely that this sense of specialness arises out of the particular mixes of the everyday, the routine domestic and caring tasks, and the special, those areas of emotional or moral significance.

References

Allan, G. (1985) *Family Life*, Oxford: Blackwell.

Allan, G. (ed.) (1999) *The Sociology of the Family: A Reader*, Oxford: Blackwell.

Backett, K.C. (1982) *Mothers and Fathers*, London: Macmillan.

Barnes, G., Thompson, P., Davies, G. and Burchardt, N. (1998) *Growing up in Stepfamilies*, Oxford: Clarendon Press.

Barrett, M. and McIntosh, M. (1982) *The Anti-Social Family*, London: Verso.

Beck, U. (1992) *Risk Society: Towards a New Modernity*, London: Sage.

Beck, U. and Beck-Gernsheim, E. (1995) *The Normal Chaos of Love*, Cambridge: Polity Press.

Bell, C. (1968) *Middle-Class Families*, London: Routledge and Kegan Paul.

Bendelow, G. and Williams, S.J. (eds) (1998) *Emotions in Social Life*, London: Routledge.

Bernardes, J. (1997) *Family Studies: An Introduction*, London: Routledge.

Bott, E. (1957) *Family and Social Network*, London: Tavistock.

Boulton, M.G. (1982) *On Being A Mother*, London: Tavistock.

Bradshaw, J. and Millar, J. (1991) *Lone Parent Families in the UK*, London: HMSO.

Brannen, J. and Collard, J. (1982) *Marriages in Trouble: The Process of Seeking Help*, London: Tavistock.

Brannen, J. and Wilson, G. (eds) (1987) *Give and Take in Families*, London: Allen and Unwin.

Cheal, D. (1988) *The Gift Economy*, London: Routledge.

Cheal, D. (1991) *Family and the State of Theory*, New York and London: Harvester Wheatsheaf.

Clarke, K., Craig, G. and Glendinning, C. (1996) *Children's Views on Child Support: Parents, Families and Responsibilities*, London: Children's Society.

Crompton, R. (1993) *Class and Stratification: An Introduction to Current Debates*, Cambridge: Polity Press.

Davidoff, L., Doolittle, M., Fink, J. and Holden, K. (1999) *The Family Story: Blood, Contract and Intimacy, 1830–1960*, London: Longman.

Delphy, C. and Leonard, D. (1992) *Familiar Exploitation*, Cambridge: Polity Press.

Dennis, N., Henriques, F. and Slaughter, C. (1956) *Coal Is Our Life*, London: Eyre and Spottiswoode.

Devine, F. and Heath, S. (1999) *Sociological Research Methods in Context*, Basingstoke: Macmillan.

Duncombe, J. and Marsden, D. (1993) 'Love and intimacy: the gender division of emotions and "emotion work"', *Sociology* 27 (2): 221–42.

Edwards, R., Gillies, V. and Ribbens McCarthy, J. (1999) 'Biological parents and social families: legal discourses and everyday understandings of the position of step-parents', *International, Journal of Law, Policy and the Family*, 13: 78–105.

Elliott, F.R. (1986) *The Family: Change or Continuity?* Basingstoke: Macmillan.

Finch, J. (1983) *Married to the Job*, London: Allen and Unwin.

Finch, J. (1989) *Family Obligations and Social Change*, Cambridge: Polity Press.

Finch, J. (1997) 'Individuality and adaptability in English kinship', in M. Gullestad and M. Segalen (eds) (1997) *Family and Kinship in Europe*, London: Cassell.

Finch, J. and Mason, J. (1993) *Negotiating Family Responsibilities*, London: Routledge.

Finch, J. and Morgan, D. (1991) 'Marriage in the 1980s: a new sense of realism?' in D. Clark (ed.) *Marriage, Domestic Life and Social Change*, London: Routledge, 55–82.

Fletcher, R. (1966) *The Family and Marriage in Britain*, revised edition, Harmondsworth: Penguin.

Frankenberg, R. (1957) *Village on the Border*, London: Cohen and West.

Frankenberg, R. (1966) *Communities in Britain*, Harmondsworth: Penguin.

Gershuny, J., Godwin, M. and Jones, S. (1994) 'The domestic labour revolution: a process of lagged adaptation', in M. Anderson, F. Bechhofer and J. Gershuny (eds) *The Social and Political Economy of the Household*, Oxford: Oxford University Press, 151–97.

Giddens, A. (1992) *The Transformation of Intimacy*, Cambridge: Polity Press.

Gillis, J. (1997) *A World of Their Own Making*, Oxford: Oxford University Press.

Goldthorpe, J. (1983) 'Women and class analysis: in defence of the conventional view', *Sociology* 17 (4): 466–88.

Gubrium, J. and Holstein, J.A. (1990) *What is Family?* Mountain View CA: Mayfield Publishing.

Gullestad, M. and Segalen, M. (eds) (1997) *Family and Kinship in Europe*, London: Cassell.

Harris, C.C. (1983) *The Family and Industrial Society*, London: Allen and Unwin.

Henricson, C. (ed.) (1994) *Crime and the Family*, London: Family Policy Studies Centre.

Horrell, S. (1994) 'Household time allocation and women's labour force participation', in M. Anderson, F. Bechhofer and J. Gershuny (eds) *The Social and Political Economy of the Household*, Oxford: Oxford University Press, 198–224.

Humphrey, R. (ed.) (1996) *Families Behind the Headlines*, University of Newcastle: Department of Social Policy.

Hunt, P. (1980) *Gender and Class Consciousness*, London: Macmillan.

Irwin, S. (1995) *Rites of Passage: Social Change and the Transition from Youth to Adulthood*, London: UCL Press.

James, A. and Prout, A. (eds) (1997) *Constructing and Reconstructing Childhood*, second edition, London: Falmer Press.

James, A., Jenks, C. and Prout, A. (1998) *Theorising Childhood*, Cambridge: Polity Press.

Jamieson, L. (1998) *Intimacy: Personal Relationships in Modern Societies*, Cambridge: Polity Press.

Jones, G. (1995) *Family Support for Young People*, London: Family Policy Studies Centre.

Jones, H. and Millar, J. (eds) (1996) *The Politics of the Family*, Basingstoke: Ashgate.

Klein, J. (1965) *Samples from English Cultures*, London: Routledge and Kegan Paul.

Leira, A. (ed.) (1983) *Work and Womanhood: Norwegian Studies*, Oslo: Institute for Social Research.

Littlejohn, J. (1964) *Westrigg: The Sociology of a Cheviot Parish*, London: Routledge and Kegan Paul.

Mansfield, P. and Collard, J. (1988) *The Beginning of the Rest of Your Life?* Basingstoke: Macmillan.

Marshall, H. (1993) *Not Having Children*, Melbourne: Oxford University Press.

McAllister, F. with Clarke, L. (1998) *Choosing Childlessness*, London: Family Policy Studies Centre.

McGlone, F., Park, A. and Smith, K. (1998) *Families and Kinship*, London: Family Policy Studies Centre.

McKie, L., Bowlby, S. and Gregory, S. (eds) (1999) *Gender, Power and the Household*, Basingstoke: Macmillan.

Mills, C.W. (1959) *The Sociological Imagination*, Harmondsworth: Penguin.

Ministerial Group on the Family (1998) *Supporting Families: A Consultative Document*, London: The Stationery Office.

Morgan, D.H.J. (1975) *Social Theory and the Family*, London: Routledge and Kegan Paul.

Morgan, D.H.J. (1985) *The Family, Politics and Social Theory*, London: Routledge and Kegan Paul.

Morgan, D.H.J. (1996) *Family Connections: An Introduction to Family Studies*, Cambridge: Polity Press.

Morris, L. (1990) *The Workings of the Household*, Cambridge: Polity Press.

Oakley, A. (1974) *The Sociology of Housework*, Oxford: Martin Robertson.

Pahl, J. (1989) *Money and Marriage*, Basingstoke: Macmillan.

Porter, M. (1983) *Home, Work and Class Consciousness*, Manchester: Manchester University Press.

Roberts, H. (1993) 'The women and class debate', in D. Morgan and L. Stanley (eds) *Debates in Sociology*, Manchester: Manchester University Press.

Saunders, P. (1990) *A Nation of Home Owners*, London: Unwin Hyman.

Shilling, C. (1993) *The Body and Social Theory*, London: Sage.

Silva, E.B. and Smart, C. (eds) (1999) *The New Family?* London: Sage.

Smart, C. and Neale, B. (1999) *Family Fragments?* Cambridge: Polity Press.

Speak, S., Cameron, S., Woods, R. and Gilroy, R. (1995) *Young Single Mothers: Barriers to Independent Living*, London: Family Policy Studies Centre.

Strathern, M. (1992) *After Nature: English Kinship in the Late Twentieth Century*, Cambridge: Cambridge University Press.

Vogler, C. (1994) 'Money in the household', in M. Anderson, F. Bechhofer and J. Gershuny (eds) *The Social and Political Economy of the Household*, Oxford: Oxford University Press, 225–6.

Waerness, K. (1987) 'On the rationality of caring', in A.S. Sassoon (ed.) *Women and The State*, London: Hutchinson.

Wallman, S. (ed.) (1979) *Social Anthropology of Work*, London: Academic Press.

Yeandle, S. (1984) *Women and Working Lives: Patterns and Strategies*, London: Tavistock.

Young, M. and Willmott, P. (1962) *Family and Kinship in East London*, revised edition, Harmondsworth: Penguin.

chapter 12

Sociology and health: creating the agenda

Anne Murcott

Introduction

Health is on everyone's agenda. It is a concern of any state – a concern that runs from assuring an orderly and productive populace to overseeing some arrangement for the disposition of the sick and infirm, from levying revenues to raising armies. It is evident in the social institutions and divisions of labour in any society such that specialists dealing with misfortune and sickness, birth and death come to be named. It is manifest everywhere in that any culture provides a repertoire of rules and symbols, theories or explanations creating conceptions of health, illness and the corporeal self, not to mention models and meanings about the origins of human life, cosmologies or the sources of suffering. And health is on anyone's personal agenda: yours, theirs, mine. Health – or its absence – is ever present, potentially a private trouble, frequently a public issue. To this extent health is as much a social (psychological, anthropological, economic, etc.) as a biological matter, as much a candidate for the sociological (psychological, anthropological, economic, etc.) agenda as it is for the medical, public or governmental agendas.

This chapter examines the development of health as an item on sociology's agenda, and – although space permits only oblique acknowledgement – pays some attention to its obverse, sociology on health's agenda. What are its origins? In what guise(s) does it appear? Where might it be going? The chapter opens by considering two alternative accounts of the beginnings of health as an item on sociology's agenda. One asserts that the origins derive primarily from 'taking' doctors' problems as the objects of study in order to help provide solutions; the other stresses the 'making' of them into sociological problems (Young 1971). Later sections trace some of the ensuing twists, turns and quarrels (what is or should be the relation between medicine and sociology?) accommodations and revisions (perhaps it should be health not medicine?). The intention is to be even-handed as to the varieties of sociology, schools or perspectives, a stance firmly not to be confused with indifference. All the same, present purposes are partisan, firmly committed to a certain version of that which is distinctively sociological.

Although all this centres on sociology and health, it is only a particular illustration of the state and status of sociology no matter what its substantive concerns. For there is no escape from the conclusion, as Everett Hughes put it long ago, in that the problem of sociology's condition as both profession and science is chronic (1958). Sociology has never really made it, if Michael Gibbons and his colleagues' criteria for the success of Mode 1 knowledge production are anything to go by. Sociologists, in Britain at least, have shied away from the 'specialisation in the cognitive realm, professionalisation in the social realm and institutionalisation of the political realm' pursued by natural/biomedical scientists (Gibbons et al. 1994: 10). The terms (devised before Gibbons et al. was published) in which this essay is couched could be revised to permit examination of the establishment of health on sociology's agenda as a candidate for Mode 2 knowledge production. The opportunity to do so here has, however, not been taken. This is not because the exercise would be uninteresting or fruitless, but because, as already indicated, the position adopted here maintains there is a value to what there is of Mode 1 sociological knowledge production and that it is this mode which needs continually to be nurtured alongside Mode 2. Introducing Gibbons et al.'s characterization of each mode is useful here, however, as a shorthand to assert that, in parallel, there is no interest in preserving Mode 1 by means of disparaging or dismissing Mode 2, let alone (were that sensible, desirable or realistic) proposing the latter's abolition.

All these considerations come back to the simple insistence with which this essay begins and ends. Sight should never be lost of that which is disciplined, what in Eliot Freidson's words are the 'systematic and self-conscious methods of data-collection and . . . theoretically organized methods of analysis' (Freidson 1983: 219). It is this which must be cultivated, otherwise the value of being 'congenitally and deliberately outside' (Freidson 1983: 219) will be lost to health and to sociology alike.

Just before turning to consider British beginnings of the health agenda in sociology, one or two qualifications need to be mentioned and a broader context noted. First, what follows is not a review, nor is the coverage comprehensive – the field has become sufficiently intricate, nuanced and dispersed for such an attempt to be foolhardy – and the vocabulary adopted sometimes elides, without comment, 'sociology', 'medical sociology' and 'health', leaving the reader to make the appropriate inferences. Although not a formal history, a historical thread is arbitrarily fastened to 1969 and parochially not just to Britain but to the formation of the British Sociological Association's (BSA) Medical Sociology Study Group (hereafter the Group). The Group was founded in November that year when forty-nine self-styled sociologists assembled in a now forgotten small hotel in York in the north-east of England. Representing a mixture of sociological attitudes, theoretical outlooks, preferred styles of research methods and designs, we had responded to John McKinlay's invitation issued from his base at the Medical Research Council (MRC) Medical Sociology Unit in Aberdeen, to attend a weekend conference. Meeting annually every since, the Group's conferences rapidly attracted large numbers (as compared with meetings of other BSA study groups), more than doubling in size after only a couple of years, now steadily consisting of well over three hundred with the presentation of some two hundred papers. Such developments are not peculiar to Britain – on the contrary. Similar rapid growth was witnessed significantly earlier in the United States and has been paralleled in Australia, the Nordic countries and, unevenly, across mainland Europe. Undoubtedly developments elsewhere display other similarities as well as distinctive differences (cf. Nuyens and Vansteenkiste 1978; Willis 1982; Palosuo and Rahkonen 1989; White 1991; Pearlin 1992; Davis and George 1993; Cleary and Treacy 1997; and see also addresses by recipients of the Leo G. Reeder Award for Distinguished Scholarship in Medical Sociology, e.g. Levine 1987; Olesen 1989; Bloom 1990; Pearlin 1992) though pursuit of either is a separate exercise, which will have to be postponed for the moment. Last there is a difficult question as to what the boundaries were, or are to be, between sociology, or medical sociology, other disciplines – especially medical social anthropology (see Good 1994) or social history of medicine – or between health professions, occupations and trades. In the process, the terms of the discussion risk begging several questions in implicitly relying on a notion that somehow identifiable and unshifting boundaries exist – all of which is also set aside for now.

Medical sociologists and doctors – British beginnings

One account has it that, in Britain, the agenda was initially created by doctors, administrators and others outside sociology (e.g. Stacey and Homans 1978). No doubt the formation of a new Study Group, with the

title Medical Sociology, under the auspices of the discipline's national association serves as one signal that health was an item on sociology's agenda.
But a closer look shows it owed precious little else to sociology or sociologists in Britain – whether represented in its literature or journals, its
topics of investigation, its economic support or its institutional bases. Only
a small minority of those who attended the Group's inaugural meeting
were based in university departments of sociology. Most were attached to
freer-standing centres or institutes or located in medical departments, e.g.
psychiatry, obstetrics or social medicine, with one or two in colleges of
technology. Most were funded from health/biomedical science sources, the
Medical Research Council (MRC), the (then) Department of Health and
Social Security (DHSS) or the occasional medical charity rather than any
agencies devoted to supporting the social sciences. And a good proportion
of those associated with the Group at the outset were on 'soft' money (Group
Register 1969–70).

Certainly, this last altered somewhat in the following few years with
the creation of a series of lectureships to introduce sociology teaching
(accompanying a parallel innovation introducing psychology) to the medical undergraduate curriculum. These posts were, however, almost invariably
located in medical not social science faculties. For the spur came not from
sociology, but from a Royal Commission on Medical Education (Todd 1968).
Its members included no sociologist, though between them Richard Titmuss
(as Professor of Social Administration in London) and G. Morris Carstairs
(whose work, long before he became Professor of Psychiatry at Edinburgh
University, had a strong affinity with social anthropology) were bound to
have represented a sensitivity to social sciences. It may be noted that the
British Psychological Society is listed among those who submitted evidence,
but the British Sociological Association is not: a reminder of their rather
different attitudes to professionalization and institutionalization and that
the former is a qualifying association.

Likewise, the literature available to the Group in the early years of its
existence reflected barely any sociological work. If the literatures consulted
dealt with health, they emanated in Britain from social medicine and
public health, social epidemiology or social policy and administration. An
honourable exception that is well worth re-reading is *Sociology in Medicine*,
first published in 1962. All the same, it was the product of a collaboration
between a physician who had worked in epidemiology and clinical practice
and a sociologist who had also worked in social anthropology, both with
experience of teaching in medical schools (Susser and Watson 1971: ix).

Sociological work at large appeared, at the time, to bypass health. That
which did address it and did seem to arise from distinctively sociological

concerns – the functionalism of Talcott Parsons, the social psychology of David Mechanic, the interactionism of Julius Roth or David Sudnow – was virtually exclusively North American (e.g. Parsons 1951; Koos 1954; Apple 1960; Roth 1963; Mechanic 1968; Sudnow 1968). Referring even to this body of work's topic as 'health' is deliberately anachronistic. Far more appropriate is to describe the topics they covered in phrases such as: the social positions of the sick and their doctor; feeling ill and having something clinically wrong but getting on with it; living and dying in hospital. Ill health was more apt.

Further, the topics on Group members' research agendas were more often than not directly geared to the solution or illumination of practical problems in healthcare provision and organization (Group Register 1969–70). The work was sociological more by virtue of using methods sociologists also used and because the data collected were social, than by the manner in which the research was conceived. Even research of the very early period in the Group's life that was less plainly applied and formulated in more sociological terms still bore a strong imprint of extra-sociological definitions of the problem; paths to medical care, pre-patient behaviour, decision making prior to consultation with professional medical authorities. And the imprint derived from quite specific medical interests. Like members of any occupation providing a personal service, doctors could not avoid noticing how their clientele behaved, and were especially conscious, censorious even, when they behaved inappropriately. Patients neglected to take the medicines prescribed; they put off going to see the doctor, despite suspecting serious illness; they knowingly damaged their own health and wasted general practitioners' (GP) time with trivial ailments and non-medical complaints. Framing the work in terms of patient behaviour or pathways to the doctor had overtones of complicity with the doctors' desire to discover why patients failed to conform to what was required of them. Even if more gently expressed, gearing efforts in these directions still looked very like serving doctors' purposes, and still seemed to require setting aside intellectual enquiry to subsume sociological identities under quests for answers to medical professionals' questions and solutions to public health or health service problems. Answering these questions, solving these problems was and is important to everyone. But that does not, of itself, make them sociological. Put another way, the sociological contribution appeared to accept their being cast in ways which were neither self-evidently, nor primarily, sociological.

That, then, is how one account of the early creation of the agenda in Britain runs. There is a second. The alternative version turns the first inside out. Even if work still bore initial hallmarks of extra-sociological definitions of the problem, once begun it was nevertheless being re-formulated sociologically. The trick was to take doctors' problems for which a solution was to be produced, but then to make them into sociologists' problems for which understanding or explanation was to be sought. So doing introduced additional angles on the matter to the perspectives which doctors saw, or, perhaps more probably, saw as relevant and legitimate. Investigating paths to medical care took the use of alternatives to orthodox medicine seriously rather than dismissing them as patients' foolishly falling prey to quackery. Studying pre-patient behaviour catered for good reasons for not consulting the doctor, regarding would-be patients as rational rather than misguided – and paved the way for later examination of the sources of doctors' judgements of non-conformity among their patients (e.g. Murcott 1981; Dingwall and Murray 1983).

The point about the origins of health on the agenda can, then, just as easily be made the other way round. Work was indeed being formu-lated in sociological terms but simply had to be packaged appropriately for extra-sociological consumption (and funding). Once chances opened up and salaries, however short-term, became available, they could and were used to 'make' problems *inside* the business of 'taking' problems (Young 1971). Without doubt, items on health agendas outside sociology con-tinued to make their mark on the work of members of the Group, and were more often than not the source of many livelihoods. Those intent on making sociological problems, however, had to content themselves with life on the margins. As one of those who attended the original 1969 Group meeting later implied, much that was sociological in conception was undertaken as Ph.D. or even undergraduate dissertations, 'one-offs', offshoots from other studies or from voluntary work, think-pieces and programmatic reflections; if they were empirically based, they commonly took the form of 'small-scale, here-and-now ethnography', manageable as single-handed studies (Horobin 1985: 103). So that even if the second account of early beginnings is adopted, making rather than taking prob-lems had to be done away from the swim of things, incidentally, furtively even.

That two such versions are possible is nothing new. Indeed, something like it was a common item on the Group's own agenda from the outset. For amongst the American literature to which the Group was heir, was Straus's (1957) paper 'The nature and status of medical sociology' exam-ining the work of 110 medical sociologists. The part of his paper most commonly quoted is his suggestion that the work could be classified in terms of a logical division of medical sociology into two categories: the soci-ology *of* medicine, and sociology *in* medicine (cf. the distinction between *critical* and *clinical* medical anthropology (Leslie 1990); also that between *description* and *prescription* in policy analysis (Hogwood and Gunn 1984)). The former consists of studying 'such factors as the organizational structure, role relationships, value systems, rituals, and functions of medicine as a system of behaviour . . . best carried out by persons operating from independent positions outside the formal medical setting'; the latter describes 'collaborative research or teaching often involving the integration of concepts, techniques and personnel from many disciplines' (Straus 1957: 203).

Straus went on to suggest that these two types of medical sociology tend to be incompatible with one another. If sociologists of medicine identify too closely with medical teaching or clinical research they may lose objectivity. But if sociologists in medicine try to study their colleagues, they risk jeopardizing a good working relationship. Put another way, the former are to be scientists, needing to be able to stand back from their object of study. The latter are to act as professionals serving a clientele, whether it be the medical students they teach or, by proxy, the patients needing medical care.

Straus was far too sophisticated to suppose that the two types of medical sociology could be cleanly separated, although it has to be said that anyone who has discovered textbook references to the distinction without knowing his original paper could be forgiven for thinking otherwise. Indeed he recognized that, in practice, medical sociologists have to move between different degrees and combinations of each, chameleon-like, to match whichever (medical) surroundings they are in at the time. If the sociologist 'become[s] a good chameleon, he should be able to do so without sacrificing either his integrity or his professional identification' (Straus 1957: 204). But if Straus had provided a convenient vocabulary for a retrospective classification of the American agenda of the 1950s, his survival strategy was unlikely to be acceptable in creating any post-1968 sociological agenda.

Both versions of the origins of the agenda were evident in work that followed. The difficulty, at the time, lay in deciding which was which. For instance, a good slice of medical sociological research undertaken in the 1970s was about the medical profession and its work. The inspiration of American work was evident and clearly acknowledged – notably Freidson's analysis of the medical profession (1970) and his investigation of professional self-regulation (1976), as well as one of the classics among studies of medical training by Becker *et al.* (1961). All the same, the contribution of this decade was not simply to mirror work from the US but to develop a distinctively British sociological style, much in an interactionist tradition.

There were examinations of the allocation of identity in out-patient therapeutic encounters (Davis and Strong 1976) and in emergency departments (Hughes 1977; Jeffery 1979). There were studies of medical professional socialization (Atkinson 1977, 1981), extended to health visiting (Dingwall 1977) and nursing (Melia 1987) among other health professions a little later. And there was a prime concern with professional autonomy (Bloor 1976), contrasts and contradictions between doctors' and patients' views of one another (Stimson 1974; Bloor and Horobin 1975) and the boundaries between specialties and professions (Garmarnikow 1978; Eaton and Webb 1979), while studies in the nature and routines of medical work itself supported the publication of a volume of eleven papers just into the next decade (Atkinson and Heath 1981).

Review of these studies could conclude that, like the first account of the agenda's origins, they were still aligned with a medical viewpoint and they still revolved around the medical professions, mostly doctors, mostly clinicians. Hindsight makes it even easier to suggest that the large extent to which (with a small handful of honourable exceptions) the studies inclined to neglect occupational therapists, theatre nurses or dentists, only underscores sociologists' thrall to the medical professional view of the world. Equally, though, they could be said – in line with the second version – to show signs that sociologists were making their own sociological problems rather than simply taking problems made by non-sociologists. Merely, it could also be said, that their work just happened to be about one set of occupations in the contemporary division of labour. It was less that remnants of a sociology *in* coexisted with moves towards a sociology *of* medicine, more that proponents of one or the other were forced into a messier dialogue with each other than even a close reading of Straus's logical division might have predicted.

Medical sociologists and doctors – dependence and power

The theme running throughout a large body of this work about doctors and nurses as well as their patients was the power, the autonomy, the dominance of the medical profession.

Medical sociologists were fascinated, even mesmerized by the power doctors could wield. This is nothing peculiar to medical sociologists; sociologists generally are enormously interested in power. And it would be very odd had doctors not loomed large in medical sociologists' field of vision. So in one sense it is simply that in the case of medical sociology it was the power of the medical profession that held their attention transfixed. Except, as many medical sociologists might well have argued, it was more than that, for the simple reason that, according to their analyses at the time, doctors were an unusually powerful profession. Apprehensions of that power were formulated in one or other sociological mode represented amongst sociologies *of* medicine. Yet despite the apparent incompatibility between an *in* and an *of*, these apprehensions were bolstered by, rather than separate from, sociologies *in* medicine – or more to the point, sociologists supposedly *in* medicine. The everyday life of a medical sociologist (of either type) gave them a picture of doctors in close-up. The picture has two, interlinked elements: one originating in their private and personal lives, the other occupationally derived.

The former element involved being a (potential) patient themselves, or a relative or friend of a patient, like any other citizen. The sociological point to be remembered is that people do not ordinarily split themselves tidily according to the shorthands devised (largely perhaps by marketing) to make sense of mass society – shorthands such as motorist, taxpayer or owner-occupier and also sociologist, patient or expectant mother. It is probably only extraordinary occasions that prompt commentary in such terms: when a budget is laid before Parliament, when a routine visit to the GP falls short of expectations. What is remarked upon, what makes news, is the out of the way, the extraordinary. Thus good news is relegated to being no news. Medical sociologists (along with doctors or nurses themselves) are likely to be exceptionally conscious of any bad news in their own personal dealings with doctors. And like anyone else, it would mean seeking to make sense of the experience, drawing on whatever sources were to hand. Doing so slides across to what had become their stock in trade; by virtue of being medical sociologists the repertoire of sources at hand was extended. They had been admitted to the medical library. There they found literature on the limitations of medicine; discovered that the medical dictionary listed iatrogenesis, medicine's own term for doctor-induced disease; and came across disaffected and despairing doctors' fictional exposés of medical under-life (Hejinian 1974; Shem 1985). Strong put it aptly when he commented that Davis and Horobin's (1977) edited collection (to which he too was a contributor) of sociologists' personal accounts of their own ailments was a fascinating blend of 'analysis and animosity' (Strong 1979a: 213).

The second element derived from sociologists' positions as researchers and teachers. They had to apply to doctors (among others) for research access. They were (and continue to be) interviewed for posts in sociology by panels wholly composed of doctors and/or other non-social scientists already drawn into the medical circle. They found themselves heavily out-numbered by doctors on curriculum committees. And any sociologist who had taught in a medical school ruefully recognized what lay behind Una Maclean's (a doctor herself) choice of metaphor when she described medical sociologists as 'facing undergraduates in the front line' (Maclean 1975: 4). Securing remarkably good access, being offered the job, feeling surprised and exhilarated by a tutorial of hard-working, highly intelligent medical students fascinated by a nice sociological point, could readily become the good, i.e. no, news of day-to-day working life. It was hard to ignore, and harder still not to magnify, the bad news of facing the scarcely concealed contempt for sociology and startling rudeness that some med-ical colleagues, with neither embarrassment nor apology, quite openly displayed. Few sociologists were well placed not to risk having their professional self-confidence undermined by such blatant antagonism.

Both these types of everyday concern reminded medical sociologists of the extent of their dependence on doctors. The particular form it took was in part a product of the newness of the Group coupled with its members' sense of the youth of medical sociology. Not only were many of the sociologists themselves either, or both, young and inexperienced, they were also academically junior and lacked the colleagueship of others in the self-same position into the bargain. Furthermore, doctors (in Britain at least) were as much prey to popular misconceptions about sociology as any other non-sociologists. First-hand experience includes a familiar catalogue of epithets and descriptions of sociology as: 'social work'; 'motivated by political extremisms'; 'just common sense'; 'overly subjective'; ' "soft" science'; 'inhumanely reducing everyone to a statistic'. Medical sociology had not been in the medical field of vision long enough for doctors reasonably to be expected to know otherwise, especially as sociology goes public in so many different guises. Even those doctors who championed the discipline could not help but be relatively ignorant of it. Ironically, their well-intentioned support could – and in some cases probably should – readily be interpreted as dictating the terms on which sociology should operate.

Such an interpretation of the terms of engagement for creating the agenda was a product of the immediacy of day-to-day work. Accordingly, a parallel interpretation – such as, for example, maturely contemplating it all as just the beginning of a very long process of mutual education – was far less obvious. So it was hardly surprising that medical sociologists were tempted to regard medicine as imperialistic, seeking to extend its sphere of control over what they could regard as their own terrain. Whether primarily sociologist *of* or *in* medicine, they were obliged to recognize doctors as sponsors, patrons or paymasters. Small wonder they were pre-occupied with imbalances of power.

If many medical sociologists were short of the day-to-day colleague-ship of their own kind, at least the Group's conferences could serve as possible compensation. By the same token those meetings provided a forum for the expression and attempted analysis of incompatibilities and contradictions in doing medical sociology. Discussion could get heated and in the mid- to late 1970s, often enough boiled over in accusations of 'doctor bashing' and counter-accusations of succumbing to cooption by medicine.

Margot Jefferys (who had held the only named chair in medical soci-ology in Britain since 1965, to be relinquished only on retirement in 1982) could praise new work and applaud the enterprise and energy in medical sociology. But she was also concerned about the juncture which the agenda had reached. Certainly she recognized the incomprehension with which medical sociologists' work could be received and drew attention publicly to the low status as well as low pay of those who produced it. At the same time, she detected 'a barely veiled hostility to, and indeed contempt for, the medical profession' among many young sociologists (Jefferys 1974).

Military metaphor and reports of mutual aggression gave way just a few years later to colonial analogy in attempts to characterize who held sway over, and offered judgement on, creating the agenda. Drawing on a view of professions which sought to expand their empires, Strong was prompted to offer a self-styled polemic that castigated everyone in sight (Strong 1979a). Although on 'soft' money, he enjoyed the sturdy socio-logical colleagueship of the MRC Medical Sociology Unit in Aberdeen, at the same time as the conduct of his research brought him into close contact with senior members of the medical profession, observing both British and US consultant paediatricians at close quarters over a prolonged period (Strong 1979b). Yes, analyzed as a profession, medicine was imperialistic. But, in so far as it was also a profession, so too was sociology. Yes, medicine was powerful (far more so than sociology), and its capacity for harm was 'pro-foundly disturbing' (Strong 1979a: 201). Yes, medical sociologists were often 'forced to do hack work of little sociological value', and their developing a properly theoretical approach was inhibited by being excluded 'from the ultimate formulation of the problems which they investigate' (Strong 1979a: 204). But take care: sociologists' preference for a 'social model of health' carries its own, and far greater dangers.

It was a bold piece of work, one that is much cited. But, as is often the fate of such efforts, it was to be used by sociologists further to bash doctors and by doctors to retaliate, as Strong would later complain (personal communication 1992). Rather more seriously, his main point has far too often been bypassed completely, and, in the view of Simon Williams, Ellen Annandale and Jonathan Tritter (1998), continues to be so.

On the face of it, much has altered in the twenty years since Jefferys and Strong captured the spirit of those times. The uncertainties of 'soft' money became widespread with the far-reaching policy and political and economic changes of the 1990s, not just among academic researchers but university teachers more generally, never mind in the wider job market. Some would argue that short-term contracts keep employees on their toes. It may also be that now that far more are in the same employment position, less is to be lost by speaking out boldly, for so doing might just provide the very basis on which the next short-term contract is to be offered. Moreover, analyses of professional power and power imbalances are points well taken. They have seeped into and settled as the stuff of journalistic recognition, management training and industrial tribunal, not just in the therapeutic encounter, but in school pupil–teacher relationships, the counselling trades, and business and organizations of all kinds. Medicine *qua* medicine is perhaps investigated rather less of late, relative to the study of a far wider range of health-related topics. No ready answer presents itself to pondering whether the analysis and workings of power have submerged or been normalized, disappeared or become so engrained as no longer to be noticed. Is it because medical sociologists themselves are more senior and less sensitive to power imbalances? Maybe, reminiscent of George Homans' hypothesis that the longer people work alongside each other the greater the chance of friendship, sheer longstanding association between doctors and sociologists in the medical schools has had some effect. Perhaps it has meant they are more used to one another, better able to understand one another, developing if not a shared understanding at least an accommodation rather than mutual hostility in collaborative efforts to secure joint funding and joint futures.

In any case, the world is changing. The public image of doctors has undergone dramatic shifts in the UK and elsewhere; deference and submissive acquiescence is becoming outgrown as the population of both patients and sociologists ages. The analytic centre of gravity might just have shifted too, such that attempts are made to identify power alongside other dimensions in the therapeutic encounter. This may be as a result of studying professions other than doctors, e.g. notably nurses, who are being seen to bring to that encounter different histories, assumptions and attitudes to the task in hand. Important too may be efforts at understanding agency among members of the public in general, as for instance in Charlie Davison's propositions about lay epidemiology among the public in general (Davison *et al.* 1991) or among patients in particular (May 1992). Again, analyses of power may be diffusing along with the dispersal of topics in medical sociology to reappear under other sub-divisional headings, behind newly emergent vocabularies: women and healing (Clarke and Olesen 1999), health and emotions (James and Gabe 1996). Michael Bury, however, is clear that power is an area that continues to require attention. He concludes his delicate examination of health and postmodernity with the cautious suggestion that power 'is now seen to be giving way to more pluralistic structures in which voices once unheard now emerge as new sources of influence' (Bury 1998: 24–5).

Medical sociologists and doctors – a shift of emphasis

In warning against unthinking adoption of a social model of health, Strong was referring to a switch in the creation of the agenda that was already attracting attention and tends to remain predominant. Reviewing the origins and development of medical sociology, Stacey and Homans (1978) called for a sociology neither in nor of *medicine*, but of *health and illness*. The implications were far-reaching. Not only would any particular connection to the medical profession fall away, not only would the whole array of health-related knowledge and beliefs, institutions, workers paid and unpaid be encompassed, but the effects on social relationships of suffering and associated dependence could no longer be ignored.

In Britain this move was set against a 1970s' backdrop that included a Royal Commission on the NHS, the creation of Community Health Councils in 1974 and a Labour government's emphasis on preventive medicine and on citizens' own responsibility for looking after their health. The movement towards a sociology of health rather than medicine was not peculiarly British, and though reported to have met with little success at the time, had earlier been proposed in the US (Olesen 1975). But by the late 1970s it did catch on, and rapidly. And when the international journal that is associated with (but not the organ of) the Group was launched in 1979, its founders judiciously sought to court all-comers with the title *Sociology of Health and Illness: A Journal of Medical Sociology*.

A sociology of health and illness promised to be far more congenial. It can handily encompass all that has gone before without drawing attention to the difficulties of sociology's stance *vis-à-vis* medicine. For it conveniently abolishes having to fret about distinctions between sociologies *of* and *in* medicine – overtly at least (Jefferys 1996). Indeed it no longer so noticeably links sociology to doctors or ties sociologists to difficult questions of whether modern medicine is a good or bad thing. It means that doctors and sociologists can line up side by side, with health and illness instead of one another in their sights. After all, everyone can agree that health is a good thing. And it neatly chimes with the invention, and rise to prominence, of health promotion.

All the same, doubts were registered. I had pointed out (Murcott 1977) that while renaming might resolve one set of contradictions it ran the risk of creating other problems. A sociology of health rather than a sociology of medicine did not dispose of premature definition of the object of enquiry. Of itself it was no guarantee against prejudging where and how concern with health and illness arose and the manner in which thereby social constructions of either were constituted; health is, after all, a state valued not in nature but in society (Murcott 1979). More eloquently, Gordon Horobin came at the same point another way. He warned that calls for alliances with patients against a medical paternalism carry the danger of replacing it with another, and potentially nastier, form of paternalism transferred to researchers and other health experts in licensing them to determine what is good for us. Whichever way it goes, he said, we are assigning to health, no matter how it is to be defined, some pre-eminence among human values: 'Medical sociologists, being in the health trade as much as doctors, are inclined to take that primacy for granted; most people, most of the time, do not' (Horobin 1985: 99).

Horobin was, albeit obliquely, reminding medical sociologists to include themselves and their own viewpoint in their field of investigative vision, gently pointing out that whether embraced with alacrity or reluctance, they were members, by association and material circumstances, of the health industries. His point may well serve as a programmatic basis for asking about the circumstances under which valuing health was and was not accorded primacy, by which social groups, with what sort of appeal to legitimacy in so doing, with which degrees of success, and with what consequences.

Medical sociologists and sociologists at large

So far, creating the agenda has been discussed as a view of and from inside medical sociology. This chapter now turns to a handful of developments from a rather different standpoint.

Suppose for the moment that the inauguration of the Group signalled that health was on some general sociological agenda. It is possible to point to an assortment of ensuing events in support of this supposition. Health was the theme of the 1976 BSA annual conference for the first time in twenty-three years. Unlike its 1953 predecessor, when only some sessions were concerned with health, in which the majority of papers were in any case presented by doctors, the 1976 conference was dominated by the medical sociologists who regularly attended the Group's annual conferences (a steady presence, sustained in the 1991 BSA Annual Conference on Health and Society when the theme came round again). *Sociology*, as the Association's journal, was carrying stoutly sociological work on health as well as Stacey and Homans' (1978) assessment of the state of the sub-discipline. By the end of the 1970s, the Study Group had become (and probably still is) the largest of any in the BSA. With that growth, more of its members were based in university and the then polytechnic sociology departments, responsible, presumably, for the medical sociology options springing up in bachelor's and master's degree sociology programmes. A crude count of the institutional affiliation of those listed in four of the Group's registers suggests, though, that the proportion in sociology depart-ments of the doubly self-selected total continues to be overshadowed by those in medical and related faculties (see Table 12.1).

No one should depend very heavily on these figures, especially since, among other changes through the 1990s, the university sector has been expanded with the creation of the new universities from the earlier poly-technics and since nurse education has been moved into the university sector. All the same, the figures go in the same general direction as Horobin's (1985) observation that medical sociology is separated from academic sociology.

It is one thing to suppose that health was on a wider sociological agenda, quite another to know whether it was noticed or what anyone thought about it. While medical sociologists could be severely discomfited in their relation to medicine, there is hearsay evidence that they could be equally troubled by their relation to sociology at large. For some, the trouble was so profound they became wholly disenchanted with mainstream soci-ology, so impatient with what they regarded as, at best its irrelevance, at worst its self-absorption and self-satisfaction, that they absented them-selves altogether. Others were piqued, believing themselves marginalized within the sociological enterprise, hypersensitive to their inferior status as 'merely applied', empiricist (in the pejorative sense), atheoretical, and consigned to service teaching. Yet others, accepting a place apart, could display to sociology in general the deference and reverence reserved for elders and betters. Ironically, some published attempts to reconcile medical sociology and sociological theory served only to perpetuate a separation

Table 12.1: Institutional affiliation of those who submitted a return for inclusion in the BSA Medical Sociology Group Register of Research and Teaching, first, fourth, sixth and eighth editions (per cent)

	1969/70	1982	n.d.[c. 1990]	1998
	N = 102	N = 189	N = 251	N = 252
University[a] departments, sociology	9	15	12	17
University[a] departments, other social sciences	1	12	9	21
Polytechnic[b] and colleges, health studies, social studies	1	12	11	15
Independent centres and institutes	31	18	21	8
University medical schools nursing schools and faculties	18	23	23	31
Other	40	20	24	8

[a] 1998 includes new universities.
[b] 1998 includes old universities.

Source: Group Register (1969–70; 1982; n.d. [c. 1990]; 1998).

between them (e.g. Johnson 1975; Scambler 1987). Either way medical sociologists were perhaps too readily beset by a 'cultural cringe' (the self-mocking epithet Australians apply when catching themselves venerating, against their better judgement, the distinction, taste and manners of the English simply because they are English) in the face of sociology at large.

Several obvious factors are likely to be related to a medical sociologist's stance *vis-à-vis* sociology in general. These include: a medical sociologist's institutional base; the relation of their work for which they are employed to the medical and health enterprises; their job title; whether their employer recognizes all their sociological work/publications as relevant or only those parts the employer deems relevant; the extent to which their research runs across several sociological sub-specialties at once (see also Jefferys 1996). They may also include whether or not the sociologist in question is willing to describe themselves as a medical sociologist, a sociologist of health or anything else or simply seeks to be no more than a sociologist *tout court*. Caricaturing the case for brevity's sake, the first of these can be illustrated as follows. Those located in sociology departments, at one extreme, are more likely to be able to adopt an investigative research stance that absolves them of having to divide themselves in half, at least in print (e.g. Atkinson 1995; Elston 1997), while those based in medical or nursing schools and faculties of health, at another extreme, may be obliged to split themselves into demonstrating they are both teachers who can be 'relevant' to medicine's interests (e.g. Armstrong 1994; Scambler 1997) and thinkers capable of engaging in sociological theorizing fashioned in stylish images of successive periods of sociology *à la mode*, be it Foucauldian, Habermasian or the postmodern (e.g. Armstrong 1983; Scambler and Higgs 1998).

Revising history is one way of quelling any lingering sense of being an upstart, and an invitation to do so was issued from amongst sociologists at large. Presumably it was Turner's longstanding interest in a very wide range of sociological concerns that brought him to follow Foucault's lead in examining the manner in which the social and the medical meet inscribed in the body (Turner 1987). He picks up Foucault's comment that sociology's own origins lie in nineteenth-century medicine and they are thus so inextricably linked that modern medicine is (or should be) applied sociology and sociology is applied medicine (1987: 5). Turner makes a direct claim to the peculiarly sociological agenda that is to follow: 'Medical problems force sociological theory to confront constantly the problem of the relationship between human biology, physiology and socio-cultural phenomena' (1987: 5). By these lights, and contrary to the previous pages of this chapter, the conventional history of medical sociology as a latecomer is shown to be mistaken.

Creation myths can always provide a source of comfort, re-viewing a history as more venerable – and thus demanding it commands respect – than previously thought. Turner does, of course, do far more than revise medical sociology's history. From some viewpoints, his contribution is a rare example of a recognition of health as on a broader sociological agenda than those who one way or another find themselves more closely associated with medical sociology. His is a theoretical synthesis offering a sociology of medicine, health and illness in political economic context that focuses in particular on a Foucauldian apprehension of the body. In this last lies the strength of the synthesis in that it raises 'in an acute form the whole debate on the relationships between body and mind, culture and nature, self and society' (Turner 1987: 218).

His agenda is self-evidently of sociological interest, but one that can unduly overemphasize the theoretical at the expense of the empirical. To the extent that he engages with medical sociologists rather than with medical sociology, Turner repeats the warning about social models of health Horobin had already offered. But (wisely, some might suggest, as an author who had hitherto served little or no time in the field) he limits his suggestions to advising that their contribution be modest, circumspect and judicious, offering no sense of how this might be achieved or alternative directions to take.

Freidson, however, had already indicated both, in a paper to which Turner refers but otherwise neglects. Although published not far short of twenty years ago, it is still as pertinent today as it was then, not just in its analysis of the state of health and healthcare, not just to sociology and health, but to sociology at large. As a visitor to Britain for a year from the Department of Sociology at the University of New York where he had held a full professorship for more than a decade, Freidson was a sympathetic observer who could rise above the domestic fray. He had long been much admired among British medical sociologists, especially for his hugely influential *Profession of Medicine* (Freidson 1970) that appeared when the Group was barely a year old. It was in his polemical address delivered at St Thomas's Medical School in London, and published in revised form as a 'Viewpoint' in *Sociology of Health and Illness* (Freidson 1983) that he came to give what must stand as one of the most considered accounts of the agenda for sociology and health that is available. It is an elegant, beautifully crafted piece and since, like Jefferys and Strong before, he too bangs a great many heads together, it is all the more effective for being so.

It is, he began, a time of economic reckoning in the industrialized world that makes increasingly expensive public institutions vulnerable. With more wealth and privilege to lose, coupled with an increase in public scepticism about their actions and their motives, medical institutions face serious crisis. Trained in medical sciences, its practitioners are utterly ill equipped to tackle the creation of a health system providing humane and decent care at an affordable cost to individuals and their nation's economy. The contribution of other specialists, including sociologists, is needed. But sociology does not look equal to the task. It too is in crisis, so 'seriously fragmented into . . . mutually hostile intellectual segments' (Friedson 1983: 210) that its identity will be lost, either absorbed into philosophy and history or becoming a merely technical enterprise.

In dealing with the crisis faced within each, medicine and sociology need each other. Studying health affairs is one arena in which sociology can engage with the real world. Medicine has to conserve what is valuable in its institution and engage creatively in remoulding it to meet force of circumstances. 'Each needs the other, yet each alienates the other by self-serving and essentially dishonest conceptions of itself and the other' (Freidson 1983: 212). Since all concerned are in crisis and all 'participate in the same crumbling of previously secure assumptions', we would do well to put each other to better use. More than a decade later, the crises may be different but the advice is indispensable.

Sociology and health: coming of age

Writing thirty years after attendance at that inaugural meeting of the Group, it is neither just the passage of time, nor simply the normal complement of retirements, funeral orations, obituaries and Festschrifts that promotes a powerful sense in which British medical sociology/sociology of health and illness has come of age. The Group flourishes: anyone interested in keeping up with its newsletters, conferences and other activities can, these days, visit its website htttp://medsocbsa.swan.ac.uk. Undergraduates now can treat the presence of an optional course in the sociology of health in their degree schemes as unremarkable, just as their predecessors of the 1960s could treat a course in the sociology of the family, of work, of community, or of politics. Those teaching currently have a respectable choice of texts – seven published in a single year being sufficiently numerous to support a whole review article (Cox 1999) – of which as many are geared to a readership in sociology as in the health professions, while textbooks specifically aimed at medical students have reached their fourth editions.

The sheer volume of research has expanded dramatically, encompassing a gamut of contemporary topics and problems far too extensive to begin listing here. The field is clearly visible in the proliferation of new academic journals founded in the 1990s (e.g. *health* and *Qualitative Health Research* edited from the UK and the US respectively). Yet *Sociology of Health and Illness* has not suffered. Instead it has not only continued steadily to reach volume 22, but has grown from three issues a year when it was founded to six, and extends to an accompanying monograph series. One of these (Elston 1997) is devoted to the long overdue investigation of medical sciences and technologies (Atkinson 1995) which, after all, many declare, make modern healthcare what it is. Representing a sociologically distinctive and sophisticated line of enquiry, this volume includes work representing fine examples of just the Mode 1 sociological knowledge production that needs to be well tended. Testimony to persistent effort, these impressive developments alone are reason enough to make bracketing sociology with health unexceptionable, a sociological sub-specialty come of age.

It is also the sheer scale of these developments that makes ever more precarious the present attempt to capture the manner in which the agenda is created. Coming of age may be a suitable time to develop adequate analyses (cf. Webster 1994) – as distinct from the speculative reflections presented here – of the process and relationships involved in the creation of agendas all the better to see what is going on. Certainly it is important to cater for several agendas and different styles of socio-logical study, even within Mode 1 knowledge production, never mind the different angle on agenda construction introduced by engagement in Mode 2. Equally it is intelligent to recognize that new and different agendas emerge out of old ones, that new generations take for granted the novelties welcomed or rejected by their predecessors, and that newly configured collaborative working relationships play their part. But the old, uncomfortable suspicions persist. Theorizing for what too often looks like its own sake is still rewarded and seemingly highly regarded. And, how-ever competently and assiduously pursued, the agenda is still swamped by extra-sociological interests – inequalities in health, the voice of the laity, the viewpoint of the patient, the experience of disability, healthcare pro-vision and the social origins of human activities which epidemiologists report promote or risk health. As indicated in the opening passage of this chapter, everyone has an interest in these, including sociologists person-ally and perhaps professionally. But without energetic 're-making', doing no more than 'taking' these problems no matter how committed and concerned a citizen the researcher may be, will neither adequately exploit sociological possibilities nor nurture the distinctively sociological.

The point Freidson made in 1983 was not new at the time. Particu-larly regrettably, for a discipline like sociology which, with social anthro-pology, urges reflexivity, it needs to be said time and again. Despite the growth of medical sociology, despite its proliferation, despite the emer-gence of devastating new disease (e.g. Bloor 1995), despite the employment, alongside health service researchers, health promotion practitioners and public health doctors, of those trained in sociology and/or acquainted with the medical sociology literature, despite altered opportunities for contribu-tions to the medical curriculum (GMC 1993), despite changes of name to emphasize health and illness rather than medicine, despite some excep-tionally classy contributions that already strive to steer a course between C. Wright Mills' Scylla of Grand Theory and Charybdis of Abstracted Empiricism, none of us should neglect what makes sociology quite so dis-tinctive. If we are looking for a lead in creating our agendas, no matter what the substantive focus, no matter what our working conditions, free-dom (or lack of it) for manoeuvre in deciding our topics of investigation, we can do no better than require ourselves to take Freidson's stinging admonition and wise counsel very seriously indeed when he wrote:

> In order to rebuild its intellectual coherence, sociology must be engaged in the real world as something other than a mere technical enterprise at the service of the highest bidder or a scholastic enterprise of parasites

hypnotizing themselves with mere talk while depending on support from universities who supply them with captive audiences. Sociology needs the challenge of data to keep theorizing honest, and of theory to keep data honest.

(Freidson 1983: 212)

Acknowledgements

I am indebted to Bob Burgess for his encouragement to reflect on this field of sociological work and for his helpful observations on the result. And I am especially grateful to: the late Phil Strong for his remarks about the early 1992 draft; Virginia Olesen for so generously troubling to commit to paper her insightful comments on the first full version of this chapter written in 1993; Erica Haimes, Virginia Low and also Colin Hutchens for practical encouragement and support; and Ronnie Frankenberg for thirty-one years of intermittent but inspiring conversations about social anthropology, sociology and medicine. Mistakes and oversights remain my own.

References

Apple, D. (ed.) (1960) *Sociological Studies of Health and Sickness*, New York: McGraw-Hill.

Armstrong, D. (1983) *Political Anatomy of the Body*, Cambridge: Cambridge University Press.

Armstrong, D. (1994) *An Outline of Sociology Applied to Medicine*, fourth edition (first edition, 1980), Bristol: Butterworth-Heinemann.

Atkinson, P. (1977) 'The reproduction of medical knowledge', in R. Dingwall *et al.* (eds) *Health Care and Health Knowledge*, London: Croom Helm.

Atkinson, P. (1981) *The Clinical Experience*, Farnborough: Gower.

Atkinson, P. (1995) *Medical Talk and Medical Work*, London: Sage.

Atkinson, P. and Heath, C. (eds) (1981) *Medical Work: Realities and Routines*, Farnborough: Gower.

Becker, H.S., Geer, B., Hughes, E.C. and Strauss, A.L. (1961) *Boys in White*, Chicago: University of Chicago Press.

Bloom, S.W. (1990) 'Episodes in the institutionalization of medical sociology: a personal view', *Journal of Health and Social Behavior* 31 (March): 1–10.

Bloor, M. (1976) 'Professional autonomy and client exclusion: a study in ENT clinics', in M. Wadsworth and D. Robinson (eds) *Studies in Everyday Medical Life*, London: Martin Robertson.

Bloor, M. (1995) *The Sociology of HIV Transmission*, London: Sage.

Bloor, M. and Horobin, G. (1975) 'Conflict and conflict resolution in patient interaction', in A. Cox and A. Mead (eds) *A Sociology of Medical Practice*, London: Macmillan.

Bury, M. (1998) 'Postmodernity and health', in G. Scambler and P. Higgs (eds) *Modernity, Medicine and Health*, London: Routledge.

Clarke, A.E. and Olesen, V.L. (1999) *Revisioning Women, Health and Healing*, New York: Routledge.

Cleary, A. and Treacy, M.P. (eds) (1997) *The Sociology of Health and Illness in Ireland*, Dublin: University of Dublin Press.

Cox, D. (1999) 'Review article: normal science? Texts for teaching the sociology of health and illness', *Sociology of Health and Illness* 21 (4): 485–93.

Davis, A. and George, J. (1993) *States of Health*, Pymble NSW: Harper Educational.

Davis, A. and Horobin, G. (1977) *Medical Encounters*, London: Croom Helm.

Davis, A.G. and Strong, P.M. (1976) 'Aren't children wonderful? – a study of the allocation of identity in developmental assessment', in M. Stacey (ed.) *The Sociology of the National Health Service*, Sociological Review Monograph 22, Keele: University of Keele.

Davison, C., Davey Smith, G. and Frankel, S. (1991) 'Lay epidemiology and the prevention paradox: implications for coronary candidacy and health education', *Sociology of Health and Illness* 13 (1): 1–19.

Dingwall, R. (1977) *The Social Organisation of Health Visitor Training*, London: Croom Helm.

Dingwall, T. and Murray, T. (1983) 'Categorisation in accident departments: "good" patients, "bad" patients and children', *Sociology of Health and Illness* 5 (2): 127–48.

Eaton, G. and Webb, B. (1979) 'Boundary encroachment: pharmacists in the clinical setting', *Sociology of Health and Illness* 1 (1): 69–89.

Elston, M.A. (ed.) (1997) *The Sociology of Medical Science and Technology*, Oxford: Blackwell.

Freidson, E. (1970) *Profession of Medicine*, New York: Dodd Mead.

Freidson, E. (1976) *Doctoring Together: A Study of Professional Social Control*, Amsterdam: Elsevier.

Freidson, E. (1983) 'Viewpoint. Sociology and medicine: a polemic', *Sociology of Health and Illness* 5 (2): 208–19.

Garmarnikow, E. (1978) 'The sexual division of labour', in A. Kuhn and A. Wolpe (eds) *Feminism and Materialism*, London: Routledge.

General Medical Council (GMC) (1993) *Tomorrow's Doctors: Recommendations on Undergraduate Medical Education*, London: General Medical Council (Education Committee).

Gibbons, M., Limoges, C., Nowotny, H., Schwartzman, S., Scott, P. and Trow, M. (1994) *The New Production of Knowledge*, London: Sage.

Good, B.J. (1994) *Medicine, Rationality, and Experience*, Cambridge: Cambridge University Press.

Group Register (1969–70) *Medical Sociology in Great Britain 1969–70*, London: BSA Medical Sociology Group.

Group Register (1982) *Medical Sociology in Britain*, fourth edition, London: BSA Medical Sociology Group.

Group Register (n.d.) *Medical Sociology in Britain*, sixth edition, London: BSA Medical Sociology Group.

Group Register (1998) *Medical Sociology in Britain*, eighth edition, London: BSA Medical Sociology Group.

Hejinian, J. (1974) *Extreme Remedies*, London: Pan.

Hogwood, B.W. and Gunn, L.A. (1984) *Policy Analysis for the Real World*, Oxford: Oxford University Press.

Horobin, G. (1985) 'Review essay. Medical sociology in Britain: true confessions of an empiricist', *Sociology of Health and Illness* 7 (1): 94–107.

Hughes, D. (1977) 'Everyday and medical knowledge in categorising patients', in R. Dingwall *et al.* (eds) *Health Care and Health Knowledge*, London: Croom Helm.

Hughes, E.C. (1958) 'Professional and career problems of sociology', in E.C. Hughes, *Men and their Work*, New York: Free Press.

James, V. and Gabe, J. (eds) (1996) *Health and the Sociology of Emotions*, Oxford: Blackwell.

Jeffery, R. (1979) 'Deviant patients in casualty departments', *Sociology of Health and Illness* 1 (1): 90–107.

Jefferys, M. (1974) 'Social science and medical education in Britain', *International Journal of Health Services* 4: 557.

Jefferys, M. (1996) 'The development of medical sociology in theory and practice in Western Europe 1950–1990', *European Journal of Public Health* 6: 94–8.

Johnson, M.L. (1975) 'Medical sociology and sociological theory', *Social Science and Medicine* 9: 227–232.

Koos, E.L. (1954) *The Health of Regionville*, New York: Columbia University Press.

Leslie, C. (ed.) (1990) 'Critical medical anthropology: theory and research', special issue *Social Science and Medicine* 30 (2): v–260.

Levine, S. (1987) 'The changing terrains in medical sociology: emergent concern with quality of life', *Journal of Health and Social Behavior* 28 (March): 1–6.

Maclean, U. (1975) 'Medical sociology in Great Britain', *British Journal of Medical Education* 9: 4–16.

May, C. (1992) 'Individual care? Power and subjectivity in therapeutic relationships', *Sociology* 26 (4): 589–602.

Mechanic, D. (1968) *Medical Sociology*, Glencoe IL: Free Press.

Melia, K. (1987) *Learning and Working: The Occupational Socialization of Nurses*, London: Tavistock.

Murcott, A. (1977) 'Blind alleys and blinkers: the scope of medical sociology', *Scottish Journal of Sociology* 1 (2): 155–71.

Murcott, A. (1979) 'Health as ideology', in P. Atkinson, R. Dingwall and A. Murcott (eds) *Prospects for the National Health*, London: Croom Helm.

Murcott, A. (1981) 'On the typification of "bad patients"', in P. Atkinson and C. Heath (eds) *Medical Work: Realities and Routines*, Farnborough: Gower.

Nuyens, Y. and Vansteenskiste, J. (1978) *Teaching Medical Sociology*, Leiden: Martinus Nijhoff.

Olesen, V.L. (1975) 'Convergences and divergences: anthropology and sociology in health care', *Social Science and Medicine* 9: 421–5.

Olesen, V.L. (1989) 'Caregiving, ethical and informal: emerging challenges in the sociology of health and illness', *Journal of Health and Social Behavior* 30 (March): 1–10.

Palosuo, H. and Rahkonen, O. (1989) 'Sociology of health in Finland: fighting an uphill battle?' *Acta Sociologica* 32 (3): 261–74.

Parsons, T. (1951) *The Social System*, Glencoe IL: Free Press.

Pearlin, L.I. (1992) 'Structure and meaning in medical sociology', *Journal of Health and Social Behavior* 33 (March): 1–9.

Roth, J.A. (1963) *Timetables*, Indianapolis: Bobbs-Merrill.

Scambler, G. (1987) *Sociological Theory and Medical Sociology*, London: Tavistock.

Scambler, G. (1997) *Sociology as Applied to Medicine*, fourth edition (first edition 1982), London: Saunders.

Scambler, G. and Higgs, P. (1998) *Modernity, Medicine and Health*, London: Routledge.

Shem, Samuel (1985) *The House of God* (first edition 1978), London: Black Swan.

Stacey, M. and Homans, H. (1978) 'The sociology of health and illness', *Sociology* 12 (2): 281–307.

Stimson, G.V. (1974) 'Obeying doctor's orders: a view from the other side', *Social Science and Medicine* 8: 97–104.

Straus, R. (1957) 'The nature and status of medical sociology', *American Sociological Review* 22 (2): 200–4.

Strong, P.M. (1979a) 'Sociological imperialism and the profession of medicine', *Social Science and Medicine* 13A: 199–215.

Strong, P.M. (1979b) *The Ceremonial Order of the Clinic: Doctors, Parents and Medical Bureaucracies*, London: Routledge and Kegan Paul.

Sudnow, D. (1968) 'Dead on arrival', *New Society*, February: 187–9.

Susser, M.W. and Watson, W. (1971) *Sociology in Medicine*, second edition, Oxford: Oxford University Press.

Todd Report (1968) *Royal Commission on Medical Education*, London: HMSO.

Turner, B. (1987) *Medical Power and Social Knowledge*, London: Sage.

Webster, A. (1994) 'University–corporate ties and the construction of research agendas', *Sociology* 28 (1): 123–42.

White, K. (1991) The sociology of health and illness, *Current Sociology* 39 (2): 1–134.

Williams S., Annandale, E. and Tritter, J. (1998) 'The sociology of health and illness at the turn of the century: back to the future?' *Sociological Research Online* 3 (4): 1.1–6.7, http://www.socresonline.org.uk/socresonline/-1995/

Willis, Evan (1982) 'Research and teaching in the sociology of health and illness in Australia and New Zealand', *Community Health Studies* VII (2): 144–53.

Young, M.F.D (ed.) (1971) *Knowledge and Control*, London: Collier-Macmillan.

part 3

Policy and problems

chapter 13

Poverty and the welfare state at century's end: paradoxes and prospects

Mick Carpenter

That in this land of abounding wealth, during a time of perhaps unexampled prosperity, probably more than one-fourth of the population are living in poverty, is a fact which may well cause great searching of heart.   (Rowntree 1902: 304)

Introduction: the sociology of problems and policies

In this chapter I will consider one of the central questions confronting contemporary social policy, the paradox of widespread poverty among riches, and what sociology has to offer by way of explanation and prescription. Why has this pressing question at the beginning of the century, which by mid-century appeared to have dwindled to insignificance, returned by century's end? Does it cause as much heart searching now as then, and is there much confidence today that it can be tackled?

I will seek to address this issue in explicitly sociological ways. In Britain, Sociology and Social Policy[1] have often been seen as separate disciplines, the former more concerned with theory and explanation, the latter eschewing theory building for empirical investigation focused on pragmatic questions of intervention. This is an unhelpful dichotomy, as many of the key questions which Social Policy addresses are sociological, while the exercise of 'sociological imagination' itself necessarily has practical consequences. In this chapter, there are three major ways in which I assert the need to tackle social policy issues from sociological directions. First and foremost, identifiable social problems and issues such as poverty, child abuse, alcoholism, ill health, old age, etc., cannot be simply treated as discrete and isolated matters for pragmatic intervention, but need locating within a wider social totality. Following C. Wright Mills, there is a need to analyze the extent to which 'personal troubles of milieu' may also be 'public issues of social structure' (Mills 1970: 15). Thus the central sociological 'structure–agency' question concerning the extent to which society produces individuals or individuals society, lies at the heart of policy debates about the degree to which social problems are socially caused or open to individual influence, determining the extent and nature of public responsibilities. Mills used the examples of unemployment and divorce to illustrate these issues, both of which are highly relevant to contemporary Social Policy.

Second, as a consequence of the 'New Sociology' of the 1960s onwards, initially through labelling theory and more latterly through 'social constructionist' analysis, it has become clear that social problems cannot be treated in naturalistic terms simply as Durkheimian 'social facts'. Labelling theory, originating in criminology, asserts that social behaviour becomes externally defined as problematic and reinforced by the very professionals and agencies set up to tackle the problem (Becker 1963; Lemert 1967). Therefore the police and the legal system produce criminals as well as combating crime, and by extension doctors manufacture illness and the welfare system generates poverty. As well as indicating that social intervention may produce the opposite of what is intended, it also draws attention to the possibility that professional and institutional actors may have vested interests in creating and perpetuating 'social problems'. This creates difficulties for both the 'pragmatic' and 'structural' approaches to Social Policy because they both in different ways have a bias towards intervention, without fully appreciating the complexities involved. However, labelling theory itself has deterministic tendencies in emphasizing 'societal reaction' and downplaying the agency of those who become defined as 'deviants'. It has therefore largely been superseded since the 1980s by other forms of social constructionist analysis, particularly 'discursive' or 'poststructural' approaches inspired by Michel Foucault (see Rabinow 1991). Discourse theory draws attention particularly to the role of 'expert' knowledge about social problems in framing some possibilities and excluding others. It suggests that the classic distinction between fact and value judgement, between 'is' and 'ought' cannot be sustained, because forms of action involving the exercise of social power over persons are embedded in definitions. However, in contrast to labelling theory, emphasis is on the way that discourses can be challenged by intellectual deconstruction and practical resistance.

Social constructionism has important implications for Social Policy, requiring analysis of why some social phenomena are framed as 'problems' and not others: for example, that poverty is seen to be a problem for society but not necessarily wealth. The discursive framing of acknowledged problems in particular ways also has social and political implications, which is why we shall see that the debate between 'absolute' and 'relative' definitions of poverty is of more than scientific interest. Similarly the turn since the 1980s to associating poverty with a self-generating urban 'underclass' not only implies a shift away from structural explanation, but highlights the need to analyze from whose point of view something is deemed to be a problem. Are policy debates focusing on the problems experienced by the poor, or presuming the poor are a burden or threat to others?

Thirdly, then, Social Policy is sociological in that practitioners need to be reflexive, critically aware that the frameworks they adopt are necessarily influenced by socially situated values and interests, which structure the ways that one identifies, explains and proposes to deal with social policy issues. In Social Policy, sociological reflexivity has been particularly represented by the 'perspectives of welfare' tradition (George and Wilding 1976, 1994). However, reflexivity raises difficult problems about whether anything definite can be stated about the causes and remedies to social problems such as poverty, especially when the discursive turn in social thought denies the existence of absolute truth. In other words, is poverty a 'real' problem with identifiable causes and remedies, or is it simply 'in the eye of the beholder'? My reflexive position is a 'realist' one in scientific terms, drawing among others on Bhaskar (1989) and Layder (1998), and acknowledges the discursive dimensions of poverty but defends the validity of structural analysis. This in turn is politically allied to a radical social democracy which seeks to synthesize pragmatic and structural policy approaches. However, in this chapter I will be less concerned to articulate this analysis or associated policies than to review poverty debates from Rowntree to Tony Blair, seeking to show how the shifts in sociological theorizing are paralleled by broader political economic changes. Thus while Rowntree's 'objective' analysis of poverty was associated with the political triumph of social democracy in 1945, challenges to it were closely associated with the break-up of the political as well as scientific consensus from the 1960s onwards, and the radicalization of both left and right. I will show how the left regarded his definition as too stringent but retained a notion of structural causes which it developed further in more radical directions, and also how the right retained Rowntree's stringency but disputed structural explanations of poverty. At the same time, the emergence of new social movements such as feminism and anti-racism radically challenged the terms of left–right debates. Towards the end of the chapter I also critically examine the ways in which sociological theorizing, particularly by figures such as Anthony Giddens and Amitai Etzioni, has influenced the approach taken in Britain by the 'New Labour' government elected in 1997.

A very British subject: the empiricist approach to poverty

In conventional accounts of the development of state welfare – the kind that I read as an undergraduate in the early 1970s (e.g. Bruce 1968) – Rowntree's study of poverty in town life at the beginning of the century was seen as a major landmark along the road to the welfare state. It provided the objective 'facts' concerning poverty and its 'structural' causes which socialist reformers such as Sidney and Beatrice Webb were able to utilize to campaign for an end to a poor law based on a liberal political economy and individual responsibility for poverty, that finally bore fruit in the welfare reforms of the 1945–51 Labour government. Sociologically, the sense of an unstoppable onward march was encapsulated by T.H. Marshall's conception of the welfare state as a natural evolution from a liberal-democratic society, in which the 'social rights of citizenship' were built upon the foundations of civil and political rights (Marshall 1950).

Rowntree's research provided the discursive evidence for the creation of the welfare state, the poverty standards on which benefit rates were based, and also the basis on which it was claimed that its utopian expectations of 'security from the cradle to the grave' had been realized. He conducted two more surveys of York, one in 1936 and the final one in 1950. Whereas, at the beginning of the century, low wages combined with large family size had been found to be the major cause of poverty, and in 1936 unemployment had risen in significance alongside them, by 1950 neither of these figured. The numbers in poverty had dwindled, from 17,185 in 1936 to 1746 in 1950. What remained was now primarily due to old age and sickness, and Rowntree had no doubt that the welfare state was the major reason for this change (Rowntree and Lavers 1951: 66). This was undoubtedly the moment of greatest triumph for the British Social Policy tradition, which could claim to have brought the reforms about and been responsible for their beneficial effects. It reinforced an uncritical stance to state welfare by a subject defined as 'Social Administration', since fundamental problems had been solved and only those requiring technical adjustment remained.

From a sociological point of view, it is important to analyze historically how this tradition developed. One of the major influences, which perhaps itself begs the question, is the weak political and intellectual influence of Marxism in Britain. In Europe, Marxism had a strong influence on rising labour movements, compelling social theorists to address 'big questions', and theorists such as Durkheim and Weber certainly responded to the challenge. By contrast, in Britain the Labour party grew out of a class-conscious but pragmatically oriented labour movement, and was intellectually influenced by the Webbs and a Fabian commitment to gradualist change. The Webbs promoted faith in parliamentary democracy allied to an efficient state run in the interests of all by expert officials and professionals, administered on neutral scientific principles derived from Comte's positivism. This was also combined with a strong ethical appeal to the middle-class conscience for a just settlement with the exploited, by figures such as Rowntree and Tawney (see Sullivan (1998) for a more detailed exposition). It can therefore be seen that Rowntree's scientific and objective approach to poverty connected to this discursive framework, in which the objective 'facts' tugged at the emotions, pulling them in a particular political direction.

Although it is not explicitly stated in such terms, Rowntree's research developed a particular conception of structure and agency in relation to poverty. This centred primarily on the extent to which poverty is 'primary' or 'secondary', in the context of a poverty 'line' set deliberately low in terms of the 'minimum necessary expenditure for the maintenance of merely physical health' (Rowntree 1902: 87). The most significant feature of Rowntree's claim to being scientific was thus its reliance on the latest nutritional and medical evidence. Rowntree showed that in these terms about half of the poor were in primary poverty and did not obtain enough to live on, for whom the dominant poor law strategy of remoralizing the poor was significantly wanting. However, this was not the case with the remainder who were deemed to be in secondary poverty because they had sufficient money but spent it on inappropriate items. Rowntree's approach to policy research is a classic Enlightenment approach, claiming to suspend value judgements or abstract theories, to examine the social 'facts' which through careful observation will of course readily present themselves to the senses. Nevertheless, Rowntree's approach is brimming with value judgements and a priori assumptions. These include the implication that the claim of the poor on society is limited to mere physical survival;

and by taking household income as his starting point he implicitly endorses the male-headed patriarchal family. His positivistic concept of causes focuses only on immediate influences such as low wages, family size, irregular employment, sickness of a breadwinner, and family budgeting decisions. It fails to account for their linkage to underlying causal processes connected to employment and family relations in an urban capitalist setting, or what Bhaskar (1989) would call 'generative structures'. We are not told why so many working-class people in York existed on low wages, became unemployed or were ill. In other words, neither he nor the modern tradition of empiricist 'poverty line' research adequately identifies poverty as an embedded *social relation* (Novak 1995). The Rowntree tradition is thus a prime example of what Mills (1970) calls 'abstracted empiricism', which he sees as necessarily tied to political projects of 'liberal practicality'.

In more explicit ways, however, Rowntree shares the moralizing discourse which his evidence otherwise challenges, especially his judgement that secondary poverty is the fault of the poor themselves. Of one poor person he states that she is a 'disreputable old woman, ill; ought to be in Workhouse', the cleanliness of the home receives particular attention in judgements of working-class life, and drinking and gambling are denounced (Rowntree 1902: 15–35). Such moralizing is also a prominent feature in pronouncements by Sidney and Beatrice Webb, in the way that they elaborated their assault on 'destitution' in 1911, by which they meant 'not merely a lack of food, clothing and shelter, but also a condition of mental degradation' or 'coarseness and bestiality, apathy and cynical scepticism of every kind' which resulted, they argue, when the poor are 'practically segregated in "cities of the poor"'' (Webb and Webb 1911: 1–2). They also endorse the notion that the poor reproduce their own kind, as

> there is certainly a very potent family tradition and 'class atmosphere' of slovenliness, physical self-indulgence, and irresponsibility – it may be actually of 'parasitism' which is quite unmistakably transmitted from one generation to the next.   (Webb and Webb 1911: 49)

Linkages thus exist between these founding figures and the modern 'underclass' theory that will be examined later in this chapter. Finally, within this tradition, the poor are very much objects of concern who may be pitied or blamed, but need to be socially administered, which relates to a conception of the welfare state as produced and delivered, as Le Grand (1997) puts it, by altruistic 'knights' to passive 'pawns'. There is no acknowledgement that poor people themselves might have views on their situation and needs, as called for by Beresford and Croft (1995).

Poverty, inequality and the welfare state: extending or transforming the paradigm?

Either the deficiencies of the empiricist and pragmatic tradition can be addressed from within, or the tradition itself can be seen as just one possible starting point whose epistemological and value frameworks are open to challenge. If the empiricist tradition is regarded, in Kuhn's (1970) terms, as a consensual paradigm within which 'normal science' was conducted, this helps to explain why the initial response in the 1950s and the 1960s was to question aspects of it as contrary findings appeared. However, as these accumulated, and became less compatible with the old paradigm, more radical challenges and forms of deconstruction emerged. In this sense, too, New Labour can be seen as associated with a new discursive paradigm which, as we shall see, seeks to shift concern from poverty and inequality to 'social exclusion'. A full review of conceptual and methodological debates is not feasible here (for which, see Stitt 1994). The main point I wish to make therefore is that the consensus Rowntree created has now broken down, and this is not only a social scientific but also a political issue.

Thus the initial 'rediscovery of poverty' in the 1960s started to stretch Rowntree's original paradigm, by redefining poverty in terms of 'relative deprivation' or exclusion from a culturally defined 'normal' standard of living rather than mere subsistence. This was the conscious effort of left-wing Fabians such as Peter Townsend to extend the welfare state's formal commitment to equality in more substantive ways, and extend rights of social citizenship. They sought to do this in the time-honoured way by unearthing new scientific evidence on which to base renewed appeals to the public conscience. Abel-Smith and Townsend (1965) therefore set the poverty line 40 per cent higher than Rowntree's, and found that poverty levels were actually increasing in the 'golden years' of the 1950s. This evidence was used as a means of launching the 'poverty lobby', through the creation of the Child Poverty Action Group (CPAG) in 1965, to put pressure on the then Labour government to raise benefits.

The growing calls to extend the egalitarian agenda came at a time when the welfare state was experiencing a combination of rising expectations and growing political economic difficulties. These became increasingly difficult to manage in the 1970s' oil recessions when traditional Keynesian means of regulating the economy broke down as *both* inflation and unemployment rose in tandem. This was also a political space in which new welfare discourses emerged and old ones returned. In academic Social Policy this was marked by a significant theoretical breakthrough – the emergence of the 'perspectives of welfare' approach of George and Wilding (1976, 1994), which asserted that starting points are inherently value laden rather than purely objective constructs. In the most recent edition of their work, George and Wilding helpfully identify four features associated with welfare ideologies as linked to wider political and philosophical positions: a view of human nature as either cooperative and altruistic, or selfish and individualistic; an associated critique of existing institutions in these terms; a utopian vision of the future which inevitably becomes simplified; and guidance on political methods to be used to achieve the ideal society (George and Wilding 1994: 6). At this point we can note two things. First, that by identifying them as ideologies their underlying assumptions can be laid bare and disputed. Second, the emphasis on competing ideologies tends towards relativism and an idealist explanation of social change. While the former breaks with the British Social Policy tradition, the latter is quite consistent with it.

Nevertheless the perspectives of welfare paradigm do enable us to link debates about the extent, causes and remedies of poverty and other social problems to wider ideological frameworks. For example, Townsend's (1979) attempt to broaden the notion of poverty to embrace both 'material' and 'social deprivation' has produced two responses within the social demo-cratic paradigm. First, from a centre-left perspective, Townsend's broad approach has been disputed by a more traditionally pragmatic and 'scientific' preference for a more modestly drawn poverty line based on 'adequate' budget standards (Bradshaw *et al.* 1987; Piachaud 1987). Second, however, more 'populist' approaches have sought to base the concept of relative poverty on more subjectivist foundations. Thus Mack and Lansley (1992) base poverty standards on baskets of 'necessities' identified by public opin-ion surveys of the general population, while other surveys have for the first time drawn up scales by asking poor people themselves what they need (see MacPherson and Silburn 1998). These adaptations are, however, to be distinguished from more radical challenges from left and right. On the left, there was support among Marxists for Townsend's approach, in shifting the concern from traditional Fabian concerns with benefit levels and the poor as a defined group, to a focus on the social inequality gener-ally experienced by the working class within capitalism (Gough 1981). However, as Williams (1989: 33) points out, Townsend still proposed to deal with this by redistributive measures *within* capitalism.

While all these debates have centred around concepts of class and citizenship, a concerted and sustained critique by feminists also emerged, pointing out that by taking 'family poverty' as its starting point, the

Table 13.1   Comparison of causes of poverty, 1899 and 1987 (per cent)

	Among all persons		Among women	
	1899	1987	1899	1987
Old age, sickness and disability	12	32	22	49
One-parent family	9	15	18	14
Unemployment	5	31	6	23
Large family[a]	22	14	14	6
Low wages	52	8	40	8

[a] 1899 = 5 or more children, 1987 = 3 or more children.

Source: Lewis and Piachaud (1992: 42).

situation of women had been largely ignored. Men also had preferential access to social rights deriving from 'citizenship' from which women had often been excluded. Marxists, in examining the structured workings of the capitalist system had largely neglected its gendered aspects in ensuring that women related to the labour market and distribution of income and wealth in disadvantaged ways (Glendinning and Millar 1992). The 'feminization' of poverty is not in fact a new phenomenon, but its social dimensions have changed since Rowntree's survey, as Table 13.1 illustrates. The two main frameworks which have been developed to explain these empirical patterns are not necessarily mutually exclusive: the 'radical feminist' perspective which focuses attention on unequal distribution of resources within households (Delphy 1984); and 'socialist' feminist analysis which emphasizes the disadvantages women experience in the labour market, the devaluing of unpaid household labour, and the role of the state in compounding these (Bryson 1992).

Yet both Marxist and feminist analyses often ignore the issue of 'race' and ethnicity. While this was centrally addressed by Williams's (1989) review of the 'perspectives of welfare' tradition, even the most recent edition of George and Wilding (1994: 7) dismissed the anti-racist critique of welfare as not sufficiently significant to merit inclusion as an 'ideology'. Oppenheim and Harker (1996: 115) point out that many key government statistics relating to poverty, such as households below average income, are not broken down by ethnic origin. Nevertheless they are able to present evidence on a range of social indicators such as unemployment, low pay and working conditions, benefits and discrimination in society, and through the immigration control system, which shows a strong empirical association between racial disadvantage and poverty (see also

Amin 1992). The question remains of how this relates to 'structured' social divisions. Rex (1973) was the first major theorist to refer to black migrants as a distinct 'underclass' located at the base of the social structure, experiencing poverty and other forms of exclusion associated with material disadvantage and racial discrimination. While identifying key influences such as access to income and housing, some have argued that his Weberian framework downplays the links between disadvantage and the capitalist labour market (Anthias 1995). Another problem is that by equating black-ness with the underclass he fails to recognize that sections of the white working class may be undergoing comparable experiences of social mar-ginalization, while significant numbers of black people may be upwardly socially mobile.

In the 1980s, however, the whole issue of the 'underclass' took on a new dimension as a central plank of new right critiques of the welfare state, which also dismissed relative concepts of poverty as scientifically mean-ingless. The re-emphasis on an absolute standard of poverty represented an attempt to rein in efforts to expand citizenship rights. As Sir Keith Joseph put it in 1976, 'a family is poor if it cannot afford to eat . . . By any absolute standards there is very little poverty in Britain today' (cited Oppenheim and Harker 1996: 8). Relative poverty was simply inequality which in neo-liberal discourse is seen as functionally necessary. This approach is not compatible with the approach taken in this chapter, which in principle views all definitions of poverty as discursively constructed, including 'absolute' conceptions. Such a view had a direct effect on social security policy in the early 1980s, when the Thatcher government abolished the link established between state pensions and earnings, and tied it merely to prices, ensuring that pensions fall progressively behind rising average incomes (Tinker 1997: 45). Within this model, to the extent that poverty is acknowledged, it increasingly becomes associated with notions of a self-perpetuating underclass, which is, it is claimed, primarily caused by 'welfare dependency'.

New right underclass theory, premised on the view that humans are inherently selfish, posits that the growth of poverty is primarily due to the 'moral hazard' of easy availability of benefits, and is behaviourally rather than structurally caused. The American political scientist Charles Murray conducted research which deemed to 'prove' that by undermining the sense of responsibility and the social obligations which go with citizenship, wel-fare has been the main reason for the growth of poverty, unemployment, divorce, single parenthood and crime. Although this was initially applied to the USA he claimed this was equally the case for Britain in the 1990s

(Murray 1984, 1994). According to this paradigm the poor have, with some well-meaning but misguided assistance from the state, excluded themselves rather than been excluded. According to Novak:

> The construction of an 'underclass' as an explanation for Britain's grow-ing poverty . . . serves the two purposes of shifting attention away from other explanations for deep-rooted social problems by blaming the poor themselves, and provides legitimation for a harder, more coer-cive and much reduced welfare state.   (1997: 227)

Yet underclass theory and the 'welfare dependency' paradigm has also captured the centre-left ground as at least a partial explanation, alongside structural changes, of the persistent problem of poverty (e.g. Field 1995). As a result it has therefore also had a significant influence upon the evo-lution of New Labour's social policies.

However, it needs also to be acknowledged that government policies since 1997 have been officially framed more in terms of a relatively sophisticated European discourse of poverty as 'social exclusion' than crude underclass theory, a concept whose origin therefore needs to be traced. It first emerged in 1984 with the adoption by the European Union (EU) of a definition of people as poor 'when resources (material, cultural and social) are so limited as to exclude them from the minimum acceptable way of life in the Member States in which they live' (cited Abrahamson 1998: 146–7). This corresponds with Townsend's definition of poverty as a multi-dimensional phenomenon broader than living standards, affecting people's ability to participate in society. However, since then, and particularly in the wake of the 1991 Maastricht Treaty and the 1994 EU White Paper on Social Policy, poverty has been defined less in terms of living stan-dards and more in terms of encouraging labour market participation or 'insertion', with policy focusing on how the various barriers – structural, behavioural and discriminatory – might be removed by supply-side meas-ures which enhance skills and labour market adaptability (Abrahamson 1998). Increasingly, therefore, there has been a reduced emphasis on redistributive measures and more on measures to secure participation in paid work, involving the danger, as Saraceno (1998) sees it, that poverty is *equated* with 'social exclusion'.

Given these wider European influences, it is necessary to situate British welfare developments in an international context. In doing so, I will argue is that the policies of the late 1990s, though borrowing from the language of European social policy, were in practice more closely modelled on US neo-liberal models and strategies.

The changing British welfare state in international perspective

As noted above, the 'perspectives of welfare' approach was a significant breakthrough, but still tends to view policy as caused by shifts in
ideology, a strong characteristic of the British Social Policy tradition.
Another deficiency is the narrow 'anglocentric' focus on the British case,
in a world where social policy in Britain is increasingly affected by events
beyond the English Channel.

There have been two broad alternative theoretical starting points to
the British empiricist tradition. The first, American structural functionalism,
argued that the welfare state was primarily a response to the systemic needs
to enhance the smooth workings and social stabilization of advanced capitalist societies. Thus Rimlinger (1971) saw state welfare as investment in
the productivity of labour, while Wilensky and Lebeaux (1965) emphasized its role in social stabilization by covering wage workers against the
'risks' associated with unemployment, old age and ill health. Functionalism was severely critiqued for being deterministic and failing to account
for significant and enduring differences between societies (Mishra 1981).
It thus became superseded by theories which emphasized political mobilization, of which the most influential has been the Scandinavian 'power-
resources' model of Esping-Andersen (1990). This argues that up to 1980
the extent to which states ceded rights of social citizenship depended
crucially on the solidity of the political alliance between the traditional
manual and growing number of salaried workers. Where the alliance was
strongly represented in social democratic parties, as in Scandinavia, universalistic and generous social security was achieved. In continental countries
such as Germany and Italy, where working-class cohesion was weakened
by religious mobilization on the right, this led to well-developed but
'conservative' welfare states, in which salaried workers received more
enhanced benefits. Manual workers in countries like the USA failed to forge
effective alliances with salaried workers, producing residual or 'liberal'
welfare states in which benefits were low and highly conditional.

Within this model Britain's system has been seen by some as closer
to a 'liberal' than a 'social democratic' system, with Ginsburg (1992)
depicting it as a hybrid 'liberal collectivist' welfare state. This is largely
because in contrast to other European countries Britain failed to build
significantly on the platform established by the 1945–51 Labour government. Seen in this way the election of the Thatcher government in 1979
was not such a dramatic ideological break from the past. Nevertheless,
significant policy shifts have taken place, and the fact that the Labour

government at the end of the 1990s is seeking to modify rather than dismantle its neo-liberal inheritance also requires explanation. There are two
possible explanations which may not in fact be mutually exclusive. First,
from a structural perspective, the functional conditions may have changed;
second, an emphasis on agency might suggest that the changes have been
influenced by shifts in ideology and the conditions of political mobilization.

One form of structural explanation which was influential in the 1970s
was neo-Marxist 'crisis' theory. For example, O'Connor (1973) argued
that a contradiction had emerged in capitalist welfare states between the
functions of 'accumulation', or welfare necessary to capital, and 'legitimation', or welfare to meet peoples' needs and secure social peace. This was
potentially dysfunctional in that it threatened the profitability of capital
which was essential to the 'health' of the system. This would either be
resolved by a transition to socialism or a radical retrenchment of welfare.
In hindsight, crisis theory was too apocalyptic, for even under Thatcher
it was not dismantled. This can in part be seen as due to political
resistance, although Klein (1993) sees many of the Conservative reforms
since 1979 – more conditional welfare, greater efficiency and consumer-
ism in state services, a more significant role for the voluntary and private
sectors – as an 'organizational adaptation' towards a more 'pluralist' system
in the face of 'economic stringency' and criticisms of a 'self-serving welfare bureaucracy imposing their own preferences on captive consumers'
(Klein 1993: 13). Thus a new strain of left and centre-left analysis emerged
which saw the neo-liberal reforms not just as the result of ideology and
the political mobilization of capital, but in quasi-functionalist terms.

This form of analysis can be said to have helped to pave the way for
New Labour's accommodation to the Thatcher inheritance. Much of it was
initially disseminated through the now defunct journal *Marxism Today* (for
a compilation see Hall and Jacques 1989), whose most influential sociological thinker was Stuart Hall who, it is only fair to state, subsequently
distanced himself from New Labour thinking (Hall 1998). The essential
element of the journal's analysis of Thatcherism was that it was partly in
tune with 'new times', both in the sense of where capitalism as a mode
of production was moving and where people's ideological inclinations were
shifting. Although its Marxism was informed by a Gramscian emphasis
on politics and ideology, there was nevertheless a strong insistence that
changes in the productive system were exerting a powerful influence on
political developments, of which Thatcherism was one manifestation. In
particular, it was claimed that society was moving from a 'Fordist' to a
'post-Fordist system of production, and traditional left politics which had
been in tune with the former was now out of synch with the latter. Fordism

is seen as more than a system of mass production, and also as an associated form of nation-based Keynesian regulation ensuring stable full employment and institutional welfare states. It is argued that this form of regulation reached its limit in the late 1960s for a variety of reasons, including the revolt of alienated labour and the development of more sophisticated consumer tastes, in the context of breakdown of the international currency system, and pressure of oil recessions. From that point, capitalism needed to shift to 'flexible accumulation' based on global production, decentralized systems of labour management, and more responsiveness in competitive situations to rapidly changing consumer tastes (Aglietta 1979; Piore and Sabel 1984).

Post-Fordist theory took some time to focus centrally on social policy and what systems of 'regulation' most appropriately 'fit' this new situation (Burrows and Loader 1994). Thus Lash (1992) sees the US underclass as produced by post-Fordist de-industrialization and removal of new jobs in expanding high technology and service sectors to new and inaccessible areas. In response to this, parallel 'regulatory' institutions, from public bureaucracies to family structures, become stripped away. In the wider economy itself, a shift to competitive 'lean production' is associated with a shrinking 'core' of stable jobs and a broader mass of insecure, low-paid workers. Lash recognizes that these tendencies are most manifest in the neo-liberal countries like the USA and Britain and that in 'corporatist' Germany a large 'underclass' has not emerged both because of constraints on capital and strong family relations among Turkish migrants. Jessop (1994) focuses directly on emerging systems of welfare regulation, arguing that capitalist requirements have led to the hollowing out of the state at the supranational and regional levels, undermining the Keynesian welfare state (KWS). The state, rather than being able to guarantee jobs and benefits, is now under pressure to reintegrate workers into labour markets by conditional forms of benefit based on 'workfare' rather than unconditional social security.

Postmodern social theory is another allied development of the late 1990s (see Carter 1998). Though diverse, it extends the emphasis of the 'perspectives of welfare tradition' upon the role of ideologies and discourse on social policy, by arguing that these have a tendency to fragment. The 'grand narratives' of change and progress represented by both Marxism and reformist socialism, are necessarily giving way to a more fragmented social structure, a post-industrial 'knowledge-based' society, and an associated pluralistic and pragmatic set of politics (Lyotard 1984). In line with this, postmodern Social Policy emphasizes the potentially oppressive character of universalist discourses of welfare promoted by Fabianism as insufficiently adjusted to needs of women, black people, gays, lesbians and other marginalized groups and individuals. In its place it celebrates particularism and 'difference'. Marxism is also criticized for its overemphasis on class and its economic determinism, with preference expressed for Foucauldian analysis of fragmented social identities, and the decentralized and contingent nature of power relations (Penna and O'Brien 1996). Despite the emphasis on a 'cultural turn', however, there is sometimes a tendency towards technological determinism, in that computer and media technology are seen as creating a socially deconstructive milieu, which lends itself to the fragmentation and decomposition of 'expert' systems of welfare (Loader 1998). Postmodernism thus often argues similar things to post-Fordism, if from different premises, especially where 'flexible accumulation' is seen as part of the 'condition of postmodernity' (Harvey 1990).

A postmodern perspective on poverty has started to emerge with the view that it is less closely associated with social class than in the past, which is consistent with a discourse of 'social exclusion' as multi-dimensional rather than simply associated with material deprivation. Thus the 'new' poverty is seen as highly differentiated, linked to long-term unemployment, part-time working, increased divorce and single parenthood, discrimination towards disabled people and people from ethnic minority groups, and so on. Abrahamson suggests that this may be seen as characteristic of a fragmenting society which is less associated with vertical hierarchies of class. Echoing Touraine, he suggests there may be a transition to a society in which 'today it is no longer a case of being "up or down" but "in or out"' (Abrahamson 1998: 148). Such a view is consistent with the view that there is a contemporary problem of political agency which has perhaps been most graphically put by Galbraith (1992), who argues that in contemporary society the 'core' majority enjoy material prosperity in circumstances where an increasing number have been expelled to the 'periphery', and who are feared rather than pitied. Thus, rather than policies to remedy poverty, there are increasing shifts towards policies of containment and control.

Needless to say, these claims are controversial. For example, Navarro (1991) has criticized post-Fordism as a productivist theory which does not satisfactorily account either for the politically constructed development of the welfare state by struggle from below, or for its contemporary decay through a political attack from above by capital. Postmodernism's emphasis on trends to pluralism and social fragmentation has been portrayed by Taylor-Gooby (1996) as a 'great leap backwards', serving unwittingly as an ideological 'smokescreen' obscuring a world where the universalizing discourse of the new right is increasingly triumphant, and behind which the balance of power has shifted in capital's favour. Levitas (1996) has critically reviewed changing policy discourses on social exclusion and the preferred solution of insertion into paid work as devaluing the contribution of women's unpaid labour in the 'private' sphere, and the continuing importance of class divisions in the public sphere. She argues that such discourses represent a shift back to a functionalist sociology, and express a Durkheimian concern to secure social cohesion by integrating people into the existing unequal division of labour, abandoning social policy's traditional concerns with social justice. Ratcliffe (1999) argues that as far as 'race' and ethnicity are concerned the concept of social exclusion should be rejected in favour a structure–agency approach to social divisions, as it can end up labelling the 'socially excluded' in stigmatizing ways. My own view is that social structures are changing in complex ways, and that both processes of fragmentation *and* polarization are at work (Bradley 1996). This means that traditional redistributive agendas still have relevance, as the social structure has not changed so much that collectivist class politics has lost its force, particularly as the salaried classes are experiencing insecurity and being subjected to processes of capitalist rationalization. However, the interesting thing to note is that sociological theorizing has had a direct influence upon politics and policy in the late 1990s, in ways I will now specify.

Sociology and New Labour social policies

The advent to power of New Labour in 1997 led to the unveiling of a much vaunted 'Third Way' in politics between neo-liberalism and social democracy, and much activity in social policy, including a pledge to abolish child poverty in Britain within twenty years. In September 1999 this led to the announcement of thirty-two poverty indicators and a yearly audit against which government progress will be judged (DSS 1999). In approaching this topic I want to distinguish between the Social Policy *of* and *for* New Labour, although assigning commentators to one or the other is fuzzy at the edges. I will focus on three theorists who have publicly been 'for' New Labour: Anthony Giddens, Amatai Etzioni and Ruth Lister, though the last has combined this with criticisms of its strategies.

Finlayson (1999) argues that although the Third Way was named before it was given shape by Tony Blair (1999), it nevertheless has strong sociological underpinnings, including *Marxism Today*, and more recently the 'late modern' social theorizing of Giddens (1998). Despite differences, a common theme is that the world has radically changed and politics needs to catch up: to the global economy, the computer revolution, the decline of the manual working classes, the flexible labour market, the demands of women for equality, the individualism of the middle classes, the disenchantment of people with welfare professionals, and much else besides. Rather than approaching politics through traditional socialist ideology, it needs to be approached pragmatically, by facing up to realities or what Finlayson dubs 'social facts'. A second feature of the two contributing traditions is what Finlayson calls 'technological futurism', in which the aim of politics is not so much to direct or rechannel the accelerating pace of social change, as to adapt and manage it within the framework of the global market, and to help individuals to do the same.

A third dimension, however, which Finlayson's otherwise excellent review omits, is the way in which the Third Way rediscovers the social, often expressed as 'community', in ways that align it closely with the conservative tradition in sociology. Giddens is on the social democratic left flank of Third Way thinking, seeking to reconcile a reflexive individualism with support for reasonably robust regulation of the global economy, and social measures to reduce inequalities rather than merely widen opportunities, which to some extent distances him from Blair (Calinicos 1999). Etzioni, and the 'communitarian' tradition which he promotes, is an American import which seeks by contrast to find a middle way between neo-liberalism's emphasis on individual freedom and the Conservative imperative to assert authority. Echoing Durkheim, communitarianism acknowledges that an economy based on unbridled individualism can have damaging effects, but rather than seeking to regulate it through interventionist measures, the aim is to ensure that market decisions are subject to moral considerations, through inputs from 'stakeholders' such as workers, the community and the government (Etzioni 1988). Communitarianism has, however, had less of an impact on economic policy, because it would represent a significant shift away from neo-liberalism to European corporatist forms of governance, as advocated notably by Hutton (1995). However, it has made a significant impact on the government's social policies, which echo its concern that neo-liberalism is corroding the collective institutions of civil society, but the social democratic welfare state is castigated for doing the same by offering 'too many rights, too few obligations'. Instead it wishes to encourage voluntary effort and family responsibility (Etzioni 1995). It should be noted, however, that communitarians do not argue for a simple 'rolling back of the state', but state interventions to reinforce community self-capacity. We can see this in Etzioni's claims that many modern social problems are due to a 'parenting deficit' (he is careful not to blame it solely on women) which needs to be remedied by state intervention. He also wishes to see strong law-and-order policing to avoid communities taking matters into their own hands (Hughes 1996). Thus, while one dimension of Third Way thought, as Finlayson suggests, appeals to a 'reflexive' left pragmatics represented by Giddens, Etzioni's is more conservative and even at times authoritarian.

It is important not to exaggerate the impact of theorizing upon politics, which clearly reacts to events and circumstances. Clearly the failure of Labour to win the 1992 election with a mildly redistributive manifesto was crucial in the final jettisoning of an 'ethical' politics based on appeals to middle-class altruism. Also important has been New Labour's perception that the global economy and supranational institutions significantly constrain its political choices. A prime political effect of globalization, claim Crouch and Streeck (1997), is to foster a 'symbolic politics', involving a cynical pretence that national decision making is shaped by domestic democratic politics rather than international finance markets and requirements of multinational companies. Looked at in this light, the Third Way can be seen as a way of sweetening a bitter pill and reassuring people that the state is still in charge. Thus the state pursues anti-poverty policies but without taking money away from the middle classes, or departing from the tight monetary restrictions imposed by the European Union on public expenditure and debt. It can, however, safely pursue rhetorical 'moral' campaigns through the media on crime, marriage, parenting, paedophiles, gypsies, etc., and intervene on populist issues such as whether there should be a memorial to Princess Diana.

In their different ways, the sociology of Giddens and Etzioni represents a shift from sociology as a radical challenge to the status quo associated with the 'New Sociology' which C. Wright Mills played a key role in inaugurating. There remain tensions, however, between the sociological community and the government, especially since in practice the Amercian conservative version of the Third Way has appeared more hegemonic in practice. We can see this explicitly in the work of Ruth Lister who occupies an ambiguous position as both one of the architects and a persistent critic of Third Way Social Policy. Lister was one of the academics who helped to frame the Labour party's review of its traditional commitment to redistributive tax and benefit strategies following the 1992 election defeat, the semi-independent Borrie Commission (Commission on Social Justice 1994). This advocated the creation of an 'investors' Britain' in which economic prosperity and social justice go hand-in-hand, against both a neo-liberal 'deregulators' Britain' and a 'Levellers' Britain' which prioritizes redistribution over economic renewal. Its main proposals were for training and education aimed at improving 'supply-side' skills and adaptability, with a floor provided by a minimum wage, a welfare system that encourages integration into the labour market and protects against the effects of insecurity, and a tax system that benefits rather than penalizes the working poor. Many of the measures advocated by Borrie, or variants of them, were implemented by the Labour government after 1997, particularly the overriding emphasis on welfare to work.

Nevertheless, Lister subsequently emerged as a critic of New Labour social policies. She was one of fifty-four Social Policy professors who signed an open letter to the *Financial Times* in October 1997, criticizing the government's abandonment of redistribution and calling for a rise in benefit levels. In a more analytical vein, she notes that New Labour's approach formed part of a 'paradigm shift' in government discourse 'from equality to social inclusion', and a focus on 'social exclusion/inclusion' *instead* of poverty, with paid work and education as the prime mechanism. She focuses particularly on the work of the government's Social Exclusion Unit which works directly under the Prime Minister, the main aim of which is to tackle poverty outside the framework of redistributive measures (Lister 1998). Improving benefit levels had been dismissed by Gordon Brown, the Chancellor of the Exchequer, as treating the symptoms rather the causes of poverty (cited Lister 1998: 219). Thus the traditional welfare state was seen as purely ameliorative, with New Labour proclaiming its intention to tackle the 'root causes', mainly identified in terms of promoting 'joined up' solutions across government departments, in partnership with individuals and communities: seeking, in other words, to liberate the agency of the poor. As Lister comments: 'The question has to be whether, in the context of entrenched structural inequalities, genuine social inclusion, including the eradication of poverty, is possible without greater equality' (Lister 1998: 224). Lister, therefore, within a basic agreement of the shift to New Labour, has attempted to add in the traditional concerns of social democracy with greater equality. Giddens (1999), too, without openly criticizing government policy, has argued that the Third Way must also involve strategies for 'equality of outcome' otherwise it is no better than 'warmed-over porridge'.

Conclusion: a future for the welfare state?

This chapter has reviewed the way that sociologists have conceptualized the 'poverty problem' and the responsibility of the state from Rowntree onwards. The structure–agency issue has been a constant preoccupation of theories which sought to identify how much individuals could be held responsible for their situation, and also the scope for intervention to change these conditions.

I have argued against an approach which sees Social Policy and Sociology as concerned with different issues. Although the empiricist tradition did seek to separate the issue of poverty from questions of social structure, I have also presented evidence that Marshall, Townsend and others related it to more general questions of the direction in which society was moving, and the extent to which it could be tackled within existing social relationships. Similarly, sociologists such as Hall, Giddens, and Etzioni have in different ways linked theorizing to issues of pressing practical concern. Admittedly this chapter has focused less on the details of poverty itself, such as trends in how many and which people are affected by it, how it is experienced and so on. Nor have I focused on the details of policies, concerns at the growing costs of the benefits system and its effects, etc. Rather I have concentrated primarily on different forms of sociological theorizing for, as MacPherson and Silburn (1998: 17) put it, 'the seemingly academic questions of poverty – definition and measurement – have profound consequences for policy and practice, and thus for those now condemned to poverty and its consequences'.

On the whole, sociologists have targeted what Giddens (1998) calls 'market fundamentalism', although Third Way theory undoubtedly accepts the global market as a framework within which to operate. Etzioni's theory clearly has conservative roots, while both Giddens and Lister undoubtedly wish to move beyond a society based on Blairite 'equality of opportunity'. Nevertheless the danger is that 'Giddens sociology, combined with the latent Marxist functionalism of "New Times" Post-Fordism, might fall into the fallacy of empirical sociology . . . The result might be to accept economic developments as non-political, even natural phenomena, and the role of government as shaping us all up for the new world, forcing us to be reflexive' (Finlayson 1999: 278).

If this is fair comment, it is also ironic, given that reflexivity in social theory is supposed to *widen* possibilities for political choice. Certainly it does appear at times that Giddens (1999) portrays a rather cosy functionalist 'lifeworld' without hard choices, where the 'modernized' welfare state will both be 'internally reformed and brought into line with the demands of the global marketplace', and at the same time ensure 'employability, the dissolution of poverty traps and the creation of pensions systems that take account of increased worker mobility and the decline of traditional corporate employment'.

Unfortunately, however, we are not told exactly how this impressive conjuring trick is to be brought about. A more realistic but depressing scenario is presented by Esping-Andersen (1993), who argues from post-Fordist premises that there is a 'choice' between the European way of seeking to preserve welfare benefits and labour market regulation at the price of high unemployment and a large excluded population, and the American road of deregulation and forced employment in a large low-paid service sector – the road both Conservative and New Labour governments in Britain have largely followed. Although 1970s' crisis theory was too apocalyptic, it could still therefore be plausibly argued that 'there is a fundamental conflict between the needs of unregulated capital and the needs of people' (Gough 1999). As Taylor-Gooby (1999: 303) puts it, 'state welfare must construct an agenda that includes a focus on state power, class inequality and the power of capital'. This does not point to any easy way forward, but it does indicate that political mobilization and not just the 'battle of ideas' alone is likely to make a crucial difference.

These conclusions are not comfortable and reassuring nostrums, but then that is not necessarily the purpose of Sociology. If the problem of the New Sociology of the 1960s was that it could afford to criticize because it was excluded from power, this chapter points to a danger in British Sociology both in the immediate postwar period, and more latterly in the late 1990s, of getting too close to government agendas for critical comfort. In this respect, how Sociology and Social Policy deal with the continuing paradox of poverty among riches immeasurably vaster than in Rowntree's day will serve as a key test of whether they remain crusaders for social justice, or become uneasy servants of the status quo.

Note

1   I use capitals to refer to the academic subject of Social Policy, whereas social policy or policies refer to actual developments.

References

Abel-Smith, B. and Townsend, P. (1965) *The Poor and the Poorest*, London: Bell and Sons.

Abrahamson, P. (1998) 'Combating poverty and social exclusion in Europe', in W. Beck, L. van der Maesen and A. Walker (eds) *The Social Quality of Europe*, Bristol: Policy Press.

Aglietta, M. (1979) *A Theory of Capitalist Regulation*, London: New Left Books.

Amin, A. (1992) *Poverty in Black and White: Deprivation and Ethnic Minorities*, London: Child Poverty Action Group.

Anthias, F. (1995) 'Rex', in V. George and R. Page (eds) *Modern Thinkers on Welfare*, Hemel Hempstead: Harvester Wheatsheaf, 330–51.

Becker, H.S. (1963) *Outsiders: Studies in the Sociology of Deviance*, Glencoe IL: Free Press.

Beresford, P. and Croft, S. (1995) 'It's our problem too! Challenging the exclusion of poor people from poverty discourse', *Critical Social Policy* 15 (2/3): 75–95.

Bhaskar, R. (1989) *Reclaiming Reality: A Critical Introduction to Contemporary Philosophy*, London: Verso.

Blair, T. (1999) *The Third Way: New Politics for the New Century*, London: Fabian Society.

Bradley, H. (1996) *Fractured Identities: Changing Patterns of Inequality*, Cambridge: Polity Press.

Bradshaw, J., Mitchell, D. and Morgan, J. (1987) 'Evaluating adequacy: the potential of budget standards', *Journal of Social Policy*, 16 (2): 189–215.

Bruce, M. (1968) *The Coming of the Welfare State*, fourth edition, London: Batsford.

Burrows, R. and Loader, B. (1994) *Towards a Post-Fordist Welfare State?* London: Routledge.

Bryson, L. (1992) *Welfare and the State*, London: Macmillan.

Callinicos, A. (1999) 'Social theory put to the test of politics: Pierre Bourdieu and Anthony Giddens', *New Left Review*, 236: 77–102.

Carter, J. (ed.) (1998) *Postmodernity and the Fragmentation of Welfare*, London: Routledge.

Commission on Social Justice (1994) *Social Justice: Strategies for National Renewal*, London: Vintage.

Crouch, C. and Streeck, W. (1997) 'Introduction: the future of capitalist diversity', in C. Crouch and W. Streeck (eds) *Political Economy of Modern Capitalism: Mapping Convergence and Diversity*, London: Sage, 1–18.

Delphy, C. (1984) *Close to Home: A Materialist Analysis of Women's Oppression*, London: Hutchinson.

Department of Social Security (DSS) (1999) *Opportunity for All: Tackling Poverty and Social Exclusion*, London: The Stationery Office, obtainable at http://dss.gov.uk/hq/pubs/poverty/main/index.htm

Esping-Anderson, G. (1990) *The Three Worlds of Welfare Capitalism*, Cambridge: Polity Press.

Esping-Andersen, G. (1993) 'Post-industrial class structures', in G. Esping-Anderson (ed.) *Changing Classes: Stratification and Mobility in Post-Industrial Societies*, London: Sage, 7–31.

Etzioni, A. (1988) *The Moral Dimension: Towards a New Economics*, New York: Free Press.

Etzioni, A. (1994) 'Restoring our moral voice', *The Public Interest*, 115: 107–13.

Etzioni, A. (1995) *The Spirit of Community: Rights, Responsibilities and the Communitarian Agenda*, London: Fontana.

Field, F. (1995) *Making Welfare Work: Reconstructing Welfare for the Millennium*, London: Institute of Community Studies.

Finlayson, A. (1999) 'Third way theory', *Political Quarterly*, 70 (3): 271–9.

Galbraith, J.K. (1992) *The Culture of Contentment*, London: Sinclair Stevenson.

Glendinning, C. and Millar, J. (1992) *Women and Poverty in Britain: The 1990s*, Hemel Hempstead: Harvester Wheatsheaf.

George, V. and Wilding, P. (1976) *Ideology and Social Welfare*, London: Routledge and Kegan Paul.

George, V. and Wilding, P. (1994) *Welfare and Ideology*, Hemel Hempstead: Harvester Wheatsheaf.

Giddens, A. (1998) *The Third Way: The Renewal of Social Democracy*, Cambridge: Polity Press.

Giddens, A. (1999) 'Better than warmed-over porridge', *New Statesman*, 12 February: 25–6.

Ginsburg, N. (1992) *Divisions of Welfare: A Critical Introduction to Comparative Social Policy*, London: Sage.

Gough, I. (1981) 'Poverty in the United Kingdom', *International Journal of Health Services*, 11 (2): 315–28.

Gough, I. (1999) 'The needs of capital and the needs of people: can the welfare state reconcile the two?' Inaugural lecture, University of Bath, http://www.bath.ac.uk/~hssirg/inaug.htr

Hall, S. (1998) 'The great moving nowhere show', *Marxism Today*, Special New Labour Issue: 9–14.

Hall, S. and Jacques, M. (eds) (1989) *New Times: The Changing Face of Politics in the 1990s*, London: Lawrence and Wishart.

Harvey, D. (1990) *The Condition of Postmodernity: An Enquiry into the Origins of Cultural Change*, Oxford: Blackwell.

Hughes, G. (1996) 'Communitarianism and law and order', *Critical Social Policy*, 16: 17–41.

Hutton, W. (1995) *The State We're In*, London: Cape.

Jessop, B. (1994) 'The transition to post-Fordism and the Schumpeterian workfare state', in R. Burrows, and B. Loader (eds) *Towards a Post-Fordist Welfare State?* London: Routledge, 13–37.

Klein, R. (1993) 'O'Goffe's tale: or what can we learn from the success of the capitalist welfare states?', in C. Jones (ed.) *New Perspectives on the Welfare State in Europe*, London: Routledge, 7–17.

Kuhn, T. (1970) *The Structure of Scientific Revolutions*, second edition, Chicago: University of Chicago Press.

Lash, S. (1992) 'The Making of an underclass: neo-liberalism versus corporatism', in P. Brown and R. Crompton (eds) *Economic Restructuring and Social Exclusion*, London: UCL Press, 157–74.

Layder, D. (1998) *Sociological Practice: Linking Theory and Social Research*, London: Sage.

Le Grand, J. (1997) 'Knights, knaves or pawns? Human behaviour and social policy', *Journal of Social Policy*, 26 (2): 149–69.

Leisink, P. (1997) 'Work and citizenship in Europe', in M. Roche and R. van Berkel (eds) *European Citizenship and Social Exclusion*, Aldershot: Ashgate, 51–65.

Lemert, E.M. (1967) *Human Deviance, Social Problems and Social Control*, Englewood Cliffs NJ: Prentice Hall.

Levitas, R. (1996) 'The concept of social exclusion and the new Durkheimian hegemony', *Critical Social Policy*, 16: 5–20.

Lewis, J. and Piachaud, D. (1992) 'Women and poverty in the twentieth century', in C. Glendinning and J. Millar (eds) *Women and Poverty in Britain: The 1990s*, Hemel Hempstead: Harvester Wheatsheaf, 27–45.

Lister, R. (1998) 'From equality to social inclusion: New Labour and the welfare state', *Critical Social Policy*, 18: 215–25.

Loader, B. (1998) 'Welfare direct: informatics and the emergence of self-service welfare?', in J. Carter (ed.) *Postmodernity and the Fragmentation of Welfare*, London: Routledge, 220–33.

Lyotard, J.-F. (1984) *The Postmodern Condition*, Manchester: Manchester University Press.

MacPherson, S. and Silburn, R. (1998) 'The meaning and measurement of poverty', in J. Dixon and D. Macarow (eds) *Poverty: A Persistent Global Reality*, London: Routledge, 1–19.

Mack, J. and Lansley, S. (1992) *Breadline Britain: The Findings of the Television Series*, London: London Weekend Television.

Marshall, T.H. (1950) *Citizenship and Social Class and Other Essays*, Cambridge: Cambridge University Press.

Mills, C.W. (1970) *The Sociological Imagination*, Harmondsworth: Penguin.

Mishra, R. (1981) *Society and Social Policy*, second edition, London: Macmillan.

Murray, C. (1984) *Losing Ground*, New York: Basic Books.

Murray, C. (1994) *Underclass: The Crisis Deepens*, London: Institute of Economic Affairs.

Navarro, V. (1991) 'Production and the welfare state: the political context of reforms', *International Journal of Health Services*, 21 (4): 585–614.

Novak, T. (1995) 'Rethinking poverty', *Critical Social Policy*, 15 (2/3): 58–74.

Novak, T. (1997) 'Poverty and the "underclass"', in M. Lavalette and A. Pratt (eds) *Social Policy: A Conceptual and Theoretical Introduction*, London: Sage, 214–27.

O'Connor, J. (1973) *The Fiscal Crisis of the State*, New York: St Martin's Press.

Oppenheim, C. and Harker, L. (1996) *Poverty: The Facts*, London: Child Poverty Action Group.

Penna, S. and O'Brien, M. (1996) 'Postmodernism and social policy: a small step forwards?', *Journal of Social Policy*, 25 (1): 39–61.

Piachaud, D. (1987) 'Problems in the definition and measurement of poverty', *Journal of Social Policy*, 16 (2): 147–62.

Piore, M. and Sabel, C. (1984) *The Second Industrial Divide*, New York: Basic Books.

Rabinow, P. (ed.) (1991) *The Foucault Reader*, Harmondsworth: Penguin.

Ratcliffe, P. (1999) 'Housing inequality and "race": some critical reflections on the concept of "social exclusion"', *Ethnic and Racial Studies*, 22 (1): 1–22.

Rex, J. (1973) *Race, Colonialism and the City*, London: Weidenfeld and Nicolson.

Rimlinger, G. (1971) *Welfare Policy and Industrialization in Europe, America and Russia*, London: Wiley.

Rowntree, B.S. (1902) *Poverty: A Study of Town Life*, second edition, London: Macmillan.

Rowntree, B.S. and Lavers, H. (1951) *Poverty and the Welfare State: A Third Social Survey of York Dealing Only With Economic Questions*, London: Longman, Green and Co.

Saraceno, C. (1998) 'The importance of the concept of social exclusion', in M. Roche and R. van Berkel (eds) *European Citizenship and Social Exclusion*, Aldershot: Ashgate, 51–65.

Stitt, S. (1994) *Poverty and Poor Relief: Concepts and Reality*, Aldershot: Avebury.

Sullivan, M. (1998) 'Democratic socialism and social policy', in R.M. Page and R. Silburn (eds) *British Social Welfare in the Twentieth Century*, London: Macmillan, 105–30.

Taylor-Gooby, P. (1994) 'Postmodernism and social policy: a great leap back-wards?', *Journal of Social Policy*, 23 (3): 385–404.

Taylor-Gooby, P. (1999) 'Bipolar bugbears – comment on Colin Hay: "Globalization, Welfare Retrenchment and 'the Logic of No Alternative': Why Second Best Won't Do"', *Journal of Social Policy*, 28 (2): 299–303.

Tinker, A. (1997) *Older People in Modern Society*, fourth edition, London and New York: Longman.

Townsend, P. (1979) *Poverty in the United Kingdom: A Survey of Household Resources and Standards of Living*, Harmondsworth: Penguin.

Webb, S. and Webb, B. (1911) *The Prevention of Destitution*, London: Longman, Green and Co.

Wilensky, H.L. and Lebeaux, C.N. (1965) *Industrial Society and Social Welfare*, New York: Free Press.

Williams, F. (1989) *Social Policy: A Critical Introduction*, Cambridge: Polity Press.

chapter 14

Rediscovering the underclass

Robert Moore

Introduction

The idea of an underclass is not new. Although the word itself is of postwar origin, the ideas underlying it may be traced to the nineteenth century and variously to reactions to the rise of large urban populations, to the emerging demands of organized labour and to the rise of crime and pauperism. The second, short, section of this chapter looks at what I have called the 'disreputable' history of the term 'underclass'. Forerunners of the underclass idea were used not for purposes of analysis, but *against* identified groups, who were stigmatized thereby. It is for this reason that we call the history disreputable. This discussion of the history of the idea comes second because, whatever the historical credentials of an idea, it is more important for us to examine the validity and utility of an idea, unencumbered by knowledge of past usage. Perhaps underclass is an idea whose hour has come and we can leave the historical baggage behind and, taking the idea seriously, move forward with conceptual clarity to develop an idea which has powerful analytical utility in understanding our times.

Because it has been a problem for more than a century, no discussion of the underclass can claim to be original. Recent debates have entailed *rediscovering* a section of the population that was (at best) only temporarily lost from view. The first part of this chapter tries to start again, to define and measure the underclass by asking the questions 'what might an underclass be?' and 'does this stand up to empirical test?' It seeks to clarify the concept and then looks for evidence of an underclass in terms of the clarified conception. In doing this it is necessary to summarize and review the commentaries and the research findings of sociologists from the Second World War until the present. By the end of this section the relative utility to sociologists of the idea of underclass should be clear.

After the historical snapshot of the forerunners of the underclass, we return to a sociological discussion of how the underclass, or underclasses, are *made*. Here we turn to questions of industrial restructuring, the possible redundancy of sections of the population and their exclusion from what becomes the mainstream of social and economic life. Social policies may either amplify or offset this structural exclusion. The discussion is about *interests*, identifiable *actors* and *institutions* – the core subject matter of sociological enquiry. In considering questions of exclusion, domination and subordination we ask who acts upon whom, why and by what means? These questions are far removed from the attribution or denial of the moral worth of the excluded or dominated that comprises most popular discussions of the underclass. The chapter therefore concludes with a reflection upon the sociologist as social actor and the consequences for others, whether intended or not, of the way in which we use and promote ideas about the social world. In these concluding reflections the argument that has been implicit throughout the chapter is made explicit and underlined as a professional and ethical issue; the people whom the term 'underclass' is meant to describe are not the problem, it is the term itself and the way in which it is used that comprises the problem of the underclass.

Defining and finding the underclass

Defining the underclass

The earliest postwar reference by a social scientist to the idea of an underclass is in Gunnar Myrdal's *Challenge to Affluence* published in 1964 (Myrdal 1964). Looking at the booming US economy he saw unemployment as becoming less cyclical and amenable to demand stimulation. New technical developments were eliminating the need for wide categories of labour. This was creating an underclass

> of unemployed and gradually, unemployable persons and families at the bottom of a society in which, for the majority of the people above that level the increasingly democratic structure of the education system creates more and more liberty – real liberty – and equality of opportunity [. . .]
>
> Opening up more opportunities to more people has closed some opportunities for some. And now in the end it threatens to split off a true 'underclass' – not really an integrated part of the nation at all but a useless and miserable substratum.
>
> (Myrdal 1964: 40–1)

Nearly thirty years on the argument has been imported in similar terms to the UK, notably by Halsey and Dahrendorf. Halsey (1991) argues that:

> The class structure of industrial societies, including Britain, is developing an underclass of those who can not be placed in the stable workforce of the formerly employed . . . they suffer a cumulation of social pathologies – educational failure, illiteracy, broken families, high crime rates, poor housing and spatial concentration in the inner city. They are disproportionately recruited from the young and the ethnic minorities, and they lead a ghetto existence outside of the normal social contract of citizenship and with little or no stake in official society.   (Halsey 1991)

Myrdal, Halsey and Dahrendorf all raise the question of whether there is a population surplus to the requirements of the productive economy. They suggest that such a population is, or would be, outside the mainstream of society, with little or no stake in society. Later developments of the idea of an underclass took on an increasingly moral (and judgemental) tone but it is important to note that these early formulations are about social structural change.

Later, interest in the underclass derived from the work of William Julius Wilson and Charles Murray (Wilson 1987; Murray 1990). Each was interested in the emergence and persistence of the underclass, but offered quite different explanations which may, loosely, be characterized as behavioural and structural. Unsurprisingly they also offered very different policy solutions to what they separately see as the problems of the underclass.

Murray's enterprise is less an academic one than a crusade against the underclass. He attributes the origins of the underclass in part to the demoralizing and demotivating impact of welfare policies. He is mainly concerned by the behaviour and attitudes of the underclass. For him, ' "underclass" does not refer to a degree of poverty, but to a type of poverty' (Murray 1990: 1). The underclass are notable for labour market drop-out, illegitimacy and violent crime. Young women make a rational choice in having children without getting married because this makes them eligible for Aid for Families with Dependent Children. AFDC was intended for widows (especially war widows) but became a major political cost in the US welfare system through its use to support never-married women with children. Children are thus born out of wedlock and, according to Murray, little boys grow up lacking role models; they do not know about getting up and going out to work every morning and do not 'become adolescents naturally wanting to refrain from sex, just as little girls don't become adolescents naturally wanting to refrain from having babies' (Murray 1990: 11).

Because young men do not have to support families they 'find other ways to prove that they are men, which tend to take various destructive forms' (Murray 1990: 22). According to Murray: 'Marriage is an indispensable civilising force . . . young men who don't work don't make good marriage material. Often they don't get married at all . . . too many of them remain barbarians' (Murray 1990: 23).

Murray introduced his ideas to a British audience through an article in the *Sunday Times* in 1989. This was followed by a visit to speak in public in 1990. In commenting on the situation in Britain, Murray admitted that he did not know much about Britain. He went on to show that he knew rather less than he thought. He was forced to cover his ignorance by saying that Britain has an underclass which is out of sight, unquantifiable, but growing rapidly (Murray 1990: 3). In parts of Britain, young people grow up without a clear picture of the meaning and necessity of work; young men cannot picture themselves in their fathers' jobs. As Murray collected his evidence in Clydeside and Birkenhead, two locations which had experienced catastrophic collapses of traditional industries, this is not surprising.

Murray suggested that being a single mother in Britain was 'not so bad' rather than 'extremely punishing'. Having and keeping a baby is economically feasible and because the woman does not need a man to support her there is less need for a man to plug away at a job, however menial.

In discussing the underclass, Murray uses the language of contamination and disease, and amongst his remedies are the reduction of welfare and the renewal of stigma. These are strange remedies indeed for reintegrating people into the mainstream of society. This is why writers like Macnicol and others have concluded that Murray was simply renewing the use of an idea with 'a long and undistinguished pedigree' (Macnicol 1987: 315). The pedigree of the underclass idea is the subject of the second part of this chapter.

Wilson, whose arguments are confined to the United States, responded quite simply to the argument that welfare created an underclass: during the period in which Conservative analysts were correlating rising poverty with welfare benefits, rising unemployment was creating increased poverty while benefits kept an increasing number of people above the poverty line. Without welfare, therefore, there would have been even more people in poverty. It was also the case that poverty and dependency had increased as the value of welfare benefits had declined.

The dislocation of the North American ghetto areas had to be explained none the less. Wilson argued that young black males were concentrated in educational categories for whom employment opportunities were declining the fastest. Most new jobs require above-average education and those new entry-level jobs that were being created were largely in the peripheral areas of the cities. Thus the ghetto population was unable to respond to economic recovery because young men had the wrong qualifications and were in the wrong place.

Secondly, the successful civil right campaigns of the 1960s had enabled black professionals to move out of the ghetto areas. This residualized the local population by leaving behind the apparently least successful, least skilled and least educated. It also removed from these areas models of black success that could serve to motivate and encourage others to strive. Key members of the local community who managed the churches and voluntary associations that sustained vital black communities also moved away.

These changes had consequences: the young (literally) did not see the value of work, or the connection between education and employment, nor did they see many families not living on welfare. The wider social consequences included the ghetto poor becoming more isolated as others avoided the area. Furthermore, residents, and especially the young, became detached from job-finding networks and fell into patterns of life associated with casual rather than regular work, and with hustling and crime.

On the illegitimacy question Wilson argued that the *proportion* of births to unmarried women was rising because the fertility of married women was falling. More importantly, young black women find it increasingly difficult to find a marriage partner who is economically active or fully employed. Unemployment, drugs, incarceration and early (often violent) deaths had reduced the pool of marriageable men. Marriage in these circumstances would have entailed a burden for women, who would have had to support a non-working male in addition to a child and lose certain welfare benefits. Women on AFDC had already suffered a sharp decline in their real incomes in the 1960s and 1970s. The solution to the problem of the underclass as described by Wilson lies in greater intervention in the labour market and in education and training (Hughes 1989). In contrast to Murray's, Wilson's definition of underclass is structural and processual, with behaviour seen as adaptations to structural problems.

Murray argued that welfare was creating a culture amongst the poor which led to labour market drop-out, illegitimacy and crime. Wilson argued that changes in the economic and social structure of northern US cities were creating labour market exclusion to which people were adapting in ways that included greater reliance on welfare. His argument was very much in line with those of Myrdal and Halsey, and he, like them, acknowledged the cultural consequences that flowed from the exclusions he was describing. But the contrast between Murray and Wilson is stark and simple.

It is important to note that Wilson increasingly found himself in difficulty with the term 'underclass'. He substituted 'ghetto poor' for his 1989 Presidential Address to the American Sociological Association. In 1992 he said the idea of 'underclass' was inappropriate in Europe and should not be used there (Moore 1993b: 61). Hughes (1989) has suggested that the subject of Wilson's research was not the ghetto poor but the poor ghetto because he was writing about populations in specific areas. What we need to consider is whether at any time he was writing about a *class*.

Class position derives from the ownership and control of productive plant or the marketability of skills and knowledge; a class consists of people in the same or similar class positions. Classes exist within a given economic order of production and consumption and the structure of classes and class relations alter as the economic order changes. Economic opportunities, power and a wide range of life chances depend on the actor's class position. A person who is without work or skills will probably be poor; their class position is defined in terms of their non-ownership of property and lack of skills and marketable knowledge. Their small income is not secured through the labour market but through limited rights to social security benefits.

Whilst *class positions* in structured class relations might be relatively permanent, subject to the changes brought about by changes in the economic order, *class membership* might not be permanent. The extent to which the 'top' positions can be permanently monopolized by the current occupants and their descendants has been widely researched in the UK. Similar questions might be asked about the 'bottom' of the class structure. The idea of a class of people *permanently* outside the mainstream is crucial to the analyses of Murray and Wilson. The extent to which persons in underclass positions remain there is therefore important in a critique of the idea of an underclass as a class. The idea of underclass would be relatively meaningless if it described people in transition between economic or occupational statuses or temporarily removing themselves from the labour market.

It is easy, from a commonsense point of view, to see that some people are excluded, perhaps permanently, from the labour market and are detached from the main economic and social institutions. They may also, and understandably, not share the values of the majority from whom they are separated by unemployment and poverty. The political right say that such people thrive in a 'dependency culture' that misguided and generous welfare provisions have created for them. They come to lack the incentive to rejoin the mainstream.

Unemployment is found even in times of high employment. There have been phases in history when it has been especially high, notably in periods of economic and industrial restructuring. In England the Poor Law Act of 1598 was precipitated by the rise in the number of unemployed occasioned by the end of the war with Spain. The end of the Napoleonic wars set in train economic changes in town and country in which the demobilized soldiers and sailors mixed with displaced rural workers and the developing urban working classes to make demands for political change. Results included the 1832 Reform Act and the 1834 Poor Law Amendment Act. In both these postwar cases the surplus populations were largely absorbed. The early part of the twentieth century and the inter-war period were two periods of national and global restructuring that created high levels of unemployment, but the unemployed were absorbed into the workforce when labour was needed for war-fighting and war production.

Finding the underclass

The long-term unemployed are the best 'candidates' for underclass membership. This is where Buck sought the underclass (Buck 1992). He distinguished between the unemployed with a high chance of re-entering employment and those with a high chance of remaining *detached* from the labour market. Buck used the Labour Force Survey and his methods are described in Smith (1992: 12–13). The number of long-term unemployed and inactive households doubled from 1979 to 1986. In that same period unemployment doubled from under 6 per cent to nearly 12 per cent. If membership of the underclass varies with the economic cycle then it is impermanent and not class-like. Buck concluded that the 10 per cent of the working-age population in 1986 which might constitute an underclass 'were not so much stable members of an underclass as unstable members of the working class' (Buck 1992: 19). Longer-term unemployment may be related to unemployment because unemployment leads to the loss of skills and increasingly becomes a disqualification from work through employers' discriminatory recruitment policies. So the long-term unemployed will be the recruiting ground for permanent detachment from the labour market and membership of the underclass. It is not benefit levels that deter the unemployed, and certainly not their potential employers.

Smith found that there was no evidence of unemployment being connected with benefit rates. Like Wilson in the United States, he noted that the value of benefits had declined as unemployment had risen.

If we cannot clearly identify an underclass structurally, can we find underclass attitudes and define the underclass behaviourally? Heath's analysis of the 1989 British Social Attitudes Survey and the 1987 British Election Survey again encountered problems in devising simple measures of underclass membership. He defined the underclass as family units where neither partner was in paid employment and where a member had been in receipt of either Supplementary Benefit or Income Support during the past five years. He excluded respondents over 60 years of age (Heath 1992: 33). By his definition, 4.9 per cent of the sample were members of the underclass. They were mainly white and they made up only one quarter of the population of the poorest areas. They were more likely to want work than other unemployed people and less fussy about the kind of job they took. Sixty-eight per cent of them had voted in the last election. Thus the most likely candidates for underclass membership lived in conditions quite unlike Wilson's ghetto poor, were not Murray's work-shy drop-outs, and were not wholly alienated from political activity.

Dean and Taylor-Gooby searched for the underclass amongst claimants and found that most claimants were motivated to work and that this motivation was unconnected with their experience of the social security system (Dean and Taylor-Gooby 1992: 92). They found claimants not to be culturally separate; they were a heterogeneous group subscribing to mainstream culture, its prejudices and attitudes (including some who had punitive attitudes towards claimants). They were uncomfortable with and resentful of their claimant status (Dean and Taylor-Gooby 1992: 136). The 'claiming experience', according to Dean and Taylor-Gooby, may heighten the political awareness of some, but is mainly a depoliticizing experience (Dean and Taylor-Gooby 1992: 132). Dean and Taylor-Gooby's findings are consistent with the observations of those who work with or amongst claimants; people do not enjoy being on benefits, and they have many disparaging terms to describe the experience. Furthermore, they will take almost any employment in order to escape.

In spite of claimants' desire to find work, the social security system is a deterrent. This is because the acquisition of even a quite low-paid part-time job can lead to loss of benefit (at high marginal tax rates) and then to complicated and perhaps protracted measures to get benefit restored when employment ceases. Such difficulties create an incentive to undertake unreported work for cash in hand. Tighter policing of social security is making this a more risky venture.

The poverty trap ensures a very high cost in entering the labour market for low wages. The outcome may be an income not much higher than benefit, with the added expenses of working. In the case of single parents the cost of childcare can raise the threshold to the point where only a high salary or employer-provided childcare would make it worth taking a job. The lack of childcare is probably the single most import-ant factor keeping single parents out of the labour market. My own unpublished enquiries into aspects of European Objective One policies on Merseyside on behalf of the Government Office North-West showed child-care problems to be an important deterrent to women wishing to re-enter the workforce. The issue poses a problem for governments who wish both to see mothers in their 'proper' place raising children in the home, and to reduce the cost of single motherhood to the taxpayer. The answer has been to stigmatize the mother as a scrounger if she stays at home and a neglectful mother if she goes out to work. Suggested remedies floated by Labour ministers have included the suggestion that young unmarried mothers might offer their babies for adoption (Jury and Burrell 1999). By contrast, measures are also being introduced to enable women to return to work and recognition given to the higher costs of raising younger children in the tax and benefits systems.

Finally, is there evidence that the underclass and underclass attitudes create a culture of dependency that is transmitted across generations? This is a crucial question, for unless the underclass reproduces itself it cannot constitute the threat that Murray and others imagine. The underclass becomes just the poor and unemployed. It was certainly the view of Keith Joseph that poverty was transmitted and that the children of parents in poverty were themselves likely to be in poverty. Three-quarters of a million pounds were spent on research into transmitted deprivation which failed to sustain the thesis. The outcome also amplified the hostility of senior Conservative politicians to the Social Science Research Council. The findings of the extensive research are reported in Brown and Madge, who found no evidence of a culture of poverty (Brown and Madge 1982). Families and individuals broke out of poverty and two-thirds of the children of poor parents were not themselves in poverty. 'Over one half of all forms of disadvantage arise anew each generation' (Rutter and Madge 1976: 304).

Buckingham's recent study revisits these issues and tests three com-peting theories about the underclass: behavioural, structural and critical (Buckingham 1999). Behavioural approaches, as we have seen, regard the underclass as a new variant of the undeserving poor, content to live a life of dependency on benefits whilst engaging in criminal behaviour and begetting children to form the next underclass generation. Structural approaches (*labour market* approaches according to Buckingham) follow Wilson in arguing that structural features create a separated and excluded *class* which develops coping cultures that are maladaptive for re-entering employment. The critical approach suggests that there is no separate class; the 'underclass' is the unemployed and will comprise largely unskilled or low-skilled persons.

Buckingham adopts a Weberian definition of the underclass, similar to Heath's, in terms of relations to income and capital, domestic status and work attachment. It is a definition based upon members' life chances in a market-based economic order. To be a member of the underclass one must have weak work attachment, have relied on income solely from the state (or in the case of woman have a partner who has relied solely on income from the state) and not own domestic housing assets (Buckingham 1999: 52, fig. 1). He used data from the 1958 cohort of the National Child Development Study (NCDS). Buckingham found that over one half of the women under age 33 in the sample were lone parents and thus prime candidates for membership of Murray's underclass. But only one quarter of lone parents were 'underclass' according to Buckingham's definition, 'indicating that the majority [of lone parents] were successfully avoiding a career in state dependency' (Buckingham 1999: 56). A high proportion of the men had never married or formed stable relationships but only one had fathered a child out of wedlock. When they had been younger the underclass males were also more likely than other men to have truanted and to have been in trouble with the law.

The 'underclass' was compared with the lower working class in the NCDS sample. Buckingham found that his underclass men had a lower commitment to work, but not of an extreme kind. In contrast to Dean and Taylor-Gooby's sample they were more 'choosey' about jobs and were prepared to risk unemployment as a consequence. Buckingham suggested that this behaviour could equally be a response to negative work experiences rather than a cause of low work attachment. Underclass members found work, but stayed in jobs for shorter periods, a factor which seemed to lower their later chances of employment. But they were not content simply to 'live off the state'. The idea of the inter-generational stability of the underclass was not fully substantiated. Underclass members were more likely to have had unemployed fathers and there was evidence that underclass members were likely to have had a family history of illegitimacy and welfare dependency, but Buckingham concluded none the less:

> Even though underclass individuals were disproportionately likely to come from such [unemployed and welfare-dependent] families, the vast majority were brought up in two parent families where the father was employed and which were not dependent on benefits.
>
> (Buckingham 1999: 66)

The study also showed that underclass members, whilst ostensibly dismissive of politics, none the less are as likely to vote as the lower working class and to be staunchly Labour in their political allegiance. Indeed the allegiance of the underclass was not only very strong but could not be explained by their proxy class (the class of their last occupation). This finding, based on a sample of 33-year-olds, suggested to Buckingham that: 'An underclass does exist with a homogenous and distinctive political attitude and it is not the same as the long-term unemployed and the poor which is how the underclass has often been defined' (Buckingham 1999 63). A further tentative conclusion of this study was that underclass membership was slightly more associated with social and economic structural factors than behavioural and attitudinal ones.

This careful study provides a degree of conceptual clarity not always found in discussions of the underclass but its conclusions are cautious: the underclass is not simply the bottom of a system of stratification, and although low education and disadvantaged social backgrounds are important factors in underclass membership they are not the sole factors. Most importantly, Buckingham suggested that behavioural factors could not be entirely ruled out of an explanation of underclass membership. Furthermore there is *some* evidence of intra-/inter-generational continuity of underclass membership. Contrary to expectation, Buckingham also found that the underclass had the clearest political identity of any class and did not behave like marginal and excluded people.

Burchardt *et al.* (1999) used the British Household Panel Survey to study the extent and duration of social exclusion. Social exclusion is as contested a term as underclass but Burchardt *et al.* used a definition that closely parallels Buckingham's definition of underclass. The five dimensions on which people could be seen as excluded were active engagement in consumption (evidenced by low income), savings (savings, pensions and property), production (paid work, retirement, study or caring), politics (voting) and social interaction in which others provide support. The study covered the period 1991–5, over which time the sample size fell from 9912 to 8816, leaving a large sample but one from which, perhaps, the more 'excluded' would be more likely to disappear. Over 50 per cent of the sample were never excluded by this definition, over 25 per cent were excluded on one dimension only and less than 2 per cent on four. In terms of duration, only on the dimension of low wealth were more than 10 per cent excluded for the five years of the study. Like Buckingham's this analysis suggests that it is the economic factors which are most salient. Less than 0.1 per cent were excluded on all five dimensions for five years. Whether these excluded people comprise an underclass or not, they are a very small group of people unlikely to pose the threat to the social fabric envisaged by Murray.

A disreputable history

In the light of the evidence that has been presented so far, it is difficult to draw any other conclusion than that it is better not to seek to amalgamate characteristics of sections of the population into an 'underclass'.

The term 'dependency' is used selectively in debates about the underclass. Social life itself is a pattern of dependencies and reciprocities. We are all especially dependent at particular stages of our life cycle: when we are young, when we are ill and when we are old. Life-cycle impacts upon economic security have been known since Rowntree's early work in York. The welfare state was established partly in recognition of unavoidable life-cycle dependencies and the dependency which can be created by accident, or factors otherwise beyond individual control. The welfare state functions by spreading the risks and the costs of dependency between the active and the dependent and across the individual life cycle.

We all live in a dependency culture or cultures of dependency. At the abstract level dependency defines social life. At the level of daily experience we are dependent upon our employers to provide income and perhaps other work-based satisfactions and upon the domestic sphere for meeting our bodily and emotional needs. It is just as possible for people to be 'trapped' in unsatisfactory work or domestic situations as it is to be trapped in poverty or on benefits. There may be fewer trapped in dependency on the welfare state than are trapped in unsatisfactory and low-paid jobs or in unhappy marriages. *Independence* is a much more problematic concept and, for many social actors, highly abstract, because it may depend upon the subordination of others or on highly privileged material circumstances that few enjoy. Except in very limited conditions, dependency is the normal state of humankind. Recent governments have attached priority to our dependence upon a traditional form of family and to employers. In the latter case they have tried to emphasize *subordination* as well as dependence.

These two forms of dependency are approved. Dependence on the welfare state has been treated as a problem and steps taken to shift the burden of this dependence back to the family and the labour market.

That family and the labour market dependency should be approved and encouraged as 'natural' is plainly consistent with the radical right-wing agenda of recent governments (Moore 1993a, 1995). For our part, as sociologists, we should not let our sociological judgement be clouded; the dependency of those said to be in a 'dependency culture' is not unique. It is only people who are dependent on the state who are uniquely stigmatized.

The stigmatization of forms of dependency is not new. The poor have always been divided into deserving and undeserving and the division incorporated into principles of less eligibility. The unemployed have been especially stigmatized as 'the hopeless ne'er-do-well, the incorrigibly idle': 'men and women, who are quite capable of working, but who have degenerated and become demoralised, it may be by lack of work, possibly by lack of training, or by the evil conditions of their youth' (Alden 1908: 66).

In the latter part of the nineteenth century, when it was feared that the lower orders were out-breeding the better class of people, eugenic concerns were added to moral judgements. The threat lay not only in the fertility of the most degenerate but in the declining fertility of the higher orders about which Mary Gladstone wrote so breathlessly from the 1880s to the 1910s (cited in Jalland and Hooper 1986: 277 *et seq.*). Such views were held across the political spectrum and were amplified by the panic at national decline evidenced by the unfitness of men volunteering for the Anglo-Boer War and the loss of national efficiency evidenced by the failure of Britain to keep up with Germany's industrial advance. We do not speak much about one of the origins of British sociology, which lies in the eugenics movement. We have some forefathers whom we now find embarrassing and we usually erase them from our family tree. Francis Galton (1822–1911), Karl Pearson (of the *Product Moment Correlation*, 1857–1936) and Benjamin Kidd (1858–1916) advanced hereditarian causes and authoritarian and imperialist solutions to the problem of national decline (for a brief description of their work, see Jones 1998). These solutions were not unique to sociologists. Between the wars, Charles Wicksteed Armstrong expressed alarm at the pauper vote after the extension of the franchise in 1918 and was an early exponent of the thesis that welfare creates poverty (Armstrong 1927). Shaw and the Webbs expressed their eugenic views in two Fabian tracts of 1896 and 1907 and in *The Prevention of Destitution* in 1911. In *The Time Machine*, H.G. Wells presents a picture of the future in which an effete population is farmed by the Morlochs (Shaw 1987: 530), much as the modern new right sees claimants farming hard-working taxpayers.

Many solutions were proposed. Armstrong was amongst those who wanted colonies for breeding the better classes, but restricting the fertility of the lower orders was a more popular solution. Family planning crusades were not wholly for the liberation of working-class women; they were also a means of reducing the reproduction of the poor and especially the birth of children to fathers who were unemployed, drunkards or criminals. Mental deficiency was also seen as a source of national degeneration and both family planning and sterilization were solutions. Although attempts to bring 'the right to sterilization' to 3.5 million people in Britain failed, policies adopted in the USA and the Third Reich were more successful. At least 43,000 young women are believed to have been compulsorily sterilized in state institutions alone in the USA between 1927 and 1944 (Trombley 1988: 114). In Hitler's Germany 110,000 were sterilized in 1934 and 1935 before more drastic measures were adopted at the end of the decade. In both the USA and the Third Reich, ideas of degeneration and policies of sterilization and extermination had explicit racial dimensions.

A uniquely British solution to what was, in effect, an 'underclass' problem was the forced migration of 'slum children' to the Empire. About 10,000 children were sent to Australia in the postwar period alone, just one country in an Empire to which surplus children were exported. Whatever the limited benefits and extensive disbenefits to the children, the emigration schemes were used not only to remove potential underclass recruits but to punish single mothers for their fertility. Their children were simply taken away from them 'for adoption'. The children were later told they were orphans (see Bean and Melville 1989). Less malign solutions were proposed through Family Endowment and by Eleanor Rathbone who advocated a tax regime that encouraged higher-status parents to have larger families (Rathbone 1924).

Understandably, eugenic ideas had less currency immediately after the Second World War but they were revived in public by Keith Joseph in 1974 when he asserted that 'the balance of our population, our human stock is threatened'. The threat came from births to young mothers in social classes IV and V who were, according to Joseph, 'producing problem children, the future unmarried mothers, delinquents, denizens of our borstals, subnormal educational establishments, prisons, hostels for drifters' (Trombley 1988: 203). Put plainly, the children would be 'idle, thieving bastards' (Bagguley and Mann 1992).

Joseph and Murray have much in common with Marx and Engels. Marx had conventional Victorian middle-class and patriarchal views when it came to consideration of the poor and the lumpenproletariat; Engels plainly saw the most deprived as the most depraved; with only drink and sex to bring them pleasure (Mann 1992: 131). But such ideas were not the sole property of intellectuals and members of ruling classes.

Working-class organizations were obliged to adopt a pragmatic approach to the nineteenth-century 'underclass' and it was an exclusive one. The more skilled and securely employed workers formed their own self-help associations. Relatively high and regular wages were needed to maintain subscriptions to unions, friendly societies and other benefit organizations. People in irregular employment, on low pay or in poor health would be an unbearable financial burden. Drunkards and others with irregular habits would be quite inadmissible, but casual workers, women and the Irish were also excluded (Mann 1992: 54).

This is of more than passing interest because, Mann goes on to argue, the state incorporated the practices of the respectable working class into the administration of the welfare state from its twentieth-century beginnings. The trades unions and the friendly societies were eager to maintain their autonomy and to see the state take financial responsibility for the poorer insurance risks. As members of tribunals administering the Household Means Test and the Genuinely Seeking Work Test, trades unions were eager to 'search for scroungers'.

In establishing the postwar welfare state the trades unions, the friendly societies (and the Co-operative Insurance Society) played a conservative if not reactionary role in protecting their interests and in promoting the idea of a class of less worthy people below them in the social order. They wished to maintain their members' benefit levels and not to become part of a state system within which they would have to share the costs of health, unemployment and social security for the whole population. In the event the cost of the welfare state was met from rising production in conditions of almost full employment. But unemployment increased substantially from the late 1970s and full employment may not now be restored in the foreseeable future, even if significant labour market niches have to be filled by immigrants (see United Nations 2000).

Making an underclass

Creating an Underclass

Dahrendorf raised the questions of whether: 'a developed modern economy needs everybody who could conceivably be employed, to what extent it could do quite well with two, five, ten, fifteen, twenty per cent unemployment and yet produce satisfactory growth rates' (Dahrendorf 1992: 56). None of the authors of *Understanding the Underclass* (Smith 1992) were able to identify the scale of the effects of deindustrialization in creating an economically and socially surplus population. In the UK not only can a government be re-elected with unemployment in excess of 10 per cent, but we have yet to see the extent to which unemployment acts as a brake upon economic growth. Dahrendorf's question is in many respects one of the most crucial for social policy and one of the hardest for policy makers to confront because of the way in which it raises the question of redistribution. If goods and services cannot be distributed through payments from incomes earned from employment in the labour market, then upon what basis will a population be sustained?

Given long-term high unemployment, entitlements to health care, education and housing based upon taxation or purchase alone would become less feasible because many would not pay direct taxes and would also lack purchasing power. Labour markets, wages and retail markets would be less capable of distributing goods produced by those who were working. Non-market distribution would become *the* issue to be confronted by governments of all political persuasions if a half or even a quarter of the population was to become permanently surplus to capital's requirements.

The solution (of sorts), which might be open in the case of certain ethnic minorities in Europe, is to expel the surplus population, like the UK children, or to treat it as outside mainstream society and less worthy of consideration. There are contradictions in such policies. Exclusion from consumption acts as a brake upon economic growth and has already become an important issue in the EC. The Commission's poverty programmes have sought to promote the integration of some of the 45 million living in poverty not just into 'mainstream society' but into active consumption.

Because the respectable majority have benefited from an upward redistribution of income through changes to the tax and benefit system there is an interesting research question about the extent to which the promotion of ideas such as the underclass is successful in uncoupling the plight of the poor from the good fortune of the better-off. Such evidence as we have suggests that the last decade has seen *increased* sympathy for the poor and *less* punitive attitudes (except to single mothers and the unemployed). In 1976, for example, 43 per cent of people polled in the UK for *Eurobarometer* attributed poverty to 'laziness and lack willpower'; by 1989 this had fallen to 18 per cent (Commission of the European Communities 1990: 37). Perhaps the most important uncoupling takes place in the minds of the poor groups we have identified who are likely to attribute their own misfortune to bad luck rather than the good luck of others.

The idea of a threatening underclass thus enables discussion to be deflected away from serious questions of redistribution on a European scale, much as it obscures processes at work within nation-states. If the term obscures structures and processes then it is our task as sociologists to make them more transparent. In so doing we can show the extent to which an idea like an underclass is redundant.

Social exclusion is now a popular term in social policy debates in the European Union and the UK, but the underclass is still in the shadows surrounding these debates. The relationship between social exclusion, poverty, deprivation and multiple deprivation is not always made clear. Poverty and deprivation plainly refer to material conditions and social exclusion to wider forms of deprivation. These are all deprivations likely to be a feature of the circumstances of sections of the working class but, as we have seen, the evidence that these people constitute a class in or for itself is tenuous. Ruth Levitas (1999) outlines the ways in which issues of social exclusion are analyzed and the data relevant to each approach.

Levitas suggests that there are three ways of seeing those who may be characterized by their 'inability to participate effectively in economic, social, political and cultural life, alienation and distance from mainstream society' (Duffy 1995, cited in Levitas and Guy 1996: 11), and that the underclass discourse is only one of them. Her analysis enables us to set the idea of the underclass in its proper intellectual context. In summary, Levitas firstly identifies approaches that simply treat social exclusion as resulting from poverty as belonging to a redistributional debate. In this debate, raising benefits is 'crucial to reducing poverty' (Levitas 1999: 12). Secondly, there is a 'social integration discourse' in which paid work is regarded as the normal and legitimate means of social integration. Levitas makes the point that this is an approach which devalues unpaid work and ignores those who are excluded from wider social participation by virtue of low pay. The workless or those at risk of worklessness are the problems to be addressed; economic inactivity defines the problem. The market and especially the labour market is the main agency for its solution. Broadly this might describe the approach of the EU and the UK government to social exclusion.

The third approach is the 'moral underclass' approach which is centrally concerned with dependency (in its pejorative usage discussed above) and the moral, cultural and individual causes of poverty.

I have suggested that this particular 'discourse' has a less than reputable history. Given this history and the tenuous empirical basis for the use of the term 'underclass' we should use it with extreme care, if at all. Buckingham, for example, is asking serious questions about the development of 'the underclass' as a class and about the inter-generational stability of this putative class. The extent to which a 'culture of poverty' develops as either an adaptation or maladaptation to poverty and deprivation is an important issue. But Buckingham is in a minority of serious scholars addressing the issue. The term is more the property of those who would blame the poor for their poverty.

Social exclusion is not a passive state. In order to be described as excluded someone has to exclude. The use of the term therefore invites us to ask 'who is excluding whom?' Similarly the idea of underclass implies an over-class or over-classes. We could redeem the idea of underclass by seeing it as the social location of those who are dominated. The important questions are then not moral judgements but empirical questions about the means of domination.

The answer to the question 'How many classes are there in British society?' is, according to Runciman, 'seven' (Runciman 1990: 378). Class position depends, for Runciman, upon economic power. Economic power derives from the ownership, control or marketability of productive plant or skills. As he was writing about a capitalist society, Runciman did not need to add 'within or outside a given economic order'. It would be possible to derive a definition of an underclass as 'comprising those who typically have little or no control over goods and skills either within or outside a given economic order' (Moore 1990: 18). Runciman characterizes the underclass as containing the long-term unemployed and over-representing ethnic minorities and women. The underclass is largely unable to participate in the labour market. Its members are dependent on benefits supplemented by 'undeclared labour, mendicancy, barter or petty theft' (Runciman 1990: 388).

Runciman is, therefore, partly defining the underclass in terms of its relations to the social division of welfare. When he says 'benefits' he does not mean mortgage interest tax relief, company cars and occupational pensions, but state welfare. The underclass depends upon benefits different from those enjoyed by other people. Benefits are stratified and what Parkin described as a process of usurpation and exclusion has resulted in particular allocations of welfare. This social division of welfare becomes an integral feature of the stratification of modern capitalist societies. Mann sees this as a continuation of the processes started by organized industrial labour in the nineteenth century. The people at the bottom of the system of stratification do not choose to be there; they have been excluded and then blamed for their low status; they have been defined as and made into an underclass (Parkin 1979: ch. 5; Mann 1992, especially ch. 6). So now we may examine the *making* of an underclass.

Trades unions are defensive organizations with relatively little usurpatory power, but with powers of bargaining and exclusion. Beginning with the First World (i.e. European) War, trades unions and the labour movement have been incorporated into a series of compromises with the state and with capital where they have used their bargaining power to some effect. Most notably they were able to ensure 'business as usual' after each war with the re-establishment of prewar recruitment and work practices. Thus dilutees and most notably women were quickly ejected from the labour force with the impending return of servicemen to 'their' jobs.

Separating the underclass

European Voluntary Workers (postwar refugees) and later migrant workers were excluded from skilled occupations and from union membership. Unions were capable of acting directly against their own black members in industrial disputes (Moore 1976: ch. 5). Meanwhile, and especially in conditions of skilled labour shortage and periods of attempted wage restraint, unions negotiated benefit packages for their members, improved pensions, holidays, health care in some instances, contributions to travel costs and the reduction of social distinctions at work between white- and blue-collar workers. All these constituted a significant package of occupation benefits for unionized labour. Those who could afford insurance policies benefited from fiscal advantages and those who bought houses (and in increasing numbers after 1979) enjoyed the benefits of mortgage interest tax relief. They could benefit from the fiscal welfare state because their unions had secured them incomes that enabled them to do so.

Post-1979 governments addressed these interests, firstly, by more deeply incorporating the working population into the fiscal welfare state in the expansion of home ownership through council house sales. Secondly, they have played upon fears of black 'immigrants' taking employed workers' jobs and scroungers sponging off their hard-earned (and rising) incomes. Such appeals to self-interest seem to have been successful in returning governments eager to celebrate self-interest in the 1980s. Organized labour had always done so. The definition of class cleavage given by Runciman (1990) is of substantially more interest than he may have thought because of its capacity to highlight the processes by which the underclass is excluded.

If we accept a definition of underclass in these terms then the key issues to emerge concern the extent to which the underclass has developed, is developing, or accumulating, sufficient differences of interest and culture to find itself objectively in conflict with Runciman's other six classes. This is not a new issue and it is one that has been addressed in the context of European migrant workers (Miles 1982; Castles and Kosack 1973; Moore 1977, 1989). At what point do sufficient differences of interest accumulate for a radical rupture to take place within what might be thought of as the working class?

Social policy and the underclass

The processes that have increased the numbers of unemployed are in part external to any one country; there is a worldwide restructuring of commerce and industry based in part upon a new international division of labour. But locally in the UK, labour market deregulation, extensive privatization of public services and utilities, the promotion of compulsory competitive tendering and the reduction of local authority spending have all contributed to job losses. Energy policies have precipitated the collapse of coal-mining, 'efficiency savings' are reducing the size of the home civil service. No judgement needs to be passed on these policies in stating that they have and will continue to add to employment loss. The destruction of trades unions' immunities in the 1980s has disabled them from protecting jobs, and, in return for no-redundancy agreements, unions have accepted labour-saving measures which protect current members' livelihoods at the cost of the next generation's jobs.

The addition of many working people to the ranks of the poor underlines the impact of labour market deregulation, the loss of unions' power and the extent to which reconstructed industries require new forms of labour, often 'flexible' and female. The UK, alone in Europe until 1998, had no minimum wage legislation and did not require firms to recognize trades unions. Men and women who are not working full-time or are under the age of 18 may still receive wages at below poverty level in spite of the introduction of the minimum wage by the Labour government.

Income support policies have entailed cuts in the real value of benefits and a reduction in entitlements. One intention of the reduction of benefits for young people was to make them more dependent on their families and more eager to find work. The families are deemed to be receiving a contribution to rent from their children, with a consequential loss in their own Housing Benefit (Child Poverty Action Group 2000: 452–4). One result has been the rapid expansion of the numbers of young homeless people, forced to leave home but without the means to make their own home. Dependency in and on the domestic sphere is approved, even if the burden is too great for the household.

Single mothers cannot get childcare that would enable them to re-enter the labour market. If they cannot demonstrate the availability of childcare then they are not deemed to be available for work and are disqualified from unemployment benefit even if they are qualified by contributions. Those who do manage to find childcare, through limited voluntary or local authority provisions or kinsfolk, face a deep poverty trap. They also face a potential loss of benefit if they refuse to name the father(s) of their child(ren). The threat is not simply to their income but to their privacy. Their most intimate (or perhaps most traumatic) relationships are opened to scrutiny. These provisions will only be applied to parents (almost invariably women) who are on benefits and therefore amongst the poorest in society. A further element of family policy contained in the 1991 Criminal Justice Act makes parents responsible for their children's fines; they are required to attend juvenile courts and as parents may be bound over for their children's offences.

This is not to recite a litany of complaints but to identify particular policies targeting, or disproportionately affecting, identifiable groups: the unemployed, poor, homeless youth, single mothers, stressed parents. Many of these groups are blamed directly and personally for their predicament. Collectively they may be lumped into an underclass in a way that hints that they are probably the authors of their own problems. More importantly, being part of an underclass and thus part of a threatening and potentially degenerate rabble, the 'dangerous classes' of the nineteenth century, they are less eligible for humane consideration and more exposed to punitive measures. All they really have in common is poverty and powerlessness.

At the local political level the underclass may be an issue. In the 1980s the author was a member of a Labour party branch where there was strong pressure from the constituency party to give special scrutiny to the membership applications of social workers and community workers. Anyone associated with or working with the poor or the unemployed was immediately suspected of Militant tendencies and therefore liable to exclusion from the branch.

The issue of the radical potential of the underclass has been addressed by Giddens and Gallie who are concerned with the revolutionary or radical potential of this class (Giddens 1986; Gallie 1989). The long-term unemployed are a major element of their underclass but they conclude that the underclass is too heterogeneous and divided to achieve radical action. This is a peculiarly ahistorical analysis which seems to assume that other classes have been homogeneous and undivided. More importantly, they seem to overlook the radical action of which members of the nineteenth-century residuum were capable when they turned themselves into the 'mob' and drove Poor Law commissioners out of northern towns and set fire to workhouses (see Driver 1946). They have been no less passive in the twentieth century; Mann lists the National Unemployed Workers' Movement, claimants' unions, squatters and rioters as conspicuous examples of underclass action. It is the outbursts of direct action in postwar riots that have made the underclass so threatening to right-thinking people.

The underclass: an irredeemable idea?

We may now see why a term with a disreputable pedigree and capable of describing a range of disparate social groups and situations is so popular and why we need to study it as a problem. Westergaard argues that the term enables us to square the circle. We may live in a society where the great majority are said to be 'classless', sharing in rising prosperity whilst explaining the poverty of the poor in ways that exculpate the affluent.

If there is a major process of industrial reorganization under way which requires the wide-scale demobilization of labour, we might argue, the services required to reproduce labour power (health, education, housing and income support) are being stood down. Those who remain mobilized in the labour force will be serviced by the occupational and fiscal welfare states of Titmuss's 'three welfare states' (Titmuss 1963). We may have affluence and poverty, enjoy the former and feel no guilt for the latter. Power and privilege may be uncoupled from poverty and exclusion.

The term 'underclass' is ideological. Bagguley and Mann see it as serving '*in particular historical circumstances*, to establish and sustain relations of domination' (Bagguley and Mann 1992: 124, citing Thompson):

> In our view the concept of the underclass is a set of ideological beliefs held by certain groups among the upper and middle classes. It helps them sustain certain relations of domination of class, patriarchy and race towards the unemployed, single mothers and blacks through the formulation of state welfare policies.   (Bagguley and Mann 1992: 124)

From this perspective it is the *idea* of the underclass that is the problem rather than a real underclass. We should examine the structures and processes that the idea obscures and the interests that are served thereby. While the development of the idea may be media-led we cannot simply leave the field to the tabloids (see Westergaard 1990; Robinson and Gregson 1992: 48–9).

Can the idea create that which it purports to describe? The use of the term 'underclass', according to Dean and Taylor-Gooby, 'Not only defines the marginalised but marginalises those it defines' (Dean and Taylor-Gooby 1992: 44). They echoes Gans' suggestion that the use of the idea of underclass might actually create an underclass and underclass areas of our cities through the intensification of zoning policies, exclusion and control (Gans 1990). The underclass may come to have geographical locations, underclass places, 'symbolic locations' (Rose 1992: 32) where the police have to lay military-style plans to seize the territory and *impose* order on the local inhabitants. The residualization of council housing and problem estates in the UK and the proliferation of entry-phones, security guards and neighbourhood watch schemes in more 'respectable' areas might be seen as the beginning of this. A further stage would be equipping private estates with chain-link fencing, closed circuit TV, check-points and guards. The underclass would thus be territorially confined and physically excluded from respectable middle- and working-class areas.

The media meanwhile keep the term alive as a threat to the whole of society. In their hands the term becomes infinitely flexible and has at times included joy-riders and ram-raiders, meths drinkers, people sleeping rough, homosexuals, football hooligans, single mothers, rioters, the unemployed, Caribbean youth, (all) people on benefits, drug addicts, homeless young people, hunt saboteurs and anarchists. In its very imprecision the underclass concept is capable of keeping alive a threat which can be used to justify adopting punitive policies against a range of less-approved people and to extend the power of the state over ordinary lives.

Sociologists do not need the term. The discussion above has indicated the extent to which we may sensibly speak of the long-term unemployed, claimants, single mothers and homeless youth and understand their circumstances without recourse to the use of the word 'underclass'.

The use of the term 'underclass' poses important ethical questions for sociologists. If we ever had any control, however limited, over the way in which the term was used we have now lost it. But given the way the term is used in popular discourse and the ideological functions it may perform, is it really worth the cost of hanging on to such a concept? We may only pay a cost in terms of intellectual confusion but others may pay upon the streets in more physical ways. The idea of an underclass and its intellectual forebears have not been abstractions alone. They have been ideas which when implemented have had real, even fatal, consequences for those to whom they have been applied.

The idea of an underclass lacks conceptual clarity, it has the most tenuous empirical basis and has been part of a rhetoric of domination and exclusion. It is time sociologists stopped using the term except when they need to discuss the problem of the people who do use the term.

References

Alden, P. (1908) *The Unemployable and the Unemployed*, London: Headley Brothers.

Armstrong, C.W. (1927) *Survival of the Unfittest*, London: C.W. Daniel.

Bagguley, P. and Mann, K. (1992) 'Idle thieving bastards? Scholarly representation of the underclass', *Work, Employment and Society* 6 (1): 113–26.

Bean, P. and Melville, J. (1989) *Lost Children of the Empire*, London: Unwin Hyman.

Brown, M. and Madge, N. (1982) *Despite The Welfare State: A Report on the SSRC/DHSS Programme of Research into Transmitted Deprivation*, London: Heinemann.

Buck, N. (1992) 'Labour market inactivity and polarisation: a household perspective on the idea of an underclass', in D.J. Smith (ed.) *Understanding the Underclass*, London: Policy Studies Institute.

Buckingham, A. (1999) 'Is there an underclass in Britain?', *British Journal of Sociology* 50 (1): 49–75.

Burchardt, T., Le Grand, J. and Piachaud, D. (1999) 'Social exclusion in Britain 1991–1995', *Journal of Social Policy and Administration* 30 (3): 227–44.

Castles, S. and Kosack, G. (1973) *Immigrant Workers and Class Structure in Western Europe*, Oxford: Oxford University Press.

Child Poverty Action Group (2000) *Welfare Benefits Handbook*, London: CPAG.

Commission of the European Communities (1990) *Eurobarometer. The Perception of Poverty in Europe*, Brussels: EC.

Dahrendorf, R. (1992) 'Footnotes to the discussion', in D.J. Smith (ed.) *Understanding the Underclass*, London: Policy Studies Institute, 55–8.

Dean, H. and Taylor-Gooby, P. (1992) *Dependency Culture*, New York: Harvester Wheatsheaf.

Driver, C. (1946) *Tory Radical*, Oxford: Oxford University Press.

Duffy, K. (1995) *Social Exclusion and Human Dignity in Europe*, Strasbourg: Council of Europe.

Gallie, D. (ed.) (1989) 'Employment, unemployment and social stratification', in D. Gallie (ed.) *Employment in Britain*, Oxford: Blackwell, 465–92.

Gans, H. (1990) 'Deconstructing the underclass. The term's dangers as a planning concept', *Journal of the American Planning Association* spring: 271–7.

Giddens, A. (1986) *The Class Structure of Advanced Societies*, London: Hutchinson.

Halsey, A.H. (1991) 'Citizens of the future', *Guardian*, 20 September: 17.

Heath, A. (1992) 'The attitudes of the underclass', in D.J. Smith (ed.) *Understanding the Underclass*, London: Policy Studies Institute, 37–47.

Hughes, M.A. (1989) 'Misspeaking truth to power: a geographical perspective on the underclass fallacy', *Economic Geography* 65 (3): 187–207.

Jalland, P. and Hooper, J. (eds) (1986) *Women from Birth to Death*, Brighton: Harvester Press.

Jones, S. (1988) 'Social Darwinism revisited', *History Today*, August, or at http://www.britannica.com/bcom/magazine/article/0,5744,54096,00.html

Jury, L. and Burrell, I. (1999) 'Mothers urged to give up babies', *Independent*, 26 January.

Levitas, R. (1999) 'Defining and measuring social exclusion: a critical overview of current proposals' *Radical Statistics* 71: 10–27.

Levitas, R. and Guy, W. (eds) (1996) *Interpreting Official Statistics*, London: Routledge.

Macnicol, J. (1987) 'In pursuit of the underclass', *Journal of Social Policy* 16: 292–318.

Mann, K. (1992) *The Making of an English Underclass*, Milton Keynes: Open University Press.

Miles, R. (1982) *Racism and Migrant Labour*, London: Routledge and Kegan Paul.

Moore, R. (1976) *Racism and Black Resistance in Britain*, London: Pluto Press.

Moore, R. (1977) 'Migrants and the class structures of western Europe', in R. Scase (ed.) *Industrial Society: Class, Cleavage and Control*, London: Allen and Unwin.

Moore, R. (1989) 'Ethnic divisions and class in western Europe', in R. Scase (ed.) *Industrial Societies: Crisis and Division in Western Capitalism and State Socialism,* London: Unwin Hyman.

Moore, R. (1990) 'The idea of an underclass', inaugural lecture, University of Liverpool, November (unpublished).

Moore, R. (1993a), 'Citizenship and the Social Agenda, 1965–1990' in H. Martins (ed.) *Knowledge and Passion: Essays in Honour of John Rex*, London: Tauris Press, 23–50.

Moore, R. (1993b) 'Citizenship and the underclass' in H. Coenen and P. Leisink *Work and Citizenship in the New Europe*, London: Edward Elgar.

Moore, R. (1995) 'Urban policy; problems paradoxes', in H. Jones and J. Lansley (eds) *Social Policy and the City*, London: Avebury Press.

Moore, R. (1996) *Ethnic Statistics and the 1991 Census: the Black Population of Inner London*, Liverpool: Runnymede Trust.

Murray, C. (1990) *The Emerging British Underclass*, London: Institute of Economic Affairs.

Myrdal, G. (1964) *Challenge to Affluence*, London: Victor Gollancz.

Parkin, F. (1979) *Marxism and Class Theory: A Bourgeois Critique*, London: Tavistock.

Rathbone, E.F. (1924) *The Disinherited Family: A Plea for the Endowment of the Family*, London: Arnold.

Rose, D. (1992) *A Climate of Fear*, London: Bloomsbury.

Robinson, and Gregson, (1992) 'The underclass a class apart?' *Critical Social Policy* 12: 38–51.

Runciman, W.G. (1990) 'How many social classes are there in contemporary British society?' *Sociology* 24 (3): 377–96.

Rutter, M. and Madge N. (1976) *Cycles of Disadvantage: A Review of Research*, London: Heinemann.

Shaw, C. (1987) 'Eliminating the yahoos: eugenics, Social Darwinism and five Fabians', *History of Political Thought* 5: 521–44.

Smith, D.J. (ed.) (1992) *Understanding the Underclass*, London: Policy Studies Institute.

Titmuss, R. (1963) 'The social division of welfare', in *Essays on the Welfare State*, London: Allen and Unwin.

Trombley, S. (1988) *The Right to Reproduce: A History of Coercive Sterilisation*, London: Weidenfeld and Nicolson.

United Nations (2000) *Replacement Migration: Is it a Solution to Declining and Ageing Populations?* New York UN and at http://www.un.org/esa/population/unpop.htm

Westergaard, J. (1990) 'About and beyond the underclass: some notes on influences of social climate in British sociology today', *Sociology* 26 (4): 575–87.

Wilson, W.J. (1987) *The Truly Disadvantaged: The Inner City, the Underclass and Public Policy*, Chicago: University of Chicago Press.

Abel-Smith, B. and Townsend, P. 281
Adorno, T. 81–2, 83
advertising 92–3
agency/structure issues 124, 276, 279–80, 293–4
Ahmed, S. 102–3
Alexander, J.C. 57, 60, 63–4, 67
Alexander, J.C. and Colomy, P. 64–6
Althusser, L. 84, 88
Amos, A. *see* Kerr, A. *et al.*
anti-foundationalism 57–60, 71
Arber, S. and Lahelma, E. 25
Archer, M.S. 56–7, 59
architecture and art, postmodernist 104
Armstrong, C.W. 313, 314

Bagguley, P. and Mann, K. 322
Bainbridge, W.S. *see* Stark, R. and Bainbridge, W.S.
Barrett, M. 101, 102
Barton, L. 172
Baudrillard, J. 82–3, 94, 109, 110
Bauman, Z. 91
Beck, U. 208, 209, 214
Benedict, R. 88–9
Bernstein, B. 167, 169, 174, 178
Bernstein, R. 52, 60
Bhaskar, R. 57, 59, 280
Birmingham group 87–8
Blair, T., and New Labour 70, 277, 290
Blalock, H.M. Jr. 67
Bourdieu, P. 91, 165–6, 169
bovine spongiform encephalitis (BSE) 209
Boyne, R. and Rattansi, A. 103
Braverman, H. 188–9, 190, 191, 193
British Household Panel Study (BHPS) 20, 22, 27
British Journal of Sociology 168
British Journal of Sociology of Education 171, 172

British Social Attitudes Survey (BSAS) 18, 21, 22, 27
British Sociological Association 172–3, 179, 186, 222
  Medical Sociology Study Group 251–3, 254–5, 259, 261, 262–3, 267
Brodribb, S. 112
Brooks, A. 112–13
Buck, N. 307
Buckingham, A. 309–11, 318
Bulmer, M. 14–15
Burchardt, T. *et al.* 311–12
Burgess, R.G. 167, 171–2, 176, 178–9

Cannadine, D. 84
capitalism
  and culture 83, 92–4
  and gender relations 100–1
  and poverty 282–3
caring
  childcare 17, 309, 321
  as emotional labour 241–3
  gendered 130–1, 229
  Informal Carers Survey 18, 27
  responsibility for 238–9
Castells, M. 144–5
Catterall, P. *see* Obelkevich, J. and Catterall, P.
Census of Population (OPCS) 17, 18
Chernobyl 212
Chicago School 38, 105–6
Child Support Agency 229–30
childcare 17, 309, 321
Cicourel, A.V. 11, 58
citizenship, and welfare state 278, 281, 284–5
class
  and social inequality 122–3
  and sociology of education 167–8
  stratification 237, 318–19
  surveys of 15–16
  and underclass 306, 318–19

coercion 90–1
Cohen, S. 36, 87
cohort studies 19–20
Coleman, J.S. 67
Colomy, P. 64–6
communitarianism 291–2
Comte, A. 58, 59, 68
consumption
    household 234, 236
    postmodern 109–10
Creutzfeld-Jacob Disease (CJD) 209
cultural anthropology 88
culture 79–95
    complexity of 79–80
    and culturalism 86–7
    culture industry 82, 83
    ethnocentric 89
    feminism and 102, 106, 115, 130
    Marxism and 84–7
    and morality 91–2
    perspectives on 80–95
    popular 85–6
    and postmodernism 82, 90, 91,
        93–4, 105–6
    and power 84–5
    and relativism 80, 85–6, 90, 91
    and religion 80–1, 106, 144
    in workplace 189
Cunningham-Burley, S. see Kerr, A. et al.

Dahrendorf, R. 303, 315–16
Dale, R. 165, 170, 178, 180
Danton, R. 85
data analysis
    ethnographic research 38
    secondary 21–8
Data Archive, University of Essex 20,
    21–3, 26–7, 28
data collection and storage 13
    ethnographic research 39–40, 44–5
Davies, B. 167, 169
Davis, M. 82
Davison, C. 260–1
Dean, H. and Taylor-Gooby, P. 308,
    310, 323
deconstructionism 107–8
Delamont, S. 165, 167, 173, 179–80
Delphy, C. 116
dependency 312–13, 317–18
    culture 309–10, 312
    welfare 284–5, 309, 312–13
Derrida, J. 107, 130
development studies 132–3
difference, and feminism 101–2, 113,
    123

discourse
    and power 107–8, 130, 190–1,
        276–7
    sociology as 63–5
doctors
    changing image of 260–1
    and medical sociology agenda 251–6
    power of 256–61
    and sociologists 251–62
double hermeneutic 55, 62, 71
Durkheim, E. 53, 58, 59, 279, 291

Economic and Social Research Council
    (ESRC) 15, 16, 20, 22, 170, 222
    Future of Work programme 196–7
    postgraduate students 44–5, 46–7
education, sociology of 165–81
    1960's expansion 169–70
    1970's golden age 174–5
    1980's contraction 170–1
    and 1988 Education Reform Act 176
    decline of 179–80
    defining 166–8
    fragmenation 175
    institutions 167, 168–9, 171–3,
        180–1
    and policy 174, 176–7, 180–1
    and sociology in general 172–3,
        174–5, 178–90
empiricism 68–9
    perspective on poverty 278–80, 281,
        294
    and post-empiricism 61–2, 71–2
employment
    changing patterns of 186–7, 192–6
    conditions of 199–200
    and gender 124–6, 192, 194–5, 197
    potential sociology objectives
        196–200
    see also industrial sociology; labour
        market; unemployment
Engels, F. 58, 314–15
epistemology 116–17
Esping-Anderson, G. 128, 286
essentialism 123–4
ethnicity, and gender 123, 124, 129
ethnographic research
    case studies 42–5
    data collection and analysis 38,
        39–40, 44–5
    development 36–43, 46–7
    in education 178–9
    religious 144
    role of sponsorship and funding 41–3
    techniques 38–41

use of photography 45–6
see also qualitative research
Etzioni, A. 278, 291–2, 293, 294
eugenics movement 313–14
European Journal of Social Theory 70
European Union (EU)
 poverty and state welfare 285, 295,
  316, 317
 Social Chapter 199
 and women's issues 122, 124–5, 128
evaluation, research 14, 40

Family Expenditure Survey (FAS) 21
family studies 227–44
 apparent marginalization 227–9
 current developments 229–33
 emotional economy of family 233,
  241–3
 and gender issues 228–9, 235–7, 242
 moral economy of family 233,
  238–41
 political economy of family 233–7
feminism
 changing nature of 100–2
 and concepts of poverty 282–3
 and culture 102, 106, 115, 130
 and the family 228–9
 government surveys and 17–18, 126,
  127
 perspectives approach 100, 101
 and postmodernism 99–100, 111–17,
  123
 see also gender relations
field, sociological 165–6
Finch, J. and Mason, J. 16, 231, 238–9
Finlayson, A. 290–1, 292, 294
Flax, J. 114
flexible specialization 189
Fordism and post-Fordism 189, 287–8,
  294
Foucault, M. 63, 64, 107–8, 129, 130,
  190, 276
foundationalism/anti-foundationalism
  57–60
Fowler, B. 91
Frankfurt group 81–2
Freidson, E. 250, 255, 266, 268–9
functionalism
 and neo-functionalism 65, 66
 structural 167, 173, 174, 286
funding
 ethnographic research 41–3
 medical sociology 252, 259, 260
 social research 14–15, 21
 sociology departments 70

Gallie, D. 195, 196, 321
Gans, H.J. 69, 323
Geertz, C. 60, 89–90
Gellner, E. 83, 90–1
gender issues
 conceptions of the body 131–2
 and employment 124–6, 194–5
 and ethnicity 123, 124, 129
 EU and 122, 124–5, 128
 in the family 229, 235–7, 242
 globalization and 128, 132–3
 in politics 128–9
 and religion 146–8
 and sexuality 129
 violence and 126–8, 134
gender relations
 institutional development 133–4
 theoretical developments 122–4
 see also feminism
General Household Survey (GHS) 17,
  20–1, 22–3, 24–5, 26–7
genetically modified food 210–15
Giddens, A. 55, 57, 66, 129, 149, 214,
  321
 and New Labour 70, 180, 278,
  290–3, 294
Giddens, A. and Turner, J.H. 62
Gilbert, G.N. and Mulkay, M. 216–17,
  218
globalization 93, 94–5, 105
 and employment 193
 and religion 150–1
 and Third Way 291, 292, 294
 women's issues and 115–16, 128,
  132–3
Gluckman, M. 37
government, and sociology 68–9, 71–2
Government surveys 12, 13, 17–18,
  24–8
Gramsci, A. 86, 87
Gulf War Syndrome 210

Habermas, J. 59, 64
Hall, S. 86–7, 287
Halsey, A.H. 174, 304
 see also Karabel, J. and Halsey, A.H.
Hammersley, M. 165, 178–9
Harding, S. 114–15, 132
health, sociology of 249–69
 British beginnings 251–6
 misnomer 253
 move towards 261–2
 volume of research 267–8
 see also medical sociology
Hechter, M. 154

herbicides 209
hermeneutism 90–1
  double hermeneutic 55, 62, 71
Hervieu-Léger, D. 145, 149, 154–6
Hesse, M. 61–2
Hill, C. 85–6
Homans, H. *see* Stacey, M. and
    Homans, H.
Horkheimer, M. 82–3
Horobin, G. 262, 263
Horowitz, I.L. 2
households
  defining 233–4
  differences within 235–7
  distinct from families 235
  economic and social elements 234–5
  household work strategies 191–2
  surveys of 26
  see also family studies
human body, in sociology 131–2,
    148–50, 242, 265
human relations management 189
hyper-reality 109

idealist fallacy 90–1
identity
  postmodern 110, 115
  religious 144–6
  work and 190–1
  see also self
illegitimacy 303–4, 305
income support policies 320–1
individuality 82
industrial sociology 185–202
  and concepts of power 190–1
  contemporary work and
      employment 192–6
  declining academic status 185–7
  labour process debate 187–9
  Marxist perspectives 187–9
  methodology 201–2
  potential research objectives
      196–200
  theoretical 187–92
Informal Carers Survey 18, 27
instrumental positivism 66–7
interviews
  computer-assisted 12, 13
  formal 36–7
  in-depth 37–8
irrationalism 60

Jackson, S. 100, 102, 116
Jameson, F. 93–4
Jasanoff, S. 213, 215

Johnson, R. 86–7
Joseph, K. 284, 309, 314
just-in-time production 189, 190

Karabel, J. and Halsey, A.H. 173–4
Kerr, A. *et al.* 216
knowledge creation
  Big Ditch approach 90
  feminist treatment 114–15
  Modes of 250, 268
  post-empiricist 64–6
  postmodern treatment 108, 114, 116
  scientific 216–18
  sociological 250

Labour Force Survey (LFS) 12–13, 17,
    23, 27, 28
labour market
  changing patterns 186–7, 192–6
  deregulation 320
  potential sociology objectives
      196–200
Lahelma, E. *see* Arber, S. and Lahelma, E.
language
  ideal-speech situation 59–60
  language games 109
  linguistic turn 54–5, 59–60, 61, 71–2
  and poststructuralism 107
Lash, S. and Wynne, B. 209–10
Lenin, V.I. 58
Levitas, R. 290, 317
liberal feminism 100–1
Lister, R. 292–3, 294
London School of Economics 168, 173
longitudinal research
  and ethnography 45
  surveys 19–20
Longitudinal Study, ONS 20
Lyotard, J.F. 108–9

Madonna 106, 129, 130
management theory 176–7
Mann, K. 315, 318–19, 322
  see also Bagguley, P. and Mann, K.
Marcuse, H. 82
Marsh, C. 11
Marshall, T.H. 278
Marx, K. 58, 59, 187–8, 189, 196,
    314–15
Marxism
  and culture 84–7
  feminist 100–1
  and industrial sociology 187–8, 189,
      196
  and social policy in Britain 279, 287

Mason, J. *see* Finch, J. and Mason, J.
medical sociology 251–62
  dependence of sociologists on
    doctors 258–60
  in medicine or *of* medicine 254–5,
    256, 257, 258–9, 261–2
  origins of agenda 251–6
  'soft' funding 252, 259, 260
  vis-à-vis sociology in general 262–6
  see also health, sociology of
Medical Sociology Unit (Medical
    Research Council) 251–2, 259
Mellor, P. and Shilling, C. 148–9
Merton, R.K. 52–4, 55, 58, 59, 71, 219
meta-theory, and theory proper 52–4,
    63, 64–5
migration, and underclass
  forced emigration 314
  migrant workers 284, 319–20
Millett, K. 101
Mills, C. Wright 11, 230, 276, 280,
    292, 293
modernism 110, 111, 112
moral panics 87–8
morality
  and culture 91–2
  in family life 238–41
Mouzelis, N. 116–17
Mulkay, M. *see* Gilbert, G.N. and
    Mulkay, M.
multi-site case studies 39, 42–5
Murray, C. 284, 303–4, 305, 309, 314
music 81–2
Myrdal, G. 302

National Centre for Social Research
    (NCSR) 18, 21
National Child Development Study
    (NCDS) 19–20, 21
National Survey of Ethnic Minorities
    (PSI) 18
National Survey of Health and
    Development 219–20
Neale, B. *see* Smart, C. and Neale, B.
Nelkin, D. 212, 219
neo-functionalism 65, 66
New Labour 70, 177, 180, 278, 281,
    290–3, 294
new social formations 104–5
New Sociology 276, 292, 295
Newby, H. 222
Novak, T. 285

Obelkevich, J. and Catterall, P. 1
observation, participant 36–8

official statistics 12, 14
ontology of the social 55–6
organophosphates 210
Ozga, J. 176

Pahl, R.E. 16, 191–2, 197
parenting 239–40
  single 304, 321
Parkin, F. 318
Parsons, T. 53–4, 59, 71, 105–6
patriarchy 100–1
Pawson, R. 56–7, 58, 59
peer review 212, 218
performativity 109, 130
Pesticides Advisory Committee 209
photography, use in research 45–6
Policy Studies Institute (PSI) 18
post-empiricism 61–2, 71–2
postfeminism 113
postmodernism 102–17, 288–90
  in architecture/art 104
  and culture 82, 90, 91, 93–4, 105–6
  elements of 102–9
  and feminism 99–100, 111–17, 123
  new social formations 104–5
  philosophy 108–9
  and poststructuralism 107–8
  and social theory 51, 109–11
poststructuralism 107–8
  in education 178
poverty 275–95
  agency/structure issues 279–80,
    293–4
  defined and redefined 277, 281–2,
    285
  deserving or undeserving poor 280,
    313–15, 316–17
  empiricist approach to 278–80, 281,
    294
  and eugenics 313–14
  past and present 275
  postmodern perspective 289
  and race/ethnicity 283–4
  Rowntree's study of 278–80
  and social exclusion 281, 285, 290,
    311–12, 317–18
  and social policy 320–2
  see also underclass
poverty trap 309, 321
power
  and culture 84–5
  and discourse 107–8, 276–7
  of medical profession 256–61
Pringle, R. 129
Pusztai, A. 211, 212, 217–18

qualitative research
  developments 36–42, 46–7
  multi-site case studies 39, 42–5
  see also ethnographic research

race/ethnicity
  and gender 123, 124, 129
  and underclass 283–4, 305
radical feminism 100–1
rational choice theory 151–4
Rattansi, A. *see* Boyne, R. and Rattansi, A.
realism, social 56–7
relativism
  and culture 80, 85–6, 90, 91
  and feminism 115
religion
  centrality of body to 148–50
  and culture 80–1, 106, 144
  and gender 146–8
  and globalization 150–1
  and identity 144–6
  rational choice theory 151–4
  restructuring 154–6
  sociology of 143–57
risk
  risk society 207–10, 214
  science and regulation of 213–15
Ritzer, G. 63, 66
Rochefort-Turquin, A. 150
Rorty, R. 55, 58, 60
Rosaldo, R. 94–5
Rowntree, B.S. 277, 278–80, 281
Runciman, W.G. 180, 318, 319–20
Rutter, M. *et al.* 25

Samples of Anonymized Records (SARs)
  18
sampling 13, 18
Saussure, F. de 107
science policy
  public involvement in 218–21
  and regulation of risk 213–15
science and technology studies (STS)
  207–22
  expertise as monopoly 208–9
  public understanding 219
  and risk 207–10
scientific expertise 208–10, 212, 216–18
secondary analysis 21–8
  pitfalls of 25–8
  potential of 22–5
self
  deconstruction 108, 113–14
  and difference 113
  see also identity

sexuality 129
Sheffield Local Authority case study
  42–5
Shilling, C. 148, 165, 172, 173, 174,
  177–8, 179
Simmel, G. 83
single parenthood 304, 321
Smart, C. and Neale, B. 231, 239–40
Smelser, N.J. 69, 72
Smith, D.J. 307–8, 316
Social Change and Economic Life
  Initiative (SCELI) 16, 19, 195–6,
  201–2
social constructionism 276–7
social exclusion 281, 285, 290, 311–12,
  317–18
  see also underclass
social inequality
  and class 122–3
  and welfare state 281–2, 293
social policy
  academic 281–2
  interventionist 276
  and Marxism 279
  New Labour 290–3
  postmodern 288–9
  and sociology 275–8, 294–5
  and underclass 320–2
  and unemployment 315–16
social science
  and double hermeneutic 55, 62, 71
  and practical sociology 71–2
  sociology as 52
social stratification 237
social theory
  epistemology and 116–17
  fragmentation 52, 99, 110
  meta-theory and theory proper
    52–4, 63
  as modernist project 110
  and postmodernism 51, 109–11
sociological reflexivity 277, 294–5
Sociological Theory 66
sociology
  in America 66–9
  in Britain 69–71
  as discourse 63–4
  as 'impossible science' 51–2, 67–8
  levels of conceptual systemization
    53–4
  linguistic/hermeneutic turn 54–5,
    59–60, 61, 71–2
  and New Labour 177, 290–3
  New Sociology 276, 292, 295
  post-Second World War 1–2

pragmatic 71–2
and social policy 275–8, 294–5
social science and practical 52, 71–2
see also education, sociology of;
health, sociology of; industrial
sociology; medical sociology
sponsorship, research 41–3
Stacey, M. and Homans, H. 261, 263
Stark, R. and Bainbridge, W.S. 152–3
sterilization programmes 314
Straus, R. 254–5
Strong, P.M. 257, 259–60, 261
structural functionalism 167, 173, 174, 286
structuration theory 7, 56
surveys
critiques of 11–12
cross-sectional 18–19, 21
developments 12–14
future use of 28–9
longitudinal 19–20
purposes of 14–15
secondary analysis 21–8
sociological 15–17
study of time in 18–21
used by sociologists 17–18

Taylor-Gooby, P. 289, 295
see also Dean, H. and Taylor-Gooby, P.
Thatcher, M. and Thatcherism 70, 286–7
Theory, Culture and Society 70
Third Way 290–3, 294
Thompson, E.P. 84–5, 86–7, 91
timescales, research 38, 42
Titmuss, R. 252, 322
total quality control/management 189, 190
Townsend, P. 281, 282, 285
see also Abel-Smith, B. and Townsend, P.
trades unions 315, 319
training, sociological 46–7
Turner, B. 265–6
Turner, J.H. *see* Giddens, A. and Turner, J.H.
Turner, J.H. and Turner, S. 51–2, 67–8, 69

underclass 277, 280, 284–5, 288, 301–24
creating 315–19
culture dependency 309–10
defining 302–7

finding 307–12
forced emigration 314
idea of 322–4
and illegitimacy 303–4, 305
and migrant workers 284, 319–20
racial aspects 284, 305
separating 319–20
social policy and 320–2
welfare policies and 303–7, 308–9
unemployment
and social policy 315–16
surveys into 16, 17
and underclass 302–3, 304–5, 307–11

validity, of surveys 14, 25, 26–7
violence
family 229
and gender relations 126–8, 134
male 126, 127

Walford, G. 173, 178, 179
Warshay, L.H. 71
Webb, S. and B. 279, 280, 313
Weber, M. 80–1, 153
welfare
perspectives of 277, 282, 283–4, 288
structural functionalism 286
and underclass 284–5, 303–7, 308–9
welfare dependency 284–5, 309
welfare to work 292–3
welfare state
attitude of working class 315
changing British 286–90
future of 293–5
Marshall's conception 278
Rowntree's study of poverty 278–80
Scandinavian 'power-resources' model 286
and social inequality 281–2, 293
under New Labour 287–8, 292–3
Westergaard, J. 322
Whitty, G. 165, 172
Williams, F. 282, 283
Williams, J. 92
Williams, R. 92–3, 94
Wilson, W.J. 69, 303, 304–6
women
deconstructed 101, 113
and difference 123
and employment 124–6, 192, 194–5, 197
see also feminism; gender relations
Women and Employment Survey 17–18, 19

work
  culture in workplace 189
  future issues 196–200
  household work strategies 191–2
  organization 187

  sociology of work 185–202
  see also employment; labour market
Work, Employment and Society 186
Wynne, B. 209, 214
  see also Lash, S. and Wynne, B.